Cap.ᵗ Zerbino   Riciulina.   Metzetin   Cucurucu

Cucuba.   Sig.ᵃ Lucia.   Trastullo.   Cap.ᵗ Zerbino

Cucurucu.   Scapino.   Cap.ᵗ Esgangarato.   Cap.ᵗ Cocodrillo

Trillo   Sig.ᵃ Lucia.   Trastullo.   Riciulina.

822.33   Shakespearean comedy
D
S527c

Shakespearean COMEDY

Ingenio stat sine morte decus

OBIIT AP 23 1616
ÆTATIS 53

William Shakspere

POETA, PHILOSOPHVS, ACTOR,

"*Iudicio Pylium, Genio Socratem, Arte Maronem,*
Terra Tegit, Populus Mæret, Olympus Habet."

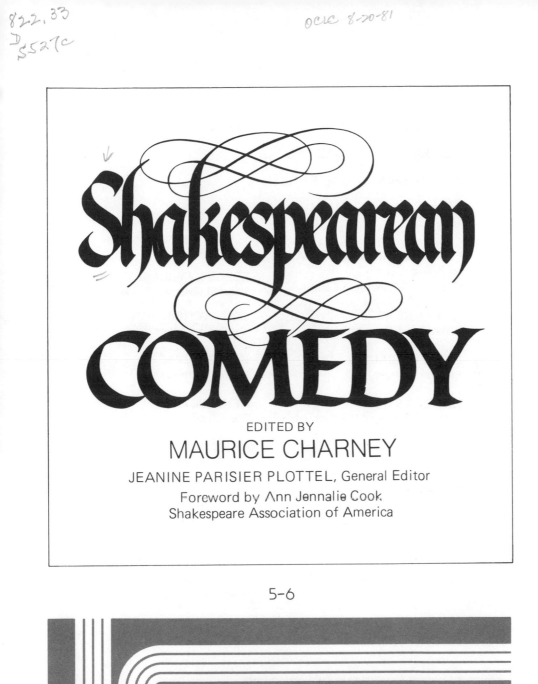

Shakespearean
COMEDY

EDITED BY
MAURICE CHARNEY

JEANINE PARISIER PLOTTEL, General Editor

Foreword by Ann Jennalie Cook
Shakespeare Association of America

5-6

NEW YORK LITERARY FORUM

NEW YORK • 1980

New York Literary Forum acknowledges the support of the Department of Romance Languages and its chairman, Professor Carlos Horgas, Hunter College, C.U.N.Y.

Library of Congress Cataloging in Publication Data

Main entry under title:

Shakespearean comedy.

   (New York literary forum;   ISSN 0149-1040)

   Bibliography: p.
   Includes index.
   1. Shakespeare, William, 1564-1616–Comedies.
I. Charney, Maurice. II. Series.
PR2981.S49   822.3'3   79-52616
ISBN 0-931196-07-8 (lib. bdg.)

CONTENTS

Foreword

Shakespearean Comedy *grew out of a seminar on comedy organized by Maurice Charney for the Shakespeare Association of America. The result, as the present volume attests, is scholarship of considerable and unusual importance.*

Shakespearean Comedy *presents essays from that seminar that were significant enough to be published together with a number of other critical studies. In a very tangible way, Professor Charney's collection of essays not only fulfills two major aims of the Shakespeare Association of America—to set the highest standards of scholarly excellence and to advance the state of Shakespeare criticism—but also makes these outstanding studies available to an even broader audience—all students and devotees of Shakespeare.*

Ann Jennalie Cook
Executive Secretary
Shakespeare Association of America

Preface

Shakespearean Comedy reflects the tremendous resurgence of interest in comedy during the past 15 or 20 years. Tragedy in our time no longer seems a viable literary form; like epic, it is too noble, too difficult, too ethically remote. Comedy now seems to represent not just literature but a way of perceiving an "absurd" existential reality. Fashions in Shakespeare change with changing mores, so that A. C. Bradleys's choice of the four "great" tragedies—*Hamlet, Othello, Macbeth*, and *King Lear*—no longer so exclusively dominates Shakespeare studies. We have become more interested in imperfect tragedies mixed with comedy, like *Troilus and Cressida*, and in comedies mixed with darker shadings, like *Measure for Measure*. Through the influence of such critics as Northrop Frye and C. L. Barber, there is once more an assertion of the imaginative vitality and integrity of Shakespeare's comedies.

The present volume had its beginnings in the Comedy Seminar of the Shakespeare Association of America but rapidly expanded in scope and purpose so that it now includes 20 essays by scholars from the United States, Canada, Great Britain, and Israel, as well as an important Latin text (with translation) and a book review section. The *New York Literary Forum* had already demonstrated its commitment to comedy as a genre by publishing, as its first issue, a collection of studies called *Comedy: New Perspectives* (1978), a volume which itself included three articles on Shakespeare.

Shakespearean Comedy continues and intensifies this lively interest in comedy and the revaluation of the comedies. None of the distinguished contributors feels the need to be apologetic about the subject; in fact, there is a strongly positive assumption that the comedies represent Shakespeare's most varied, most characteristic, and most extensive achievement—he did write more than twice as many comedies as tragedies. Our volume, too, has the special merit of stressing the roots of Shakespearean comedy in Plautus, Terence, Ovid, and other classical and neoclassical sources, as expressed in treatises on comedy like that of Donatus and Evanthius. In speaking about sources, all the authors are eager to go beyond verbal similarities to the larger parallels in imaginative conception that mark Shakespeare's indebtedness to the comic traditions, with its elaborate conventions of plot, character, and action. Shakespeare's relation to Italian comedy, for example, may now be understood as a mutual and reciprocal response to the same classical precedents. Louise Clubb introduces the very useful term "theatergram" to describe the minimum units of romance material that occur in both Shakespeare and Italian Renaissance comedy and that seem to derive from Plautus and Terence. Readers will also find in the present volume a fresh evaluation of comic romance—an acknowledgment that fabulation is at the imaginative heart of comedy. Romance is more than a genre; it is a way of conceiving the world, and romantic artifice mediates between literature and life.

The organization of this volume reflects a variety of interests in theories and traditions of Shakespearean comedy. We begin, logically, with Plautus, Terence, Donatus, and the neoclassical heritage. The authors in this section are all distinguished women— whereas the Popular Tradition in Part 5 has only male support—who speak for the intellectual roots of Shakespearean comedy in classical and neoclassical sources. All four authors are trying to establish an equilibrium in which Shakespeare uses his sources not with deference but with tact. There is an interplay between imitation of models and improvement on them.

The centrality of Ovid, and especially Ovid's *Metamorphoses*, is the theme of the second part. Both Carroll and Lamb focus on *Twelfth Night*, which is interpreted as a very Ovidian play. In this perspective, the conventions of romantic love establish the world in which the characters must function. Roberts' account of animal signs is also deeply involved in Ovidian transformations.

A darker view of romantic comedy is evident in Part 3, where Bergeron and Garber both concern themselves with the night world—tempest, shipwreck, death—of romantic comedy. Their emphasis reminds us of the assumptions of "hard" pastoral, in which the green world is closer to the rigors of the wilderness experience than the tame elegance of Watteau and Fragonard. In Peterson's theory of ideal comedy, these rigors are mitigated by a larger pattern of reconciliation and the perfecting of ordinary experience.

The discussion of Italian comedy in Part 4 returns us to the classical tradition of Part 1 but with a good deal of historical development. Italian theorists claimed to understand in detail what ancient comedy really meant, both theoretically and practically, and they did not hesitate to prescribe rules for the writing of comedy. Both Clubb and Mellamphy take it as a matter of course that Shakespeare must have been strongly influenced by Italian comedy, and they use novel ways of persuading us of the close relationship.

The popular, oral, folk tradition of comedy comes right at the center of our volume in Part 5. It represents a strong minority report by Hawkes, Charney, and Oz of a way of looking at comedy that is more indebted to experience than to literature—if such a distinction can be made at all.

Hawkes, who was born closer to Shakespeare's birthplace than any other contributor in this volume, is also the only contributor to make active use of the Coventry telephone book in discussing *A Midsummer Night's Dream*. Oz's account of doubling insists on the histrionic and improvisatory nature of playing, and the Charney article calls attention to the villain as an essentially comic figure, with deep roots in daily life.

Part 6 returns us to the topic of comic characterization, where Salingar, Freund, and Siegel take on Falstaff and Malvolio. It is interesting to note that, although Salingar is Bradleyan and Freund Hartmanesque, their conclusions are surprisingly close. Siegel reminds us that Bergson's renowned essay on laughter provides useful criteria by which to understand Malvolio. It is refreshing to find Malvolio treated as a comic character again.

Although speculative concerns enliven our volume at every point, only Part 7 is predominantly theoretical. Freedman grapples with a novel theory of farce based on psychoanalytical criteria, and Trousdale introduces semiotic assumptions about language to refute Northrop Frye. In both of these essays, the theory is applied to problems of practical criticism, and especially the interpretation of *The Comedy of Errors* and *Twelfth Night*.

Part 8, Texts and Documents, is a regular feature of the *New York Literary Forum*. By reprinting, translating, and discussing treatises on comedy by Evanthius and Donatus, Nugent provides us with texts that figure importantly in this volume and that deserve to be better known.

The volume concludes with a review article by Kiniry on the most important books of the past five years on Shakespearean comedy. The bibliography at the end gathers together references from the notes and bibliographical notes that are of general interest to students of Shakespeare and of comedy. In the interests of uniformity, Shakespeare's plays are quoted throughout from *The Complete Signet Classic Shakespeare*, general editor, Sylvan Barnet (New York: Harcourt Brace Jovanovich, 1972).

Maurice Charney

PART 1

PLAUTUS, TERENCE, DONATUS, AND THE NEOCLASSICAL TRADITION

1

Shakespeare's Comic Remedies

RUTH NEVO

Out of his Renaissance-Roman and Renaissance-romance materials, Shakespeare wrought a form of comedy unmistakably his own. It is the function of two inconstant variables: the Terentian formula for comic plots, which serves as model for a multitude of variations, and the battle of the sexes, which constitutes the underlying motivation of his variegated romantic-courtship stories. The Terentian scheme, in one of its many formulations, was expounded in the 1550 edition of the *Andria*, a text that was very possibly used in the Stratford Grammar School of Shakespeare's day. "Comedy," the formula runs, "ought indeed to be five-parted, the first of which unfolds the argument" (in another version: "contains either the perils, the anguish or some trouble"); "the second completes the same. The third has the increment of turbations and contentions" (or "brings on the perturbations, and the impediments and despair of the desired thing"); "the fourth seeks a medicine for the turbations" (or: "brings a remedy for the impending evil") "and is a preparation for the catastrophe, which the fifth demands by right for itself."[1]

The ends the plays of Plautus and Terence or rather their characters have in view are specific and concrete indeed: brides (with substantial dowries), complaisant courtesans or purchased flute girls, a parasite's pickings, the exposing of a braggart or impostor or cheating procurer, the outwitting of a heavy father or a light son. They aim at the wealth, pleasure, freedom, praise, or at least a prize, which life does not in general provide equally for all. They go about achieving these ends with the aid of tricky manipulations, disguises, pretenses, bed-tricks, simulations and dissimulations, the wily slaves themselves being the chief functionaries, if not originators, of the whole contrivance. However, far from achieving what is wished, this brings about a thickening web of accidents and miscomprehensions and is accompanied by considerable verbal violence (especially in the less polite Plautus) as abuse, threat, and invective are lavishly and hyperbolically distributed. The result is not only consonant with the original desires of the protagonists, but in excess of them. They get more, and better, than they bargained for, and this on account of a series of fortunate coincidences and discoveries: lost foundlings, wrecks, rings, caskets, birthmarks—in short, all the paraphernalia of the fortunate unforeseen, the lucky chances that our precarious existences need even more than gifts of birth or intellect.

These stratagems of the New Comedy supplied Europe with its comic fictions for two millennia—longer, if we include subtle and profound inversions like those of Ibsen and Chekhov, witty parodies like *The Importance of Being Earnest*, *Major Barbara*, and *The Confidential Clerk*, fantasias like *The Playboy of the Western World*, and the steady stream of musical comedy and soap opera, let alone the secondary proliferating life led by dramatic forms in the novel since the eighteenth century. They also provided Shakespeare with his plots from *The Comedy of Errors* to *The Tempest*.

The distinction between "plot" and "story" (roughly equivalent to "fabula" and "sjuzet" in Formalist terminology) was not unknown to the ancients. By the time of the last of the final romances, Shakespeare will have bettered his instruction in the "artificial order" recommended to dramatists by Horace,[2] whereby chronological sequence is disrupted for the sake of dramatic effects. But if Shakespearean devices for creating a simultaneity of past and present, for irradiating present by past, and for effecting multiple ironies while cunningly advancing or retarding the solutions to his characters' bewilderment finally surpass those of the ancients, it is as well to remember that the procedure is inherent in New Comedy plots, whether in their original form of drama or in the later development of narrative.

The Tempest is a palimpsest of Plautus' *The Rope*, which starts with a description of a tempest and has a prologue in which Arcturus explains how he has "stirred up a wintry storm and raised high waves in the sea" in order to wreck the ship of the wicked procurer who decamped with the slave girl, long-lost daughter of the farmer-fisherman upon whose coast the wrecked travelers are washed up. And *The Winter's Tale* is a startlingly recognizable transformation of the fragment by Menander called *The Arbitration*, in which a charcoal burner and a goatherd dispute the ownership of trinkets found by the latter when he picked up an abandoned baby, later depositing it with the former, whose wife has just given birth to a stillborn child. The arbitrator in the dispute, as it so happens, turns out to be the foundling's own grandfather, whose daughter, it seems, in the heat of a quarrel with her husband, inadvertently mislaid her baby. Whatever the obscure, primordial origins of such stories may be, whether they have their source in the myths of Dionysos or in the Athenian custom of infant exposure, the lost or abandoned child whose lot is to be found again becomes, as Kerenyi tells us, basic to the entire genre of New Comedy.[3]

In the early *Comedy of Errors*, just such a Menandrine narrative of separation and reunion encases the brisk Plautine mistakings and unmaskings of the *Menaechmi*. This has tempted criticism to become preoccupied with the question whether the meandering romance narrative of marvelous reunions (*Apollonius of Tyre*, for instance) or the tight Roman structure of mistakes and unravelings took precedence in Shakespeare's imagination. The fact of the matter is that both were contained in Plautus, and the historical bifurcation into medieval romances on the one hand and dramas of intrigue on the other was largely a matter of theatrical convenience. The plays emphasize the tangle of errors; the romances—they have the time to do so—emphasize the precedent vicissitudes. Whatever permutations and combinations come to be devised, it is to the basic linkage that the term *New Comedy* usefully applies. In application to Shakespeare, however, a further parameter comes into play.

After the initial sally of *The Comedy of Errors*, the wandering narrative of long-lost children and family reunions disappears until the final romances, save for an evocation of "sea-sorrow" vicissitudes in *Twelfth Night*, with its pair of twins fished out of the sea. The modern and fashionable emphasis in Shakespeare's day was not only upon the Roman comedies that had been enthusiastically resuscitated and interpreted by the humanist eruditi of the Renaissance and popularized by their ebullient offshoot, the commedia dell'arte, but also upon the specifically courtly branch of romance. The romance of courtship, medieval in its first impulse, had recently been trimmed and spruced up, Peele'd, Greene'd, Lylyfied, and Euphuized and had made a new and elegant debut in the theater. It is, therefore, these courtly or courtship comedies, particularly the "supposes" combination of mistakings and matings, which dominate Shakespeare's playwriting till the turn of the century. And it is in these comedies that the specific and distinctive form of Shakespearean comedy is to be discovered.

Recovery and Discovery: The Terentian Scheme

The telos of Shakespeare's early comic plots is recovery: the finding of what was missing or lacking at the start. And here the first great novelty is at once apparent—Shakespeare's protagonists do not know what they want, except in the most superficial sense. They discover as they go along, and so transform the rather arid Donatan formula into a heuristic device of immense potency and flexibility. When Shakespeare's characters, like the Romans in their happy ends, get more than they bargained for, it is not simply the bonus (admittedly considerable) of a son's light-of-love turning out to be respectable or an Athenian citizen or even the long-lost daughter of the father's best friend, but an illumination of their entire lives. Leo Salingar expresses this extremely well, if impressionistically, when he speaks of a "fundamental innovation which in its general effect distinguishes Shakespeare's plays from all previous comedies, that he gives his people the quality of an inner life. Their inner life, with their capacity for introspection, changes the whole bearing of the incidents that make up a traditional comic plot. It is as if Shakespeare separates the events that composed the plot from the centers of consciousness in his leading characters, so that the plot-machinery operates on a different plane, the plane where the characters are being 'transformed' . . . carried out of their normal selves . . . observe themselves passing into a new phase of experience."[4]

It is not only the language of the inner life, however (important though it is), which "changes the whole bearing of the incidents that make up a traditional comic plot." The effect is the consequence of a radical and consistent employment of what Bertrand Evans has taught us to recognize as a particularly subtle and pervasive form of dramatic irony: the exploitation of a gap in awareness between the characters (or some of them) and the audience.[5] This is a major technique of discovery in all of Shakespeare's plays, but in the comedies particular profit is derived from the close coordination between the audience's knowledge and the character's ignorance and from an overt display of the device as such. The audience is told matters that are concealed from the characters (or some of the characters) in such a way (or by such means) that progressive disclosures for the former are synchronous with progressive deceptions, confusions, and mystifications for the latter. Puck's application of the magic juice, for example, puts the audience in the know and the lovers into bafflement at one and the same stroke, as do the eavesdropping scenes in *Much Ado.* But to this central comic device I shall presently return.

The audience's possession of superior knowledge insures that comedies of this kind never surprise. Or rather, the "surprises" they supply are characteristic of good spectactor sports: perfectly expected in principle but always admirably unforeseen in practice. They are the fruit of the finesse, versatility, verve, and skill whereby goals are achieved, situations saved, and gambles won in spite of the difficulties set up by the conventions of the game itself. Once again the point has been made by Northrop Frye: "All art is conventionalised," he says, "but where the convention is most obvious and obtrusive the sense of play, of accepting the rules of a game, is at its strongest . . . the comedies as a single group . . .

seem more like a number of simultaneous chess games, played by a master who wins them all by devices familiar to him, and gradually, with patient study, to us, but which remain mysteries of an unfathomable skill."[6]

Shakespeare's implementation of the Terentian scheme, in the first ten comedies, runs as follows: Whatever the predicament sets forth as missing at the start, be it a twin or an obedient wife or matched couples to make up a foursome or the secret of a "living art" or requited love or love and a fortune or a good match for a daughter and a punishment for a jealous husband or a match for a wayward cousin or a place in the sun for a dispossessed young man or mastery in love, it will be found. The plot's formal coherence depends on this, and so does the audience's perception of the play's coherence. Since the protagonists are themselves seekers and only partly (or not at all) aware of what they seek, the formal development is a continual, unfolding process of disclosure, during which, however, the protagonist and audience are proceeding at different rates. The protagonist is positively retarded by tumults and confusions on the way, whereas the audience moves apace by inference and hypothesis.

When the plot is finally resolved, therefore, by some appropriate recognition that enables objectives to be attained, the *anagnorisis* or recognition is retrospective as well as immediate for the protagonists and holistic or integrative for the audience. The recognition invites, in effect, a second order or interpretative, reevaluative reading of events for both. The solving event, of which the audience, too, has not had full advance notice, produces hindsight on two levels. Scales fall from the protagonists' eyes according to whatever mistaken identity or reunion is now disclosed and from the audience's eyes according to the entire "journey into the interior" the protagonists' adventures can now be seen to have been. The manifest purposes, desires, goals, and motivations of the protagonists reveal their inner, previously concealed or veiled or latent implications. What the protagonists see will not altogether, of course, coincide with what the audience sees. The audience has more material to unify, to knit into coherence, than any single character. But the approach of the protagonists' knowledge to the level of the audience's at the end of the play is what gives the recognitions of the dénouement their telling effect. And it is one of the marks of the progressive Shakespearean mastery of dramatic speech that protagonists become more self-perceptive, more aware of themselves as having been fooled or foolish, and also as having gained in wisdom or insight.

In the Roman New Comedy the author or implementer of the comic device—the deception or pretense or bluff or imposture—which precipitates the comic process of involution and evolution and creates the gap between audience's knowledge and that of protagonist, is usually the trickster slave. In Shakespeare trickery has gone up in the world. And though he has tricky servants, like Puck, they are not markedly successful and, in the end, they have to have their chestnuts pulled out of the fire for them by their royal employers. The freeing of the comic device from its strictly utilitarian Roman deceptions, however, has great advantages for variety and flexibility. In *The Comedy of Errors* the comic device is nature's own—the freakish identicalness of twins—but thereafter in Shakespeare's comedies we have psychological one-upmanship, a girl as page, crossed letters, the delusive juice of a flower, three deceptive caskets, a wifely trick to catch a cuckold, a series of eavesdroppings, girls in disguise.

The comic device meshes in marvelously intricate, varied, and eye-opening ways with the comic disposition of human beings to be deluded, deceived, mistaken, unreasonable, perverse, irrational, and subject to every kind of folly. This produces what the neoclassical theorists of the Renaissance, following Donatus, called the *incrementum processusque turbarum*, the increase and progression of perturbations, or "the forward progress of the turmoils,"[7] that is to say, confusion worse confounded or the knot of errors. The reversals, shocks, absurdities, displacements, and disorientations of this stage strike the protagonists as having turned their world upside down, or into dream, and result eventually in a double exhaustion. The comic device is exhausted; it has fulfilled (or overfulfilled) its function. It is not usable any more, or it is about to be exposed. But also, and at the same time, the privations or perversities that bred the entanglements ultimately to be dissolved or resolved have undergone a process of hyperbolic excess that has reached the point of exhaustion.

The Comic Device—Remedies and Cures

Not only is this process itself remedial; the comic device is thematically remedial in terms of the represented world of the play. Even in early Ephesus the resolution of the enigmas follows Dr. Pinch's attempted exorcism of Antipholus' "madness." Consider, in each of the plays, who plots what and for what purpose. There is the taming of the shrew and of Titania and of the lovers' frenzies; there is the bringing to their senses of the young Lords of Navarre, one of whom is to be homeopathically cured of joking by joking in a hospital; and the bringing to their senses of the headstrong "sworn bachelors" of Messina; there is the "curing" of the love-sick Orlando and of the love-sick Malvolio. The notorious prevalence of disease in *Henry IV, Part 2* presages the replacing of a comic remedy by a deathbed scene. Then there is the remedying of Vienna's ills and the problematic medicinal skills of Helena, the French physician's daughter. The whole construction is like nothing so much as the house that Jack built. The remedial devices produce errors that trigger complications; that bring out or induce quiescent follies, instabilities, compulsions, humors; that, extruded—expressed—reach a maximum point of exhaustion that generates remedies. We have a multitude of metaphors for a process of excitation, discomposure, and reconstruction that we do not understand. We refer to this medicinal, benign, and restorative process variously in terms of exorcism, sublimation, homeopathy, safety valves, release of therapy; and the fact of the matter is that the therapeutic, rather than the didactic function of comedy, though obscured in late neoclassical criticism, had been consistently recognized in the earlier phases of the classical tradition. The medical analogy between the progress of a comedy and the progress of a disease toward amelioration is persistent. The influential Landino five-act formula of 1482 ascribes to the fourth act "the bringing of a remedy for the obstructing ills."[8] Willichius, in his commentary on Terence's *Andria* in the edition of 1550, explains the five-act Terentian scheme: "The third has the sequence of turbations with the complication of the argument, and the stirring of all the difficulties. The fourth exhibits the desperate state of the matter. . . . The fifth brings a remedy for the great ills, gives all persons what they desire, and fills them with great joy."[9] The last two formulations are slightly differently phrased in his commentary on Horace's doctrine of the five acts: "The third has the increment of turbations and contentions. . . . The fourth seeks a medicine for the turmoils and is, as it were, preparatory to the catastrophe, which the fifth demands by right for itself."

The providential remedies are, in the first instance, the immediate local solutions to the impasses created by the involutions of the plot, the enigmas and errors induced by what Donatus called "the infolding of the argument." That they come about at all is the happy chance, the good luck, the fortuitous and fortunate circumstance that is comedy's presiding genius, as the fatal error and its inevitabilities are tragedy's. Thus the presence of the disguised abbess, a convenient occasion for demonstrative obedience, true love in disguise, the healing flower, the legal loophole, cover for the elopment of the young lovers, the captured villain, the fortunate encounter and a change of heart, the arrival of a lost twin—such stuff as spells out the bitter anguish of "too late" in the tragedies—here provide solutions to the problems, dilemmas, embarrassments, mishaps, mistakings, deceptions, and imbroglios, and potential disasters, of the *processus turbarum.* This is their technical sense. But as they close the gap opened by the play's beginning, they provide the audience with means for a full and final retrospective intelligence of the nature (in all its inwardness) of the desirable, the pleasurable, the good, the absence of which motivated the story. They enable us to transcend, if we will, the comedy-game aspect of the play and to move, in the words of Paul Ricoeur, "from what it says to that of which it speaks."[10]

By study of the early plays I am persuaded that the spectacle of these follies is cathartic in a uniquely interesting way. We perceive the emergence of a mimesis that embraces both character and audience in its double interaction. As in all forms of dramatic irony, the informed audience witnesses what befalls unwitting characters. But here the process of looking before and after is so finely articulated that the audience, too, undergoes a restructuring of experience analogous to that of the characters, though from a higher and more comprehensive vantage point. The power of Shakespeare's comic creations lies in the simultaneous formal complexity and naturalistic verisimilitude with which these canonical elements of comic form are deployed. The remedies solve and resolve, illuminate the whole human condition for the audience while they enact the particular repair, or cure the particular folly or set of follies or species of folly or privation or perversity presented in a particular play. The insights that these remedies generate or precipitate are thus endowed with a double validity.

Shakespeare's Fools

It is the fools who ensure this endowment. These fools, that great company of the commonalty—menials, professional jesters, solid citizens, who carry on their quotidian, absurd, and good-natured existences in the most subtle disrelation with the official plot—grow in stature as Shakespeare proceeds. They are the catalyzers of the comic disposition to be deluded, deceived, mistaken; they are affected, conceited, pretentious, inept, maladroit, or perverse and, in short, foolish. Foolery, as Feste says, doth walk about the orb like the sun. It is the fools that, to change the metaphor, focus its rays. Because they are not the tricksters—Shakespare's orientation is aristocratic and his plotters are dukes and princes and witty heroines—they are not tied to the exigencies of plot and are, therefore, free to improvise plays and parody their betters. And they do this directly, if they are witty fools whose folly is a stalking horse, or indirectly, if they are foolish would-be wits, simply by being, in their own blithe unawareness, what their betters are in their ridiculous essence.

The question of how foolish a Shakespearean fool really is, is always a good question. Who, for instance, is mocking whom when the complacent Jaques mockingly exults at having met a fool in the forest? It is a fool, at all events, whose foolish philosophy bears an uncanny resemblance to Jaques's own nihilistic obsessions. The dramatic duplicity here is like Bottom's dream, so-called, it will be remembered, because it hath no bottom. Face and mask, illusion and imposture, are the dubieties out of which a profoundly ironic intelligence generates its ironies, the world of the theater and the theater of the world reflecting each other in manifold ways. By dissonance and by consonance, by diminishing or by augmenting, by simulation or be dissimulation, by infirmities and by recoveries, the fools entertain us ceaselessly, and we entertain them; that is to say, we entertain a diversity of perspectives and proportions. They may not themselves always be witty—some may indeed fairly be rated underachievers—but they are certainly the cause that wit is in others. And the constant mediation between opposing temptations, between head and heart, rational and irrational; between the defenses of the ordering intellect and the defenses of immersion in dissolving emotion has much to do with the exquisite equipoise of Shakespearean remedies. Through the fools, fantasies of the unconscious and fantasies of the ideal are both enacted and reduced to viable proportion.

One is often struck by the many faces of even the simplest of Shakespeare's clowns, by their complementarity with other characters, and by their refusal to be disposed of by a dichotomous wits/butts or knaves/gulls classification or through besetting and extravagant "humors." The only way I can account for this peculiarity of Shakespeare's fools is by recourse to an ancient Greek insight concerning three comic manners, or dispositions, or modes of conduct or characters (*ethoi*), namely, the Bomolochos, the Eiron, and the Alazon: Buffoon, Ironical Man, and Impostor. These are the three possible producers of the ludicrous and pleasurable, according to the fourth century *Tractatus Coislinianus*,[11] the fragment that tantalizes us with its glimpse into the missing Aristotelean treatise on comedy. Tripartite divisions of the soul are common and frequently overlap conceptually, Freud's having often been shown to have more than a superficial resemblance to Plato's. The *Tractatus* lends itself to the notion of a mock or burlesque theater of the psyche, with Plato's charioteer as Eiron/Ego, his spirited part as Alazon/Superego, and his appetitive part the buffoonish Bomolochos/Id. What the appellations mean we have a fair idea from other Greek texts, in particular Aristotle's *Nichomachean Ethics*. Alazon or Boaster is "a charlatan or impostor who pretends to have distinguished qualities which he either does not possess at all or possesses less fully than he would have us believe" (Book IV, Chapter VII). Bomolochos is a facetious wag, exhibits an excess of wit, must be funny come what may, and can't resist a joke in or out of season (Chapter VIII). Eiron is notoriously hard to pin down. In the *Nichomachean Ethics* he is the self-deprecator, the understater (like Socrates), who disclaims the possession of distinguished qualities (Chapter VII). But Socrates himself, according to Alcibiades in the *Symposium*, adds an important proviso: he is Silenus, the large-bellied, coarse, ridiculous image within which is hidden divine wisdom.

The formulations of the *Nichomachean Ethics* (and even more of Theophrastus' *Characters* in the next generation) are ethically oriented; they are descriptions and prescriptions of ways of behaving in society. Alazon and Eiron are, respectively, the excess and defect of the virtue of plain truth-speaking. Bomolochos represents the excess of affability, against the dour and humorless Agroikos, who is its defect (Chapter VIII).[12] But consider the threesome functionally, as does the *Tractatus*, as laughter-producers, and it becomes at once evident that they are all necessary and complementary elements in the perception of absurdity. Alazon is a fool for pretending to a wisdom or virtue he does not have, but there must be an Eiron present to make this apparent. Bomolochos is a fool because he is always fooling or playing the fool, but, again, always for someone's benefit and enjoyment and at someone's cost, if only his own. Eiron masks true wisdom by pretending to be a fool in order to expose the mock wisdom of wisdom's ape. All "humors," excesses, defects, fixations, and compulsions are, of course, foolish from either a rational or an ethical point of view. But what distinguishes the archetypal threesome is that they are interrelated functions, depending on, and varying with, each other. They can reflect and modify and duplicate each other in infinite combinations of deception and pretense, imitation and parody, masking and unmasking, resembling nothing so much as the antics performed, modern mythology tells us, by their equivalents—ego, id, and superego—in the comedies of our own discomfitures.

Shakespeare's fools exhibit just this complementarity of the quasi-Aristotelean triad, thus proving it as natural as folly itself (since Shakespeare had no written source) and justifying the Greek insight. And just as the three primary colors behave under the laws of optics—the complement of red being green, which is a mixture of blue and yellow; or the complement of blue being orange, a mixture of red and yellow—so, after the initial essays in the Terentian servant couple (one dumb and one clever), Shakespeare's fools tend to pair off in exactly analogous ways. The complement and opponent of a braggart like Armado is Costard, a mixture of mocker and fool. The mocking Puck has for his complement the foolish and bossy Bottom, impostor-lover of a fairy queen. Feste the wit complements the foolish Alazon Malvolio. If the complement of an ironic impostor like Sir Toby is a fool simple, Aguecheek admirably fills the bill. Don John, cunning impostor, is outwitted (ironically) by no other than the virtuous but assified Dogberry. In the darker tonality of *Troilus and Cressida*, Thersites, scurrilous mocker, stands over against Pandarus, complacent and overreaching fool. The ironic Hamlet faces the pompous fool Polonius, and when he becomes his own buffoon, it is to outwit the sardonic impostor, his uncle. One could multiply instances.

But for fear of a digression on fools of Shandyan proportions, perhaps by some contamination from the subject matter, I turn instead to Falstaff and to the question raised by that fat knight, who is composite Buffoon, Alazon, and Eiron. What does his folly enact? What do his comic energies nourish and foster? Having more flesh than another man, he has, therefore, more frailty, but what are the pleasures we derive from his easy morals and immense belly? According to Bakhtin in *Rabelais and His World*, Falstaff would be the supreme example of what he calls the "grotesque realism" of Renaissance comic art, the sole function of which is to degrade or debase the dogmatic, the authoritarian, the official or ideal, the pompous or pretentious, the "finished and polished." "Folly," says Bakhtin, "is a form of gay, festive wisdom, free from all laws and restrictions, as well as from preoccupations and seriousness."[13] This comic degradation, this "uncrowning" as Bakhtin calls it in his brilliant analysis of the language and imagery of the comic, brings down to earth, to the lower stratum of the body—belly, bowels, phallus—turns into flesh, materializes. The essence of comedy, he claims, is contained in the "Rabelaisian complex": laughter, food, procreation, abuse. It is rooted in folk carnival with its billingsgate abuse, its joyous license, its indecent irreverence, its violence and scatology, its presentation of the body not as a harmoniously proportionate form, but all belly, as a prodigy of cavities, excrescences, and protuberances, and also as itself grave and seed bed, matrix of both disintegration and renewal: Falstaff's Hallowe'en Spring.

Against Bakhtin's radical medievalism (reminiscent of Victor Hugo's Preface to *Cromwell*), it is instructive to place the neoclassical rationalism of Castelvetro, who, in 1576,[14] adduced four sources for the risible in an analysis that is startlingly anticipatory of modern post-Freudian views like Koestler's, for instance, in *The Act of Creation*.[15] As a first source for laughter, not essentially comic, such as that of a mother welcoming her children, Castelvetro placed affection. Next came deception, mainly the mishaps and miscalculations of others, but he does include self-deception, such as boasting or pretension, which rebounds boomerang fashion; third, a physical or moral defect or deficiency, wittily exposed; and lastly, obscenity, cunningly covert.

Falstaff is certainly a very prince of disinhibition and of mockery. Both these caps fit, though one fits Falstaff as object of derision; the other, as subject. But what neither Castelvetro nor Bakhtin explains is precisely the duality, the doubleness, of comic pleasure when laughter, or the risible, is deliberately, brilliantly, histrionically engineered, rather than simply embodied or expressed. Falstaff is a multi-impersonator, and in this he draws upon a source of pleasure, not exclusively and disjunctively the property of comedy, but anterior to all other comic pleasure: the art of mimicry. He impersonates "Monsieur Remorse," pious patriot, valiant soldier, and plays at being misunderstood, long-suffering. There is nothing, in fact, that he will not impersonate, and this is the secret of his wit. For the pleasure of imitation, as Aristotle knew, is the primary pleasure of knowledge as power. To imitate is to understand, to have grasped the distinguishing principle, to have stripped away all that is excrescent or accidental, to have recognized. While Falstaff thus performs, he has two audiences: the stage audience, duped or unduped, and the theater audience, unduped. Falstaff rejoices in the gulling of the dupes. The theater audience rejoices both in the gulling of the dupes and in the countergulling of Falstaff, thus emotionally having its libidinous, disinhibitory cake and eating it with a good moral conscience. The theater audience rejoices in the actor's histrionic skill, in the fictive Falstaff's skill, in Hal's greater skill (or vice versa), in Shakespeare's skill in providing the text that generates these skills, and in its own skills of perception. Since it is never oblivious for a moment of the open and palpable fabrication, it is never the victim of Plato's most heinous of all deceptions: the presentation of appearances as if they were reality. Whether we rejoice with trickster-victim or with trickster-victor, our love is really love for the artist, masked, and transferred to his creations. We love the inventor of these marvelous inventions.

Such clowning gives us double indemnity: we escape with the hare and hunt with the hounds; we mock and affirm; we delight in witty intelligence and in unwise impulse, in high spirits and low designs, in the laxities of infantile fantasy, and in the astringencies of ironic reality. For the two hours' traffic of the stage, we are not trapped in the disjunctions of our mortality, and this in itself is therapeutic. A benign doubling and re-doubling is a mark of comedy; its emblem Falstaff doubling and redoubling and multiplying his buckram men for the delectation of his double audience. There are twins and quasi-twins, double-faced rogues and jokers, double plots doubly complicating each other, double entendres and dual sexual roles for disguised heroines. But where doubling in life, we are told, is often a sign of failure in integration, in comedy, mankind's dramatized dream of a second chance, doubling is the essential vehicle for its transforming dialectic of wisdom and folly.

Notes

1. The formula originated with the fourth-century grammarian Donatus and was endlessly repeated and revised by the Renaissance humanists. See T. W. Baldwin, *Shakespeare's Five Act Structure* (Urbana: University of Illinois Press, 1947), pp. 232-33, 249, and passim; see also Marvin Herrick, *Comic Theory in the Sixteenth Century* (Urbana: University of Illinois Press, 1964).

2. *Ars Poetica*, lines 146-52, and recommended by Sir Philip Sidney, *Apologie for Poetry*, ed. Gregory Smith, *Elizabethan Critical Essays* (Oxford University Press, 1904), I, 198.

3. C. Kerenyi, *Dionysos: Archetypal Image of Indestructible Life* (Princeton: Princeton University Press, 1976), pp. 343-67.

4. Leo Salingar, *Shakespeare and the Traditions of Comedy* (Cambridge University Press, 1974), p. 222.

5. Bertrand Evans, *Shakespeare's Comedies* (London: Oxford University Press, 1960).

6. Northrop Frye, *A Natural Perspective* (New York: Columbia University Press, 1965), pp. viii and 4-5.

7. Evanthius, *De Fabula*. During the sixteenth century this essay was ascribed to Donatus and published together with his *De Comoedia* under the title *De Comoedia et Tragoedia*.

8. Baldwin, *Shakespeare's Five Act Structure*, p. 232.

9. Ibid., p. 238; see also pp. 312-46 passim.

10. Paul Ricoeur, "Metaphor and the Main Problem of Hermeneutics," *New Literary History*, 6 (1974), 106.

11. Translated and discussed by Lane Cooper in *An Aristotelean Theory of Comedy* (New York: Harcourt Brace, 1922).

12. Northrop Frye, *The Anatomy of Criticism*, p. 172, borrows Agroikos from the *Ethics* in order to make up, with the triad of the *Tractatus*, "two opposed pairs" of comic character types. Despite the appeal of symmetry, this move obscures the issues and seriously confuses Frye's account of comic character. Of course, the surly Agroikos can provide the basis for humors characters and frequently did in comedies of the Latin tradition; Surly, Morose and Malvolio are cases in point. So were Eiron, Buffoon, and Alazon susceptible of development and realization in any number of ethically based ways. Comic transformations are legion—as many as there are parameters of temperament, sensibility, and morality. They may be as rarefied and refined as Lyly's pert pages or as randy and rambunctious as Panurge. An Agroikos, in order to be funny, will have to have a touch of Eiron, Buffoon, or Alazon in his dour disposition or a neighbor to point out that he has!

13. Mikhail Bakhtin, *Rabelais and His World*, tr. Helene Iswolsky (Cambridge, Mass.: M.I.T. Press, 1968), pp. 19-23, 260, and passim.

14. Quoted in Marvin Herrick, p. 53, and in Allan H. Gilbert, *Literary Criticism: Plato to Dryden* (New York: American Book Co., 1940), p. 314.

15. Arthur Koestler, *The Act of Creation* (London: Macmillan, 1964). The theory is conveniently summarized by Koestler in his article "Humor and Wit," in the *New Encyclopedia Britannica*.

Bibliographical Note

T. W. Baldwin, *Shakespeare's Five Act Structure*, and Marvin Herrick, *Comic Theory in the Sixteenth Century*, are invaluable sources for information concerning the Donatan tradition and its ramifications during the Renaissance. Lane Cooper, *An Aristotelean Theory of Comedy*, translates and discusses the *Tractatus Coislinianus* during his attempt to reconstruct an Aristotelean treatise of comedy. Leo Salingar, *Shakespeare and the Traditions of Comedy*, and Giacomo Oreglia, *The Commedia dell' Arte*, give most thorough, detailed, and perceptive accounts of comic tradition in England and Italy respectively. C. Kerenyi's *Dionysos* is a brilliant reconstruction and analysis of the Dionysian cult festivals of antiquity, and the work of C. L. Barber, *Shakespeare's Festive Comedy*, and Mikhail Bakhtin, *Rabelais and His World*, fill out our understanding of the nature of long-continuing folk traditions of the comic upon which Elizabethan drama drew. Ian Donaldson, *The World Upside Down*, pursues a particularly central theme in this tradition; and Michael Long, *The Unnatural Scene*, develops Barber's idea to accommodate the tragedies as the contrary "traumatic perspective" of minds for which "the volatilities of unstructured experience hold terror not release." Standard works in the fields are Enid Welsford, *The Fool*, Robert H. Goldsmith, *Wise Fools in Shakespeare*, and Muriel Bradbrook, *The Growth and Structure of Elizabethan Comedy*. Bertrand Evans, *Shakespeare's Comedies*, gives a definitive account of Shakespeare's manipulation of audience knowledge in a study that deserves to figure prominently in any newer "affective" approach to the poetics of theater. The view of comedy as essentially irrational is well presented by Morton Gurewitch, *The Irrational Vision*, and its counterpart: comedy as the supreme embodiment and enactment of rationality, by James Feibleman, *In Praise of Comedy*. Arthur Koestler, *The Act of Creation*, skillfully adapts Freudian views in a comprehensive account of creativity, which includes jester, poet, and man of science. Freud himself, of course, is everywhere a mine of insight into the therapies of comedy. Northrop Frye's taxonomies and analyses of generic symbolism (in *Anatomy of Criticism*) are indispensable to any study of a genre and generate insight even when most productive of disagreement.

2

The Conscious Art of
The Comedy of Errors

CATHERINE M. SHAW

The Comedy of Errors holds a place unique in the Shakespearean canon because it shows at once the most direct derivation from Roman comedy and, at the same time, an awareness of contemporary audience and occasion. This does not mean that the drama of the intervening years, particularly that of Renaissance Italy and the native English tradition, does not show its influence. Rather, there is something to be gained by looking at either end of a creative process—the pressure of Latin comedy at the beginning and the demands of occasion on performance at the end. If we can assume that this play as we have it in the Folio text shows signs of catering to an audience at least as learned as the playwright, then awareness of specific audience and perhaps also of the specific occasion of the Christmas revels at Gray's Inn in December, 1594, encouraged Shakespeare to indulge in authorial virtuousity; perhaps even to show off a little. Many critics have dealt with *The Comedy of Errors* as a serious expression of Shakespearean sentiments even though they are couched in Plautine farce —no doubt they are there. What my interest is, however, is in viewing the play as an artistic performance whose comic success depends upon an awareness of its deliberate eclecticism and of a craft expressly designed to set up a confrontation between stage representation and audience expectation.

We might note, for example, that no other Shakespearean play has so few prose lines (230 or 1/8 of the total), and of these, as we might expect, 2/3 (165) are spoken by the Dromios and almost all the rest (58) by Antipholus of Syracuse when he engages in badinage with his servant in Act 2, scene 2 and Act 3, scene 2. This should lead us to speculate on the comic effect of the farcical sequences of mistaken identity, particularly those in which either Dromio takes a drubbing, in which the dialogue is in blank verse, or in the dinner scene mid-play (the only one except for the finale with all the major characters on stage), in which the characters caterwaul in rhymed couplets. Surely, the couching of such Plautine buffoonery in blank verse and rhyme suggests a conscious dichotomy for comic effect. Perhaps in this Shakespeare is following the lead of the courtly John Lyly, whose influence in the play shows elsewhere; but if he is, then his audience would recognize the technique of imitation as well as the deliberate juxtaposition of action and speech pattern.

Shakespeareans are indebted to editors and scholars such as T. W. Baldwin, R. A. Foakes, and Geoffrey Bullough for their investigations into Shakespeare's narrative sources for *The Comedy of Errors*, for it is upon such knowledge that we can base our assessment of the freedom with which Shakespeare adapted and added and also come to recognize when he broke with direct or indirect Plautine influence to adopt other dramatic methods and style, particularly those of Terence. T. W. Baldwin has dealt in detail with *The Comedy of Errors* and the five-act Terentian formula for play construction.[1] More recently, Richard Levin has drawn our attention to a fact about Latin comedy too often ignored. "Of the eighty-odd plays that have survived from classical antiquity, only those of Terence contain a fully developed double plot."[2] On this subject George E. Duckworth says, "Since the double plot appears in all of Terence's comedies except *The Mother-in-Law* but is scarcely ever used by Plautus, and since Terence handles the two plots with greater skill in his later plays, it seems probable that he himself developed this feature and in many cases altered the Greek originals to make his own comedies more intricate."[3] I would like to suggest that Shakespeare, whose knowledge of Plautus and Terence was at least as great as theirs had been of Menander and Apollodorus, took the same liberties with Plautine narrative and with Terence's interlocking double plots as Terence had done with his Greek forebears and that this freedom opened the way for an even greater expansion of that "comic complication" and character illumination of which Levin speaks.[4] The result is that in Shakespeare's play there are not two, but *three* levels of dramatic sensibility, each projecting a distinctive tone.

The Terentian double plot is based on the adventures of two young lovers: one more serious and romantic, the other tending toward practicality and somewhat less respectable. Little stage time is given to slap-stick. Even though *Menaechmi* is almost pure farce, however, Shakespeare found the beginnings of a Terentian bifurcation in the Plautine twins. Syracuse is more impressionable and idealistic. His response to Erotium's hospitality is, "Ye immortal gods! Did ye ever in a day bestow more blessings on a man who hoped for less."[5] Epidamus is somewhat more cynical and more of a sexual adventurer. The idea of stealing from his wife to buy favors for his mistress appeals to his sense of justice, and he appears to have been on close terms with Erotium's maid as well. The character distinction is relatively undeveloped in Plautus, but Shake-speare takes advantage of it to make over the twins into Terentian heroes whose differences in personality and in their relationships with added or adapted characters, particularly their respective women, provide the distinction in tone between the high and middle comedy of the play.

Of course, the sexual dealings found in both Roman dramatists had to be dropped or at least left ambiguous. Neither Plautus' bawdy and farcical exploitation of licentious situations nor even Terence's more sophisticated attitudes toward extramarital sex would please the Eliza-bethan audience unless they were kept subtle or dropped into the buf-foonery of the low comic plot. So Shakespeare complies by adding the Dromios and relegating much of the farce to these servants. It is true that each Antipholus beats his Dromio, or one whom he supposes to be his servant, but the emphasis in these farcical scenes is on the victim and his bewilderment. Or, in the bawdy anatomizing of the "spherical" Nell, Antipholus of Syracuse is merely the ear; the low humor is Dromio's.[6] Although the name Dromi is derived from Terence by way of Lyly (*Mother Bombie*), the idea of identical servants came from Mercury and Sosio in *Amphitryon*, from which Shakespeare also borrowed the feast scene in Act 3. In this, Shakespeare is practicing the technique known in Terence as *contaminatio*;[7] as Terence did with Menander's plays, so Shakespeare intrudes into one Plautine play characters and episodes from another.

The other characters of the farcical level are not the result of *con-taminatio* but rather of accommodation. Plautus' doctor becomes "the hungry, lean-faced" (5.1.238) Dr. Pinch, the first of Shakespeare's comic pedants. Erotium, called *amica* in *Menaechmi*, a word often used by Plautus and Terence to mean concubine, becomes in Shakespeare's play merely a nameless "courtesan," whose profession is left ambiguous and from whom Antipholus of Ephesus seeks "excellent discourse" (3.1.109) only when his wife locks him out. Her cook, a male in Plautus' comedy, not only becomes a skivvy in Adriana's household, but is translated into a female and occupies the low comic position in a hierarchal triad of feminine figures: Luciana, Adriana, and Nell (or Luce). Nell, it is true, appears only briefly on stage, but her insistent demands on her brother-in-law are rehearsed by Dromio of Syracuse and parallel those made by Adriana on her master in the middle comedy. Interestingly enough,

Antipholus of Syracuse is again the brunt of chastisement in the high or romantic level of the play when Luciana also scolds him for unhusbandly behavior. This kind of Shakespearean asymmetrical sophistication of a comic situation is unparalleled in Roman comedy—the Syracusan men stand the assaults from the women on all three levels of the play, while the Ephesians for whom they are mistaken get off almost scot-free.

Comedy in which the innocent suffer the most abuse is certainly not new, but it is when superimposed upon a familiar dramatic base that relies for its farcical effect solely upon a balanced repetition of absurd confrontations. The Menaechmian pattern of repeated and bizarre situations arising from mistaken identity is an example of the kind of comedy that Henri Bergson refers to as having been repeated so often (even by Shakespeare's time) that it had reached "the state of being a classical type or model." And Shakespeare takes advantage of the "comic *de facto*" in *The Comedy of Errors*. By superimposing his own, different pattern upon the original model, however, he doubles the comic effect and achieves additional and new "*de jure* comedy."[8] A second and more sophisticated level of laughter results from the dichotomy between the original Menaechmian farce imprinted on the audience's imagination and the Shakespearean palimpsest that it sees before its eyes on the Renaissance stage.

"Extracontaminatio"

At the upper level of the comic scale, Shakespeare practices what might be called "extracontamination," or the addition of characters and their situations from a completely different and, in this case, a nondramatic and anachronistic source: Egeon and the Abbess who, with Luciana, are totally alien to the farcical laughter usually connected with Plautine comedy. Egeon's name, from Aegeus, may have come from the father of Theseus, whom Shakespeare would have come across in his reading of Plutarch or, more likely, as R. A. Foakes suggests, from Cooper's *Thesaurus* or from *The Excellent and Pleasant Works of Julius Solinus Polyster* (1587), which would also explain the name of the Duke of Ephesus, although a Solinus also appears in Lyly's *Campaspe*.[9] The tale that Egeon tells, however, was borrowed from that of Apollonius of Tyre as it was related by John Gower in *Confessio Amantis*, which Shakespeare used again some fifteen years later for *Pericles*. This version also accounts for Emilia's being an abbess.

Shakespeare's opening of his comedy with the threat of death may have been an allowance suggested by Mercury's joking acceptance of tragicomedy in *Amphitryon*, but I think it more likely that an expansion of *Menaechmi*'s narrative and psychological limits to encompass a whole family appealed to the apprentice dramatist anxious to outdo Plautus' "very granary" (p. 367) of comic situations. Shakespeare does not, however, interweave Egeon's precarious position into the main narrative as he does with the addition of the Dromios but uses it as a time frame for the dramatic action, which begins in separation and melancholy and ends in reconciliation and joyousness. Nonetheless, by adding characters at either end of the central Plautine progression, he elongates the spectrum of dramatic coloration.

The introduction of Egeon effectively begins the separation of the two Antipholi into distinct Terentian types. The old man's tale of the tribulations that have beset his family is also his son's, and its pathos and gravity carry over to Antipholus of Syracuse when he appears in the second scene. The son is, like the father, under threat from Ephesian law, but, unlike Egeon who has a one-day reprieve and may move freely about the city, Antipholus must lose himself in an alien world to find that part of himself which is his brother. Various critics have dealt with the whole problem of identity in *The Comedy of Errors;* the point here is to recognize that at the end of Act 1 the dramatic prognosis for Antipholus of Syracuse is anything but comic. He is an alien in a bewildering world— a world that seems to be forcing an identification upon him that he does not recognize—in which his servant acts mad and the thousand marks that are his security against death have disappeared.

Luciana is the only character in *The Comedy of Errors* for whom Shakespeare clearly practices what is called, again with reference to Terence, "auto-contamination,"[10] the addition of a character of his own creation. Her name probably stuck in the playwright's mind from the details borrowed from the travails of Apollonius of Tyre for the Egeon-Emilia frame, although the name Lucina also occurs in the anonymous *Soliman and Persida* (c. 1592). Her position in the play is to introduce into the serious plot a kind of romantic love common to Terence (and through him to Lyly) but not to Plautus. Kathleen M. Lea suggests that she is provided to be a confidante for Adriana and as a "consolation prize for the deserving stranger."[11] Juxtaposed as she is to Adriana, however, Luciana makes even clearer the distinction between the romantic quality of the high comic level and the bourgeois or realistic comedy of which her sister is a part.

Adriana is neither borrowed nor created; neither is she an accommodation to a dramatic composition more sophisticated than the Plautine farce in which Shakespeare found her. Rather she is a transformation! Gone is the mere "matrona" of *Menaechmi,* and in her place stands a fully developed woman who stands at the head of a long line of Shakespeare's remarkable heroines. Luciana pales by her as Hero does by Beatrice. In fact, although Shakespeare has shifted the narrative interest in *The Comedy of Errors* to Antipholus of Syracuse, it is Adriana who prevents the serious concerns from swamping the whole play, not her husband. She even has more lines than he has. Plautus' virago may end up as the nagging wife in Jacobean city comedy, but Shakespeare's Adriana, with her spirit and independence and womanliness, goes on to become Rosalind and Kate and Beatrice and perhaps even Cleopatra. Her husband, on the other hand, never becomes other than a stock type from domestic comedy.

This view of Adriana should lead us to consider with a somewhat less serious eye the disputation on husband-wife relations in which she engages with Luciana. Adriana is clearly a crowd-pleaser, and perhaps her considerations of marriage are designed to titillate a sophisticated mixed audience. Attention has been drawn to the closeness of Luciana's argument to that of St. Paul's. L. Boronski, on the other hand, would see the whole exchange as patterned deliberately as a euphuistic dialogue.[12] There is no reason, of course, why it cannot be both or, indeed, assimilate even a third possibility. The position that Luciana takes is remarkably similar to that of Micio in Terence's *The Brothers*, in which the debate is on how to raise a son. In Terence's play, Micio and his brother, Demeo, present opposing views: Micio advises that a father be generous and patient; Demeo, that he be sparing and hard. The same opposed extremes are presented in the marriage debate in *The Comedy of Errors*, a subject that must have been of topical interest because Shakespeare comes back to it in *Love's Labor's Lost*, *The Taming of the Shrew*, and *Much Ado About Nothing*. Luciana insists that a man be "master of his liberty" and the wife patient and agreeable (2.1.7-9). Adriana takes a firm view; a man is "unruly" and "feeds from home" (2.1.101-2) and, therefore, a wife should be demanding and keep a tight rein. The joke is that Micio's position does not score a victory in *The Brothers*. In a clever and surprising conclusion, Terence shows that the wisest course avoids the weakness of either extreme, and surely this is what Adriana represents at the end of Shakespeare's play and, regardless of what scripture says, the position that would most delight an audience at once aware of the stylistics of the argument and of the Terentian compromise—to say nothing of its relationship to the *topoi* from Cicero through *The Marriage of Wit and Science* (1568), *A Marriage Between Wit and Wisdom* (1570), and *The Marriage of Mind and Measure* (1579), and the like.

Indeed, in the scene before the priory, Adriana's more worldly position ultimately converts even Luciana, for when the Abbess reproaches Adriana for causing her husband's distraction, it is the formerly Pauline Luciana who insists that her sister's behavior was but sauce for the gander:

> She never reprehended him but mildly,
> When he demeaned himself rough, rude, and wildly.
>
> (*The Comedy of Errors*, 5.1.87-88)

With this encouragement, Adriana opposes the holy woman's judgment and asserts her rights in the office of wife. This is not "merely possessive love," as John Russell Brown somewhat chauvinistically suggests, but a statement of her legal conjugal rights certain to draw approval from Shakespeare's mixed audience, particularly one versed in the law and aware, as Shakespeare so often proved himself to be, of the conflicts between secular and spiritual statutes.

Professor Brown attempts to present Adriana's love as "taking" as opposed to "giving." He says, "Adriana sees love as a system of promises, duties, and bonds,"[13] and he is quite right. By the marriage contract Antipholus of Ephesus became, as Adriana says, "Lord of me and all I had" (5.1.137). The "giving" part, both of herself and her possessions, had come much earlier, and now her demands within the marriage bond are valid and understandable. This does not, however, diminish her love and willingness to care for him nor her promptness as a practical helpmeet to "take order for the wrongs" (5.1.146) she thinks he has committed. Much more the victim of the confusions in identity than her sister or the kitchen wench, Adriana has a position at once sympathetic and admirable and entirely in keeping with the realistic level of the comic structure.

Once again, the conscious craft of *The Comedy of Errors* is not merely the result of Shakespeare's lifting the Plautine farce from its Latin setting, peopling it with more lively characters, giving a contemporary twist to a Terentian debate, and then recasting the combination into a totally new comedy palatable to English Renaissance tastes, because the Roman dramas themselves still clearly underlie the Shakespearean super-structure. Neither does Adriana's view on marriage erase that imprinted on the audience's mind from scripture because Luciana has already presented the Pauline position liberally laced with other Biblical allusions to the subservience to man expected of all created things. The comic totality of *The Comedy of Errors* and the sophistication of its response in laughter depends upon consciousness of multiple *and separate* levels of dramatic representation working at once both in dramatic point and counterpoint.

Eclecticism in *The Comedy of Errors*

Conscious eclecticism is also what makes the ending of *The Comedy of Errors* "work" in the theatrical sense, because both its comic structure and its deliberate catering to audience conditioning allow the advantage of playing off actual visual representation against audience mental precon-ceptions. The mere entrance of the second Antipholus to the rest of the cast assembled on stage would suffice to unravel the mistaken identities, as it does in the Plautine farce. Shakespeare chooses to give the narrative resolution to his comedy a distinctly Terentian twist. As Professor Duck-worth points out, "many of the pertinent facts of a Terentian plot were not revealed to the spectator until late in the action";[14] Shakespeare not only holds back knowledge of Emilia's existence, but also introduces her as an entirely new character when she emerges from the priory in Act 5, scene 1. That the Abbess turns out to be the mother of the Antipholi is another borrowing from *Confessio Amantis*, in which, after much wander-ing, Apollonius of Tyre is reunited with his wife in Ephesus. This is the same source that accounts for the resurrection of Egeon, the father reported to have died in *Menaechmi.*

The reactions of the various comic groups to the presence of double sets of twins are finely tuned. The eloquent despair voiced by Egeon when one he sees as his son denies any kinship changes to the joy of waking from a bad dream. Antipholus of Syracuse, whose fortunes were linked with the serious concerns of his father at the beginning of the play and who has throughout the action expressed his bewilderment in repeated doubts as to whether he were awake or asleep, repeats the dream imagery when he reiterates his vows of love to Luciana:

> What I told you then
> I hope I shall have leisure to make good,
> If this be not a dream I see and hear.
>
> *(The Comedy of Errors,* 5.1.375-77)

As for Adriana, one can only guess her facial expressions when first she exclaims with astonishment, "I see two husbands, or mine eyes deceive me" (5.1.332) and then later when she realizes that the Abbess with whom she had disagreed so vociferously is actually her mother-in-law. Her questions, however, are eminently practical—"Which of you did dine with me today?" "And are you not my husband?"—and she and her husband set about clearing up such realistic matters as who owes whom how much money and who gets the gold chain.

Problems in the Ending of *The Comedy of Errors*

The actual ending of *The Comedy of Errors* presents specific problems that can perhaps be explained by again giving attention to audience and occasion. Charmingly funny as the Dromios may be in the closing lines as each acts as the other's mirror, why should Shakespeare choose to end the play with the servants of the low comic action rather than with the higher ranking or main characters, as he does in most other plays he wrote? One possible answer is that Plautus closes *Menaechmi* with a speech by Messenio, the former slave of Menaechmus of Syracuse, except that Messenio's words are only a farcical announcement of the forthcoming auction of Epidamus' property, whereas the Dromios' lines have actual thematic and tonal significance for the end of Shakespeare's play. It is also very strange that Shakespeare would overlook the joyous reconciliations at the close of *The Comedy of Errors* as an opportunity for providing, or at least implying, some kind of revelry to round out the action, as was common to most Elizabethan comedies. But the ending of the play is abrupt. The actual dramatic conclusion of the action comes with the Duke's agreement to join the reunited family in their celebration, and yet there is not even a call for music to accompany the feast. Perhaps a plausible answer to these problems is that the play as we have it in the Folio text is the version designed to fit into the special entertainment for which we have record in the *Gesta Grayorum*. It would certainly explain why *The Comedy of Errors* is so short, just over 1,700 lines, hardly enough for a complete theatrical performance. In fact, the New Cambridge editor thinks that the public playhouse version was "longer than the text that comes down to us, perhaps by as much as four hundred lines."[15]

There is certainly ample precedent for using short dramatic representations as part of larger aristocratic entertainments throughout Elizabeth's reign. In addition, Geoffrey Bullough lists a number of Italian and other Continental adaptations of *Menaechmi*[16] in the sixteenth century, and both Foakes and Lea agree that Shakespeare "does seems to have been acquainted with the way in which comedy of mistaken identity was exploited on the Italian stage."[17] George Freedley and John Reeves describe an Italian performance of *Menaechmi*, which was followed by "one of the famous banquets which included a morisco (a simplified *ballet d'action*) in which Cesare Borgia acted. As the music rose for a glorious finale, the guests danced with the performers and the Pope looked on approvingly."[18] Shakespeare's play appears to have been adapted to be part of a similar larger entertainment, and there is reason to suspect that *The Comedy of Errors* was also meant to be followed by a masque.

At the entertainment planned for "*Innocents-Day* at Night" in December, 1594,[19] the Prince of Purpoole was, on behalf of his subjects at Gray's Inn, to entertain an Ambassador from the Inner Temple and his court. The King of Arms announced the arrival of the Ambassador and his attendants to the Prince "then sitting in his Chair of State in the Hall." The guest proceeded through the hall to honor the Prince of Purpoole with speeches of high compliment. However, the Ambassador was no sooner placed so he could view "something to be performed for the Delight of the Beholders," than the plans went awry, for "there arose such a disordered Tumult and Crowd upon the Stage, that there was no Opportunity to effect that which was intended." Indeed, the Gray's Inn lawyers and their company behaved so badly that the guests from the Inner Temple left in displeasure. Considering the progress of events to the disorder, the indication is that had the evening's entertainment continued as planned, the presentment, procession to state, and ceremonial compliments would have been followed by a play and a masque. Under other circumstances, the "something to be performed for the Delight of the Beholders" might have meant merely games of mumchance, barriers, or some other diversion interjected before the play, but the earlier reference to "good Inventions and Conceipts," suggests that the plan was for something more elaborate such as a masque.[20]

The end of *The Comedy of Errors* seems to support this suggestion. After the denouement—the discovering and sorting out of the Antipholi and the Dromios and the joyous reunion of parents with children and brothers with brothers—the major characters, led by the Duke, withdraw from the stage to celebrate the happy occasion. The two servants, the Dromios, are left on stage to go through a series of burlesque gestures as to who will leave the stage first, finally agreeing:

> We came into the world like brother and brother:
> And now let's go hand in hand, not one before the other.
> *(The Comedy of Errors*, 5.1.426-27)

This posturing is suggestive of an antic dance, one type of comic contrast that gave rise to the antimasque in the Court Masques and could have been intended as a prelude to the masque dances. These measures, if this were the case, would be performed by members of Gray's Inn and their ladies taking the place of the professional actors for the dance finale. The use of the lowly Dromios as masque presenters is fully in keeping as a final fillip for a play that has relied so much upon comic confrontation and juxtaposition, while, at the same time, their amusing dialogue would provide stage business during the substitution. The masque would thus fulfill two functions. It first rounds out the action of the play proper by visually symbolizing harmony achieved after confusion, and it would also act as the final sport of the entire Innocents-day night celebration.

Various other suggestions would also seem to relate the extant version to this specific occasion: an unusual amount of legal terminology that Sidney Thomas uses to support December 28, 1594, as the first performance of *The Comedy of Errors*;[21] the appropriateness of Emilia's closing line, "After so long grief, such nativity" (5.1.407); and the fact that it was thought suitable for presentation at the stylish Stuart court for the same festival in 1604.

G. B. Harrison senses a rather condescending touch about the play, "a hint that the author is above this sort of thing but if you challenge him he will show you how cleverly he can do it."[22] On the other hand, we might speculate that a beginning playwright would be flattered that his company was asked to present one of his plays before such a prestigious and learned group and go out of his way to adapt it to their tastes and formal occasion. Harold Goddard calls it "pure theatre," "a product of Shakespeare's intellect rather than of imagination."[23] Although we might not agree totally with this assessment, *The Comedy of Errors* is certainly a remarkably eclectic play, which depends for its comic impact upon knowing the theatrical game the playwright is playing. It is an Elizabethan hybrid. Although still showing the clear signs of its original farcical stock, the play has been crossbred with both the realism and romance of the English stage and the learned and dialectical wit of Renaissance thought. The multileveling of character and narrative tone and the superimposition of various layers of dramatic representation upon the Latin base have produced a Shakespearean palimpsest. Structurally and stylistically, Shakespeare uses Plautus to outdo Plautus, Terence to outdo Terence, and turns a Roman farce into a polished and sophisticated entertainment, which produces a special intellectual relation between performance and audience depending for its effect upon awareness of its conscious art.

Notes

1. *On the Compositional Genetics of "The Comedy of Errors"* (Urbana, Illinois, 1965), Chapter VI, pp. 73-87.
2. *Multiple Plots in English Renaissance Drama* (Chicago, 1971), p. 226.
3. *The Complete Roman Drama*, edited in two volumes with Introduction (New York, 1942), I, xxxi.
4. Op. cit., p. 227.
5. *The Two Menaechmuses*, trans. by Paul Nixon, *Loeb Classical Library* (London, 1917), p. 413. All quotations are from this edition.
6. T. W. Baldwin notes that "Dromio's lesson in political geography . . . was not lost on the Gentlemen of Gray's Inn, who turned it into 'Purpoole smut' " (op. cit., pp. 3-4).
7. Paradigmatic variations of the verb *contaminare* were used by Terence to describe the transference of plot elements or characters from one play to another. He defends the practice in various of his Prologues (see, for example, *The Lady of Andros* and *The Self-Tormentor*).
8. Henri Bergson, "Laughter," *Comedy*, edited by Wylie Sypher (New York, 1956), p. 122.
9. Introduction to *The Comedy of Errors* (The Arden Shakespeare: London, 1968), pp. xxix-xxx.
10. The term *auto-contamination* is first used by Gilbert Norwood (*The Art of Terence* [Oxford, 1923], p. 16). Roy C. Flickinger accepts the validity of the term with regard to Terence's stagecraft although he objects to the example Norwood cites ("The Originality of Terence," *Philological Quarterly*, VII [1928], p. 112).
11. *Italian Popular Comedy* (Oxford, 1934), II, 42.
12. For a summary of Boronski's argument and the various Biblical borrowings, see R. A. Foakes's notes to Act 1, scene 2, and Appendix 1 (pp. 113-15) in The Arden Shakespeare.
13. *Shakespeare and His Comedies* (London, 1962), pp. 54-55.
14. Op. cit., p. xxxii.
15. *The Comedy of Errors*, edited by John Dover Wilson (Cambridge, 1968), p. 77.
16. *Narrative and Dramatic Sources of Shakespeare*, I (London, 1957), 57.
17. Foakes, op. cit., p. xxxii.
18. *The History of the Theatre* (New York, 1941), p. 66.
19. *Gesta Grayorum*, edited by W. W. Greg, *Malone Society Reprints*, 42 (Oxford, 1914), 20-23.
20. It is tempting to speculate that part of this planned "Delight" was to have been a rehearsal for the *Masque of Proteus*, which was performed at Court by the gentlemen of Gray's Inn the following Shrovetide. The "Adamantine Rock," the movable device employed in the masque, would account for the necessity for "Scaffolds," which the record tells us were "reared to the top of the House, to increase Expectation."
21. "The Date of *The Comedy of Errors*," *Shakespeare Quarterly*, VII (1956), 380-81.
22. "Shakespearean Comedy," *Stratford Papers on Shakespeare* (Toronto, 1962), p. 42.
23. *The Meaning of Shakespeare* (Chicago, 1951), I, 26.

Bibliographical Note

This paper owes much to classical scholars concerned with the dramaturgy of Latin comedy, particularly Gilbert Norwood (*The Art of Terence* [Oxford, 1923]; *The Nature of Roman Comedy* [Princeton, 1942]) and George C. Duckworth (*The Complete Roman Drama* [New York, 1942]). Also seminal to the study of relationships between Latin and Renaissance comedy is Appendix A "The Double Plot in Roman Comedy" in Richard Levin's *Multiple Plots in English Renaissance Drama* (Chicago, 1971).

3

Wise Saws
and Modern Instances:
The Relevance of Donatus

SUSAN SNYDER

In the late 1580s and early 1590s, Shakespeare and his contemporaries—
men like Peele and Greene as well as the now unknown authors of such
plays as *Fair Em* and *Mucedorus*—were developing a distinctive genre of
romantic comedy on the Elizabethan public stage. In the process they
had the Roman classics and the native English tradition, festival as well as
literary, to draw on. Were they, in addition, aware of any theory, any
organic idea of comedy? In the absence of personal statements, one looks
about for ideas that were current; and none was more current than the
scheme by which "Donatus" defined comedy by opposing it to tragedy.
The essay "De tragoedia et comoedia" (actually a work in two parts, the
second written by the fourth-century grammarian Aelius Donatus and the
first by his contemporary Evanthius) regularly appeared in editions of
Terence used by school and university students.

Alas. Though so widely available and hence probably familiar to
Shakespeare and the others, Donatus (I shall from now on use the term
for both parts of the essay) seems at first inspection an unlikely source for
any organic notion of comedy. Comedy, goes the laconic formula, is

about men of middling estate; its dangers are small-scale, its outcomes are happy. In tragedy, "omnia contra": the persons and issues are great, the outcomes lamentable. Comedy begins in turbulence and ends in tranquillity; this shape tragedy quite reverses because it expresses the *rejection* of life where comedy expresses the *embracing* of life. Finally, comedies have feigned plots whereas tragedies are often based on history. As a theoretical key to romantic comedy's blend of fantasy, fortune, and multiplied plots and characters, this series of discrete oppositions seems to modern eyes a dismal failure. Nevertheless, looking at what the Elizabethan comedy writers actually created, one suspects that they found in Donatus more depth and consistency than we do. In any case, their practice—in mediocre comedies as well as masterpieces—gives depth and consistency to the grammarians' apparently arbitrary dicta.

The plays suggest, for instance, that their writers saw more than a truism in the premise that comedies end happily and tragedies unhappily. The implication is that, although dangers threaten in both kinds, it is only tragedy that follows out threat to fulfillment and chains act to consequence in unbreakable logic. To achieve its happy resolution in the face of potential ill, comedy must deal in alternatives—fresh scenes of action, new identities, alternative realities. Magicians with the power to transform landscapes and hearts at will abound in the Elizabethan comedies, along with others who effect their transformations by different means: Petruchio's corrective satire remakes Kate in *The Taming of the Shrew*, and only a few words from an "old religious man" are enough to turn tyrant Frederick in *As You Like It* into a repentant eremite. Still others, needing to gain freedom of action, take on themselves temporary alternative identities. The constant resort to disguise that Chapman later mocked in *May Day* ("by a change of a hat or cloak to alter the whole state of a comedy") did not become a comic cliché by accident. Disguise, magic, manipulation all enact a kind of "evitability" principle, as ways of creating new situations when the old ones become impossible. Reality is alterable, unfixed.

In a fixed reality, death is the unavoidable end of each human course. Romantic comedy thus has a special need to get around death somehow: by ignoring it completely or, more interestingly, by presenting it as nonfinal, illusory. The Elizabethans allow nobody important to die in their comedies; indeed, Shakespeare preserves *all* his romantic comedy characters intact, no matter how minor. On the contrary, they are fond of resurrecting people believed or feared dead. To Shakespeare's Abbess in *The Comedy of Errors*, Hero in *Much Ado About Nothing*, and Sebastian in *Twelfth Night*, we may add such examples as Sempronio in *A Knack to Know an Honest Man* and Dorothea in *James the Fourth*. So potent is this refusal of mortality that even a character who is "really" dead, Jack the corpse in Peele's *Old Wives' Tale*, is not denied a lively part in the play's action. Though he is called a ghost, he has far less in common with Banquo than with Falstaff on Shrewsbury field, rearing up irrepressibly after Hal has pronounced his epitaph.

Out of the same need for an alterable reality, romantic comedy flamboyantly rejects constraints of law and time. Northrop Frye has made us aware how frequently Shakespeare's comedies begin with a harsh law that must be evaded or openly flouted in the course of the action.[1] Not only does comedy have a Saturnalian affinity for lawlessness in general, but law in these comedies tends to be set up in opposition to life and fertility. Against the notable exception of Portia's father's will in *The Merchant of Venice*, a legal arrangement that promotes marriage at least for the winner of the casket stakes, the norm is set by laws that condemn Syracusan merchants to death in the absence of ransom (*The Comedy of Errors*) and daughters who resist their fathers' choice of a husband to death or perpetual virginity (*A Midsummer Night's Dream*); or self-imposed laws that cut off young men from the company of women (*Love's Labor's Lost*) and cloister a young woman apart from all wooing (*Twelfth Night*). Olivia, too, along with Navarre and his bookmen, must lose her oath to find herself. As the rules of life they tried to force on themselves did not suit their young natures, so the civil laws of Ephesus and Athens, initially imposed without consideration of individual cases, must bend to accommodate, in the one case, a reunited family, and in the other, a happy pairing of lovers. The two major jobs of Shakespeare's comic dukes are to lay down the law in the first place and then to wave it away in the last.

In Greene's *Friar Bacon and Friar Bungay*, Margaret seems destined, like Hermia, to spend her life in a cloister mourning disappointed love; but her "vow that may not be revok'd" is, in fact, revoked with great alacrity when her lover Lacy appears—at the very moment she is to withdraw to the convent. For time as well as law in these comedies stretches to suit, allowing not only Lacy to rescue Margaret but Orlando to save Angelica in Greene's *Orlando Furioso* and several sets of twins to confront one another when confusion has led events to the brink of madness and death in *The Comedy of Errors* and *Twelfth Night*. Once again, a later reference tells us how conventional was that opportune entrance that solves every-thing: when Edmund's plot against Edgar in *King Lear* requires his brother's presence, he laughs as Edgar comes right along on cue "pat . . . , like the catastrophe of the old comedy" (1.2.137-8). "Too late" is not in the comic vocabulary.

Donatus's Rules for Comedy

From this angle, Donatus's prescription of a made-up plot for comedy looks less arbitrary. Whether the comic writer borrows fictions or creates his own, he must not be held down to facts and probabilities. In order to supply the alternatives and second chances that life does not, he must be free like his own favorite magician-manipulators to remake reality in the image of his wish.

In this expansiveness, this refusal of limits, comedy opposes tragedy, where it is finitude that generates the intensity. Tragedy's high stakes and fateful decisions give significant form, in Susanne Langer's term, to a sense of one's own life as unique and momentous, having its own destined shape. In its lesser folk and more ordinary concerns, comedy embodies a sense of life quite different though equally familiar to us—as common and continuing, an ongoing current in which we participate without being the whole story. This is the kind of comic perspective that Shakespeare liked to introduce toward the end of a tragedy, using the relaxed, wide-ranging view of the clown to set off Cleopatra's fully perceived, fateful moment or the common humanity of the gravediggers (who, like the clown in *Antony and Cleopatra*, are given no names) to define more sharply Hamlet's special identity. Even if Elizabethan playwrights liked to dole out higher ranks to their lover-characters, the dukes and kings of romantic comedy function essentially like private citizens. Courtship, not foreign policy, is their preoccupation. Wars between Christians and Saracens or between the English and the Scots that in a tragedy would be all-important, in the comedies are displaced to the background by the loves of Orlando and James the Fourth.

Love and mating are, of course, the point. The Donatus scheme summarized above does not characterize the ordinary doings that are the stuff of comedy; but another early grammarian, Diomedes, in a treatise that parallels Donatus's at many points, declared that comedy was about love affairs and the stealing away of maidens.[2] Donatus seems to agree when, in another section of the essay, praising Terence for his double plots, he says that whereas *The Mother-in-Law* has only the love of Pamphilus, all five others have two young men (that is, lovers). Courtship is indeed the usual mainspring of the action in the Elizabethan comedies I have been examining. The occasional exceptions, like *The Comedy of Errors* or *A Knack to Know a Knave*, meet what is apparently felt as an obligation by offering a courtship subplot. When in *Love's Labor's Lost* the Princess and her ladies impose a year's delay on their marriages, Berowne could complain to an audience that knew very well how comedies were supposed to come out:

> Our wooing doth not end like an old play:
> Jack hath not Jill. These ladies' courtesy
> Might well have made our sport a comedy.

(5.2.872-4)

In the convention that a truly satisfactory ending must pair as many Jacks as possible with Jills, there is an implication that separately the Jacks and Jills are somehow incomplete, lacking the complement that rounds out identity. The marriages that end romantic comedies operate as symbols not only of procreation but of fuller being.

As two identities are better than one, so it seems clear from Donatus's praise of Terentian plot-doubling that two actions are better than one. In fact, I would argue that the principle that links together all the traditional formulas is *the rejection of singleness*. It is implicit in the sense of ourselves as participants in some larger and ongoing whole that assigns unexceptional rank to comedy's characters as opposed to the exalted rulers and heroes of tragedy. It is the basis of "evitability," for the figures we depend on to bring about comedy's happy endings are the disguisers who take on a second identity, the magicians who call up an alternative reality. The need to multiply and vary perspectives also underlies aspects of Elizabethan comedy that go beyond the prescriptions of Donatus. Far more than Terence's double plots, the multiple actions in these plays operate so as continually to be qualifying the single world view with others. At the elbows of the most romantic lovers appear homely rustics and servants who think only of eating and drinking. Even within the same social class Shakespeare will differentiate actions so that, for example, in *The Taming of the Shrew* Bianca's storybook wooing and the earthy encounters of Kate and Petruchio over beef and mustard can comment on each other.

If necessary, one character can incorporate his own opposing voice, as Touchstone does in summing up life in the Forest of Arden:

> In respect that it is solitary, I like it very well; but in respect that it is private, it is a very vile life. Now in respect it is in the fields, it pleaseth me well; but in respect it is not in the court, it is tedious. As it is a spare life, look you, it fits my humor well; but as there is no more plenty in it, it goes much against my stomach.
>
> (*As You Like It*, 3.2.15-21)

Neither truth is enough by itself, that of the pastoralist celebrating solitude, communion with nature, and content with little, or that of the urban sophisticate missing polished conversation and *haute cuisine*. Comedy must open out to find the more comprehensive view, and so several plots are better than one, and clowns will have their say as well as lovers. Even their manner of saying typically rejects the single for the double meaning. Puns, malapropisms, and portmanteau words work by superimposing one idea on another, disparate one, not so as to cancel out the first but so as to expand our awareness—to take in more life.

For *vita capessenda (est)*, the imperative to take hold of life and fully engage it, if taken seriously in Donatus's formula, can explain much more about comedy than its harmonious ending. As a driving motive *vita capessenda* applies more wholly and organically to these romantic comedies than the more didactic one so frequently cited in Shakespeare's day, which justified comedy morally as holding a mirror to all manners and exposing the defective to corrective ridicule. Surely playwrights with such an intention would not return again and again to courtship when other areas of life offer so many examples of human folly. Indeed, something quite apart from morality seems to determine comedy's rewards and punishments. Sir Toby Belch is not notably higher on the scale of virtue than Malvolio; but whereas the puritanical steward gets thoroughly humiliated, the reveller-trickster gains his satisfying revenge and a wife in the bargain. As Harriett Hawkins observes in her paper, the "moral example" theory of comedy "is a defense designed to answer specific charges, and not a primary response to comedy itself."

What we watch in *Twelfth Night* is not virtue rewarded and vice held up to scorn but the victory of festivity and flexibility over the rigid, constraining humor. Toby is a rogue, but his roguery promotes freedom and, in Donatus's formula, embraces life. It is appropriate that Shakespeare marries him off to Maria at the play's close, thus associating the not-so-young but still game knight with Orsino and Viola, Sebastian and Olivia, in the triumph of youth that recalls comedy's ancient roots in fertility ritual. Frazer, Cornford, and others have made us familiar with the various rites—an old king displaced by a young one, a dead god resurrected, a scapegoat sent out, branches of greenery brought in—which were enacted to banish death and ensure the fertility of the new growing season. The symbolic forms all have their relevance to Shakespearean romantic comedy, with its drive toward mating and its insistence (obscured in *Twelfth Night* by the absence of a real older generation but clear enough in *A Midsummer Night's Dream* and *The Merchant of Venice*) that the old give way to the fertile, vigorous young. Rites and plays alike are about life, not virtue.

Twelfth Night provides an emblem of the relative comic status of Toby and Malvolio when the one, engaged in a practical joke, looks on from concealment and comments while the other pursues, all unaware, the daydreams of his obsessive vanity. Such scenes, as Frye observes, "in which one character complacently soliloquizes while another makes sarcastic asides to the audience show the contest between *eiron* and *alazon* in its purest form." Frye's perception that the core of comedy is this contest between eiron, the knowing one who seems less than he is, and alazon, the impostor who pretends to be more than he is, has been valuable;[3] but as categories for characters who win or lose in comedy, eiron and alazon will take us just so far. Proteus in *The Two Gentlemen of Verona* and the whole quartet of lovers in *A Midsummer Night's Dream* gain the reward of marriage, but ironic awareness, of self or others, is not their strong suit. In my mind, eiron and alazon give most insight into comedy's workings when seen as *principles*, rather than as characters, in conflict: flexibility and awareness operating on all levels to shake loose the fixity of self-delusion, or, if that is impossible, to cast it out discomfited. Propelled by love (even when it is temporarily love for the wrong girl), Proteus, Lysander, and Demetrius can adjust to new conditions, improvise ways around obstacles. This potential aligns them with the eiron against the rigid alazon. Once again, the contest is not moral but vital; fixation in one position imitates death, adaptation to new situations promotes further, more abundant life. And once again, as we observe the single identity or position of the alazon falling before the eiron's shifts of stance and multiple awareness, we are led back to the same persistent principle: the rejection of singleness.

Notes

Portions of this paper are taken in adapted form from Chapter 1, "A World Elsewhere," of *The Comic Matrix of Shakespeare's Tragedies* by Susan Snyder, and are copyrighted © 1979 by Princeton University Press. Reprinted by permission of Princeton University Press.

1. *Anatomy of Criticism* (Princeton: Princeton Univ. Press, 1957), p. 166.
2. Diomedes, *De arte grammatica opus* (Paris, 1507), sig. H6v. For the availability of the Diomedes essay during the Renaissance, see Madeleine Doran, *Endeavors of Art* (Madison: Univ. of Wisconsin Press, 1954), p. 106 and p. 414 n.
3. *Anatomy*, pp. 171-5; quotation from p. 172.

Bibliographical Note

For general notions of comedy, my thinking in this essay is indebted to C. L. Barber, *Shakespeare's Festive Comedy* (Princeton: Princeton Univ. Press, 1959); Northrop Frye, *Anatomy of Criticism* (Princeton: Princeton Univ. Press, 1957); Helen Gardner, "*As You Like It*," in *More Talking of Shakespeare*, ed. John Garrett (London: Longmans, Green & Co., 1959); Susanne K. Langer, "The Comic Rhythm," in her *Feeling and Form* (London: Routledge and Kegan Paul, 1953); and Maynard Mack, Introduction to Fielding's *Joseph Andrews* (New York: Holt, Rinehart, 1948). Also illuminating in its implications for comedy is Mack's essay on Shakespearean tragedy, "The Jacobean Shakespeare," in *Jacobean Theatre*, ed. J. Russell Brown and Bernard Harris, Stratford-upon-Avon Studies, 1 (London: Edward Arnold, 1960). The formulas of Donatus, Evanthius, and Diomedes are discussed in Madeleine Doran, *Endeavors of Art* (Madison: Univ. of Wisconsin Press, 1954) and Marvin T. Herrick, *Comic Theory in the Sixteenth Century* (Urbana: Univ. of Illinois Press, 1950). Barber's book and the earlier, more controversial study of F. M. Cornford, *The Origin of Attic Comedy* (London: Edward Arnold, 1914), explore the relation between seasonal rituals and literary comedy, and Cornford in the process uses the *Tractatus Coisilianus* categories *eiron* and *alazon*, later elaborated by Frye. The *Tractatus* itself, a Greek outline closely related to Aristotle's *Poetics*, *Ethics*, and *Rhetoric*, is printed in *Comicorum graecorum fragmenta*, I, ed. Georg Kaibel (1899; rept. Berlin: Weidmannsche Verlag, 1958), as are the essays of Donatus-Evanthius and Diomedes; Lane Cooper offers an English translation of the *Tractatus* with extensive glosses in *An Aristotelian Theory of Comedy* (Oxford: Blackwell, 1924).

4

What Neoclassical Criticism Tells Us about What Shakespeare Does Not Do

HARRIETT HAWKINS

Many scientific theories have, for very long periods of time, stood the test of experience until they had to be discarded owing to man's decision, not merely to make other experiments, but to have different experiences.

Erich Heller

And one wild Shakespeare, following Nature's lights, Is worth whole planets, filled with Stagyrites.

Thomas Moore

"What," asked Dryden, could be "more easy than to write a regular French play, or more difficult than to write an irregular one, like those of Shakespeare?" In their manifest "irregularity," Shakespeare's plays were impossible to imitate. Moreover, they also defied analysis in terms of the orthodox and, indeed, the only body of critical theory available to Dryden: Classical antiquity had always provided the "ideal" models of what literary and dramatic forms ought to be. Some of the best minds in western Europe had articulated and affirmed those critical principles that could be deduced from the practice of the ancients. And many great playwrights had conformed to the consequent tradition amenable to analysis in terms of those rules. Shakespeare, of course, did not. Thus, the transcendent greatness of "the man who, of all modern, and perhaps ancient poets, had the largest and most comprehensive soul" seemed a wonder of nature—an object of reverence not subject to critical examination. Dryden, therefore, chose one of Jonson's comic masterpieces, not one of Shakespeare's, for the most detailed analysis given to a single play in his *Essay of Dramatic Poesy*.

Like all critical theories, neoclassical theories of the drama can be compared to prescription lenses that obscure what lies outside their focus even if they clarify things within it. Thus, the same theories that provided major playwrights and critics, like Dryden and Jonson, with practical rules for application, as well as topics for critical inquiry, effectively impaired critical consideration of Shakespeare's plays. This is why reading, say, Rymer's discussion of *Othello* seems comparable to reading a dog's criticism of the behavior of a cat, or—to borrow Isaiah Berlin's distinction—following a blinkered hedgehog into wild fox country. Thus, the example of neoclassical criticism would seem to suggest that our vision of much great literature will only be distorted by the lenses of theory. Conversely, one could argue that the idea that such theories do, in fact, promote observation and interpretation carries more (not less) weight if it can be shown that under certain circumstances they have impeded both. In any case, the circumstances whereby far the most long-lived and widely held of all critical theories at first impeded, but subsequently promoted, a critical understanding and appreciation of Shakespeare's unique accomplishment are what remain significant still.

What needs accounting for, first, is the way in which, by a kind of emergent, if not miraculous, novelty, Shakespeare's masterpieces finally brought about perhaps the most radical reversal of values in the history of literary criticism.

Finding it impossible either to explain or to judge the works of Shakespeare in terms of neoclassical theory, Dr. Johnson used Shakespeare's plays as criteria by which to criticize the theory itself. Given the usual intellectual propensity to analyze and judge literary practices in terms of theory (and not vice versa), and given the tendency of most critics to confuse their own criteria for analysis with criteria of value, one can only look back at *The Preface to Shakespeare* with astonishment. Here (to my mind, anyway) is the best possible use of a critical theory— and yet that use is paradoxical. By using the tenets of neoclassical criticism to show precisely what Shakespeare did *not* do, Dr. Johnson opened up a new world of speculation as to how and why Shakespeare did what he does do. It is through Dr. Johnson's application-of-it-in-reverse that neoclassical theory can truly be said to illuminate Shakespeare's practice.

Whether Shakespeare knew all the rules "and rejected them by design or deviated from them by happy ignorance" is, as Johnson observed, "impossible to decide, and useless to inquire." The ways in which he deviated from them and the dramatic impact of those deviations are what count. He does not (for instance) present us with an intrigue "regularly perplexed and regularly unravelled"; he does not endeavor "to hide his design only to discover it"; to the unities of time and place he shows little regard; he is "so much more careful to please than to instruct" that he seems to write without any moral purpose. He makes no "just distribution of good or evil," nor is he always careful to "show in the virtuous a disapprobation of the wicked"; he carries his persons indifferently through right and wrong "and leaves their examples to operate by chance." His plays are neither strict tragedies nor strict comedies, but compositions that purposely mingle hornpipes and funerals. His plots are often so loosely formed that "a very slight consideration may improve them." When he found himself near the end of his work and in view of his reward, "he shortened the labor to snatch the profit." He, therefore, remits his efforts when he should most vigorously exert them, and his catastrophe "is improbably produced or imperfectly represented."

Judged according to the rules he violated, Shakespeare's plays must needs plead guilty as charged, defying justification on either aesthetic or on moral grounds. Dr. Johnson, therefore, challenged the laws themselves, treating them not as criteria of judgment, but as points of departure from whence to launch his appeal from criticism to "nature," to the supreme court of human experience, to Pope's "source and end and test of art" itself. Boldly judging plays and rules alike in terms of their conformity to the truths of human experience, Johnson concluded that it was Shakespeare's very adherence to "general nature" that rendered him most vulnerable to critical attack: "*Dennis* and *Rhymer* think his *Romans* not sufficiently *Roman;* and *Voltaire* censures his kings as not completely royal." But Shakespeare "thinks only on men": "He knew that *Rome,* like every other city, had men of all dispositions; and wanting a buffoon, he went into the senate house for that which the senate house would certainly have afforded him." Likewise, Johnson observed that those plays that had incurred censure by mixing comic and tragic scenes do accurately "exhibit the real state of sublunary nature, which partakes of good and evil, joy and sorrow . . . in which at the same time, the reveller is hastening to his wine, and the mourner burying his friend; in which the malignity of one is sometimes defeated by the frolick of another; and many mischiefs and many benefits are done and hindered without design."

Thanks to Dr. Johnson, it seems blindingly obvious that its conformity to, or deviations from, the dictas of neoclassical theory have nothing whatsoever to do with the merit of an individual play. Significantly, however, the same thing may be said of any critical criteria—including one's own. Like any other criticism, the criticism of our own time inevitably tends to confuse its own criteria for analysis with criteria of merit. Thus, for me to have proved that an Elizabethan play has iterative imagery, thematic and structural unity, a metadramatic substructure, Christian overtones—or Freudian undertones—would, at various times in the second half of the twentieth century, seem to have demonstrated that it was, therefore, better than it had appeared to be before this-or-that facet of it was acknowledged. Yet a play might have all the components favored by the criticism of our own age and still be deadly dull, while another play that lacks them may blaze with light. What critical theory did not dictate, that theory cannot fully explain, and it goes without saying that the greatest plays were all, without exception, written to be experienced by an audience, not to be analyzed by critics. Moreover, no theory, however distinguished its advocates, is itself beyond criticism. Are critical theories truly conducive to an understanding of literature? As the minatory example of neoclassical theory indicates, only when they serve it by showing precisely what goes on in individual works (as in Dryden's "Examen" of *The Silent Woman*) and only when the critic remains free to say how and why they do not, and need not, apply to others. Conversely, criticism becomes formulaic, sterile, and boring when it is simply a matter of applying some reigning theory to works of radically different kinds and when its arguments are directed against each other rather than at the human and literary problems posed by individual authors and works.[1]

Here are two such arguments:

> Comedies make men see and shame at their own faults.
> (Thomas Heywood, *An Apology for Actors* [1612])

> Comedy . . . corrupts the mores of men and makes them effeminate and drives them towards lust and dissipation . . . and the habit of seeing them affords the spectator the license of changing for the worst.
> (I. G., *A Refutation of the Apology for Actors* [1615])

Neither of these generalizations is directed at any specific comedy. Neither has anything whatsoever to do with, say, *The Comedy of Errors* or *As You Like It* or any number of other contemporary comedies that, in effect, prove it false.

Looking back at the long history of comic art (as opposed to comic theory), one might decide that it reflects man's determination not merely to make new experiments in comic form, but to create new forms of comic experience. Thus, while (almost?) everyone would agree that *The Frogs, The Menaechmi, The Miller's Tale, A Midsummer Night's Dream, Twelfth Night, Bartholomew Fair, Love for Love, The Beggar's Opera, The Importance of Being Earnest, My Little Chickadee*, and *Some Like It Hot* are all, indisputably, comedies, their individual shares in the total glory of comic art could more readily be explained in terms of their differences—in subject, frame of reference, vocabulary, characterization, and so on—than by any (whether or not there are any is another question) generic features common to all of them. On the other hand, after reading through neoclassical discussions of the genre, one might well conclude that, somewhere over the rainbow, there is the perfectly realized Ideal of Pure Comedy, to which all earthly efforts aspire and by which they all may be judged.

Here, chosen from any number of other critics who parrot the same idea, is Minturno's account of what comedy is and ought to do: "Now comic poets imitate the life of private persons so as to induce everyone to correct the manners which he sees criticized in others and to imitate those which he sees approved" (*The Art of Poetry*, 1563). And here is Thomas Shadwell, writing a century later: The comic playwright should "adorn his images of *Vertue* so delightfully to affect people with . . . an emulation to practice it in themselves: And to render their Figures of *Vice* and *Folly* so ugly and detestable, to make People hate and despise them, not only in others, but (if it be possible) in their dear selves" (*Preface to The Humorists*, 1671). Even when confronted with comedies (like those of Shakespeare) that wildly diverged from its tenets, this particular theory of comedy held its sway. So did the equally irrelevant countertheory: by the same token and at the same time, a whole chorus of commentators insisted, along with I. G. and Stephen Gosson, that the examples of comic characters corrupt our morals. One reason for the tenacity of these theories is that, however individual *comedies* may differ from each other in intent or in effect, critical discussions of "comedy" have, over centuries, served essentially the same purposes and, therefore, followed similar patterns: seeking to define comedy in terms of its generic characteristics, they trace its origins, name its parts, and finally either denounce or defend the genre in terms of the moral effect that it has, or ought to have, upon its audience. And over all such arguments falls the titanic shadow of Plato.

Plato on Comedy

Concluding that comedy served no good purposes at all, Plato banished poets from *The Republic* and started the controversy about the moral effect of drama that raged throughout the Renaissance and Restoration (attacks on poetry and drama by Gosson, I. G., Jeremy Collier, and their host of followers can best be seen as footnotes to Plato) and that rages on in certain twentieth-century discussions of Elizabethan and Restoration drama. Since it is so obviously true that what we look at and admire may influence what we do, Plato argued that our "uninhibited pleasure in buffoonery and bad taste on the stage" may lead us into "becoming buffoons" ourselves: "When you enjoy on the stage jokes that you would be ashamed to make yourself you are giving rein to your comic instinct, which your reason has restrained for fear that you may seem to be playing the fool." Poetry has "the same effect on us when it represents sex and anger, and the other desires and feelings of pleasure and pain" which accompany all our actions: "It waters them when they ought to be left to wither, and makes them control us, when we ought, in the interests of our greater welfare, to control them." Since poetry so powerfully elicits admiration or sympathy for characters who ought, morally, to be condemned, Plato ordered poets to portray good characters or not to write at all.

To write only about good characters and thus attempt a sinless literature of sinful man is, however, a contradiction in terms. To portray human experience as it is, literature must display human passions, follies, frailties, and crimes. Therefore, examples of bad behavior will, alas, abound in any drama. Consequently, if one accepts the premise that characters on the stage inevitably incite us to emulation, there seems to be only one defense of the drama left, and that is the counterargument that comic and tragic characters instruct us as object examples of how not to behave. Recurring over and over again, in defense after defense of the drama, is the same refrain (here taken from Sidney's *Defense of Poesy*), according to which comedy, virtually by definition, represents the common errors of our lives "in the most ridiculous and scornful sort that may be, so as it is impossible that any beholder can be content to be such a one."

The major weakness in the "example" theory of comedy, whether used by witnesses for the prosecution or for the defense, would at first glance appear to be its major strength: It is all-purpose. The effect of any drama whatsoever may be either deplored or commended, depending on who is doing the moralizing. Ever since Plato, this theory has served as an easy weapon in the hands of puritans who attack comic writers for creating characters attractive enough to seduce the audience itself. On the other hand, defenders of the drama could cite exactly the same theory, claiming that the affectations, follies, and vices of those characters are condemned rather than recommended. So, to the charge that, say, Falstaff is so engaging as to drive us toward dissipation, one need only argue that he is the incarnate figure of the vices we should banish.

Obviously, the long life and the continuing appeal of this defense of comedy are impressive. Nonetheless, it is a purely theoretical defense designed to answer critical charges, not a primary response to specific works of art themselves. Of course, the theory that comedy is an instrument of moral instruction does serve, albeit speciously, to dignify the genre and to refute Plato's charges of triviality. It still serves twentieth-century criticism by lending moral profundity to works that otherwise would seem to lack high seriousness. Thus, to read *The Miller's Tale* as a sermon against avarice, vainglory, and lechery (see D. W. Robertson, Jr., *A Preface to Chaucer*, 1962) or to prove that Restoration comedies exhort us to eschew double-dealing, avarice, hypocrisy, and so on (see Ben R.

Schneider, Jr., *The Ethos of Restoration Comedy*, 1971), is to attribute stern didactic content to comedies that appear to be hilariously obscene, blithely amoral, or frivolously profane. Still, one does wonder how many people have, in truth, read *The Miller's Tale* or bought tickets to any comedy because of the moral instruction there. Do we, in fact, read and watch comedies like so many Malvolios, solemnly classifying their characters as idle, shallow, rude things who are not of our element? And, having contemplated their noxious examples, do we therefore determine, henceforth, to confine ourselves within the modest limits of order? I think not.

As Richard Levin has observed, the recent critical effort to invest them with a spurious philosophical profundity has amounted to the "decomicalization" of Shakespeare's comedies. One critic quoted by Levin insists that *The Comedy of Errors* instructs us that "throwing off of bonds of society . . . leads to a lower, animal, level of existence. Humanity requires society; society requires social restraints." Another argues that, while watching *Twelfth Night*, we recognize that "the right attitude to the world is centered neither in the natural wants of the flesh nor in the artificial constructs of the imagination, but in a religious awe before the unearned bounty which the world bestows on man, an awe akin to man's perception of God's grace." Yet another critic decomicalizes *As You Like It* by insisting that its ending is ironic: In its "ambiguous, question-begging" conclusion, virtually "all the relationships manifest a sense of unease, of latent or open hostility."[2] One wonders if these critics seriously believe that Shakespeare's comedies, as comedies, would be the better for it if their assertions were true.

Must we forever deny the differences between comedy and other genres (like satires and sermons) in order to justify it? One thinks of Auden's lines:

> By all means let us touch our humble caps to
> *La poésie pure*, the epic narrative;
> But comedy shall get its round of claps, too.
> According to his powers, each may give;
> Only on varied diet can we live.
> The pious fable and the dirty story
> Share in the total literary glory.
>
> ("Letter to Lord Byron")[3]

The share in the total literary glory that comedy rightly claims is not, to my mind, explained by turning its dirty jokes into pious fables.

Plato's account of the explosive, excessive, undignified, and infectious pleasures of comedy seems far more accurate to me than neoclassical and modern discussions of it that set out to bring its energies under the control of a solemn didacticism. Surely, it seems too obvious to need saying that all the undignified, excessive, and infectious energies of

Twelfth Night do, in fact, join forces against Malvolio. Plato is also right in observing that life occasionally does imitate art and that impressionable members of an audience may well seek to emulate the more glamorous sinners portrayed on the stage—or screen. Young girls in the twentieth century tried, in turn, to "talk tough" like Harlow, look world-weary like Garbo, walk like Monroe and pout like Bardot, none of whom were notable for portraying paragons of virtue. And who would be like Octavia if she could be Cleopatra?

It is most profoundly true, as Plato knew and the Kremlin knows, that the energies of art are often subversive of those ideals upheld by the state. It is also true that, given the freedom to do so, life may imitate art. Moreover, given its freedom to do so, art *will* imitate life. This fact allows for a whole range of drama (a range that includes a very large number of English comedies) wherein playwrights set out to exhibit, rather than to judge, the varieties of human behavior, and thus fly in the face of the "example" theory whereby their characters must, necessarily, incite us to emulation. Certain plays by Shakespeare prove that theory false since they provide us with any number of characters where no mimetic responses are called for either one way or the other. What follies and vices do we determine to eschew while watching *As You Like It*? Which characters in *The Comedy of Errors* do we aspire to emulate? In this connection, neoclassical discussions of what comedy ought to do may, yet again, serve to underline precisely what Shakespeare does not do.

In his comedies he often seems, as Dr. Johnson said, to write without any direct moral purpose. He is not always careful to show in the virtuous a disapprobation of the wicked, and he leaves the example of his characters to operate by chance. His comedies do not represent the common errors of our life in the most ridiculous and scornful sort that may be. Nor does he render his comic figures of vice and folly so ugly and detestable to make people hate and despise them. Quite the contrary. We cannot but respond with pleasure and appreciation to any number of unsavory individuals like Falstaff and Lucio. Even his villains, like Shylock and Caliban, claim their proper share of understanding and sympathy. Shakespeare does not himself hate and despise those of his characters who misbehave (like Sir Toby), misapprehend (like Olivia), or make fools of themselves (like Sir Andrew). Nor does he encourage us to do so. To scorn even those who are absolutely determined to make asses of themselves, like Bottom, Holofernes, and Don Armado, is, so far as Shakespeare seems concerned, "not generous, not gentle, not humble" (*Love's Labor's Lost*, 5.2.627). It is, surely, the praise of folly, not its condemnation, that resounds throughout the comedies themselves. And rightly so. For the frailties, follies, and vices portrayed on the comic stage—and these include even the incorrigible pomposity of Malvolio, which it might seem the use of the comic action to correct—have to be amusing and interesting enough to hold an audience in the theater for several hours and to be engaging enough to do that is to be, in one sense at least, praiseworthy.

One might conclude that, as opposed to making us "see and shame at our own faults," Shakespeare allows us to accept and to relish the human weaknesses manifested by his comic characters with the same generous measure of tolerance with which we accept our own frailties. Does he not encourage us to share the attitude of amused acceptance directed toward themselves and each other by Rosalind and Touchstone and to enjoy (even as we recognize) the faults of Jaques, Sir Andrew, and a host of other characters as well? Even his "much-abused" Malvolio gets summoned back in the end. One could, therefore, argue that the primary message of Shakespearean comedy has been reiterated most recently by Joe E. Brown in the immortal end-line of *Some Like It Hot*:

OSGOOD. Nobody's perfect.

If we must have a moral, perhaps, this is the main one conveyed, as Shakespeare transforms us from spectators to participants in his comic recognition.

This was, of course, precisely the point of the drama to which Plato most strongly objected: it creates an "undue tolerance" for human folly, sin, and error. The defenses of comedy designed to argue that it ought not, and does not, do so simply beg the great question raised by Shakespeare's merriest works: What's so bad about tolerance? In the context of the comedies themselves, it seems (at least) as valid a moral response to human frailty as the righteous indignation called for by Plato. Once this is granted, then those comedies of Shakespeare, in which the liveliest effusion of wit and humor, and the happiest delineation of the varieties of human nature are conveyed to the world in the best chosen language will need no apology, require no defense.

Notes

1. Some of the arguments here are more fully developed, with reference to tragedy, in my essay "The Morality of Elizabethan Drama: Some Footnotes to Plato," in *English Renaissance Studies in Honour of Dame Helen Gardner,* ed. John Carey—forthcoming at the Clarendon Press, Oxford.

2. Quotations are from Richard Levin's *New Readings vs. Old Plays: Recent Trends in the Reinterpretation of English Renaissance Drama* (Chicago: Univ. of Chicago Press, 1979), pp. 58, 107.

3. *The New Oxford Book of Light Verse* (Oxford: Oxford Univ. Press, 1978), p. 264.

Bibliographical Note

Books to which I am most indebted are: *Theories of Comedy,* ed. Paul Lauter (New York: Anchor Books, 1964); *Neo-Classical Dramatic Criticism: 1560-1770,* by Thora Burnley Jones and Bernard de Bear Nicol (Cambridge: Cambridge Univ. Press, 1976); *Plato: The Republic,* trans. Desmond Lee (Harmondsworth: Penguin Books, 1974); Iris Murdoch, *The Fire and the Sun: Why Plato Banished the Artists*

(Oxford, Oxford Univ. Press, 1976); Eric A. Havelock, *Preface to Plato* (New York: Grosset and Dunlap, 1971); K. R. Popper, *The Open Society and Its Enemies: The Spell of Plato* (London: Routledge and Kegan Paul, 1966); Andrew Bear, "Restoration Comedy and the Provok'd Critic," in *Restoration Literature: Critical Approaches*, ed. Harold Love (London: Methuen, 1972); Richard Levin, *New Readings vs. Old Plays: Recent Trends in the Reinterpretation of English Renaissance Drama* (Chicago: Univ. of Chicago Press, 1979).

PART 2

OVIDIAN TRANSFORMATIONS

The Ending of
Twelfth Night and the
Tradition of Metamorphosis

WILLIAM C. CARROLL

Ben Jonson saw the problem right away: he had intended, he told Drummond of Hawthornden, "to have made a play like Plaut[us'] Amphitrio but left it of, for that he could never find two so like others that he could persuade the spectators they were one."[1] Minor technical difficulties like this rarely stopped Shakespeare, of course, who was not as literal-minded as Jonson and who had a fondness for twins out of all proportion to their occurrence in nature or even in literature. Yet the recognition scene in *Twelfth Night*, the reunion of the separated twins Sebastian and Viola, stretches even Shakespeare's limits. Antonio's confusion is partly our own:

> How have you made division of yourself?
> An apple cleft in two is not more twin
> Than these two creatures.

> (5.1.222-4)

How literally are we to understand this moment? How original is it? Can the history of Renaissance comedy show us anything new about it? I propose to look again at the background of the play in the hope of seeing the ending anew.

The sources of *Twelfth Night* have been exhaustively if somewhat inconclusively studied. The play's indebtedness to the Plautine tradition has been clear from at least 1602, when John Manningham described the play as "much like the *Commedy of Errores*, or *Menechmi* in Plautus, but most like and neere to that in Italian called *Inganni*." Did Manningham really mean *Gl'Ingannati* rather than *Gl'Inganni*? What other Plautine sources are there? I refer the reader to Geoffrey Bullough and the New Arden edition for an answer, and rest for the moment with Bullough's generalization that "*Twelfth Night* belongs to a tradition in which the Plautine twins became differentiated in sex, thus affording a greater variety of intrigue."[2] We might further distinguish two familiar motifs that Shakespeare has fused together here. The first is the Plautine convention of lost or separated twins brought to the same location, unknown to each other or anyone else, thus leading to much confusion and raising questions of identity and knowledge. The Shakespearean prototype is found in *The Comedy of Errors*, where Shakespeare gives us not one but two sets of twins. The second motif, which is broadly Plautine but also associated with romance, has a girl disguised as a boy (occasionally but rarely the reverse) and disguised parties of the same sex falling in love with one another. The resulting "errors" or "supposes" become sexual as well. The typical resolution of these familiar confusions is found in the unexpected (except by the audience) encounter of the separated twins: the Antipholi and Dromii finally meet in *The Comedy of Errors*, and Sebastian and Viola in *Twelfth Night*; or the disguised maiden reveals her identity and gender, as do Julia in *The Two Gentlemen of Verona*, Portia and Nerissa in *The Merchant of Venice*, Rosalind in *As You Like It*, and, again, Viola in *Twelfth Night*.

Sexual Metamorphosis

But in *Twelfth Night* Shakespeare takes the usual baroque complications even further—in part, I believe, because of his adaptation of yet another theatrical precedent: the drama of metamorphosis. Shakespeare did not lack for examples in which the disguised maiden, and occasionally a male, undergoes actual sexual metamorphosis as a way out of elaborate Plautine plot difficulties. The tradition seems to begin with Ovid's story of Iphis and Ianthe. Raised as a boy by her mother lest she be destroyed by her father, who wanted a son, Iphis eventually is matched by her father with Ianthe. It is a given in these stories that the sexual disguise always holds good, even to a parent, until the girl falls in love, after which a metamorphosis is required. The suggestion is strong: love, if not puberty itself, is the cause of metamorphosis. Under love's pressure, disguise becomes "reality." In Ovid's story, Iphis is just one night away from the wedding, and consequent exposure, when her mother Telethusa stops to pray at Isis' temple:

> With that word the teares ran downe her cheekes amayne.
> The Goddesse seemed for to move her Altar: and in deede
> She moved it. The temple doores did tremble like a reede.
> And hornes in likenesse to the Moone about the Church did shyne.
> And Rattles made a raughtish noyse. At this same luckie signe,
> Although not wholy carelesse, yit ryght glad shee went away.
> And Iphys followed after her with larger pace than ay
> Shee was accustomd. And her face continued not so whyght.
> Her strength encreased, and her looke more sharper was to syght.
> Her heare grew shorter, and shee had a much more lively spryght,
> Than when shee was a wench. For thou, O Iphys, who ryght now
> A modther wert, art now a boay.
> ·
> *The vowes that Iphys vowd a wench he hath performd a Lad.*
> (*Metamorphoses*, 9.918-33)[3]

Just so easily can it happen, if you know the right people.

In his 1632 edition of the *Metamorphoses*, George Sandys glossed the meaning of this episode thus: "By this the Ancient declared, that men should despaire of nothing; since althings were in the power of the Gods to give; and give they would what was justly implored." Sandys then offers examples of several such changes from Pliny, Licinius Mutianus, Pontanus; relates an anecdote from the time of Ferdinand King of Naples; and quotes Montaigne's example of Mary German, who was a woman until her twenty-second year, when she jumped too hard one day and "sodenly felt those parts to descend," after which she promptly grew a beard. But Sandys concludes skeptically, "it is with out example that a man at any time became a woman."[4]

The sixteenth-century Renaissance stage offered similar examples of such changes. In addition to prose antecedents in Huon de Bordeaux and in the story of the *"Reina d'Oriente"* (in which Camilla, disguised as Armadio, becomes a man and marries the king's daughter), Violet M. Jeffrey cites the change in Luigi Groto's *Calisto* from maid to man and back again.[5] Beyond the academic comedy, we find much greater reliance on metamorphosis, and all forms of magic, in the *commedia dell'arte*. As the extant scenari show, the characters are routinely metamorphosed on stage into fountains, trees, stones, flowers, bears, bulls, lions, oxen, asses, frogs, anything, and everything. A sexual change is certainly simple enough, as we see in this excerpt from *The Three Satyrs*:

> *Magician* from C learns that Filli loves Burattino and is surprised

at her lack of discernment. Annoyed at her repulse he contrives a spell to turn Burattino into a woman. He summons *Satyrs* from the grotto to carry off Burattino by B. . . . [Enter] *Burattino* from B in the likeness of a woman transformed by the Magician's spell plays tricks with Pantalone and Zanni who wish to enjoy him against his will. . . . The Magician makes a spell and strikes on the ground with his rod; all stand still. He then orders Burattino, Gratiano, and Coviello to drink at the fountain so that they may return to their proper shapes. They drink and are changed; thanking the Magician they recognize each other joyfully.[6]

Shakespeare, however, could have gotten everything "Italian" he needed from his comedic predecessor John Lyly. The record of Lyly's indebtedness to Italian drama has been well documented, as has Shakespeare's indebtedness to Lyly. In two of Lyly's plays he gives us a sexual metamorphosis that will cast light on what happens in *Twelfth Night*. In *Gallathea* Lyly brings the convoluted plot to a crisis in which Gallathea and Phillida, two girls disguised as boys, have fallen in love with one another and wish to marry. Neptune, Diana, Cupid, and Venus discuss the problem after the girls have sworn eternal love for one another:

> NEPTUNE. An idle choyce, strange, and foolish, for one Virgine to doate on another; and to imagine a constant faith, where there can be no cause of affection. Howe like you this *Venus*?
> VENUS. I like well and allowe it, they shall both be possessed of their wishes, for never shall it be said that Nature or Fortune shall over-throwe Love and Fayth. . . . Then shall it be seene, that I can turne one of them to be a man, and that I will [2.470].[7]

The metamorphosis, which once again is directly caused by Love, will be an explicitly Ovidian one, as Venus describes her previous efforts:

> What is to Love or the Mistrisse of Love unpossible?
> Was it not *Venus* that did the like to *Iphis* and *Ianthes*?
> howe say yee? are ye agreed? one to bee a boy
> presently? [2.470]

The parents can't agree on which one shall become the boy, and so Venus leaves them all in doubt:

> Then let us depart, neither of them shall know
> whose lot it shal be til they come to the Church-dore.
> One shall be [2.471].

The Epilogue, spoken by Gallathea, drives home the point: "for this is infallible, that Love conquereth all things but it selfe" (2.472). Moreover, we have already seen the power of love himself, Cupid, sexually disguised in "Nimphes apparell" (2.441). The popularity of the Iphis-Ianthe theme was at least great enough to produce an entire play on this Ovidian subject, "*Iphis & Iantha, or a marriage without a man, a Comedy,*" allegedly written by one "Will: Shakespeare"; Harbage dates the play "c.1591-1616(?)."[8]

In his *Loves Metamorphosis* Lyly shows the very aptly named Protea, daughter of Erisichthon, assume the powers of metamorphosis in order to escape the lecherous advances of a Merchant. She becomes, first, "A Fisherman on the shore, with an Angle in my hand, and on my shoulder a net" (3.321). A moment later, to save her lover Petulius from the clutches of a Siren, she becomes an old man, in fact, "the Ghost of *Ulisses*" who can of course defeat the Siren (3.323). Most of this story Lyly took, as before, from Ovid—the story of Erisichthon and his daughter:

> yit he [Neptune] turnd hir shape and made hir man,
> And gave her looke of fisherman.
>
> (Metamorphoses, 8.1059-60)

Lyly did not borrow all her possible metamorphoses from Ovid ("now a Mare / And now a Cow, and now a Bird, a Hart, a Hynd, or Hare"—8.1082), just the masculine one, adding the ghost of Ulysses and giving her a more suggestive name.

In *The Maydes Metamorphosis*, once attributed to Lyly but now disputed and published (1600) about the time *Twelfth Night* was written, Eurymine is importuned by Apollo. She angrily challenges him to prove his identity:

> If sonne thou be to *Jove* as thou doest faine,
> And chalengest that tytle not in vaine:
> Now heer bewray some signe of godhead than?
> And chaunge me straight, from shape of mayd to man? [3.366]

Foolishly Apollo agrees—"I graunt thy wish, thou art become a man"— and the new Eurymine confuses those around her. She has become a Cesario or Ganymede, as Viola and Rosalind disguise themselves. Eurymine's suitors encounter her changed shape in a scene (too long to quote here—3.376-77) that recalls the end of *Twelfth Night* in its tone of wonder, as they confront a male version otherwise identical to the woman they love. In the next scene, Eurymine must reject her former lover, Ascanio, who then prays to Apollo to restore her as a woman. This time the change occurs offstage: "You have not sude nor praide to me in vaine: / I graunt your willes, she is a mayd againe" (3.384). She appears again at last "in her right shape instalde" (3.385).

My point is this: that in addition to the by now routine discovery scenes of the Plautine tradition, Shakespeare also had available much more spectacular and implausible models of magical sexual metamorphosis. The ending of *Gallathea* especially, a play Shakespeare clearly knew,[9] as well as some of the *commedia* scenari, represents one dramatic possibility. Such a possibility, however, is in the case of *Twelfth Night* the road only halfway taken. As we might expect, Shakespeare modifies and transforms everything he touches; he rejects an explicitly "magical" resolution while offering something comparable at the same time. The ending of *Twelfth Night* can be seen in part as a metamorphic resolution, though not as explicit as its contemporaries could be.

The final scene of the play begins with a comic roundup of characters but quickly brings together as well all the questions about metamorphosis. Feste offers to the (as usual) puzzled Orsino an explanation as to how he can be "the better for my foes, and the worse for my friends" (5.1.12-13). This explanation is also a figure of metamorphosis, employing the frequently invoked "ass" trope:

> Marry, sir, they [his friends] praise me and make an ass of me.
> Now my foes tell me plainly I am an ass; so that by
> my foes, sir, I profit in the knowledge of myself,
> and by my friends I am abused; so that, conclusions
> to be as kisses, if your four negatives make your
> two affirmatives, why then, the worse for my friends,
> and the better for my foes [5.1.17-23].

Turning "negatives" into "affirmatives," or men into asses, is all one. Orsino doesn't get it, even when Feste responds to the gift of a gold coin, "But that it would be double-dealing, sir, I would you could make it another" (1.29). But when he gives the other coin, Orsino is able to joke that he "will be so much a sinner to be a double-dealer" (5.1.34-35). This is a minor moment in a long scene, but these parables of transformation and doubling anticipate much of what is to come.

When the confusion mounts, Olivia must call in the Priest to prove her marriage to Cesario, and his description of the marriage suggests yet another kind of metamorphosis:

> A contract of eternal bond of love,
> Confirmed by mutual joinder of your hands,
> Attested by the holy close of lips,
> Strength'ned by interchangement of your rings;
> And all the ceremony of this compact
> Sealed in my function, by my testimony.

(5.1.156-61)

Already two have become one. The two lovers are never distinguished in this description—"your hands," "lips," and "your rings" represent a single figure. A subtle alliteration—contract, confirmed, compact—stresses the coming together of two into one. The language of the passage, by turns legal and formal—contract, bond, joinder, attested, interchangement, ceremony, testimony—witnesses the ritualistic joining together symbolized in this ceremony. Such a reminder of the meaning of marriage and its transfigurative power has an emblematic status in this scene; so complete and so carefully crafted a description is certainly unnecessary for the plot alone. "Our two souls, therefore, which are one": Donne also articulates the metamorphosis that marriage, or even love alone, constitutes. The final scene of *Twelfth Night* moves through this revelation of two-in-one—marriage—to the discovery of still another two-in-one—Cesario. Sir Andrew, for example, complains of the double nature of "one Cesario," not realizing there are two of him: "We took him for a coward, but he's the very devil incardinate" (5.1.180-82). The malapropism accentuates the notion of incarnation, of two-in-one, which best describes Cesario himself. And perhaps we remember here as well that Twelfth Night marks the Eve of the Epiphany, the announcement of yet another incarnation.

At the moment of greatest confusion, threatened harm, and accumulated paradox, Sebastian enters and the twins confront one another, and the others in Illyria. Orsino's words have become famous, and they resonate with echoes from earlier parts of the play:

> One face, one voice, one habit, and two persons—
> A natural perspective that is and is not.
>
> (5.1.216-17)

In some plays contemporary with Shakespeare's, a simple discovery scene suffices to clarify confusion and reveal identity; in others, such as Lyly's *Gallathea*, a full metamorphosis is required, as we have seen. In *Twelfth Night*, Shakespeare finds still another way, offering instead of an actual metamorphosis, which he had already employed in *A Midsummer Night's Dream*, a series of equivalent transformations. The moment gains power by our recognizing its antecedents, and its difference from its antecedents.

Sebastian and Viola question each other as if they had been separated a lifetime. As Anne Barton says, they "put each other through a formal, intensely conventional question and answer test that comes straight out of Greek New Comedy."[10] Viola even wonders if Sebastian is a ghost, but he explains to Olivia the nature of the dual paradox:

> So comes it, lady, you have been mistook.
> But nature to her bias drew in that.
> You would have been contracted to a maid;
> Nor are you therein, by my life, deceived:

> You are betrothed both to a maid and man.

(5.1.259-63)

And Orsino echoes the paradox in saying to Viola,

> And since you called me master for so long,
> Here is my hand; you shall from this time be
> Your master's mistress.

(5.1.326-28)

"Incardinate," "Maid and man," "master's mistress," "one habit and two persons": the paradoxes all bespeak a mysterious transformative process, in which two become one and one becomes two. Marriage itself is perhaps the supreme paradigm of this process.

Lyly could solve the "maid and man" problem in *Gallathea* simply by invoking metamorphosis, and presto: maid and man. But Cesario undergoes fission: a maid for Orsino, a man for Olivia, one for the master, one for the mistress. As has been pointed out, this fission is the perfect fulfillment of the play's subtitle, "What you will."[11] But the fission is also a nod toward, a transformation of, earlier and even contemporary magical resolutions. However, the magic here is all Shakespeare's. What *Twelfth Night*, and especially its ending, offers us are successive moments of (to continue the nuclear metaphor) fusion and fission.

Much recent criticism of the play has rightly focused on the question of "perspective," natural or unnatural, both as a specific optical instrument and as a more generalized way of seeing.[12] Such perspective instruments or paintings are, of course, themselves metamorphic, or anamorphic. The position and disposition of the viewer are necessarily crucial to a proper viewing, and Shakespeare hints at our inclusion when Feste asks Toby and Andrew, "Did you never see the picture of We Three?" (2.3. 16-17), a picture in which the spectator becomes the missing third of three asses. As King, Gilman, and others have shown, the play as a whole offers a series of perspectives to the audience, which can view it in a number of different ways. Gilman goes on to an even greater claim: "The exercise and refinement of that double vision [which is exemplified in the 'natural perspective'] is one of the main tasks Shakespearean comedy imposes on its audience."[13]

The Paradox of Two-in-One

I would like to shift the emphasis, however, to the second half of Orsino's famous words, from the "perspective" to the paradox "that is and is not."[14] In one sense, the two halves of the sentence are not synonymous, for the 'double' perspective shows two identical figures, neither of which "is not." Rather, the whole tableau may seem something "that is and is not," something evident to the senses but impossible to credit. But the paradox also epitomizes the whole mystery of two-in-one. Both Sebastian and Viola are and are not themselves; Cesario is and is not Cesario. The strangeness of metamorphosis is revealed in this cryptic phrase. Throughout the play, moreover, similar paradoxes have been expressed. Viola-Cesario has twice given Olivia a veiled warning: "I am not that I play" (1.5.182); "I am not what I am" (3.1.143). And she has said of Olivia, "you do think you are not what you are" (3.1.141). Mistaking Sebastian for Cesario, Feste will reveal the extent of the confusion:

> No, I do not know you; nor I am not sent to you
> by my lady, to bid you come speak with her; nor
> your name is not Master Cesario; nor this is not
> my nose neither. Nothing that is so is so.

(4.1.5-9)

Feste's speech in one sense merely reflects the conventions of the usual appearance-reality theme, yet his speech has deeper resonances. There is a logical difficulty, for example, in the structure of the sentence "Nothing that is so is so," which seems to be curiously self-canceling and redundant at the same time: that which is so is also not so. These cryptic, paradoxical references gain even more force from Feste's parody of them in the fourth act:

> *Bonos dies*, Sir Toby; for, as the old hermit of
> Prague, that never saw pen and ink, very wittily
> said to a niece of King Gorboduc, "That that is is";
> so, I, being Master Parson, am Master Parson; for
> what is "that" but that, and "is" but is?

(4.2.13-17)

The reply comes in the fifth act: something "that is and is not."

Few characters in the play have been merely themselves; they have also become not-themselves through some kind of metamorphosis—through disguise and trickery or through the power of love. We find another confirmation of this doubleness when Malvolio's long-delayed letter is read. What follows is a demonstration of metamorphic powers as a species of mimesis:

> OLIVIA. Open't and read it.
> CLOWN. Look then to be well edified, when the fool delivers
>   the madman. [*Reads in a loud voice*] "By the Lord,
>   madam"—
> OLIVIA. How now? Art thou mad?
> CLOWN. No, madam, I do but read madness. And your lady-

ship will have it as it ought to be, you must allow *vox*.
OLIVIA. Prithee read i' thy right wits.
CLOWN. So I do, madonna; but to read his right wits is to
read thus.

(5.1.290-300)[15]

The suggestion, then, is that to read a text is necessarily to *become* the author as well as the reader. Thus Feste is and is not himself, and by extension Malvolio has become the forgery he has read, cross-gartered and in yellow stockings. Viola, too, has become the fiction or counterfeit "Cesario"; and as she tells us earlier, she consciously "imitate[s]" her brother (3.4.395). And beyond the characters there are the actors themselves, the technicians of the mimetic, who read a text in *vox* and become what they are not.

The next stage of discovery is to reveal Maria's forged letter to Malvolio, a *vox* persuasive enough not only to fool Malvolio but also to make Toby marry its author ("In recompense whereof he hath married her," 1.366). But the spirit of forgiveness and the whirligig of time cannot assuage Malvolio's rage. His eruption into the final scene, after the "natural perspective" has been created, reminds us of everything that refuses to be transformed, of that streak of vindictiveness and obstinance that will not change and so is less than human (as Bergson might argue), but, of course, is all too human. Malvolio has been shown throughout to be unable to see—that is, he sees only his own reflection wherever he looks, whether in writing or in "practicing behavior to his own shadow," as Maria tells us (2.5.76). When he looks in a glass, he sees only himself; but when Viola looks in the "perspective" glass, she sees both herself and also a loving other. To show Malvolio imprisoned within himself and finally locked in a dark room and therefore unable to see, marks the sharpest difference from Viola and Sebastian. Malvolio's inflexibility registers the necessity for their flexibility. The capacity for self-transformation seems to be one sign of human health. Malvolio's only glimmer of such powers is his denial of the possibility of Pythagorean metempsychosis in Feste's comic catechism (4.2.50 ff); in orthodox terms, Malvolio's denial is "right," but in the play's terms he is wrong.

I would like to return to Ben Jonson's refusal to write such a play as *Twelfth Night*, in part because he "could never find two so like others that he could persuade the spectators they were one." Northrop Frye reports an even more pedantic anecdote of this sort: "A doctor once remarked to me that he was unable to enjoy a performance of *Twelfth Night* because it was a biological impossibility that boy and girl twins could resemble each other so closely."[16] Shakespeare had had Antonio call attention to how *like* the two are: "An apple cleft in two is not more twin / Than these two creatures." (There is some ambiguity in relating a divided apple to a doubled image.) But Jonson was, in a narrow sense, right, which is undoubtedly the reason Shakespeare went ahead and wrote the play. No two actors, perhaps not even boy and girl twins, could be "so like." The *difference* between Sebastian and Viola is almost as important as the similarity. It allows Cesario to be two different things, depending on one's "perspective." But it also requires a critical transformative act by the audience, presumably not wholly filled with geneticists, to bridge the difference. Shakespeare has displaced the metamorphic principle from the stage itself into the mind of the audience; the *commedia* scenari, even Lyly's plays, presume a far more passive audience than Shakespeare does.

The ending of the play is constructed so as to reveal similarity: twinship, the harmony of marriage, forgiveness, an unexpected commonality of interests, blood relation. But in addition to establishing what "is," the ending insists as well on what "is not," on the differences. Puffed full of injured merit, Malvolio will separate himself from the vulgar, and Viola, when she comes to swear her own love to Orsino, invokes an image of astronomical separation:

> DUKE. Boy [though he now knows Cesario to be a woman]
>   thou hast said to me a thousand times
>   Thou never shouldst love woman like to me.
> VIOLA. And all those sayings will I over swear,
>   And all those swearings keep as true in soul
>   As doth that orbed continent the fire
>   That severs day from night.
>
> (5.1.267-72)

The principle of separation seems rather ironic here, for Viola is still dressed as a boy (through the end of the play) though now known to be a girl and further known by the audience to be a boy actor. The scene thus ends with that peculiarly Shakespearean tension between such images of division and identity. Orsino's pledge that "A solemn combination shall be made / Of our dear souls" (5.1.385-86) cannot be fulfilled literally. The rule of transformation yet lingers so powerfully that Viola has still not quite returned:

> DUKE. Cesario, come—
>   For so you shall be while you are a man,
>   But when in other habits you are seen,
>   Orsino's mistress and his fancy's queen.
>
> (5.1.387-90)

Thus Viola leaves the stage both as herself and not herself.

Feste's song concluding the play offers us not only a vision of the Four Ages of Man but also yet another moving, if somewhat cynical, vision of mutability, suggesting the inevitable nature of change and the great final metamorphosis which awaits us all. It has been frequently noted that in the song Feste breaks character: he seems to be both clown and, toward the end, actor ("our play is done"). This fusing could almost be predicted: Feste is and is not Feste. As Feste, the singer of the epilogue presents a distant, even bleak view of human life, marked by foul weather, drunkenness, "knaves and thieves." But as an actor, the singer concludes with the cheerfully dismissive "But that's all one, our play is done," while announcing that this melancholy song, and the whole play, form part of the actor's creed: "And we'll strive to please you every day" (5.1.409-10). Both visions can be encompassed in the song because the singer offers in himself another natural perspective by being and not being Feste and by enfolding his vision of natural mutability into a sophisticated verbal form.

Much of the final scene of *Twelfth Night*, then, can be seen as governed by the various powers of metamorphosis: mysterious energies that turn two into one and one into two, and mimetic energies that lead people to become actors, donning disguise and *vox*, willfully turning themselves into what they are not. Shakespeare appears to have found any number of ways to match, indeed outdo, the magical endings of his colleagues.

Notes

1. Ben Jonson, *Works*, ed. C. H. Herford and Percy Simpson (Oxford: Clarendon Press, 1925), I, 144. Renaissance quotations have been slightly modernized.
2. Geoffrey Bullough, *Narrative and Dramatic Sources of Shakespeare* (New York: Columbia Univ. Press, 1968), II, 270. See also II, 269, and the lucid discussion in Leo Salingar, *Shakespeare and the Traditions of Comedy* (Cambridge: Cambridge Univ. Press, 1974), pp. 238-42.
3. *Ovid's Metamorphoses: The Arthur Golding Translation*, ed. John Frederick Nims (New York: Macmillan, 1965), p. 248. Hereafter cited in the text.
4. George Sandys, *Ovid's Metamorphoses* (Lincoln: Univ. of Nebraska Press, 1970), pp. 449, 450.
5. Violet M. Jeffrey, *John Lyly and the Italian Renaissance* (New York: Russell & Russell, 1969; reprint of 1928), pp. 83, 92.
6. K. M. Lea, *Italian Popular Comedy* (New York: Russell & Russell, 1962; reprint of 1935), II, 667-69.
7. Quotations from Lyly, and from *The Maydes Metamorphosis*, are from *The Complete Works of John Lyly*, ed. R. Warwick Bond (Oxford: Clarendon Press, 1902). Hereafter cited in the text.
8. Alfred Harbage, rev. S. Schoenbaum, *Annals of English Drama 975-1700* (London: Methuen, 1964), p. 102.
9. Bond (2.569) points out the echo of *Gallathea* 3.2.36-40 (2.450) at *Twelfth Night* 2.4.120-23. See also Leah Scragg, "Shakespeare, Lyly, and Ovid: The Influence of 'Gallathea' on 'A Midsummer Night's Dream,' " *Shakespeare Survey* 30 (1977), 125-34.
10. Anne Barton, " 'As You Like It' and 'Twelfth Night': Shakespeare's Sense of an Ending," *Shakespearian Comedy*, Stratford-upon-Avon Studies 14 (New York: Crane, Russak, 1972), p. 175.
11. Walter N. King, "Shakespeare and Parmenides: The Metaphysics of *Twelfth Night*," *Studies in English Literature*, 8 (1968), 283-306.

12. See, for example, Ernest B. Gilman, *The Curious Perspective* (New Haven: Yale University Press, 1978), pp. 129-66, and Maurice Charney, "*Twelfth Night* and the 'Natural Perspective' of Comedy," in *De Shakespeare à T. S. Eliot: Mélanges offerts à Henri Fluchére* (Paris: Didier, 1976), pp. 43-51. For a history of the idea of "perspective," see Samuel Y. Edgerton, Jr., *The Renaissance Rediscovery of Linear Perspective* (New York: Harper & Row, 1975).

13. Gilman, p. 161.

14. Cf. Helena in *A Midsummer Night's Dream*: "And I have found Demetrius like a jewel, / Mine own and not mine own" (4.1.192-95).

15. The Folio shows the line "By the Lord, madam" in italics, without any stage direction, but it is clear from the context that Feste reads like a madman. I am indebted to my colleague Stuart H. Johnson in my discussion of this passage.

16. Northrop Frye, *A Natural Perspective* (New York: Harcourt, Brace, 1965), p. 18.

*Research time for this essay was provided by a fellowship from the National Endowment for the Humanities.

Bibliographical Note

This essay is based on two kinds of source material. First is the vast literature on Italian Renaissance drama, particularly the *commedia dell'arte*. I have profited from several of the better-known works: K. M. Lea, *Italian Popular Comedy* (New York: Russell & Russell, 1962; reprint of 1935); Marvin T. Herrick, *Italian Comedy in the Renaissance* (Urbana: Univ. of Illinois Press, 1960); Winifred Smith, *The Commedia dell'Arte* (New York: Columbia Univ. Press, 1964); Henry F. Salerno, trans., *Scenarios of the Commedia dell'Arte* (New York: New York Univ. Press, 1967); and Douglas Radcliff-Umstead, *The Birth of Modern Comedy in Renaissance Italy* (Chicago: Univ. of Chicago Press, 1969). A convenient bridge to the plays of Lyly is provided by Violet M. Jeffrey, *John Lyly and the Italian Renaissance* (New York: Russell & Russell, 1969; reprint of 1928).

The second kind of source I have used is that small but growing group of first-rate critical essays on *Twelfth Night*. It begins with the final chapter in C. L. Barber's *Shakespeare's Festive Comedy* (Princeton: Princeton Univ. Press, 1959) and continues with such essays as Joseph H. Summers, "The Masks of *Twelfth Night*," *The University Review*, XXII (1955), 25-32; John Hollander, "*Twelfth Night* and the Morality of Indulgence," *Sewanee Review*, LXVII (1959), 220-38; and the final chapter of Alexander Leggatt's *Shakespeare's Comedy of Love* (London: Methuen, 1974).

6

Ovid's *Metamorphoses* and Shakespeare's *Twelfth Night*

M.E. LAMB

The contradictory attitudes held toward Ovid in the Renaissance complicate the relationship between Ovid's *Metamorphoses* and Shakespeare's
Twelfth Night, or *What You Will*. According to one tradition-rooted in
the Middle Ages and continuing vigorously into the seventeenth century,
Ovid was a didactic teacher whose tales were really allegorical lessons
about the human soul. *Twelfth Night* can be interpreted as a play about
change within the souls of Orsino, Olivia, and Viola,[1] and metamorphosis
serves as a metaphor for an inner spiritual state revealing that love can
lead to either stasis or transcendence. The second Ovid, the urbane Ovid
of the epyllia or erotic narratives still in fashion at the time of *Twelfth
Night*, is diametrically opposed to the first. Delighting in his own verbal
gymnastics and narrative poses, he is reflected in the interpretation of
Twelfth Night as a play about characters who only perform roles and lack
absolute identity.[2]

These opposite views of Ovid in the Renaissance are both valid.
Many metamorphoses reveal spiritual states, and the narrator's attitude
toward his material is often playful. In the end, the antithetical nature of

Ovid's influence arises not from Renaissance literary traditions or modern interpretation, but from the complexity of the *Metamorphoses* itself.[3]

Metamorphosis

Metamorphosis is a complex word: it refers both to the process and the product of the change. Ovid's *Metamorphoses* treats "of shapes transformde to bodies straunge"[4]; it portrays reality as an unstable chimera where gods become animals, women become trees, men become wolves, dragon's teeth become men. These changes are final, and mortals who undergo transformation will never again be human. These transformations sometimes occur at moments of extreme stress, when the normal identity is destroyed under the force of some unendurable emotion, such as Niobe's grief over the death of her children. Her physical transformation into a rock is merely the realization of what has already occurred on the emotional level.

Other transformations, like that of Io into a cow, proceed from a petty motive of a god or goddess, such as Jove's fear that Juno might discover his attempted rape of Io. If there is a meaning in Io's metamorphosis, it is in its senselessness, its portrayal of a world without order or justice. But most metamorphoses, whether they are inherently connected to an emotional state of the person transformed or not, do serve an etiological function. Marble "sweats," for example, because Niobe continued to weep even after her transformation into stone. Taken together, the metamorphoses relate the history of the world from creation until the time of Augustus. They culminate in Caesar's transformation and Augustus' projected transformation, into a star, representing deification, transcendence of the mortal state.[5]

Medieval readers reasoned that the subject of the *Metamorphoses* could not truly be the apparently foolish tales of humans transformed into trees or birds or rocks. The tales must have some deeper meaning, or, if they were to be read at all, they at least must be given some use to repay the reader for his time. Consequently, readers allegorized the *Metamorphoses* on historical, physical or astrological, moral, and theological levels. By the Renaissance, these four levels began to yield to the moral level, which usually operated according to a fairly simple formula: the transformation of a man into a beast meant that his soul had become bestial; a god was simply a virtuous man; a metamorphosis into a star was an honor accorded to the righteous. Arthur Golding, who translated the *Metamorphoses* read by Shakespeare, related the system this way:

> But if wee suffer fleshly lustes as lawlesse Lordes too reigne,
> Than are we beastes, wee are no men, wee have
> our name in vaine.
> And if wee be so drownd in vice that feeling once bee gone,

Then may it well of us bee sayd, wee are a block or stone.
This surely did the Poets meene when in such sundry wyse
The pleasant tales of turned shapes they studyed too devyse.

(Preface to the Reader, 11.111-16)

For Golding, Ovid's metamorphoses referred to spiritual states.
Turning into a beast or stone was a metaphor for becoming less than
human, and this kind of meaning took precedence over the etiological or
historical framework important in Ovid's time. In some cases, the allegorical treatment produces an unforced meaning. In the example of Io's
metamorphosis into a cow, however, the allegory works against the
natural response to the tale. Jove, not Io, was guilty of bestial desires,
yet Golding blames Io. Ovid's work was too complex for any rigid system,
including that used by Golding and other Renaissance readers. The alle-
gorizers posited a world that made sense in which the virtuous were rewarded and the evil punished; and according to this view, sexuality was
especially to be abhorred. This was not Ovid's world and, while he was
influenced by the allegorical method, it was not Shakespeare's either.

The opening scene of *Twelfth Night* provides us with an example
of Shakespeare's use of Ovidian metamorphosis, as Orsino dignifies his
love melancholy with the epic precedent of Ovid's Actaeon, the hunter
who was changed to a deer and eaten by his own hounds as punishment
for his accidental glimpse of the naked Diana:

O, when mine eyes did see Olivia first,
Methought she purged the air of pestilence.
That instant was I turned into a hart,
And my desires, like fell and cruel hounds,
E'er since pursue me.

(1.1.20-24)

Orsino's comparison of himself with Actaeon is trite, and it shows him in
the stereotype of courtly lover. It also borrows a habit of mind from
medieval and Renaissance commentators on Ovid's *Metamorphoses.* He
has internalized an Ovidian tale to describe his own emotional state, with
the hounds as his desires and the chase as taking place within his own soul.

This interpretation of the Actaeon myth had become commonplace
by the late sixteenth century, when it appears in English sources. Geoffrey
Whitney's popular *Choice of Emblemes and Other Devises* (1586) ex-
pounds its meaning under the heading "Voluptas aerumnosa" (sorrowful
pleasure):

By which is ment, that those whoe doe pursue
Theire fancies fonde, and thinges unlawfull crave,
Like brutishe beastes appeare unto the viewe,
And shall at lengthe, Actaeons guerdon have:

And as his houndes, soe theire affections base,
Shall them devowre, and all their deedes deface.[6]

Orsino's implied analogy between Olivia and the goddess Diana gives us more insight into his character. He compliments his mistress for those very qualities, including inveterate virginity, which cause his suit's persistent lack of success; and his parallel between hounds and his desires shows his love to be a self-destructive force. Orsino's application of the Actaeon myth to himself reveals his own state of spiritual metamorphosis. He is stuck; he has reached a point of inner stasis from which there is no apparent rescue.

Orsino's name may point to another metamorphosis, less explicit than the Actaeon myth but perhaps still worth exploring. Orsino means "bear." In Ovid's *Metamorphoses*, Juno, in her anger over Jove's seduction of Callisto, turned that beautiful maiden into a bear. The innocent Callisto had herself been deceived, for in order to approach her, Jove had transformed himself to resemble Diana, the goddess Callisto served. This ruse perhaps recalls Viola's disguise as a man to bring her into Orsino's presence. In fact, Orsino explicitly compares Viola to Diana at one point:

For they shall yet belie thy happy years
That say thou art a man. Diana's lip
Is not more smooth and rubious.

(1.4.30-32)

Like Actaeon, Callisto became a hunter hunted. Unlike Actaeon, however, she is rescued by Jove. When her own son Arcas is unknowingly about to kill his mother, she and her son both are transformed into stars, the highest honor possible for a mortal, an event which causes Juno disgruntlement:

I have bereft hir womans shape, and at this present howre
She is become a Goddesse.

(2.2.647-48)

The commentators on this tale agree that Callisto's metamorphosis into a bear proceeds from her moral deformity. Even though Ovid's tale portrays her as an innocent victim, the formula that anyone turned into a beast is really bestial wins out.[7] Most of the commentators do not explain her metamorphosis into a star, except for Bersuire, who interprets it to mean that great and noble persons can sometimes come from paupers.

At the risk of committing the same kinds of excesses as my medieval predecessors, I am proposing the following line of inquiry: the implied metamorphosis in Orsino's name points to the dual potentiality towards subhumanity and transcendence possible through love. Callisto's change to a bear provides a judgment about Orsino's spiritual state similar to

From Ovid's *Metamorphoses* (1632 edition). At the bottom left, Phaeton's sisters are seen being transformed into trees while mourning over Phaeton's body; in the middle, Juno is transforming Callisto into a bear; at middle right, Callisto's son Arcas is about to kill her before they are both transformed into stars. *Courtesy of the University of Nebraska Press, publishers of* Ovid's Metamorphosis *(1970) by George Sandys.*

Actaeon's change to a stag. In each case the mythographers are more severe on the Ovidian characters than Shakespeare's play gives us warrant for Orsino, but there is a grain of truth in what they say. Although Orsino is not bestial, in his self-preoccupation he has become a stereotype of a lover. In this sense, perhaps, he is not fully human. In his rage over Olivia's love for Cesario, he becomes dangerously predatory like a bear: "I'll sacrifice the lamb that I do love/To spite a raven's heart within a dove" (5.1.124-25). These are the unfortunate effects of his love for Olivia, which is really a form of self-love. Yet the star metamorphosis points to another kind of love which he seems to feel for Viola, a love that leads to the marriage proposal typical of comic endings and to his regeneration.

Like the name Orsino, the name Olivia also perhaps implies a dual metamorphosis. At the beginning of the play, she fits both classic Ovidian myths of maidens transformed into trees. Like Daphne pursued by Apollo, she insists on her chastity despite Orsino's persistent suit; and like the sisters of Phaeton, in mourning her dead brother, she gives up a portion of her life. Golding follows the traditional interpretation of the Daphne tale by praising her as a "myrror of virginitie."[8] The fate of Daphne is however, threatening in a comic world. Prolonged virginity, a virtue esteemed by the predominantly religious community interpreting Ovid's tales, assumes a different value in the context of comedy, for it menaces the expected marriages at the end of the play and ultimately endangers the regeneration of the community itself. The lesson of the metamorphosis of Phaeton's sisters into willow trees to teach moderation in mourning[9] fits the comic world without strain: Olivia's extreme vow to mourn her brother for seven years, abjuring the company of men the while, means giving up the most fertile years of her life.

Like the metamorphoses of Actaeon into a stag and Callisto into a bear, these transformations point to inner stagnation. At the beginning of *Twelfth Night*, Olivia's treelike spiritual state becomes explicit, ironically enough, when she declares her love for Cesario: "A cypress, not a bosom,/ Hides my heart" (3.1.123-24). However, as with the Callisto myth implied in Orsino's name, the myth implied in her name holds out comic possibilities. She is not a laurel or a willow; she is an olive, a tree of peace and fertility. These qualities are released in her through her love for Cesario/Sebastian.

Viola explicitly describes her feelings in terms of internalized metamorphosis when she tells Orsino of her father's daughter's unrequited love for a man much like Orsino:

> She never told her love,
> But let concealment, like a worm i' th' bud,
> Feed on her damask cheek. She pined in thought;
> And, with a green and yellow melancholy,
> She sat like Patience on a monument,
> Smiling at grief.   (2.4.111-16)

Viola's description of her inward self as "Patience on a monument" evokes an Ovidian metamorphosis like Niobe's transformation to stone in her grief over her dead children. Critical to the metamorphosis of each is their inability to speak. One effect of Niobe's grief is that "even hir verie tung/And palat of hir mouth was hard, and eche to other clung" (6.388-89). "Patience on a monument" cannot speak either; like Niobe, she cannot even cry out in pain. She must, in fact, go one step beyond Niobe; she must smile.

Moreover, Viola's image is dynamic. A decay of natural growth is revealed by her metaphor of concealment as a "worm i' th' bud;" and Patience's monument suggests a love ending in the grave rather than the wedding bed. This image of inner stasis and decay is all the more moving because it contrasts so dramatically with Viola's behavior, which is so entertaining and sympathetic. Yet this description of her inward self reveals that Viola has reached an inner state not unlike Olivia's or Orsino's. The reasons for her emotional situation are admirable rather than neurotic. She is honor-bound not to reveal her identity to Orsino and to court Olivia for him; yet she is finally, like Olivia and Orsino, denying life rather than affirming it. At this point, her love for Orsino is as fruitless as his for Olivia. There is no apparent solution for any of them. Like Orsino's bear and Olivia's tree, Viola's "Patience on a monument" is an another internalized metamorphosis that reveals that her love for Orsino, like his for Olivia, has caused stasis and even decay within her soul.

Even though she has reached the same emotional state as Orsino and Olivia, Viola's behavior is quite different. Far from being preoccupied with her own problems, she can laugh with Feste and feel sympathy for Olivia. She has enough perspective to avoid confusing the present moment with the future; she trusts to Time: "O Time, thou must untangle this not I;/It is too hard a knot for me t'untie" (2.2.40-41). In this faith she resembles an Ovidian character whose love situation parallels hers. The moral of the story of Iphis, a woman loved by a woman, is that we must not become desperate even in the greatest difficulties, but we must trust to divine help.[10] Iphis was a woman raised as a man because her father had ordered that any daughters her mother bore should be put to death. The goddess Isis, however, appearing in a vision to Iphis' mother, ordered her to save her infant by rearing her as a boy. Obeying the goddess, Iphis' mother raised her daughter to maturity, at which time she was betrothed to the lovely Ianthe, who loved her passionately. As the marriage date approached, Iphis and her mother prayed to Isis for help. Suddenly Iphis' stride grew longer, her face darkened, and she became a man and a happy bridegroom. This presents parallels with what happens between Olivia and Viola. Viola, a woman disguised as a man and loved by another woman, suddenly "becomes" her twin brother Sebastian, whose sudden appearance and wedding to Olivia are a providential solution to an impossible love situation.

The names and epithets of Viola and Sebastian point to an even closer relationship than that of twins. They are the male and female aspects of one function through which harmony is restored to society and love becomes a transcending power. John Hollander has already pointed out the significance of Viola's name: she is an instrument of "rhetorical music," restoring balance in Orsino and Olivia and in the country of Illyria.[11] Sebastian's harmonizing power is implied in the sea captain's description of him as Arion:

> I saw your brother,
> Most provident in peril, bind himself
> (Courage and hope both teaching him the practice)
> To a strong mast that lived upon the sea;
> Where, like Arion on the dolphin's back,
> I saw him hold acquaintance with the waves
> So long as I could see.
>
> (1.2.11-17)

In this description, the sea captain was comforting Viola with the possibility of her brother's survival of the shipwreck through the agency of divine providence. In fact, his likening Sebastian to Arion implies more. In Ovid's *Fasti*, Arion, a talented lyre player, was about to be murdered for his money by a greedy ship's crew. As a last request, he asked to play his lyre; the beauty of its music summoned a dolphin, which carried him safely ashore.[12] The universal power of music, even over wild beasts, was a commonplace: Orpheus, for example, tamed animals with his music, and this tradition was implicit in Ovid's tale. In both Ovid's time and Shakespeare's, music was an emblem and an agent of divine order. Its power derived from its correspondence to the music of the heavenly spheres, manifestations of the divine order of the mind of God.[13]

The tempest that swallowed the ship carrying Viola and Sebastian, was a common Shakespearean representation of disorder, corresponding to disorder or madness in the human soul. Sebastian was not saved by providence entirely, for in the face of disaster he maintained his own sanity; the order of his own soul gave him the "courage and hope" to bind himself to a mast. Both the mast "that lived upon the sea" and the waves, with which he holds "acquaintaince," are described as alive and friendly agents within a death-threatening chaos. He found them out, he trusted them, and they saved him. These same characteristics that save Sebastian are found in Viola. Her actions also reveal "courage and hope." Never giving in to despair in the bleakest of circumstances, she trusts to time and she is saved. Together, Viola and Sebastian/Arion are emblems of divine music, both in the order of their own selves and in their ability to restore order to others. In this sense, they are one.

The identity of Viola and Sebastian is further revealed by Viola's assumed name Cesario, or "little Caesar," which forms a pair with

Caesar's metamorphosis into a star, also from *Metamorphoses* (1632). *Courtesy of the University of Nebraska Press.*

"Sebastos," "the Greek equivalent of Octavian's epithet, 'Augustus.' "[14] Cesario and Sebastian represent a significant reference to the culmination of the *Metamorphoses*, Caesar's metamorphosis and Augustus' projected metamorphosis into stars. In Ovid's work, transformation into a star signified deification. According to allegorical tradition, as expressed by Golding, it signified the glory due virtuous acts: "The turning to a blazing starre of Julius Cesar showes,/That fame and immortalitie of vertuous doing growes" (Epistle to Leycester, 11.292-93).

In *Twelfth Night*, this transformation into a star also implies virtue, although in the living rather than the dead. Like the other metamorphoses in *Twelfth Night*, transformation into a star is internalized to represent a spiritual state. Viola's love for Orsino was a source of grief for her for much of the play; her inward self was static, like Patience on a monument. Now her love has a different kind of stasis, transcendence. Her love has transcended the turmoil and change usual in human lives to become like the star in Sonnet 116, one of Shakespeare's most profound statements on ideal love:

> It is an ever-fixed mark
> That looks on tempests and is never shaken;
> It is the star to every wand'ring bark,
> Whose worth's unknown, although his height be taken.
>
> (11.4-8)

Metamorphoses into stars imply the same happy fortune for Sebastian's love for Olivia and Orsino's for Viola, through the Callisto myth.

Rhetoric

The most remarkable transformations in the *Metamorphoses* belong to the narrator, whose continually changing postures toward his own material play havoc with the responses of any sensitive reader. Absurd tales are told seriously; serious tales are told absurdly. Even within a single tale, his tone can change at the most unpredictable moment. Just as a reader is drawn into a tragic vision, the narrator jolts him with a comment that is flippantly incongruous. For example, when Phaeton's ill-fated attempt to drive the chariot of the sun sets the earth on fire, causes his own death, and creates such grief in his father that he prefers to leave the earth in darkness rather than to drive the chariot himself, the narrator points out the utility of these destructive conflagrations: "The brightnesse of the flame/Gave light: and so unto some kinde of use that mischiefe came" (2.419-20). Just when we had gotten absorbed in the tale, the narrator reminds us of his presence with a ridiculous sentiment appropriate to a Pollyanna of ancient Rome. Through such means he makes us highly aware of his role as narrator and in the process often makes fun of the essentially serious tales he has collected. And integral to his poses is his wit. Continually calling attention to itself through puns, small elegancies, clever ironies, his language often distances the most moving tales.

Ovid's manipulation of narrative role and his highly self-conscious use of language were valued and imitated in the Renaissance. They are primary characteristics of the Ovidian epyllia or little epics written at the end of the sixteenth century by authors like Thomas Lodge, Christopher Marlowe, as well as Shakespeare himself. Ovid's techniques were ideally suited to their attempt to embrace complexity and to portray reality through a variety of perspectives.[15] For the writers of epyllia, as for Ovid, the primary subject of poetry is not the narrative material, but the varying attitudes toward it. Shakespeare, for example, often plays with incongruous narrative poses in his Ovidian *Venus and Adonis* when Venus' eyes, beholding her dead Adonis, are likened to snails whose tender horns are hit. In *The Rape of Lucrece*, the lustful Tarquin's hand, "smoking with pride," "did scale" her bare breast whose veins suddenly left their "turrets" to tell Lucrece of her danger (11. 438-41). These bizarre comparisons inevitably draw attention to themselves, not unlike Ovid's "jerks of invention" admired by Shakespeare's pedant Holofernes (*Love's Labor's Lost*, 4.2.125-27).

Interest in manipulating roles perhaps accounts for the frequent presence of the female wooer in both Ovid and Shakespeare. The female wooer inevitably creates two feelings: a usually sympathetic reaction to her love and an awareness, sometimes humorous, of her reversal of roles. As Helena exclaims in *A Midsummer Night's Dream*: "We cannot fight for love as men may do,/We should be wooed, and were not made to woo" (2.1.242-43). Olivia's proposal to Sebastian, surprising enough as the proposal of a man to a woman, becomes hilarious because it comes from a woman to a man. Both sympathy and humor result as she enters with a priest to perform the ceremony. The female wooer is an ideal inhabitant of the essentially rhetorical reality portrayed in the *Metamorphoses* and in *Twelfth Night*. Just as Ovid's language constantly calls attention to the role of the narrator, so we become especially conscious of the role of lover when the expected roles are reversed. Our reaction is inevitably complex.

The Ovidian succession of roles is nowhere more apparent than in Viola's dazzling performance for Olivia. Disguised as Cesario, she begins her speech, intended to court Olivia for Orsino, with the expected flattery, "Most radiant, exquisite, and unmatchable beauty" (1.5.168), only to interrupt it by an ingenuous request to know which veiled lady is Olivia, for she doesn't want to throw away her speech, "excellently well penned" and difficult to learn, on the wrong person. First she flatters Olivia, and then she calls attention to her role as flatterer, one who must laboriously write and memorize compliments. In reacting to Olivia's unveiled face, she plays the role first of admirer and then of cynic: "Excellently done, if God did all" (1.5.236). Her response to Olivia's beauty is both admiration and criticism for leaving "the world no copy" (1.5.243). Finally, she embarks on an exquisite speech on how she would win Olivia if she (Cesario) were Orsino: she would "Hallo [Olivia's] name to the reverberate hills/And make the babbling gossip of the air/Cry out 'Olivia!'" (1.5.273-75). Her role-playing is clear. Crying Olivia's name is not what she is doing; it is only what she would do if she were Orsino.

Her performance is splendid and highly self-conscious. She does not let Olivia forget for a moment that she is just role-playing. She even admits "I am not that I play" (1.5.182). Yet Olivia falls in love with her, and so in most performances does the audience, which is aware of the additional aritifice that Cesario does not exist except as a role adopted by Viola as a way of protecting herself in Illyria. In her succession of poses, in her distancing of her message by constantly pointing to her language and her role, she is brilliantly Ovidian. No one, not even Olivia, could mistake her for being "sincere." Viola is real to us not in spite of her role-playing, but because of it. It is Viola's skill as an actress which marks her off from the other characters: Aguecheek, who is unable to portray the roles of "drinker, fighter, wencher," as Joseph Summers points out;[16] Olivia, who is at first confined to the limited role of mourner; Orsino, who is acting out the role of unrequited lover—they are all one-dimensional not because they are acting instead of being, but because they are limited actors.

Malvolio defines the Ovidian character by contrast. No character could be more artificial than the Ovidian narrator; no one could act more roles or parody his own role more. The difference between the Ovidian narrator and Malvolio is not between acting and being, artificiality and sincerity but between good acting and bad acting. A good actor like Viola can play many roles and regard them all with irony, and so she is a full character, able to respond to many different situations. A bad actor like Malvolio is doomed to be one-dimensional. And Malvolio is a bad actor. When he attempts the role of smiling lover, a part much easier than Cesario's role of courting an unwilling lady by proxy, Olivia misunderstands the nature of his attempted role. She thinks he is insane.

Malvolio's predictable, unimaginative responses make him an easy target for Feste's gulling. His refusal to believe in Pythagoras' theory of the transmigration of souls, for example, is the expected academic answer. It is, in fact, Golding's response in his Epistle to Leycester (11. 49-54), commenting on Pythagoras' oration, which makes up much of the last book of the *Metamorphoses.* Yet far from proving Malvolio's sanity, it points to his special form of madness: his rigidity. Malvolio stands against more than Pythagoras' theory of the transmigration of souls; he stands against change itself. Change is the essence of sanity in *Twelfth Night,* whether we view it as a play about transformations within the inward self or about actors performing roles. According to Pythagoras, all creatures change; change is our stay against annihilation; change is the essence of life itself. In this way, microcosm seems to mirror macrocosm.

The constant change necessary to maintain order in the world is also necessary to maintain order within the self. In this sense, Malvolio is mad in his refusal to change; and we must, with Feste, doubt his sanity until he holds the opinion of Pythagoras concerning wild fowl.

The consequences of his failure are these. Because he cannot act, he cannot change, and he is stuck with a single role: Malvolio, humorless and righteous conserver of his mistress' possessions, stifler of undue merriment. He cannot understand how Olivia, with the help of Feste, can laugh at her role of mourner; he certainly cannot share in the laughter. He most certainly cannot step outside his role for a moment to laugh at himself. But perhaps most important, he cannot forgive. He cannot imagine the roles of the other characters; he cannot act them out in his own imagination; he cannot imagine himself in their places. Thus their playing a practical joke on him is inconceivable. He cannot accept Olivia's proffered reparations, and he must leave vowing revenge.

Feste, of course, is the most Ovidian of all. He can assume any role: gentle yet thorough critic of Olivia; reveler with Sir Toby Belch; singer of melancholy songs for Orsino; Sir Topas, curate to Malvolio. Much of his humor is self-parody, on the nature and function of fools. Regarding the drunk Toby, he exclaims, "The fool shall look to the madman" (1.5. 136); in reference to Viola's master Orsino, "The fool should be as oft with your master as with my mistress" (3.1.41); to Malvolio, "Then you are mad indeed, if you be no better in your wits than a fool" (4.2.92-93). Totally artificial, he is yet a sympathetic character whose effect on the play is profound.

To Feste is given the final song, ending this comedy on a melancholy note, reminding us that "the rain it raineth every day." In his final stanza, he breaks down the difference between character and actor, play and reality beyond the stage: "our play is done,/And we'll strive to please you every day" (5.1.409-10). The ramifications of this dissolution of the barrier between stage and life are tremendous. Not only is the real actor playing Feste's part in Feste's situation, earning a small living from pleasing and perhaps instructing others with his performance, but the essentially dramatic reality in *Twelfth Night* flows out to the audience and real life. We are all actors assuming various roles with various degrees of competence. Like Viola and Malvolio, we are defined not by our "real selves," but by our ability to play our roles, to step outside them, to understand the roles of others. Absolute reality and even absolute identity are illusory. This is the Rome celebrated by Ovid, and it seems much like Shakespeare's Illyria.

Notes

1. See Don Cameron Allen, *Mysteriously Meant: The Rediscovery of Pagan Symbolism and Allegorical Interpretation in the Renaissance* (Baltimore: Johns Hopkins Press, 1970), pp. 163-200; Douglas Bush, "Ovid Old and New," *Mythology in the Renaissance Tradition in English Poetry* (New York: W. W. Norton, 1932, rev. 1963),

pp. 69-73; L. P. Wilkinson, *Ovid Recalled* (Cambridge: Cambridge University Press, 1955), pp. 399-438. For allegories of Ovid's tales influential in the Renaissance, see *Metamorphosis Ovidiana Moraliter a Magistro Thoma Walleys Anglico* (Paris, 1511) (this work was really a fourteenth century allegory by Pierre Bersuire or Berchorius: see Allen, p. 168); *Metamorphoseon. Libri XV. Raphaelis Regii . . . cum novis Jacob Micylli Viri eruditissimi additionibus* (Venice, 1549); Shakespeare's *Ovid Being Arthur Golding's Translation of the Metamorphoses (1567)*, ed. W. H. D. Rouse (Carbondale, Ill: Southern Illinois University Press, 1961); Abraham Fraunce, *The Third Part of the Countesse of Pembrokes Ivychurch* (London, 1592); P. *Ovidii Metamorphosis, seu Fabulae Poeticae: Earumque interpretatio ethica, physica, historica Georgii Sabini* (Frankfort, 1593) (this work was written by George Schuler: see Allen, p. 179); George Sandys, *Ovid's Metamorphoses, Englished, Mythologized, and Represented in Figures*, ed. Karl K. Hulley and Stanley T. Vandersall (Lincoln: University of Nebraska Press, 1970).

2. See Elizabeth Donno, *Elizabethan Minor Epics* (London: Routledge and Kegan Paul, 1963); William Keach, *Elizabethan Erotic Narratives* (New Brunswick: Rutgers University Press, 1977); Richard A. Lanham, *The Motives of Eloquence: Literary Rhetoric in the Renaissance* (New Haven: Yale University Press, 1976), pp. 48-64, 82-110. A third Ovid, philosopher of mutability, has been demonstrated in *Twelfth Night* by D. J. Palmer, "Art and Nature in *Twelfth Night*," *Critical Quarterly*, 9 (1967), 201-12.

3. See G. Karl Galinsky, *Ovid's Metamorphoses: An Introduction to the Basic Aspects* (Oxford: Basil Blackwell, 1975); Lanham, pp. 48-64; Brooks Otis, *Ovid as an Epic Poet* (Cambridge: Cambridge Univ. Press, 1966).

4. *Shakespeare's Ovid Being Arthur Golding's Translation of the Metamorphoses*, p. 21; I, 1; all quotations from Ovid will be taken from this translation, hereafter called Golding's *Ovid*.

5. See especially Galinsky, pp. 45-69; and Otis, pp. 122-51, 260-63, and his argument (pp. 298-300) that the deification of Caesar and projected deification of Augustus were merely compliments and not meant to be taken seriously.

6. *Whitney's Choice of Emblems*, ed. Henry Greene (London: Lovell Reeve, 1866); p. 15; see also Fraunce, M1. Other popular interpretations include Actaeon as a man whose estate was consumed by usurers, and the son of God pursued by cruel persons (Walleys/Bersuire, D2, D2v). A man whose patrimony is consumed by hangers-on appears in Regio-Micyllus, E2; Golding, Epistle to Leycester, 11. 97-100; Fraunce, M1; Sandys, p. 151. The tale is moralized as a warning to avoid curiosity into the affairs of princes in Fraunce, M1 and Sandys, p. 151. Written after *Twelfth Night*, Sandys shows the conservatism of allegorical interpretation.

7. Walleys/Bersuire, C5, repeated word for word in Regio-Micyllus, D7, translation by Allen, p. 173 quoting from Paris, 1515 edition; Sabinus/Schuler, E1v; Sandys, pp. 112-13. Regio-Micyllus adds that her change to a bear is also able to signify her change from prosperity to poverty.

8. Epistle to Leycester, 1.68. See also Walleys/Bersuire, B8v; and Sandys, p. 74, who moralizes the tale to show what "immortall honour a virgin obtaines by preserving her chastity."

9. Walleys/Bersuire, C4; Regio-Micyllus, D7; Sabinus/Schuler, D6v; Sandys, p. 110.

10. Sabinus/Schuler, X7; Sandys, p. 449.

11. "Musica Mundana and *Twelfth Night*," *Sound and Poetry*, ed. Northrop Frye, *English Institute Essays, 1956* (New York: Columbia University Press, 1957), pp. 80-82.

12. Ovid's *Fasti*, ed. and trans. James George Frazer (London: Macmillan, 1929), I, 59.

13. See, for example, S. K. Heninger, *Touches of Sweet Harmony; Pythagorean Cosmology and Renaissance Poetics* (San Marino, Calif.: Huntington Library, 1974), pp. 6-7, 179-89.

14. John S. Lawry, "*Twelfth Night* and 'Salt Waves Fresh in Love,' " *Shakespeare Studies*, 6 (1970), 108, n.17.

15. Keach, pp. 5-24; Lanham, pp. 48-64. Through these techniques they were able to express a quality Keach calls "ambivalence," "the coexistence in one person of opposing emotional attitudes towards one subject" (p. xvi).

16. "The Masks of *Twelfth Night*," *University Review*, 22 (1955), 28.

Bibliographical Note

The works of special use in my study of Ovid are Brooks Otis, *Ovid as an Epic Poet* (Cambridge: Cambridge University Press, 1966); G. Karl Galinsky, *Ovid's Metamorphoses: An Introduction to the Basic Aspects* (Oxford: Basil Blackwell, 1975); Richard A. Lanham, *Motives of Eloquence: Literary Rhetoric in the Renaissance* (New Haven: Yale University Press, 1976), pp. 48-64. For Renaissance understandings of Ovid, I was most impressed by William Keach, *Elizabethan Erotic Narratives* (New Brunswick: Rutgers University Press, 1977) and Don Cameron Allen, *Mysteriously Meant* (Baltimore: Johns Hopkins Press, 1970). Essential works on Ovid's influence on Shakespeare include Lanham, Stephen Booth's edition of Shakespeare's *Sonnets* (New Haven: Yale University Press, 1977); Eugene Waith, "The Metamorphosis of Violence in *Titus Andronicus*," *Shakespeare Survey*, 10 (1957) 39-49. Articles on Ovid's influence on *Twelfth Night* include D. J. Palmer, "Art and Nature in *Twelfth Night*," *Critical Quarterly*, 9 (1967), 201-12, and Anthony Brian Taylor, "Shakespeare and Golding: Viola's Interview with Olivia and Echo and Narcissus," *English Language Notes*, 15 (1977), 103-6.

7

Animals as Agents of Revelation: The Horizontalizing of the Chain of Being in Shakespeare's Comedies

O be thou damned, inexecrable dog,
And for thy life let justice be accused!
Thou almost mak'st me waver in my faith
To hold opinion with Pythagoras
That souls of animals infuse themselves
Into the trunks of men. Thy currish spirit
Governed a wolf, who hanged for human slaughter,
Even from the gallows did his fell soul fleet,
And whilst thou layest in thy unhallowed dam,
Infused itself in thee; for thy desires
Are wolvish, bloody, starved, and ravenous.
The Merchant of Venice 4.1.128-38

In cursing Shylock, Gratiano entertains momentarily the philosophical position Ovid seems to embrace at the end of his *Metamorphoses*—an acceptance of Pythagoras' doctrine of metempsychosis. The doctrine led Ovid to advocate a benign vegetarianism, which would prevent a man from being faced with the regrettable possibility of eating his brother. Gratiano, on the other hand, resorts to metempsychosis to express the most extreme revulsion and wonders whether the souls of men and animals could indeed be interchangeable because this is the only explanation he can offer for the bestiality of the Jew. *The Merchant of Venice* presents the idea of the mingling of species as shocking, and Christian doctrine viewed it as heretical. Even the union of human and animal forms in costume was forbidden by the medieval church;[1] and, in spite of abundant evidence of the popularity of animal representations on the Elizabethan stage, as late as 1615 one I. H. inveighs in *This World's Folly* against players "barbarously diverting *Nature* and defacing God's owne image, by metamorphising humane shape into bestiall forme."[2]

And yet, for most Elizabethans there was clearly fascination and humor in metamorphic variations on the human form. In his early comedies, Shakespeare's intermingling of human and animal figures reflects the ambiguity of his age, but it shows considerably stronger affinity with the humorous reaction than with the piety embodied in the anti-Semitic fervor of the Venetian. Gratiano's virulence is beyond question, but *The Merchant of Venice* appears between two of Shakespeare's plays that use Ovidlike metamorphoses for primarily comic effect—*A Midsummer Night's Dream* and *The Merry Wives of Windsor*. Paradoxically, the same certainty of divine order that makes Gratiano's suggestion of kinship between man and wolf so devastating provides, in a lighter context, a framework for comic incongruity. Some tension and uneasiness about the true nature of man-animal relationship may help to trigger the comic explosion in an audience at the appearance of Bottom as ass and Falstaff as deer, but the laughter depends finally on a secure confidence in the superiority of man and the absurdity of the conjunction. When an audience's values become confused or the barriers between species are suddenly eroded, the loss of human form is no longer funny—witness the terror of Kafka's *Metamorphosis.* Both *A Midsummer Night's Dream* and *The Merry Wives* retain for their duration the balance of comic certainty, but each permits some sense of rising doubt at its end.

Similarly, humor remains dominant over latent horror in Shakespeare's use of man-animal analogy in the images of the love hunt in the pre-1600 comedies, especially *The Merry Wives* and *As You Like It*. Comic enjoyment diminishes, however, with dawning recognition of unpleasant similarities in these comparisons, and with the fading of comic effect comes a blurring of the clear hierarchy pictured by the Chain of Being. A new sort of shock now galvanizes the mind—not that of witnessing, seriously or in fun, the violation of divine order, but the shock of entertaining the frightening suspicion that, in fact, the assumed order might not exist. Finally, in *The Tempest* the strange monster Caliban, with his mysterious melding of bestial and human, hardly evokes laughter at all. As Prospero acknowledges responsibility for Caliban and severs himself from Ariel, we are forced to admit to consciousness, albeit reluctantly, the thought planted by the earlier comedies that man's "special" place in the universe may be beside the animals rather than above them—that the two coexist as parts of a horizontal continuum rather than as a vertical hierarchy.

The use of animal figures seems, then, to become decreasingly a source of humor for Shakespeare and more and more a way of thinking about the true nature of man. We may trace in these comedies sequences of man-animal associations that begin as spectacles enhancing comic vision and lead to revelations that, in bringing men ever closer to animals, work to dismantle the traditional hierarchy and put an end to laughter. In each case the animals are both objects of attention and agents of revelation. Real animals, animal metamorphoses, animal metaphors, and a wide variety of animal figures generate excitement in themselves but at the same time seem to serve as catalysts to facilitate the progression of ideas.

Shakespeare's animals range from the presentation on stage of such a "real" animal (he may or may not have been played by a man) as Crab, the dog of *Two Gentlemen of Verona*, through the visibly artificial bear of *The Winter's Tale*. The dramatist uses a variety of animal forms, from costumed figures to fleeting verbal evocations, which pass almost without reaching conscious perception, such as the reference in *Troilus and Cressida* to Ajax's "long-eared evasions" (2.1.70). I have chosen not to distinguish between these varied animal messages but to draw freely from them. My assumption is that all share the duality of metaphorical comparison—implicit or explicit—of man and animal. What is important is the potential in this metaphoric language (visual or verbal) for dynamism, growth, and progressive revelation. Because I want to emphasize particularly the element of change and movement of ideas in Shakespeare's metaphorical structures, I use the word *sign* (rather than *image*) in referring to animals. They are directional pointers, symbolic indicators, masks for truths instinctively avoided.

One of the theories of metaphor is that its roots are found in taboo.[3] What cannot be faced directly is approached obliquely. As agents of revelation, animals operate effectively because they offer human beings a built-in duality, a haunting combination of the recognized and the strange. Because they are both familiar and mysterious, they can often serve as links between the known and the unknown. In literature and in art, animals often function as guides to previously unexplored psychic landscapes—regions hitherto unsuspected, ignored, or avoided. They serve as foils for recognition of comic incongruity, and even when the animal comparisons are playful, they guide the audience from one level of perception to another. What seems like an innocent world of fantasy leads to a leap of insight, wherein the familiar is transformed when the known and the mysterious meet. In such cases comic devices cease to function comically, and the comic dramatist stops or seeks new directions.

In the discussion that follows I shall consider first the metamorphoses of Bottom and Falstaff in *A Midsummer Night's Dream* and *The Merry Wives of Windsor*, then turn briefly to the use of the deer in the love hunts of the early comedies, and finally attempt some analysis of the tantalizing and unsettling animals of *The Tempest*, with particular focus on Caliban. In each case I will argue that the use of animal patterns marks a stage in the evolution of Shakespeare's ideas and actually facilitates the imaginative leap from one level to another. Viewed in sequence, these patterns reveal a progression of thought that moves from the secure hierarchy of the Great Chain of Being, characteristic of the earlier plays, to the fleeting recognition at the end of *The Tempest* that the chain may be horizontal rather than vertical, and to the acceptance of the narrowing gap between man and animal. Briefly, the sequence is as follows: (1) the metamorphoses of Bottom and Falstaff make us laugh because man is superior to animal and joining the two forms seems absurd. Such a mechanism is degrading to man, reveals flaws in the characters, and ultimately destroys their comic usefulness. The Chain remains intact: (2) the love hunt in the pre-1600 comedies balances at first the comic and tragic potentialities of man-animal analogies. It turns toward the tragic with the revelation that sexual man may indeed be like an animal in his violence and uncertain fidelity. The Chain is threatened: (3) the status of the man-monster Caliban ceases to be comic and becomes increasingly ambiguous, whereas Ariel, the airy spirit, makes a virtue of metamorphosis. The hierarchy disintegrates as Prospero renounces Ariel, acknowledges Caliban, and declares that he depends on the audience for release from the isolation of his island. The Chain is turned on its side: whatever gap between species remains is between man and God.

The Metamorphoses of Bottom and Falstaff

The pattern of human-to-animal metamorphosis is unusual in Shakespeare. *A Midsummer Night's Dream* and *The Merry Wives of Windsor* are the only plays to present such a change with an explicit visual representation. Puck gives Bottom the head of an ass in order to implement Oberon's revenge on his wife. Falstaff goes to the forest in a buck's head disguise for what he imagines to be an illicit assignation with the two wives of Windsor. Both Bottom and Falstaff appear then with their "rational" human heads supplanted by animal heads, Bottom involuntarily and Falstaff deliberately. In both cases, there is an initial shock which relaxes into comedy and then moves beyond. The nearly farcical tone with which the changes are treated allays the shock and apprehension that might accompany the appearance of the drastically transformed lovers, and the tension itself causes laughter. Only gradually does the comic delight of the audience change into fears about what the transformation can mean.

The same disjunction between tone and content is markedly present in Ovid, Shakespeare's favorite classical author. In both, the implications of human metamorphoses are profoundly important. The loss of human form is shocking because it indicates a decline from a godlike image and

A Midsummer Night's Dream, Act 3, scene 1. An engraving by R. Rhodes from a painting by Johann Heinrich Fuseli. *Courtesy of The Folger Shakespeare Library.*

the loss of the human ability to communicate. Human-animal confusion can be tragic, and in *King Lear* it signifies madness. But in the two Shakespearean comedies under consideration its comic impact continues throughout the performance. Only in retrospect does metamorphosis appear to be an ironic metaphor for stasis. What seems to be change is revealed to be in actuality a sign of paralysis. In Ovid, transformations are terrifying because they are nearly always terminal. Despite the rare cases where the characters turn into exalted constellations or even return to their former selves, the cumulative effect of story after story of human form lost and human growth frozen becomes increasingly painful. In spite of apparent variations, real transformations fail to take place. People become animals or plants or stones, either because of random caprice of the gods or because they cannot move freely, cope with their problems creatively, or change. But in every case, the transformation marks the end—no further possibilities of development remain. (Perhaps the growing recognition of the failures of human existence drew Ovid to Pythagorean metempsychosis—a theory that permits some long-term hope for progress).

By contrast to the climate of Ovid, the world of Shakespearean comedy favors growth and maturity. Change, even highly unlikely change, is possible, but Bottom and Falstaff, two of the characters most infatuated with role-playing, change hardly at all. In each case the animal metamorphosis is a penultimate stage in a series of illusionary changes that culminates in a restored reality in which the characters remain the same. Bottom has been eager, in our first glimpse of him, to experience the widest possible spectrum of identities—lover, tyrant, lady, and lion. He has wanted to play all the parts in the mechanicals' play of *Pyramus and Thisbe*, promising rhapsodically to "move storms" as a lover, to play Hercules rarely as a "part to tear a cat in," or to "speak in a monstrous little voice" as Thisbe. It is Bottom, in his next scene, who insists that Snug must avoid terrifying the ladies when he appears as a lion, because "a lion among ladies is a most dreadful thing, for there is not a more fearful wild-fowl than your lion living" (3.1.29-31). Bottom's solution is that Snug must be named by his human name and "half his face must be seen through the lion's neck." This can be understood as a prevision of Bottom's own more complete transformation.

Bottom's appearance as ass should be, I think, electrifying and disquieting as well as funny. (Fuseli's painting vividly captures this ambiguity.) The tension Bottom generates is prepared for by the emphasis on the bestial in Oberon's instruction that Titania "Wake when some vile thing is near," "Be it ounce, or cat or bear/Pard or boar with bristled hair" (2.2.30-34). The nearly speechless terror of the mechanicals at Bottom's appearance is glimpsed briefly at first hand (3.1.111-23) and described at some length (in bestial terms of derogation) by Puck:

> When they him spy,
> As wild geese that the creeping fowler eye,

> Or russet-pated choughs, many in sort,
> Rising and cawing in the gun's report,
> Sever themselves and madly sweep the sky,
> So, at his sight, away his fellows fly. . . .
> And, at our stamp, here o'er and o'er one falls;
> He murder cries, and help from Athens calls
> Their sense thus weak, lost with their fears thus strong . . .
> I led them on in this distracted fear,
> And left sweet Pyramus translated there. . . .
>
> $\qquad\qquad\qquad\qquad\qquad\qquad\qquad$ (3.1.19-32)

Only as his concluding lines focus on the reaction of the fairy queen does terror dissolve safely into secure absurdity, "When in that moment, so it came to pass,/Titania waked, and straightway loved an ass" (3.1.33-34).

By contrast to the normal human terror at metamorphosis, Puck revels in the prospect of his mischievous disguises:

> Sometime a horse I'll be, sometime a hound,
>   A hog, a headless bear . . .
> And neigh, and bark, . . . and roar . . .
> Like horse, hound, hog, bear, . . .
>
> $\qquad\qquad\qquad\qquad\qquad\qquad\qquad$ (3.1.107-10)

Similarly, the translated Bottom takes a rather disconcerting comfort in beasts as he improvises his song about woosel cock, throstle, wren, finch, sparrow, lark, and cuckoo. The cluster of assembled animals in these lines, as well as Bottom's appearance, seem to signal a dawning recognition for characters and audience. Bottom has, quite literally, passed into another mode of experience. As in Puck's account of his achievements, the balance between terror and pleasure in Bottom's transformation is tipped decisively toward laughter as Titania rouses to inquire, "What angel wakes me from my flow'ry bed?" The incongruity becomes irresistibly ludicrous, and it furnishes dependable comic situations for several scenes to come. The ass-headed weaver is entertained most royally, but inevitably the vision fades. He becomes for Oberon and Puck, and in the end for Titania, a scapegoat whose "sacrifice" reunites the fairy king and queen. The mysterious power of his "most rare vision" does not change him and cannot be conveyed by the power of his words. His behavior implies that he ends as he began, still engagingly if childishly enjoying his "play" as he "dies" most pathetically for love. His transformation has not altered his destiny but merely made visible what even the most doting audience has known from the start—that he is an ass.

The case of Falstaff is similar but sadder. Its implications extend beyond the limits of *The Merry Wives.* We have reveled earlier in Falstaff's riotous play with Prince Hal in *Henry IV, Part 1,* but we have also been warned that Hal will change as he grows into the kingship. The scene in *The Merry Wives* prepares us for the inevitable severing of the relationship in *Henry IV, Part 2*. Since Falstaff is incapable of change, he is doomed to rejection by the inevitably altered Prince Hal as he becomes Henry V. In Falstaff's story as in Bottom's the recurring theme of transformation is present. In the tavern scene in *Henry IV, Part 1*, we have seen Falstaff alternately in the role of the King and as Prince Hal. He has played at being highwayman, and we first have a hint of his future as a deer in Hal's epitaph over his supposedly dead friend, "Death hath not strook so fat a deer today." Like Hal's jocular rejection of Falstaff in the tavern, the lines have a prophetic knell.

In *The Merry Wives* Falstaff sees himself as lover and cuckolder, but the audience sees him as degraded first into a basket of dirty linen and then into an old woman. His climactic fantasy in Windsor forest, as he approaches the final erotic triumph he expects, shapes itself in images of himself as Jove. Disguised with his buck's head, he waits impatiently for the ladies, musing:

> The Windsor bell hath strook twelve; the minute draws on.
> Now the hot-blooded gods assist me! Remember, Jove, thou
> was a bull for thy Europa, love set on thy horns. O powerful
> love, that in some respects makes a beast a man; in some other,
> a man a beast. You were also, Jupiter, a swan for the love of
> Leda. O omnipotent love, how near the god drew to the com-
> plexion of a goose! A fault done first in the form of a beast
> (O Jove, a beastly fault!) and then another fault in the sem-
> blance of a fowl—think on't, Jove, a foul fault! When gods
> have hot backs, what shall poor men do? For me, I am here a
> Windsor stag, and the fattest, I think, i'th' forest.
>
> (5.5.1-13)

Very soon, however, Falstaff's fantasies of himself as Jovelike lover who changes shape at will fade when he realizes that he is an ox (a castrated beast of burden) and an ass (a fool). But even this does not signal a real change. By the end of *Henry IV, Part 2*, he is, sadly but ineluctably, a surfeit-swelled, profane old man (5.5.50), whom the young king understandably rejects. His epiphany as deer has simply confirmed that he has always been the lustful spirit ready to be "dishorned," the hunter unwittingly prepared to become the prey. In the experience of both Falstaff and Bottom, the audience is entertained by dalliances with metamorphosis, but it must accept that what has actually diverted it is two hopeless cases of arrested development. It is as if Shakespeare himself, in conjuring up the humorous visions of the merged man and beast, had suddenly seen the inevitable limits of the comic *alazon*, the braggart who pretends or tries to be more than he is.

The punishment of Falstaff, *The Merry Wives of Windsor*, Act 5, scene 5. An engraving from a painting by Robert Smirke, published 1795 by John and Josiah Boydell, in the Shakespeare Gallery, London. *Courtesy of The Folger Shakespeare Library.*

The Deer in the Love Hunts

The second use of animal signs in comedy also focuses on deer. This central image is one of the richest and most provocative of recurring animal motifs in Shakespeare. In many contexts besides the Falstaff metamorphosis the deer is associated with movement and change that touch on courtship and cuckoldry. The deer in rut is reputed a lustful animal, but, for Shakespeare, the central link with courtship seems to be the hunt.[4] The effectiveness of the hunt as a mirror for the pursuit of love is delicately balanced from the start between comedy and tragedy. The comparisons are funny because of the incongruity of godlike man behaving like a beast of prey, but the inevitable overtones of violence and victimization are disquietingly obvious.

It is significant that Shakespeare uses the figure freely in both his early tragedies and his early comedies. Hunting scenes appear together in proximity with sexual encounters in *Venus and Adonis, Titus Andronicus, Love's Labor's Lost*, and *A Midsummer Night's Dream*. In *Twelfth Night* the mention of hunting makes Orsino think of his passion for Olivia but also turns his thoughts to Actaeon, the young hunter turned into a deer by Diana and torn apart by his hounds; Orsino "moralizes" the hounds as passion. Deer are referred to as sex objects—willing and unwilling—and it is significant that the hunted may be either male or female. Chiron and Demetrius speak of Lavinia as a "dainty Doe" they hope to pluck to ground, but in *Love's Labor's Lost* the Princess is the hunter and the killer of the deer. She is, of course, hunting the King of Navarre, and the hunt becomes the occasion of sustained bawdy dialogue that glances at the real subject. The easy availability of puns such as "deer-dear," "hart-heart," and the double-entendres constantly yoked with the word *die* further the identification already implied in the two meanings of the word *venery*, the art of pursuing the deer and the art of pursuing the love object.

Finally, the deer's horns, linked in the figure of Actaeon to both desire and infidelity, become the manifestation of cuckoldry.[5] Shakespeare makes this association clear in *Titus* when Bassiano, after mockingly identifying Tamora with Diana and being threatened with Actaeon's fate, credits the unfaithful queen with "a goodly gift in horning" (2.3.67) and hopes her husband will escape the fate of a stag. The connection of deer horns and cuckoldry is suggested in *Love's Labor's Lost*, repeated in *As You Like It* and *All's Well That Ends Well* (1.3.52), and Actaeon is twice invoked as the type of the cuckold in *The Merry Wives*. In early Shakespeare the images of sexual pursuit as a hunt and of horns as signs of cuckoldry provide humor in part because of the tensions associated with sexual behavior, but the outcome determines the tone. If we are confident of the happy ending, we can say, "Lovers behave like animals, isn't it funny?" But if we are seriously confronted with the actual destruction of the prey, or with the casual and inconstant coupling rightly or wrongly associated with animals, chaos threatens and we can no longer laugh. That is what seems to happen in Shakespeare's comedies of the late 1590s.

The two links of the chain of deer association, the deer hunt as sexual pursuit and the deer's horns as signs of cuckoldry, join together most dramatically and most overtly in *The Merry Wives*. The horned Falstaff fancies himself as sexual aggressor but is revealed as the prey of the wives. In attempting to cuckold Ford (with the husband's collusion), he himself becomes the very symbol of cuckoldry. The lustful intruder doesn't die but is condemned to a pseudocastration as Falstaff is pinched by the fairies. At the same time the young lovers are united in preparation for the sexual "death" embodied by marriage.

How very closely intertwined the themes of courtship and cuckoldry are is spelled out even more clearly in *As You Like It*, 4.2. The scene is a curious one. Its only apparent purpose is to provide for the passage of time between Rosalind's parting from Orlando (she says, "I'll go find a shadow, and sigh till he come") and the news of his misadventure with the lioness. The scene includes the recognition of the killer of the deer, the transformation of the killer of the deer into a deer himself (he shall have the "leather skin and horns to wear"), and the celebration of cuckoldry as a natural and inevitable phenomenon. The scene prefigures the moment at which Orlando conquers Rosalind, who has been identified earlier with a deer by Touchstone ("If a hart should lack a hind,/Let him seek out Rosalinde" 3.2.95-96) and by herself ("He comes to kill my heart" 3.2. 234). The moment of victory arrives when she swoons, "dying" for love. In a sense Orlando has then, even though he is not present, "killed the deer."

The scene shows, as did the climax of *The Merry Wives*, Shakespeare's sense of the indivisible union between sexual victory and cuckoldry—an insight soon to be pursued in *Troilus and Cressida*. The merged man-animal vision indicates an unpleasant fact: success in love inescapably brings the risk of betrayal. Man may behave like an animal in reality as well as in jest. It is perhaps not surprising that in *The Merry Wives of Windsor* and *As You Like It*, marital discord is no longer a subject of comedy, and the theme of jealousy, touched lightly in *The Comedy of Errors*, *A Midsummer Night's Dream*, and even in *The Merry Wives of Windsor*, assumes fatal dimensions in *Othello*, *Cymbeline*, and *The Winter's Tale*.

The new understanding achieved and shared with audiences through these two disparate ways of using animal signs reveals a dark side of two standard features of Shakespearean comedy: the figure of the *alazon*, who has seemed a richly rewarding stock character, and the hunt of love, which has provided the reliable foundation of plot in the tradition of New Comedy. Both reappear in comic mutations for the last time in *Twelfth Night* and *All's Well That Ends Well*.

Animals in *The Tempest*

Shakespeare was certainly indebted to the universe of Ovid, but there are significant differences in the world views of the two poets. Implicit in Ovid's *Metamorphoses* is a Chain of Being, which he himself outlines in his introduction (pp. 22-23). In spite of the light tone, I think it is clear that he regards almost all of the transformations he describes as painful. Man is unique in his "stately looke repleate with majestie" (Ovid, p. 23). Its loss is a disaster. But in the end Ovid's work incorporates an acceptance of fluidity of forms. The insistence on a rigid hierarchy with a crucial chasm fixed between man and animal is foreign to him. Such a vision of living things is a legacy of the Christian tradition.

The early church fathers, anxious to destroy primitive nature worship, rigidified the hierarchy suggested in *Genesis* and emphasized the differ- ence in kind between man and beast. Advancing this view, Augustine wrote:

> Christ himself shows that to refrain from the killing of animals and the destroying of plants is the height of superstitition, for, judging that there are no common rights between us and the beasts and trees, he sent the devils into a herd of swine and with a curse withered the tree on which he found no fruit.[6]

With the authority of the *New Testament* and the church behind it, this doctrine became axiomatic; and its emphasis on the gulf between species provides the shock of recognition which energizes Shakespeare's comic success with metamorphoses and hunt analogies and adds savage power to the animal signs in such plays as *King Lear* and *Timon of Athens*.

By the time he wrote *The Tempest*, however, Shakespeare had al- most certainly read Montaigne. I do not want to enter into the contro- versey about how detailed and specific his knowledge of Montaigne was, or to argue a narrow and decisive influence, but the derivation of Gon- zalo's commonwealth from the essay "Of the Caniballes," as trans- lated by John Florio in 1603, has long been acknowledged. Eleanor Prosser has recently demonstrated very persuasively that Prospero's speech on forgiveness echoes "Of Cruelty," the essay immediately pro- ceeding "An Apologie of Raymond Sebond," with which links to Shake- speare have also been suggested.

If Shakespeare did read "Of Cruelty," he found Montaigne debating Pythagoras' metempsychosis, first rejecting the kinship of man and animal, insisting, "Ase touching that alliance between us and beasts, I make no great accompt of it, nor do I greatly admit it," but later coming around to the admission of a bond:

> But when amongst the most moderate opinions, I meet with some discourses that goe about and labour to shew the neere resemblance between us and beasts, and what share they have in our greatest Privileges, and with how much likely-hood they

are compared to us, truly I abate much of our presumption,
and am easily removed from that imaginary soveraigntie that
some give and ascribe unto us above all other creatures.
. . . There is a kinde of enter-changeable commerce and mutuall
bond betweene them and us

(2.124-25).

It is not necessary to insist that Shakespeare learned to elevate the
animal from Montaigne. But I suggest that a parallel progression of
thought is to be found in *The Tempest*, that the progression is revealed
through animal signs, and that the changing view moves author and
audience through comedy to a sober acceptance of a different reality.
The coincidental use of specific passages from Montaigne and the reluctant acknowledgment of a human-animal kinship similar to that de-
lineated by Montaigne is striking. The struggle to redefine the relationship
between the orders of being is evident at least as early as *King Lear*, but the
overt statement of close kinship is delayed until *The Tempest*.

Although the world of *The Tempest* is hierarchical, its order is different from the rigid hierarchies that characterize the early comedies.
Fluidity and movement are signaled from the start by the tempest and are
reinforced throughout by the emphasis on air and water and by references
to birds and fish. The merging and blurring of figures is characteristic of
the whole play. The opposing qualities of stasis, paralysis, and isolation
are restraints and punishments. Caliban is confined by Prospero, and
the enchanter uses the threat of a return to that condition to subdue
Ariel. But played off against these images of stasis are figures of movement and transformation. The metaphorical movement is activated by
the yoking of surprising opposites, one of which is often animal. Miranda
is both a worm and a goddess. Bones are made into coral and eyes are
linked with the pearl-creating oyster. Alonso wonders what strange
fish has eaten his son. Prospero compares Ferdinand to a slightly worm-
eaten blossom, and both the noble Ferdinand and the bestial Caliban
are lowly carriers of wood. The song of Ariel, the airy spirit, carries a
refrain of prosaic dogs and cocks. Spirits appear as strange shapes, monstrous figures, but also as dogs, as nymphs, and as domesticated reapers,
dissolving orderly hierarchies. Iris is linked with sheep; Juno (appropriately enough) with peacocks, Cupid with wasps and sparrows.

Ariel himself is the essence of motion. He flies, swims, dives, rides,
and he is linked with winds and flying things: owls, bees, bats, chicks.
Puck's casual pleasure in transforming himself is greatly elaborated in
Ariel. He is given to changing his form more than the plot really requires: he appears rather inexplicably as a water-nymph, and as a harpy—
both hybrid forms; but far from being terminal metamorphoses like
those of Bottom and Falstaff, they are signs of life and power. Although
his music is often described as "solemn," with no instrument specified,
the tabor and pipe that he plays for the benefit of Stephano and his

company (and for the audience) certainly conjure up the image of a martial human being. Prospero himself suggests that Ariel outdoes him in "humanity" with his forgiving spirit towards Prospero's enemies. Ariel emerges then as a figure poised between sea and air, moving freely among the assorted forms of life with reward rather than penalty.

Against this background of fluidity and interchangeable forms, certain earlier, characteristically Shakespearean uses of animal signs remain predictable and conventional. The characters whom he wishes to denigrate are identified with animals, as Yoder says they regularly are in Shakespeare. Thus Sebastian is very early linked with dog, cur, cock, fowl, bulls, and lions. Antonio is connected with rats, crow, cockrel, sort (fish), chough, cat, and monster. Together they are beasts and devils, associated with roaring, shrieking, and howling. Stephano and Trinculo are similarly joined with devils, monsters, savages, geese, monkeys, ducks, fish, colts, calfs, and horse piss. In an unconventional revision of the love hunt they also become the prey of the spirits who appear as hounds to harry them. These traditional man-animal fusions contribute comic incongruity and shape the audience's attitude toward the characters.

And yet, curiously, the character who draws to himself by far the largest number of animal signs in the play is much more ambiguous than those characterized by these standard analogies. Yoder (p. 67) tabulated a total of animal comparisons for Caliban second only to those for Falstaff (in three plays). Caliban appears from the start as a man-animal hybrid comparable in some ways to the metamorphosed Bottom and Falstaff. He is not a cause of laughter in himself, but he is the butt for other people's coarse humor. As Hallett Smith points out, he is more grotesque than comic.[7] Modern critics and adapters have perceived that it is on him that the mystery of the play centers.[8] Caliban is not a man become monster, he is monster born; and although his appearance must have become specifically "fish-like" and "puppy-headed" on the stage, the text renders his true nature elusive. Shakespeare loads the dice against him from the beginning, and yet Caliban insistently and progressively rises in our esteem. He is prejudicially "a savage and deformed slave," "a freckled whelp," "not honored with a human shape," and a rapacious "villain." He is "filth," "brutish," "vild," "bestial," devilish "hag-seed." Ravens, toads, beetles, and bats are his allies and the wholesome bee his enemy. And yet he has learned human arts, he responds to music, and he knows the locations of fresh springs, brine-pits, barren and fertile places, of crab-apples and filberts and peanuts; he has mastered the arts of survival, and he learns to distinguish drunkards from gods.

His ambiguity has been well chronicled, and there is no need to belabor it here. The whole play seems an effort to come to terms with his paradoxical nature. Like Ariel, Caliban is a hybrid and no longer funny. But Ariel has been freed from the pejorative connotation of metamorphosis from the start. Airborne animals have always had some

Caliban.   An engraving by Birrell from a painting by
Thomas Stothard for *The Tempest*, published in 1798 by
Edward Harding, London. *Courtesy of The Folger Shake-
speare Library.*

relish of salvation.[9] Caliban's shape, however, begins as deformity. Our laughter when he is made the butt of Trinculo and Stephano depends initially on our sense of his inferiority. Thus our mirth at Trinculo's choosing to join the strange fishlike man under his gaberdine (a cloth that interestingly links him with Shylock) arises from the incongruity of the union and reaches a crescendo at the absurdity of the drunken Stephano's inability to distinguish man from monster.

What I am suggesting, then, is that in *The Tempest* we are witnessing a dawning perception in Shakespeare of a Great Chain of Being that does not hang from heaven but stretches horizontally over the earth. Prospero, Ariel, and Caliban are not so much a hierarchy as a rather unorthodox committee. Prospero obviously prefers Ariel, but he needs both of them; and he must give up the "tricksy spirit" before he can return to the real world. The rigid order of *A Midsummer Night's Dream* has been turned on its side, and living beings must seek new relationships. In the history of thought (as well as in *The Tempest*), the dismantling of the Chain of Being has been a slow and erratic process, one not yet fully completed in our own time. The sketching out of the process in this play should be particularly fascinating to us. We sense that the relinquishing of the old secure hierarchy must have been as painful for Shakespeare as it was for Prospero. We witness the magician's reluctance to give up the magic control exercised through his aerial "slave" and to acknowledge the "thing of darkness" that is his earthly slave. It is extraordinary that he sees the necessity of both. Natural powers are the endowment of man and animal. Supernatural control can be extended only through grace.

Prospero's position at the end of *The Tempest* is remarkably like Montaigne's at the end of "Raymond Sebond." After a sustained encomium of the beast and an insistence on man's possible inferiority, Montaigne sums up his argument:

> To this so religious conclusion of a heathen man, I will only add this word, taken from a testimony of the same condition. . . . "Oh what a vile and abject thing is man" (saith he) "unlesse he raise himselfe above humanity!" Observe here a notable speech, and a profitable desire; but likewise absurd. It is impossible and monstrous . . . that man should mount over and above himselfe or humanity; for he cannot see but with his owne eyes, nor take hold but with his owne armes. . . . He may elevate himselfe by forsaking and renouncing his owne meanes, and suffering himselfe to be elevated and raised by meere heavenly meanes. It is for our Christian faith, not for his Stoicke vertue to pretend or aspire to this divine Metamorphosis, or miraculous transmutation [2.332].

Consciously or unconsciously, Shakespeare has moved from the world of Ovid and his more rigid Christian successors toward the "so religious conclusion of a heathen man'' that characterizes Montaigne. The poetic imagination has given him, in fact, a way of "seeing with more than his own eyes" and of "taking hold with more than his own arms." His creative unions of men and beasts have engendered mutations that have indicated directions and made possible at every difficult turning point the discovery of a new terrain. The movement of metaphor has enabled him to push beyond the limtations of the *alazon* and the love hunt and has finally forced him to think the unthinkable and to accept the unacceptable: man must acknowledge his kinship with the beast. For his audience, laughter at the absurdity of metamorphosis has sobered into a poignant recognition of a new vision of the human condition; and the Chain connecting heaven and earth has begun to re-form itself into a bridge uniting earthly orders of being.

Notes

1. Beryl Rowland, *Animals with Human Faces: A Guide to Animal Symbolism* (Knoxville: Univ. of Tennessee Press, 1973), p. xvi.
2. Quoted in E.K. Chambers, *The Elizabethan Stage*, 4 vols. (Oxford: Clarendon Press, 1923), IV, 254-55.
3. José Ortega y Gasset, *The Dehumanization of Art and Other Writings on Art and Culture* (Garden City, N. Y.: Doubleday, 1956), pp. 30-31.
4. The appropriateness to Falstaff is enhanced by the fact that the deer has some reputation for living for a long time and growing more lecherous as it grows older. See Marcelle Thiébaux, *The Stag of Love* (Ithaca: Cornell Univ. Press, 1974), p. 42.
5. John M. Steadman, "Falstaff as Actaeon: A Dramatic Emblem," *Shakespeare Quarterly*, 14 (1963), 231-44.
6. Quoted in John Passmore, *Man's Responsibility for Nature* (London: Duckworth, 1974), p. 111.
7. Introduction to *The Tempest* in *The Riverside Shakespeare*, ed. G. Blakemore Evans (Boston: Houghton Mifflin, 1974), p. 1609.
8. See Ruby Cohn, *Modern Shakespeare Offshoots* (Princeton: Princeton Univ. Press, 1976) for chapter on "Peopling the Isle with Calibans," pp. 267-309.
9. See Beryl Rowland, *Birds with Human Souls: A Guide to Bird Symbolism* (Knoxville: Univ. of Tennessee Press, 1978).

Bibliographical Note

The great source of information about the Chain of Being is, of course, A. O. Lovejoy, *The Great Chain of Being* (Cambridge, Mass.: Harvard Univ. Press, 1936; rept. 1964). By analogy to the *temporalizing* of the chain traced by Lovejoy, pp. 242-87, I am suggesting a process that might be called a "horizontalizing." The traditional uses of animals in art and literature are documented by Beryl Rowland, *Animals with Human Faces: A Guide to Animal Symbolism* (Knoxville: Univ. of Tennessee Press, 1973), and *Birds with Human Souls: A Guide to Bird Symbolism* (Knoxville: Univ. of

Tennessee Press, 1978). For an analysis of Shakespeare's use of animals a very helpful source is Audrey Yoder, *Animal Analogy in Shakespeare's Character Portrayal* (New York: Columbia Univ. Press, 1947). Her work contains tables and an appendix (pp. 84-98) on stage animals and how they were presented, with a detailed section on the probable appearance of Caliban. The Renaissance obviously recognized some distinction between "animal," that is, any animate creature, and "brute" and "beast," that is, animals that "want discourse of reason." However, then as now the terms were used loosely. I have used them interchangeably to indicate non-humans.

On Ovid in particular and metamorphoses in general see Irving Massey, *The Gaping Pig: Literature and Metamorphosis* (Berkeley: University of California Press, 1976). The amorous hunt in medieval literature is analyzed by Marcelle Thiébaux, *The Stag of Love* (Ithaca: Cornell Univ. Press, 1974); and the complexity of the theme in the Renaissance is explored by Michael J. B. Allen, "The Chase: The Development of a Renaissance Theme," *Comparative Literature*, 20 (1968), 301-12. For a discussion of "theriophily" in Shakespeare's time, see especially George Boas, *The Happy Beast in French Thought of the Seventeenth Century* (Baltimore: Johns Hopkins Univ. Press, 1933), and W. R. Elton, *King Lear and the Gods* (San Marino: Huntington Library Press, 1966), pp. 191-97. Eleanor Prosser summarizes the argument about the extent of Shakespeare's knowledge of Montaigne, "Shakespeare, Montaigne, and the Rarer Action," *Shakespeare Studies*, I (1965), 261-64.

I have used the versions of Ovid and Montaigne that would have been known to Shakespeare: W. H. D. Rouse, ed., *Shakespeare's Ovid, Being Arthur Golding's Translation of 'The Metamorphoses'* (Carbondale: Southern Illinois Univ. Press, 1961); and George Saintsbury, ed., *The Essays of Montaigne Done into English by John Florio, anno 1603*, 3 vols. (London: Nutt, 1892, rept. New York: AMS, 1967). In my discussion I am accepting the idea that *The Merry Wives of Windsor* was composed before the completion of *Henry IV, Part 2*. For a summary of current thinking on the date, see my *Shakespeare's English Comedy: "The Merry Wives of Windsor" in Context* (London: Univ. of Nebraska Press, 1979), pp. 41-50.

PART 3

ASSUMPTIONS OF ROMANCE: IDEAL COMEDY AND THE NIGHT WORLD

8

The Tempest and Ideal Comedy

DOUGLAS L. PETERSON

The Tempest remains a difficult play. Its subjects—the qualities of mind and heart that are requisite to prudent governance; the intractability of evil, forgiveness, and retribution; and the limits of art and nurture—are familiar to anyone who is familiar with Shakespeare. The plot, too, is scarcely unusual, except perhaps in its observation of the unity of time. And yet the efforts of the most skillful interpreters have seemed partial or reductive.

What eludes explication is a feeling of sadness and resignation that pervades the play but that emerges most succinctly in specific passages; for instance, in Ariel's song of "sea change," in Prospero's speech announcing his decision to give up his "rough magic," and again in his observation that reality is no more than the stuff that "dreams are made on." It eludes paraphrase and yet it is in some way essential to the play's meaning. Perhaps those critics are right who insist that no interpretation will ever do justice to a play in which style expresses so much. On the other hand, our appreciation and chances of understanding the play more fully will surely be increased by whatever we can discover in the play that has gone unnoticed or by whatever reasonable solutions we can offer to the problems it presents.

I come now to my thesis: the problem of interpretation that *The Tempest* presents is essentially a problem of *kind*. Its meaning continues to elude us because we are unfamiliar with the principles by which it was conceived and written.

That the play ends happily was sufficient reason for the editors of the First Folio to place it among the comedies; but to conclude that it is a comedy raises at least as many questions as it settles. It still seems to belong more properly with the so-called romances. Even though the earlier comedies contain moments in which the emotions that are typical of these last plays come to the surface—for instance, in Puck's song of real night in the closing moments of *A Midsummer Night's Dream*, in the final songs of mutability at the close of *Love's Labor's Lost*, and again in Feste's song at the end of *Twelfth Night* of the rain that "raineth everyday"—their tone is much lighter. They are filled with youthful enthusiasm and laughter. They are festive and, above all, freely, even jubilantly, optimistic. There is optimism, too, in the last plays, but it is of a much different kind. Their protagonists, seasoned in the ways of the world, have known evil. They have also experienced or come close to experiencing, despair. If these last plays finally affirm a purposeful universe in which men are capable of living in concord, that affirmation is deeply qualified and is reached only after it has been deeply tried. In *The Tempest* it comes only in the final moments of the action and then only as an existential alternative to despair.

Indeed, tragicomedy seems a more appropriate designation than comedy for these last plays. But although it acknowledges the darker thoughts and feelings they contain, to call them such tells us little about the formal principles they share and which, in turn, distinguish them from other forms of comedy. What are those principles and where do they come from? They are those of an important comic form which Shakespeare adopted at the outset of his career and that he found sufficiently flexible to accommodate his continually evolving interests. The form, which I shall designate *ideal comedy*, has, unaccountably, gone unnoticed in even the most comprehensive accounts of the development of Tudor drama. I shall begin, then, with a definition of the form. I shall next provide a brief account of its development, stressing only its most important components: its purpose, the nature of its subjects, and progression and resolution of its action, and the nature of its fiction. I shall then conclude with a brief discussion of these characteristics that distinguish *The Tempest* from Shakespeare's earlier ideal comedies and that are, I suggest, crucial to the meaning of the play itself.

Ideal Comedy Defined

Ideal comedy shares with mirror comedy, the form officially sanctioned by humanist pedagogues, principles of progression and closure that according to medieval authorities distinguish comedy as the exact contrary of tragedy: in comedy all is disturbed at the beginning and tranquil at the close.[1] Here, formal resemblances between the two modes cease. Mirror comedy is a drama of the ordinary and the probable. Its purpose is dissuasion; its method, ridicule. It is "an imitation of the common errors of our life which he [comedy] representeth in the most ridiculous and scornful sort as may be, so as it is impossible that any beholder can be content to be such an one."[2] Its actions, moreover, normally observe the old stipulation that comedy should be "without dangers to life" (*sine pericula vitae*)[3] and are happily concluded when folly and vice are purged or appropriately punished.

In contrast, ideal comedy is persuasive rather than dissuasive. It is devoted to the depiction and praise of exemplary instances of virtue. Dangers to life, moreover, are not only common to its action; they constitute the difficulties that must be overcome for the action to end happily and are therefore definitive. They are manifestations of the forces that in a fallen world pose a constant threat to the well-being, and even the survival, of its inhabitants. The happy ending won through virtuous action is, therefore, a celebration of the victory of life over evil and its wages which is possible for all men. The dangers to be overcome in ideal comedy take many forms. They may be simply personal, ranging from the inconstancy and lust of a Proteus in *The Two Gentlemen of Verona* to the hateful vindictiveness of a Shylock. Or they may be manifest in an unjust law, for instance, the law which in *The Comedy of Errors* demands Egeon's death or that of Claudius in *Measure for Measure*. They may also be manifest in the tyrannical abuse of civil authority by a usurper, as in *As You Like It* or by an Angelo in *Measure for Measure* or a Leontes in *The Winter's Tale*. But in every instance they threaten both the well-being of the individuals immediately involved and of the communities to which they belong.

The virtues celebrated in ideal comedy, on the other hand, are less varied. They are always an expression of love and trust: constancy to a lover, friend, parent, country, or the gods; contrition for one's mistakes and the desire to repair them; and forgiveness. Love and the trust in which it is grounded are, in brief, the agencies in ideal comedy that make its happy endings possible.

Ideal comedy, because it is devoted to the depiction and praise of exemplary instances of virtue, requires a special kind of fiction. Again a comparison with mirror comedy is helpful. The dissuasive purpose of mirror comedy depends upon audience identification. Its audiences must recognize that the vices and follies it depicts are indeed "common errors," errors that are their own, and, therefore, that they, too, are likely targets of ridicule. The form of fiction traditionally used to depict the ordinary is *argumentum*, a form that, according to Boccaccio, is "more like history than fiction" and is well illustrated by the works of "the better comic poets, Terence and Plautus." Its effectiveness resides in its verisimilitude: "By their art" they "portray varieties of human nature and conversation, incidentally teaching the reader and putting him on his guard." Although "the events they describe have not actually taken place, yet since they are common, they could have occurred, or might have at some time."[4] In contrast, ideal comedy precludes audience identification. It depicts the possible rather than the probable, the extraordinary rather than the ordinary. We may watch and admire Belarius and his foster sons in *Cymbeline* holding the Roman legions at bay and by their exemplary courage and patriotism inspiring the fleeing Britons to reform their lines or in *Measure for Measure*, Isabella forgiving Angelo for executing Claudio; but we do not identify. Such extraordinary actions are distanced from us by the very fact they are extraordinary. At the same time, we may watch with interest; for the unusual, in our own lives as on the stage, invariably arouses our interest. We may also find the artfulness of invention in such scenes admirable and entertaining. (The differences between the two modes of representation in ideal and mirror comedy are suggested by scenes from Robin Phillips' production of *The Tempest* and Michael Langham's production of *The Taming of the Shrew*.)

The characters of a drama devoted to the extraordinary must also be extraordinary. They are typically narrow or flat. They are conceived to represent the forces of good and evil, which are in conflict and which give rise to the action of the play and disclose through what they say and do only what the plot requires of them. They are also frequently paired as opposites: Valentine and Proteus in *The Two Gentlemen of Verona*; in *As You Like It* Duke Senior and his usurping brother, Orlando and Oliver; and in *Much Ado About Nothing* Don Pedro and Don John. In later plays in which the evil to be overcome is more formidable, this paralleling of characters with opposite traits verges upon the allegorical. The legacies of renewing and self-destructive love in *Pericles* are represented by Pericles and Marina and the incestuous Antiochus and his daughter. Similar opposites are evident in *Cymbeline* in Posthumus and Cloten.

What we ordinarily refer to as "realism" in the depiction of character is of no relevance in ideal comedy. Character traits are determined normally by the roles characters are assigned in the action. Nor is verisimilitude to be expected in the plotting of the action. Aptness replaces probability, for the plots of ideal comedy are also ideal. In celebrating evil and misfortune overcome and happiness won, they figure forth perfect justice achieved. The dramatist through his own inventiveness administers that justice, suiting the reward exactly to the virtue and the

The difference between the modes of representation in ideal comedy and mirror comedy is suggested by these scenes from the productions of The Stratford Festival (Canada). Above: Robin Phillips's production (1976) of *The Tempest* as ideal comedy. Below: Michael Langham's production (1962) of *The Taming of the Shrew* as mirror comedy. *Photographs by Robert C. Ragsdale. Courtesy of Stratford Festival Archives.*

punishment to the crime. The apt invention is thus an instance of poetic justice or artful equity.

Shakespeare affords numerous and often brilliant instances of such equity. There is, for example, Malvolio's demise. Blinded and isolated by self-love from the rest of the household of which he is steward, he is locked up in a darkened room and treated as mad or demonically possessed. What could be more apt? It is the skill of Feste's art that the punishment he administers to his humorless and self-righteous enemy teaches while at the same time it makes us laugh. In the mirror of his art we see figured forth the consequences of the blinding pride that at the play's close prevents Malvolio from joining the newly integrated community of Illyria. Virtue's rewards are equally apt. Olivia, purged of her foolish mourning for his long-dead brother and in love with Cesario-Viola, is happily provided with Viola's twin; in turn, Viola wins the man she has unselfishly served and, in matters of the heart, instructed so well. *Pericles*, too, affords striking examples. Evil is appropriately punished when Antiochus and his daughter are struck down by a bolt of lightning from the heavens and when Dionyza and Cleon are put to death by their own subjects. Virtue is rewarded when Pericles, who has brought food to the starving people of Tarsus, receives, in turn, food and clothing from the fishermen who find him shipwrecked upon their shore. Ideal comedy, then, is literally a drama of the ethically possible. While acknowledging things as they are, it depicts things as they can and ought to be. Its purpose is to inspire belief in the possible and to spur men to emulate the exemplary actions it depicts.

The Sources and Purpose of Ideal Comedy

Where are the sources of ideal comedy and what general purpose did it serve within the culture that developed it? The pattern of action that is essential to ideal comedy, the progression from a troubled beginning in which the protagonist is threatened by death to a happy ending in which he is victorious over death, originated in the efforts of a group of writers, now collectively known as Christian Terence,[5] to transform Roman Comedy into a mode of moral instruction. The conflict in the plays they produced is simply conceived: the issue is eternal life or everlasting death; the outcome, an exemplary instance of the victory of life over sin and its wages that religious faith makes possible. Typical examples include *Appius and Virginia* (1564) and *Conflict of Conscience* (1572). The former, "a new tragical comedie . . . wherein is lively expressed *a rare example* of the virtue of chastitie," celebrates martyrdom as a victory over death; the latter presents in its protagonist's last-minute recovery from suicidal despair "*a strange example* done of late which might . . . stir minds to godliness." Other examples include *Calisto and Melebia* (1527), *The Life and Repentance of Mary Magdalene* (1566),

The Commodye of pacient and meek Grissill (1565), and *A Commody of the Most Vertuous and Godlye Susanna* (1578).

What emerges in these plays is a way of proceeding that needed only to be adapted to secular ends to allow writers committed to the humanist enterprise of social and cultural reform at all levels to depict paradigms for courtiers and governors to emulate. That such a form was developed by English humanists is hardly surprising. In fact, it is what might be expected of a society whose literature from the beginning of the sixteenth century on is informed by humanist ideals. The new emphasis upon the temporal order and the claims its institutions make upon the well-born is everywhere evident. From *Fulgens and Lucrece* and the earliest translations from Petrarch to *The Faerie Queene*, ideal exemplars abound in all of the major literary forms.

Among the early attempts to adapt the way of proceeding established in the early religious comedy to temporal concerns, Richard Edwards' *Damon and Pithias* (1565)[6] is the most important for the precedents that it establishes. They are precedents that prove to be of special interest to students of Shakespeare. Edwards' play begins with Damon and Pithias having just arrived in Syracuse, city of unhappy and frightened people governed by the tyrant Dionysius. When Damon is accused of spying and the tyrant sentences him to death, he requests only that he be allowed to journey home to Greece to settle his affairs. Pithias volunteers to serve as his hostage and even to die in his place, and the amused Dionysius agrees. When the time that Damon has been granted to make his journey is up and he has not returned, plans for Pithias' execution proceed. Just as Pithias is being led to the place of execution, Damon returns. The scene that ensues contains the "rare example of friendship true" that Edwards has promised in the play's preface. Each of the young men argues eloquently that he be allowed to die in his friend's place. Dionysius is so struck by the "rare example" that he repents, frees the young friends, and completely reforms his government and court. An exemplary act of selfless love has transformed the governor who has witnessed it from tyrant to benevolent ruler, brought concord out of civil disorder, and joy out of sorrow.

Both the specific pattern here, of an action brought to a happy ending by a governor who has been inspired by an extraordinary action he has witnessed to temper a severe sentence he has previously issued, and the general pattern, of an action beginning with dangers to life and concluding with those threats eliminated and civil harmony restored, are common in Shakespeare. In *The Comedy of Errors* the Duke of Ephesus, after witnessing Egeon's reunion with his family, rescinds the sentence he had earlier given him for violating a law denying citizens of Syracuse entrance into the city. In *The Two Gentlemen of Verona* the Duke of Milan, after being rescued by Valentine from the outlaws, forgives him, proclaims him worthy of his daughter, and grants Valentine's request that the outlaws be pardoned and allowed to return from exile.

The value of exemplary actions is the desire to emulate them that they inspire in those who witness them. The "perfect" or "rare" example evokes wonder in those who witness it. Here, too, Edwards appears to have been the innovator. Dionysius, who after remaining silent while witnessing the rare action of Damon's and Pithias' friendship, finally speaks, revealing his amazement:

> Eubulus, my spirits are suddenly appalled; my limbs wax weak:
> This strange friendship amazeth me so that I can scarce speak.
>
> (11.1651-52)

And again moments later:

> My flesh
> Trembleth. Eubulus, what shall I do?
> Were there ever such friends on earth as were these two?
> A noble friendship, I must yield! At thy force I wonder.
> My heart this rare friendship hath pierc'd to the root
> And quenched all my fury. (11. 1662-66)

Instances of wonder-evoking actions inspiring social reform or the correction of injustice are evident in *A Midsummer Night's Dream*, *As You Like It*, and *The Tempest*. When Theseus in Act 4, Scene 1, of *A Midsummer Night's Dream* discovers the young lovers sleeping together peacefully, he is moved to wonder:

> How comes this gentle concord in the world,
> That hatred is so far from jealousy
> To sleep by hate and fear no enmity? (11. 147-49)

When Egeus reminds him of the law—

> I beg the law, the law upon his head.
> They would have stolen away . . . (11. 158-59)

Theseus rejects his demand, reversing his earlier decision and officially sanctioning the marriages of the realigned couples. Again, a severe judgment has been tempered by a governor who has witnessed a rare and wonderful action.

In *As You Like It* the convention is varied but nonetheless obvious, once we have been alerted to it. Oliver, after witnessing his brother's exemplary act of forgiveness, suddenly repents. After twice being tempted to leave Oliver to fend for himself, Orlando proves he is able not only to love his sworn enemy, but even to risk his life for him. In *The Tempest* Ariel is exemplar. His response to the "sorrow and dismay" of Alonzo and his retinue inspires Prospero to choose "the rarer action" of forgiveness over vengeance and retribution.

The more general pattern in *Damon and Pithias* of an action beginning with a threat of death and concluding with the threat eliminated and civil harmony restored is also common in Shakespearean comedy. In all but *The Taming of a Shrew* and *The Merry Wives of Windsor*, threats of death in one form or another are the obstacles to be overcome for the action to end happily. In eight of these plays (*The Comedy of Errors, Love's Labor's Lost, A Midsummer Night's Dream, As You Like It, Measure for Measure, Pericles, Cymbeline,* and *The Winter's Tale*), threats of death are introduced at the outset or early in the action. In each instance, except for *Love's Labor's Lost*, to which I shall return presently, those threats are eliminated by extraordinary means; in *The Comedy of Errors* and *A Midsummer Night's Dream*, by chance and a fairy fiction, respectively; in the five other plays of this group, by extraordinary instances of virtuous actions. Four other plays (*Twelfth Night, Much Ado About Nothing, All's Well That Ends Well,* and *The Tempest*) begin immediately *after* dangers to life have subsided—Viola in *Twelfth Night* and the royal party in *The Tempest* survive storms at sea, *All's Well That Ends Well* begins with the miraculous cure of a mortally stricken king, and *Much Ado About Nothing* begins with the safe return of young men from a recently ended war—only to arise again, suddenly and in unexpected forms. Other variants of the pattern are evident in *The Two Gentlemen of Verona* and *The Merchant of Venice*.

In every instance, regardless of variations in the fundamental pattern, closure is an affirmation of a temporal happiness that can be won, in spite of the legacy of mortality. It is the promise, too, at the close of *Love's Labor's Lost:* if Navarre confronts the implications that Mercade's message has for him personally, if he will withdraw from the world for a time to reflect upon what being human and mortal means, he, too, can win temporal happiness through love. He will also have discovered that love and not fame is the way to defeat "cormorant time." In each of the plays of Shakespeare that I have mentioned above (with the arguable exception of *Twelfth Night*) the conflict between the forces of life and death that are so starkly drawn in the old religious form of ideal comedy is clearly evident. In each instance closure celebrates the triumph of life through love over the forces that constantly threaten it. Each is also a play in which an improbable or "rare" fiction figures forth an ideal pattern and which affirms in the aptness of its resolution ideal justice.

Classifying *The Tempest*

But what of *The Tempest*? I have indicated above that all but two of Shakespeare's comedies, *The Taming of the Shrew* and *The Merry Wives of Windsor* (or three, if we consider *Troilus and Cressida* a comedy) are ideal. What distinguishes *The Tempest* from the earlier comedies and

---

at the same time identifies it with the other last plays? And how does an awareness of those characteristics illuminate its meaning? That *The Tempest* is conceived as an ideal comedy is evident from the characteristics it manifests. Its action originates in a conflict between good and evil. It is only through the efforts of Gonzalo that Prospero and Miranda survive the initial conspiracy that cost Prospero his governorship. Dangers to life during the action included within the play itself are constantly to be contended with; they confront Prospero himself finally with a challenge that almost destroys his faith in man's power to resist them. The resolution of the action is effected by an exemplary act of forgiveness. The characters, too, are typical of ideal comedy. They disclose in the main only those traits that are required of them by the parts they have to play in the action: the legacies of destructive and renewing love are represented, respectively, by Caliban and Miranda; the practice of white and black magic by Prospero and Sycorax; good and evil brothers by Prospero and Sebastian; love and lust by Ferdinand and Caliban; the contrite by Alonzo and the unrepentant by Sebastian and Antonio. The fiction, too, is ideal in its depiction of the cyclical progression of time that assures the patient man that he will have the opportunity to recover what he has lost through his former negligence, in its depiction of Prospero as exemplar of prudence, and, finally, in its depiction of poetic justice.[7]

What distinguishes the play from the earlier comedies and identifies it with the other so-called romances? There is, first of all, the seriousness with which the obstacles to comic closure are taken. In the earlier comedies those obstacles never come directly under scrutiny. Their resolution, too, is little more than a matter of convenience. Theseus simply settles matters in *A Midsummer Night's Dream* by arbitrary decree. In *As You Like It* the repentance of Oliver and Duke Senior's brother are not even depicted; they are reported. Occasionally, as in *The Merchant of Venice*, issues of a more serious kind arise, only to be dismissed in favor of focusing upon the positive aspects of love and forgiveness. Shylock, who by the end of the trial scene has become something more than a scapegoat clown, is dismissed without any attempt to deal with the challenge his humanness presents to the ideals of love and forgiveness that are celebrated in the closing scene of the play.

The situation is quite different in the last plays. In ways anticipated by *Measure for Measure*, the protagonists of the last plays confront the full force of human depravity, and, in *Pericles*, mischance as well. In this respect the dangers to life depicted in these plays challenge the very premises on which ideal comedy is grounded. Pericles' faith in the justice of the gods is challenged by the seeming capriciousness of the elements and their seeming indifference to the actions of men. In *Cymbeline* and *The Winter's Tale* both the madness and destructive power of jealousy are set forth so powerfully that the victories finally won challenge the credulity of their audiences. In *The Winter's Tale* the credulity of its fiction is explicitly raised. Whether as members of the audience we conclude that the play we have seen is anything more substantial than an old tale fit for passing the time on a long winter night, depends on whether or not we accept the premises of the form of which it is an instance.[8]

The question of belief that is overtly, although indirectly, raised in *The Winter's Tale* brings us to a final characteristic of *The Tempest*, which distinguishes it not only from the earlier comedies, but also from the other last plays as well. It is the character Prospero and what his presence in the play permits Shakespeare to express. As manipulator he has numerous predecessors in earlier plays. Duke Vincentio in *Measure for Measure* and Camillo in the renewing action of *The Winter's Tale* come immediately to mind. But Prospero dominates the action in which he appears in a way which none of the earlier manipulators do. Prospero provides the play with its beginning, he controls its action throughout, and he finally determines how it will end. At the same time he is the major subject of dramatic interest, not only as father and governor, but also as master illusionist and controller of the action. His emotional responses to the events he initiates and supervises and over which he finally perceives he has only limited control, together with the emotional responses his art evokes in others, determine the emotional tone of the play.

Here, then, is the matter that I noted at the outset as critical to the play's interpretation. Prospero's decision finally to resolve the play's action happily and thus to define it as comic is made with the full knowledge that there will always be Calibans and Sebastians biding their time and awaiting the opportunity to destroy, scheme, and disrupt, and that it is a governor's burden to keep such agents under constant surveillance. It is also a decision made with the full knowledge that a world without death and winter, in which spring emerges out of harvest, is only an insubstantial dream, that the world and its inhabitants are transient, that people grow old and die. It is his knowledge of these things that accounts for the sadness that pervades the final scenes and that in the play's epilogue elicits the plea for the compassion and mercy of which all men stand in need. That sadness though profound is not despair, although in the moments immediately following his remembrance of Caliban's "foul conspiracy," Prospero is despair's temporary victim. It is, rather, a sadness tempered by the simple acceptance of what is inevitable and the belief that love and renewal are also a legacy. It is a legacy that makes possible the triumph of life over death, even though all of us must die, and of good over evil.

And so Prospero's "rarer action" of forgiving that gives comic shape to *The Tempest* is, I suggest, an affirmation of the playwright's own belief in the viability of the form of Ideal Comedy. It is an affirmation of man's capacity for good, even in the face of intransigent evil and death, and also of his capacity to change, to seek idealistically to realize what can be. The alternative is the view expressed by Prospero in his moments of ennui—a view in which neither the world nor ideal comedy itself is anything more than "an insubstantial pageant" and their actors merely "such stuff as dreams are made on."

Notes

1. These definitions have been frequently translated. I have used those of J. V. Cunningham in " 'Woe or Wonder': A Study of the Emotional Effects of Shakespearean Tragedy," in the *Collected Essays* of J. V. Cunningham (Denver, Colorado: Swallow Press, 1977). See pp. 30-31, 36-37.
2. Sir Philip Sidney, *An Apology for Poetry*, ed. Geoffrey Shepherd (Edinburgh: Nelson's Medieval and Renaissance Library, 1965), p. 176.
3. Diomedes, *Ars Grammatica*, 3; quoted by Cunningham, pp. 36-37.
4. *Bocaccio on Poetry*, trans. C. G. Osgood (Princeton: Princeton Univ. Press, 1930), pp. 48-49.
5. For a discussion of Christian Terence, see Marvin T. Herrick, *Tragicomedy* (Urbana, Illinois: Univ. of Illinois Press, 1962), pp. 16-62.
6. I have used John Quincy Adams' edition of the play in *Chief Pre-Shakespearean Dramas* (Cambridge, Mass.: Houghton-Mifflin Co., 1924, 1952).
7. See Douglas L. Peterson, *Time, Tide and Tempest* (San Marino, Calif.: Huntington Library Press, 1973), pp. 67 (n.32), 222-23, 228, 244.
8. *Ibid.*, pp. 205-10.

Bibliographical Note

It is not possible to list here all of the works that have been useful in my study of Shakespeare's comedies. Among those that come immediately to mind are: T. W. Baldwin, *Shakspere's Five-Act Structure* (Urbana: Univ. of Illinois Press, 1947); Madeline Doran, *The Endeavors of Art* (Madison: Univ. of Wisconsin Press, 1954); Marvin T. Herrick, *Tragicomedy* (Urbana: Univ. of Illinois Press, 1955); Marvin T. Herrick, *Comic Theory in the Sixteenth Century* (Urbana: Univ. of Illinois Press, 1962); R. G. Hunter, *Shakespeare and the Comedy of Forgiveness* (New York: Columbia Univ. Press, 1965); C. L. Barber, *Shakespeare's Festive Comedy* (Princeton, New Jersey: Princeton Univ. Press, 1959); Leo Salingar, *Shakespeare and the Traditions of Comedy* (New York: Cambridge Univ. Press, 1976); Joan Hartwig, *Shakespeare's Tragi-Comic Vision* (Baton Rouge, La. : Louisiana State Univ. Press, 1973).

I am, however, specifically indebted to several essays by J. V. Cunningham and to two monographs by Wesley Trimpi. Cunningham's *"Woe or Wonder": A Study of the Emotional Effects of Shakespearean Tragedy* has been a formative influence in my study of Shakespeare's plays. More recently, I have found his essays "Plots and Errors: *Hamlet* and *Macbeth*" and "Ideal Fiction: *The Clerk's Tale*," especially helpful in my explorations of ideal comedy. Cunningham's essays are available in *The Collected Essays of J. V. Cunningham* (Chicago, Ill.: The Swallow Press, 1976).

Wesley Trimpi's monographs, *The Ancient Hypothesis of Fiction* (New York: Fordham University Press, 1971) and *The Quality of Fiction* (New York: Fordham University Press, 1974), deserve far greater attention than they have received. No one who is professionally interested in fiction and mimesis in the literature of the Renaissance can afford to ignore Trimpi's work. The second of Trimpi's monographs led me to the discovery of ideal comedy.

9

Come Hell or High Water: Shakespearean Romantic Comedy

DAVID M. BERGERON

Calling the English poets of the early nineteenth century "romantic" has done a disservice to an earlier understanding of the word *romance*. For us, romantic poetry recalls Wordsworth's line in *Tintern Abbey:* "Nature never did betray/The heart that loved her." This mystical, quasi-worshipful attitude toward nature characterizes much of romantic poetry; but it is far removed from the "romance" of medieval and Renaissance England, where the emphasis is not so much on man's relationship to nature as on his quests of love and chivalry, fraught with dangers and improbable events.

Improbable events—the landscape of romance flourishes with unlikely action, whether in medieval romances, Elizabethan prose romances (such as Robert Greene's *Pandosto*, a source for Shakespeare's *The Winter's Tale*), Sidney's *Arcadia*, or Spenser's *The Faerie Queene*. In the latter, for example, the various knights encounter giants, monsters, speaking trees, loathly ladies, and a whole panoply of strange and exotic characters and events as they journey in quest of service and love. In a play like John Lyly's *Gallathea*, gods and goddesses mingle with human characters while Gallathea and Phyllida, each disguised as a boy, fall in love with one another only to have Venus finally promise to change the sex of one of them so that their love may grow appropriately. As Shakespeare has Fabian say in *Twelfth Night*: "If this were played upon a stage now, I could condemn it as an improbable fiction" (3.4.131-32). Of such stuff romances are made.

In a brief, clearly romantic tale, Jonah of the Old Testament sought to avoid his prophetic duties, imposed by God, by fleeing to the sea to escape. But, as we know, God caused a fierce storm at sea; and the sailors, seeking to appease this angry god, threw Jonah into the water, where he was, improbably, swallowed by a fish. After residing in the fish for three days, he was belched ashore, alive to carry the prophetic warning to the city of Nineveh. It is all so wondrous strange that some version of this myth crops up time and again whether in the story of Arion tossed overboard and rescued by a friendly dolphin or in Shakespeare's plays. Journey at sea-disaster-rescue—this pattern is of enormous importance in Shakespeare's romantic comedy.

A seventeenth-century French critic observes that "authors make tempest and shipwreck at will"; further, "the sea is the most fitting scene for great changes. . . ."[1] He might well have had Shakespeare in mind. Experience at sea and its consequences help delineate Shakespeare's romantic world, a world that he inherited in which problems, especially love problems, are solved, come hell or high water (there being much of the latter). Such difficulties underscore Northrop Frye's view that there are "two worlds" associated with romance: the "idyllic world" of happiness, security, peace, and the "demonic or night world" of exciting adventures, "but adventures which involve separation, loneliness, humiliation, pain, and the threat of more pain."[2] By looking at several plays, with initial emphasis on *Comedy of Errors* and *Twelfth Night*, I will explore the relationship of idyllic and night worlds of romance in Shakespeare's comedies.

The Comedy of Errors and Twelfth Night

The earliest eye-witness account of a performance of *Twelfth Night* is that of John Manningham, who, seeing a production in February 1602, made the link between this play, Plautus, Italian comedy, and Shakespeare's own *The Comedy of Errors*. In his mind and in the minds of many spectators and readers since that early performance, *Twelfth Night* seems a repository of several comic traditions. Leo Salingar skillfully traces such traditions and summarizes them in three broad categories: "the romantic elements in his plots spring from the Middle Ages, while his sense of comic irony stems from the Roman playwrights and his feeling for comedy as festivity expresses the culture of the renaissance."[3] The whole is, of course, greater than the sum of these parts. And my concern is with that romantic tradition. To generalize, I suggest that *The Comedy of Errors* represents the night world of romance whereas *Twelfth Night* contains the idyllic world. Indeed, *The Comedy of Errors* may seem "antiromantic," thanks, I believe, to its reliance on Plautine comedy as a model.

Shakespeare's primary business in *The Comedy of Errors* is plot, complicating and then unraveling the tangles of mistaken identity. Ultimately the resolution hinges on physical identity; such a relatively simple approach to the plot derives, of course, from Plautus. But Shakespeare overlays the business in Ephesus with a veneer of romantic background; indeed, it forms the "frame" of the play. The night world of *The Comedy of Errors* is nowhere more apparent than in its opening scene.

Egeon sounds the gloomy tone of the scene in his opening two lines: "Proceed, Solinus, to procure my fall,/And by the doom of death end woes and all" (1.1.1-2). The language pulsates throughout with words of hopelessness. That feeling is exacerbated by the scene itself, about which one is tempted to say: no one ever wished it longer. Having endured a production in which additional pointless stage business prolonged the first scene, I am ready to concede that Shakespeare probably nodded while writing this. The problem is not just length—some 158 lines—but that Egeon speaks 107 of the lines. He does a 90-line stretch, interrupted only once by the Duke, who perversely urges: "do not break off so" (1.1.96)—the Duke is no friend of theater!

What Egeon rehearses at length is the expository narrative of the family's separation and seeming destruction, those problems in the romantic night world engendered by storm and shipwreck—hell and high water. In his determination to leave no stone unturned, he starts at the beginning: "In Syracuse was I born" (36). Surviving the full terror of the storm when even the sailors had left the ship "sinking-ripe" (77), the family is literally split asunder "by a mighty rock," so that "Our helpful ship was splitted in the midst" (103). From that moment the family members have sought one another. But having come to Ephesus, Egeon has been arrested and will be executed in a few hours. Often in *The Comedy of Errors* it seems that this story has little to do with the rest of the play, and I think that part of Shakespeare's difficulty in the play is in fact to reconcile this dark romantic story with the rest of the plot.

The hell of separation and the hell of potential execution are put aside in the play's last scene, where Shakespeare responds fully to the romantic impulse by adding the Abbess, who just happens to be wife of Egeon, mother of the brothers Antipholus. He literally frames the play, beginning and end, with romance, while much of the internal action seems antiromantic with its lack of love quest, its preoccupation with time and material objects, and perhaps even its frenetic pace. In one line, however, the Abbess sounds the idyllic note to counter the night world of romance: "After so long grief such nativity" (5.1.407). It is both a definition of romance and of much Shakespearean comedy; it also looks forward to

Shakespeare's last plays where Pericles, having suffered much grief, will also find his lost wife as a priestess in Ephesus, or Cymbeline, reunited with lost sons and daughter, can proclaim in wonder and joy: "O, what am I?/A mother to the birth of three? Ne'er mother/Rejoiced deliverance more" (5.5.368-70). In those last plays the dark and idyllic moods of romance will be held in solution, often vying with one another. Having survived their individual hells and much high water, most of the characters will experience a nativity. *The Comedy of Errors* may fleetingly look forward to this, but it is not yet itself a full-blown romantic comedy.

Twelfth Night is like *The Comedy of Errors*, except that it is different. Obviously, it varies in many ways, but one contrast is in the opening scenes. Orsino does not face potential execution, though he is half in love with death: "If music be the food of love, play on,/Give me excess of it, that, surfeiting,/The appetite may sicken, and so die" (1.1.1-3). The word *love* crops up six times in the scene's mere forty-two lines, whereas it appears only twice in the 158 lines of the opening of *The Comedy of Errors*. This radical difference spells the contrast between the world of Ephesus, caught in the prosecution of the law, and the idyllic world of Illyria, where one may pursue love. Even though the course of true love does not run smooth in *Twelfth Night*, it at least runs.

We learn in scene 2 that Viola has endured the hell of a tempest and the high water of apparent separation from her brother Sebastian. Viola's boat, like Egeon's, has also split; but the Captain explains that her brother, bound to "a strong mast," may have survived: "I saw him hold acquaintance with the waves/So long as I could see" (1.2.16-17). Viola, never one to bewail her woes, moves swiftly into the present world, not lingering on the fact of shipwreck and loss. In a few lines she has put on the disguise of a young man and has set out in Illyria to seek her fortune. The demonic world of pain gives way to the idyllic world of the search for love, as Shakespeare moves us into the latter romantic world.

By Act 2, scene 1, we learn that Sebastian has indeed survived the high water of shipwreck, though his spirit lingers in hellish thoughts. He explains to Antonio: "My stars shine darkly over me; the malignancy of my fate might perhaps distemper yours" (3-5). He acknowledges that Antonio has rescued him but is convinced that his sister has drowned: "She is drowned already, sir, with salt water" (30). Shakespeare's dramatic problem resembles that of *The Comedy of Errors*, namely, to get these separated twins together. Like Viola, who at the end of her first appearance is off to Orsino's court, so Sebastian: "I am bound to the Count Orsino's court" (42-43). The seeds of potential discovery inhere in the movements of sister and brother. The nightmare of shipwreck will be countered by the benign world of Illyria. By introducing Sebastian as he does, Shakespeare reminds us of the fact of shipwreck (hell and high water), something he makes little of in *The Comedy of Errors*. The festive, indulgent world of Illyria will eventually dispel even Sebastian's early melancholy.

When Antonio attempts to rescue Viola (believing her to be Sebastian) from the sword fight, we get an essential development in the romance: Viola realizes the likelihood of Sebastian's survival. Antonio insists when he is arrested: "This youth that you see here/ I snatched one half out of the jaws of death;/ Relieved him with such sanctity of love..." (3.4.362-64). He even calls her "Sebastian" (369). Thus Antonio is the romantic agent: having saved Sebastian from the sea, he now rescues Viola from a fight and gives her new life by letting her know of her brother. If it prove true that Sebastian lives, Viola says, then "Tempests are kind, and salt waves fresh in love!" (388). There is no better definition of romance than this voiced by a Shakespearean character, whether one refers to *Pericles*, *The Tempest*, or *Twelfth Night*.

Sebastian has romance thrust upon him by Olivia, who snatches him away and marries him while his head swims, clear evidence of how the world of *Twelfth Night* is idyllic as love solves problems in this play, unlike *The Comedy of Errors*. Olivia has earlier unknowingly announced the principle that governs the development of Sebastian's role: "Love sought is good, but given unsought is better" (3.1.158). It remains in the play's final scene to unravel the play's entanglements and bring Viola and Sebastian together and ascertain the true identities of the characters. It is interesting that Antonio again refers to his act of saving Sebastian: "That most ingrateful boy [Viola] there by your side/ From the rude sea's enraged and foamy mouth/ Did I redeem" (5.1.76-78). And the bewildered Sebastian insists: "I had a sister,/ Whom the blind waves and surges have devoured" (227-28). But we and Viola know that the tempest has been kind, throwing them ashore in Illyria where reunion and love have prospered.

At the end the Duke refers to "golden time" (5.1.383), a statement appropriate for romance and the world of *Twelfth Night* but misleading for the urban world of Ephesus in *The Comedy of Errors*. Time is a concern in Ephesus, but not so in Illyria, where in Toby's words, "Not to be abed after midnight is to be up betimes" (2.3.1-2). Early on Viola says: "What else may hap, to time I will commit" (1.2.60); and later, as her disguise creates problems, she remarks: "O Time, thou must untangle this, not I" (2.2.40). It is easy to imagine that, like the forest of Arden, there is no clock in Illyria. In the benign romantic world one surrenders to time and lets events unfold. The structure of *The Comedy of Errors*, observing the unity of time, seems to militate against the leisurely pace typical of romance. *The Comedy of Errors* and *Twelfth Night* may, in the perspective sketched here, show the two worlds of romance, as enunciated by Frye. The issue is one of emphasis, with love paramount in *Twelfth Night* and insignificant in *The Comedy of Errors*.

The Merchant of Venice

Varying the pattern of these two plays and achieving a balance of night and idyllic worlds, Shakespeare in *The Merchant of Venice* counters the harsh, urban, commercial world of Venice with the beautiful, harmonious, musical, place of Belmont. The dominant voice of the former is the insistent, shrill cry of Shylock, whereas in the latter it is the dulcet, loving tone of Portia. In some way each world intrudes into the other; but the idyllic mode ultimately triumphs, thanks to the victory of Portia in the courtroom of Venice, where she overcomes the threat of Shylock, removing him from the play's action. No matter how strong and convincing Shylock's role may be, the play is not his. But the threat that he represents creates a tension greater than that in *The Comedy of Errors* and *Twelfth Night*.

Though there are no shipwrecks in *The Merchant of Venice*, experiencing the hell of high water and ships running aground are crucial in the play's development. As the play opens and various characters try to account for Antonio's inexplicable melancholy, Salerio suggests that it derives from fear of what might happen at sea to his ships, "What harm a wind too great might do at sea" (1.1.24). But Antonio brushes aside the suggestion: "Believe me, no, I thank my fortune for it,/ My ventures are not in one bottom trusted,/ Nor to one place" (41-43). Shylock decides that Antonio is a "good man" to enter into a bond with because he is "sufficient"; that is, he has many ships at sea, and Shylock enumerates and locates them (1.3.16-20). But Shylock adds, "ships are but boards" (21), and there are dangers of pirates, "and then there is the peril of waters, winds, and rocks" (24). It is precisely this peril that does Antonio in, as we learn in Act 3, scene 1, that his ships have "wracked on the narrow seas" (3).

Having sailed safely to Belmont, Bassanio makes the right choice and gains Portia. But he has no sooner accomplished this than Antonio's letter arrives, informing Bassanio of his plight. The incredulous Bassanio asks Salerio: "Hath all his ventures failed? What, not one hit?/ . . . not one vessel scape the dreadful touch/ Of merchant-marring rocks?" (3.2.267-71). The sea that split ships asunder in *The Comedy of Errors* and *Twelfth Night* has done its worst again, not directly producing human separation but causing Antonio to forfeit the bond and nearly to lose his life.

Without the ravages of the sea, the cruel expression of the night world, Shylock would be an idle threat. But Portia transforms the potential harshness into joy as she frees Antonio, dropping "manna in the way/ Of starvèd people" (5.1.294-95), as Lorenzo puts it. And improbably she informs Antonio that "three of your argosies/ Are richly come to harbor suddenly" (276-77). We are likely to agree with Antonio's response: "I am dumb!" (279). Nothing seals the triumph of the idyllic world more than this virtually gratuitous information, reminiscent of the "epilogue" to the Book of Job, where Job, after incredible, patient suffering, has most of his material goods restored to him. If nothing else, Antonio, the merchant of Venice, can be confident that there may be life after Belmont.

Pericles: Prince of Tyre

When Ben Jonson dismissed *Pericles* with contempt as a "mouldy tale," he hit upon a partial truth, for the basic story is an adaptation of the old romantic tale of Apollonius of Tyre, dating from at least the ninth century and first used by Shakespeare for the frame device, the Egeon story, in *The Comedy of Errors.* Nearly twenty years after that comedy he returns to the story in *Pericles*, reminding us that this last phase of Shakespeare's career is a harkening back to earlier, romantic impulses. For lack of a better term, the last plays, *Pericles, Cymbeline, The Winter's Tale*, and *The Tempest*, are designated "romances." The romantic theme that binds them together is that of family separation but ultimate reunion. When Gower, the chorus figure in *Pericles*, says in his first speech that he has come "To sing a song that old was sung" (Act 1, Chorus 1), he refers only to the story of Pericles; but the comment seems appropriate for the dramatist, who, in his final plays, sings an old song about romantic quests, exotic places, improbable events. Woven throughout the texture of such a song is a representation of demonic and idyllic worlds.

Events in *Pericles* easily document a night world of romance: they include such things as incest between Antiochus and his daughter (opening scene of the play), attempted murder of Pericles and later his daughter Marina, famine in Tharsus, the presumed death of both Thaisa (Pericles' wife) and Marina, prostitution, envy that leads Cleon and Dionyza to attempt Marina's murder, profound depression experienced by Pericles, and, of course, the hell and high water of shipwreck and family separation. Of the last much can be said, for Pericles seems to spend most of his life at sea, traveling from Tyre to the court of Antiochus, to Tharsus, to Pentapolis, to Mytilene, to Ephesus. The journey at sea becomes a symbol for the spiritual journey that his family makes.

Though Pericles sails safely away from the perils of Antiochus and sails triumphantly into Tharsus, where with corn he rescues the city from famine, what we are likely to remember are the tempests and shipwrecks. Leaving Tharsus, he encounters a storm in which the ship that "Should house him safe is wracked and split" (Act 2, Chorus 32)—so says Gower. And the simple stage direction at the beginning of Act 2 is: "*Enter Pericles, wet.*" As is true in *The Comedy of Errors* and *Twelfth Night*, so here the sea causes destruction but manages somehow to cast the characters ashore, if barely alive. The caprice of the water leads to Pericles' metaphor: "A man whom both the waters and the wind/ In that vast tennis court hath made the ball/ For them to play upon entreats you pity him" (2.1.62-64). But the night world of hell and high water gives way here at Pentapolis to the successful wooing of the lovely Thaisa, whom Pericles marries.

But, alas, when Pericles and his now pregnant wife set sail for Tyre, "Their vessel shakes/ On Neptune's billow; half the flood/ Hath their keel cut" (Act 3, Chorus 44-46)—says Gower. So savage is the experience that Thaisa, who gives birth in the storm, presumably dies. Dead mother-new-born child—emblem of what the Shepherd in *The Winter's Tale* refers to: "things dying, . . . things new born" (3.3.111). Reminding us of Jonah's story, the sailors want to take action to appease the storm; the first Sailor says: "the sea works high, the wind is loud, and will not lie till the ship be cleared of the dead" (3.1.47-49). Thus Thaisa in a coffin is thrown overboard and quite improbably and wonderfully lands in Ephesus, where she is restored to life by the benign and skillful physician Cerimon. Though the high waters have receded, the hell of separation remains.

It remains for at least fourteen years until Marina comes aboard Pericles' ship off the coast of Mytilene. Their identities established, father and daughter experience idyllic joy, what Pericles appropriately calls "this great sea of joys" (5.1.196). Appreciating the romantic formula of journey at sea-disaster-rescue, Pericles says of Marina: "Thou that wast born at sea, buried at Tharsus,/ And found at sea again!" (5.1.200-01). Spurred by a vision, they sail (safely this time) to Ephesus, where in Diana's temple they find Thaisa, reminiscent of the ending of *The Comedy of Errors*. This reunion chases away the shadows of the night world; grief has led to nativity. Gower in the Epilogue sums up the plight of the Pericles family: "Although assailed with fortune fierce and keen,/ . . . Led on by heaven, and crowned with joy at last" (5.3.87-89).

The Tempest

What has seemed capricious in *The Comedy of Errors*, *Twelfth Night*, and *Pericles*, namely, the sudden raising of a storm at sea, has become in *The Tempest* purposeful. If this is indeed Shakespeare's last play, the title may seem all the more appropriate in light of the frequent pattern of tempest and shipwreck. Prospero, the masterful dramatist and magician, causes the storm so that kinsmen, enemies, and friends may come to his enchanted isle. An unconscious narrowing of focus can be seen as one observes that the storm in *The Comedy of Errors* is of the remote past, in *Twelfth Night* of the immediate past, in *Pericles* current, and in *The Tempest* fully realized on the stage in the opening scene, beginning with the stage direction: "*A tempestuous noise of thunder and lightning heard.*"

If, as Frye suggests, "The romantic tendency is antirepresentational,"[4] then scene one of *The Tempest* is not at all romantic; indeed, it is strikingly realistic, complete with elaborate and specific instructions from the sailors about what should be done to ride out the storm. But all is despair as we hear a confused but consistent cry from within the boat: " 'We split, we split, we split!' " (1.1.61). Good old Gonzalo manages an understatement: "The wills above be done, but I would fain die a dry death" (65-66). A hellish storm, high water, splitting ship, certain death—this seems no romance at all but a faithful rendition of an actual shipwreck. Gone are the aura and mystique of romantic shipwrecks of long ago. It is impossible to know, as one might with the opening of *The Comedy of Errors*, where the dramatist intends to go.

Though violent, the storm is blessedly brief. As scene two unfolds, we learn that Prospero (and Shakespeare) has caused the storm only to transform this night world into a romance of idyllic proportions. He assures his distraught daughter, Miranda, about the effects of the tempest: "There's no harm done" (1.2.15). Somewhat like Egeon, he rehearses for her their past when he was cast from his kingdom and they were placed in a small boat, "A rotten carcass of a butt, . . . the very rats/ Instinctively have quit it" (146-48). The wonder is that they survived. To Miranda's question, "How came we ashore?" Prospero answers simply but impressively, "By providence divine" (159). Their past, evoking the night world of romance, has nevertheless given way to a state of peace and security on the island.

That sense of wonder carries over to the shipwrecked group who, in Act 2, scene 1, puzzle over their fortune. Gonzalo notes with amazement that their garments, though drenched in the sea, "hold . . . their freshness and glosses" (2.1.65-66). Alonso fears that his son Ferdinand, separated from them by high water, has drowned; but Francisco gives assurance that Ferdinand survived: "I not doubt/ He came alive to land" (126-27)—an interesting echo of the assurance given to Viola by the Captain in *Twelfth Night* that Sebastian has overcome the storm. Ferdinand himself, a few hours later when all are reunited, says in words that recall Viola: "Though the seas threaten, they are merciful./ I have cursed them without cause" (5.1.178-79).

The miracle of their survival leads to the wonder of Prospero's forgiveness and reconciliation, as his "nobler reason" has conquered his own storm of passion, "my fury" (5.1.26). One improbable event, sometimes overlooked, is that reported by the Boatswain in the play's closing moment: that the ship split by the tempest is in fact "tight and yare and bravely rigged as when/ We first put out to sea" (224-25). We agree with Alonso: "These are not natural events" (227). Of course not: they are events of a romantic world, a brave new world in which fear and loneliness have subsided into peace and harmony. We may want to echo Gonzalo: "O, rejoice/ Beyond a common joy" (206-7). One of Prospero's final acts is especially interesting in light of what has happened in this play and in those that precede it; he promises "calm seas, auspicious gales" (315), and he charges Ariel to carry out the order. No more hell or high water.

Conclusion

Classical, festive, and romantic elements help make up Shakespeare's comedies—these three, but the greatest of these is romantic. Romance is not sentimental but indeed acknowledges the facts of hell and high water, where the wonder of the characters' survival and reunion may become our wonder. The sea with its contradictory possibilities is one of the principal forces in Shakespeare's romantic comedy: whimsical and purposeful, serene and tempestuous. One may sail safely to Belmont, or one may be shipwrecked on the way to Tyre. But is not the idyllic world of love, happiness, and peace appreciated all the more by Egeon, Viola, Pericles, Prospero, and others precisely because they have known the night? It is a romantic vision that allows for seemingly improbable outcomes where restitution, reformation, and reconciliation can occur, come hell or high water. Northrop Frye puts the issue eloquently: "The improbable, desiring, erotic, and violent world of romance reminds us that we are not awake when we have abolished the dream world: we are awake only when we have absorbed it again."[5]

Notes

1. De Scudéry, preface to *Ibrahim* (1641), cited in Leo Salingar, *Shakespeare and the Traditions of Comedy* (Cambridge: Cambridge Univ. Press, 1974), p. 23.
2. Northrop Frye, *The Secular Scripture: A Study of the Structure of Romance* (Cambridge: Harvard Univ. Press, 1976), p. 53.
3. *Shakespeare and the Traditions of Comedy*, p. 26.
4. *Secular Scripture*, p. 38.
5. *Secular Scripture*, p. 61.

Bibliographical Note

The following works have been used in preparing this essay: Peter G. Phialas, *Shakespeare's Romantic Comedies: The Development of Their Form and Meaning* (Chapel Hill: Univ. of North Carolina, 1966); E. C. Pettet, *Shakespeare and the Romance Tradition* (London: Staples Press, 1949); Carol Gesner, *Shakespeare and the Greek Romance: A Study of Origins* (Lexington: Univ. Press of Kentucky, 1970); Stanley Wells, "Shakespeare and Romance," in *Later Shakespeare*, Stratford-upon-Avon Studies 8, ed. John Russell Brown and Bernard Harris (London: Arnold, 1966; New York: St. Martin's, 1967), pp. 49-79; Northrope Frye, *A Natural Perspective: The Development of Shakespearean Comedy and Romance* (New York and London: Columbia Univ. Press, 1965); Frye, *The Secular Scripture: A Study of the Structure of Romance* (Cambridge: Harvard Univ., 1976); Leo Salingar, *Shakespeare and the Traditions of Comedy* (Cambridge: Cambridge Univ. Press, 1974).

10

"Wild Laughter in the Throat of Death": Darker Purposes in Shakespearean Comedy

MARJORIE GARBER

I don't want to become immortal through my work. I want to become immortal through not dying.

Woody Allen

It may seem perverse to argue that Shakespearean comedy is really about death and dying, but that is nonetheless what I should like to propose. More precisely, Shakespearean comedy is about the initial avoidance or displacement of the idea of death, the cognition and recognition of one's own mortality—and then, crucially, the acceptance, even the affirmation, of that mortality. In a sense, therefore, what we are speaking of is a process of neutralization, in anthropological terms a removing of the experience of death from a sacred to a neutral zone—a desacralization, a normalization, a refusal to privilege death. Shakespearean comedy is a ritual of the lifting of mourning, and the revels moment of applause that marks its close is the comic theater's counterpart to the shared feast of the mourner.

Let me explain. One significant hallmark of Shakespeare's comedies is that no character ever brought to life in them will suffer death by the play's close. There are numerous threats of death: Egeon is to die by sundown if he is not ransomed, Hermia to "die the death" or accept the living death of the nunnery if she refuses to wed Demetrius, Antonio to forfeit the pound of flesh, Claudio to die by Angelo's order. But none of these threats is fulfilled. Oliver, menaced at once by a snake and a hungry lioness, is rescued by his brother, Orlando, who happens to be passing by. Even Bottom-Pyramus, having elaborately dispatched himself with a sword thrust to the left pap, leaps to his feet a moment later to perform a Bergomask dance. In the romances real deaths occur: Mamillius dies in earnest, as does Antigonus, torn to pieces by a bear; Cloten is decapitated, his head thrown in the creek and washed to the sea. In the comedies, however, such dangers are always averted. In *Measure for Measure* the charming reprobate Barnardine is appointed to die in the place of Claudio, but even he is miraculously spared, his place taken by a hitherto unmentioned prisoner, Ragozine, whom we never see and who dies naturally, "of a cruel fever."

Like Ragozine's, the deaths we do hear about in the comedies happen offstage, in a time-frame and space-frame adjacent to, but not within, the play. As *Twelfth Night* opens we hear that Olivia is mourning her brother, but we feel nothing of this death, and it soon becomes plain that Olivia's obsession with her brother is really a narcissistic obsession with herself. Ragozine, as a prisoner ex machina, undergoes a death ex machina that allows us to rejoice in the sparing of Barnardine. The "deaths" of Claudio and Hero are revealed as artifice, devices contrived to educate those who think they have killed them. Perhaps the most striking intrusion of an offstage death onto the playing space of comedy occurs at the close of *Love's Labor's Lost*, when the French messenger Marcade enters with the news of the death of the King of France. Visually, this scene must be extremely striking. The stage is crowded with brightly costumed figures: the "worthies" in their togas and swords, the lords and ladies in elegant court dress. To them, in the stark blackness of mourning Marcade enters—and becomes, as he does so, a visible *memento mori*, a reminder of death.

Indeed, in each of the comedies there is at least one *memento mori*, one character or speech that throws a dark shadow across the play, one reminder that all holiday is bounded by everyday—and that the ultimate truth of everyday is the reality of death. The bound Egeon is such a figure, framing the comedy with a visual emblem of mortality. The mechanics of farce, the mechanics of near-miss (as when the two Dromios stand one on each side of a door and speak to, but do not see, one another), is given a somber tinge by the ironic juxtaposition of the play's first two scenes. In Act 1, scene 1, we hear that Egeon needs a thousand marks to ransom him; in Act 1, scene 2 we learn that Antipholus of Syracuse has a thousand marks—but he does not even inquire about the identity of his imprisoned countryman, "a Syracusian merchant." Such self-absorption, the play suggests, may lead to death—one's own or another's. The many images of binding, of rope's ends and marriage ties, that animate *The Comedy of Errors*, find their first and principal referent in the literally bound merchant; here marriage, comedy's traditional close, as the alternative to death.

As we have already seen, this is also true in the case of Hermia and, in a different way, of Olivia. In *The Merchant of Venice* the successful Bassanio, who wins the bride, is preceded by two unsuccessful suitors, each of whom, by choosing wrongly, condemns himself to celibacy and sterility—the forgoing of marriage and therefore of heirs. The golden casket actually contains a death's head—"a carrion death," as Morocco calls it—and the verse it presents speaks of "gilded tombs" that "worms infold." The traditional association of women's bodies with caskets or boxes, as pointed out by Freud and others, underscores the polarity of the choice: Morocco chooses death; Bassanio, sexuality, marriage, and life.

By the time of *Measure for Measure*, the covert has become overt, and the subject of death occupies the center of the play. In fact, the two kinds of "dying" have there explicitly become one; Claudio is to be executed for the sin of "dying" sexually with Juliet, and the sentence of decapitation is, again in Freudian terms, a symbolic castration. With this act of coming face to face with his subject, it may be noted, the playwright ceases to write comedies. The displaced subject of death, so agilely fended off by the masques and dances of the earlier comedies, is finally admitted to center stage. It will no longer be denied. The maddened Malvolio, the embittered Shylock, and the melancholy Jaques, who is "for other than for dancing measures," reveal themselves as the other face of revelry and marriage, no longer contained, no longer containable, by the play. *The Merchant of Venice* ends in Belmont, but the audience's mind remains upon the shocking events in a courtroom in Venice. The play fails of closure; so does *Measure for Measure*. *All's Well* ends arbitrarily; it does not end well. The fool's song at the close of *Twelfth Night* does not close, either; it articulates the limits of comedy and feasting—it leads directly to that other fool, those other fools, on the heath.

Modern criticism of the comedies has relied to some extent upon concepts like Northrop Frye's "green world" and C. L. Barber's distinction between "holiday" and "everyday." In anthropological terms both of these concepts are related to the threshold or portal ritual, as Arnold Van Gennep describes it in his seminal study *The Rites of Passage* (1908). According to Van Gennep, "the door is the boundary between the foreign and domestic worlds in the case of an ordinary dwelling, between the profane and the sacred worlds in the case of a temple. Therefore to cross the threshold is to unite oneself with a new world" (p. 20). For this reason Van Gennep offered an alternative series of terms for the progression of rites he had identified as separation, transition, and incorporation; he called them preliminal, liminal (or threshold), and postliminal rites. Such rites are themselves related to magico-religious ideas about zones of neutrality and zones of sacredness. Whoever passes from one zone or territory to another crosses a neutral area that corresponds to the door or portal.

The "green world" or world of holiday is in dramatic terms such a sacred territory—a privileged territory protected from the stresses and excesses of the diurnal—that is to say, of mortality. The winter wind in *As You Like It* blows only in a song; the unfaithful lovers cited by Lorenzo and Jessica in the fifth act of *The Merchant of Venice* are only literary cliches, whose infidelity stands in strong contrast to the truth of love in Belmont. Adjacent to such worlds and sacred in a different way is the world beyond the grave—a world we see principally in the tragedies, through the ghosts of Old Hamlet, Julius Caesar, and Banquo—a world to which Puck makes a brief allusion and which Claudio in *Measure for Measure* will imaginatively explore as he waits for death. Prince Hal passes from the one to the other in the course of *Henry IV, Part 1*, as he travels from the tavern to the battlefield, from a play world in which Hotspur kills six or seven dozen Scots before breakfast to a "real" world in which Hotspur himself becomes food for worms. In fact, in that play displacement operates directly and repeatedly. The confrontation of King and Prince is delayed until Act 3, scene 2, displaced by the mumming of Hal and Falstaff in Act 2, scene 4; the confrontation of Hal and Hotspur, Harry to Harry, so often anticipated, does not occur until the final moments of the play, displaced by comparisons and contrasts drawn by each of them, by the King, and by numerous other speakers; the rejection of Falstaff is postponed all the way to the end of Part II, displaced by Hal's "I do, I will." Comedy holds death at arm's length, but cannot do so indefinitely. The undiscovered country must be discovered and explored.

The tensions implicit in Shakespearean comedy are tensions of willed ignorance followed by knowledge. Its holiday worlds are fevered and feverish, places of danger as well as of release, each one a golden casket concealing a death's head. The plays are full of dark moments. Proteus, wooing Silvia, claims that Julia is dead; she overhears him. His suit denied, he threatens Silvia with rape and is restrained by Valentine, who is conveniently by. Then Valentine, forgiving his friend, offers him "all that was mine in Silvia"; Julia faints away. Count Claudio, deceived by Don John, accuses Hero of infidelity; she swoons and is thought dead. Olivia's self-imprisonment in her chamber of mourning is matched and balanced by the forced imprisonment of her steward, Malvolio; he, like her, is a prisoner of self-regard. But Olivia crosses the threshold. Her marriage to Sebastian is, significantly, to be celebrated in a nearby "chantry"—that is, a chapel where priests perpetually chant masses for the souls of the dead. Marriage and death here coexist in the same space. Olivia's mourning has been displaced, not erased; perpetual mourning is a task for priests, not for sisters or marriageable young women. The chantry remains as a *memento mori*, an acceptance of death as intrinsic to the course of life.

"Die to live"; "seeking death, find life." These are not mystical pro-
nouncements, but eminently practical ones. Like Perseus' shield, Shakespearean comedy deflects the horrid visage of the Medusa that is each
man's death and, in doing so, makes it possible for us not only to gaze upon
it but to approach it. Shakespeare's comic characters must each gain an
awareness of their own fragility, their own mortality. For Hermia and
Helena in the wood, for Orlando and Oliver attacked by the lioness, the
threat is present. For Berowne the entrance of Marcade with his message
of death is succeeded by the ordaining of his own penance: "to move wild
laughter in the throat of death." Berowne himself complains against his
play's lack of closure: "Our wooing doth not end like an old play." That
is the point. The acknowledgement of death beyond the privileged world
of revelry enforces—requires—the failure of closure. There is always something else, something beyond. The precariousness of the world of Shakespearean comedy is intrinsic to its meanings. The plays are anchored,
grounded, in the possibility of death—and in its certainty. The first is
avoided, the second confirmed. The play itself becomes the portal. Just
as its characters "play" at death and do not die, so the play plays with the
idea of dying, lets us experience death imaginatively, as Claudio does—
and escape it, as he does. All drama is displacement. Shakespearean
comedy is in a sense a double displacement: fictive characters, fictive
deaths. But the subject of death is there and will not be denied. It is the
thing that does not happen, the thing that looms. The offstage deaths we
hear about delimit the place of comedy: out there, they die; in here, we
do not. But the knowledge of death, and its inevitability, the way in
which it shapes and informs life, are essential to the workings of Shakespeare's comedies. Just as the tragic or threatening events presented in
these plays are encapsulated in artifacts—songs, masques, plays within the
play—so the plays themselves protect as they present, conceal as they
confront, the fact of death.

My students occasionally claim that a play like *As You Like It* is
"trivial"; they do not see the skull beneath the skin. They prefer the
robust agonies of *Romeo and Juliet*, where the skull is on the table in
plain view. But Shakespearean comedy is like a Dürer engraving, in
which the loving couple, arm in arm, share the pictorial space with a little
grinning death. It is he that gives meaning to their passion. Thus we hear
that the Princess of France in *Love's Labor's Lost* had a sister who died of
love. We are startled; the detail does not seem to fit. But it does fit—in
fact, it is crucial, prefiguring both the entrance of Marcade and the tasks
allotted to the suitors. Viola-Cesario invents a similar sister, who never
told her love and pined away like Patience on a monument, smiling at
grief. The sister is a fiction, but she demonstrates a truth. Titania clings
to the changeling boy for love of his mother, who once sat and gossiped
with her on the sands; "but she, being mortal, of that boy did die." There
the antic sits, an undeclared, essential character in every comedy, awaiting
his cue. In the development of Shakespearean drama his part grows larger

and larger, until finally he transforms comedy from the thing it was—and leads the way to the darker genres of tragedy and romance.

Bibliographical Note

Like so many commentators on Shakespearean comedy, I am indebted to C. L. Barber's seminal study, *Shakespeare's Festive Comedy* (Princeton: Princeton Univ. Press, 1959). Other works that have influenced my thoughts on the plays include two that I admire as much for their methodology as for their particular perceptions: Sigurd Burckhardt's *Shakespearean Meanings* (Princeton: Princeton Univ. Press, 1968) and Rosalie Colie's *Shakespeare's Living Art* (Princeton: Princeton Univ. Press, 1974). Other useful works on the comedies include Alexander Leggatt, *Shakespeare's Comedy of Love* (London: Methuen, 1974); Northrop Frye, *A Natural Perspective* (New York: Columbia Univ. Press, 1965); David Young, *The Heart's Forest* (New Haven: Yale Univ. Press, 1972); and Larry S. Champion, *The Evolution of Shakespeare's Comedy* (Cambridge, Mass.: Harvard Univ. Press, 1970). John Hollander's essay, " 'Twelfth Night' and the Morality of Indulgence" (*Sewanee Review*, LXVIII, [1959], reprinted in Alvin Kernan, ed., *Modern Shakespearean Criticism* (New York: Harcourt, Brace, 1970) has many interesting things to say about that play.

In matters art historical, I have gained valuable information and insights from Erwin Panofsky, *The Life and Art of Albrecht Durer*, 4th Ed. (Princeton: Princeton Univ. Press, 1955); Roy Strong, *The English Icon* (London: Routledge and Kegan Paul, 1969); and Ernest B. Gilman, *The Curious Perspective* (New Haven: Yale Univ. Press, 1978).

Anthropological works that bear upon the subject include Arnold Van Gennep, *The Rites of Passage*, trans. Monika B. Vizedom and Gabrielle L. Caffee (Chicago: Univ. of Chicago Press, 1960—orig. pub. 1908); Victor Turner, *Dramas, Fields, and Metaphors* (Ithaca: Cornell Univ. Press, 1974); and Clifford Geertz, *The Interpretation of Cultures* (New York: Basic Books, 1973).

PART 4

ITALIAN COMEDY:
MIXED GENRES
AND THE
PROFESSIONAL
TROUPES

Shakespeare's Comedy and Late Cinquecento Mixed Genres

LOUISE GEORGE CLUBB

The twenty-five years since Madeleine Doran's *Endeavors of Art* have produced signs of change, largely on grounds of genre, in the scholarly view of Elizabethan-Jacobean response to Italian drama, signs that are heartening despite a lack of consensus or of communication among those participating in the re-evaluation. If G. K. Hunter and Arthur Kirsch diverge from each other and from J. W. Lever in defining Italian tragi-comedy, if Richard Cody and Jackson Cope reach no common ground while finding evidence of neoplatonic dramaturgy in Italy and England, or if Leo Salingar, following an established practice of Italian criticism, slights the late cinquecento theater nearest in time and importance to Shakespeare in favor of comedies written before Elizabeth's birth, they are nevertheless cooperating indirectly to acknowledge the international nature of Renaissance drama and the scale on which Italian innovations infiltrated the English stage.[1]

In the history of Italian Renaissance theater there was a development in the late sixteenth century that has been little studied by Italianists but is of interest to Shakespeareans. It consisted in a movement, along several paths, toward mixed genres; it gave rise to the pastoral play and brought tragedy and comedy closer together. Traditionally, critical attention has lingered on early vernacular *commedia erudita*, the work of the generation of Ariosto, Bibbiena, Machiavelli, and the members of the Sienese Accademia delgi Intronati that produced *Gli ingannati* in 1531. To this privileged body the less "erudite," that is, less neoclassically regular, plays of Ruzante also have been admitted, but the chronological limitations set by scholarly habit have not thereby been overcome. *Commedie* written before 1540 have continued to absorb the lion's share of notice, whereas most of the much larger number of Italian comedies from the period coinciding with the Elizabethan age have been neglected, on the assumption that they are dim, mechanical reproductions of their precursors. As more late cinquecento plays are reprinted and engage the interest of young Italian critics,[2] the character of the mature comic genre and its international significance should become clear.

In the early sixteenth century, when humanistically educated men of letters were producing experimental solutions to the problem of defining the classical genres of comedy and tragedy for vernacular culture, the *commedia erudita*[3] frequently depended on the principle of *contaminatio*, of merging two plots, as Terence had defended doing in *Andria*. Italian writers bent on overgoing Plautus and Terence enunciated the corollary principal of complication and increased the number of ingredients recommended for *contaminatio*. In 1543, Annibal Caro praised himself for interweaving three plots in *Gli straccioni*, and as the genre developed in the second half of the century, the principles were made to support multiple intrigues, such as those in the comedies of Bernardino Pino and of Cristoforo Castelletti. The practice of conflating individual units of action, character, and language from different sources had, even in the early *commedie*, sanctioned fusions of Roman comedy with pieces of the *Decameron* and Petrarchan imagery. In time, the principle of *contaminatio* levied parts from more numerous and disparate sources and eventually led to combining generic elements and aims chosen challengingly for their seeming incompatibility within the limits of regular comedy and of regular tragedy. At the same time, those limits were still being sought. The genres of tragedy and comedy were not yet settled in vernacular art; their ideal neoclassical forms were even at mid-century in the process of being defined and substantiated for modern Italian theater.

The purpose of the calculated contaminations was to test the nascent rules of dramatic art and the possibility of inventing a third regular genre. By the late cinquecento the Italian search for mixed genres produced variations that had moved far from the types of comedy established in the first part of the century. Although their standard plots still turned on domestic strife between generations, on love pitted against interest, with trickery and fortune ultimately promoting the triumph of the former, some of the late hybrids were strong in romantic elements, often idealistic and even didactically moral. They included matters thought by Renaissance theorists to be fit for tragedy: characters of noble rank, threats of serious danger, of death or spiritual peril, occasions for heroism and pathos. Some looked back toward medieval drama, readmitting abstract content and symbolism, seeking to represent invisible realities that had been discarded in the transition from medieval to Renaissance theater, but now employing means sophisticated enough to function within contemporary structures developed for neoclassical genres. The unified urban street setting and the twenty-four hour time scheme, ensuring a tight crisis-structured action pulling characters into dramatic relationships were conscientiously maintained, as was the verisimilitude required of comedy. However, to the desired effect of physical reality, late cinquecento playwrights often added thematic indices in prologues and patterned plots and invited moral and even theological interpretations of the actions, requiring spectators to view the plots not only as pretended real events but as emblems of folly, of fortune, or of providence.

Commedia grave of this sort was distinct from other contemporary hybrids. The *tragedia di fin lieto* championed by G. B. Giraldi had little in it of comedy save the happy ending, which did not necessarily include wicked characters. The rules of the genre allowed villains to get their bloody deserts. The *tragicommedia pastorale*, in its several kinds,[4] was more like *commedia* in barring bloodshed and suffering from its universally joyful outcome. Unlike *commedia*, however, not all pastoral recipes for the generic compound necessarily included clowns and comic underlings, but they always demanded an Arcadian setting, not merely different from but antithetical to the urban scene that was prescribed for comedy.

The semitragic comedy of late cinquecento writers such as Pino, Raffaello Borghini, G. B. Della Porta, and Sforza Oddi was a continuation and reinterpretation of the humanistic idea of *commedia grave* with the *gravità* expanded to accommodate more varied and serious content and more complex and significant metaphoric form. Earlier sixteenth-century principles of *contaminatio* and complication of plots remained fundamental, indeed were invoked to the limit, and the essential materials of which the comedy was made, the structural formulae and units by which the elements of the fable acquired stage presence, came from a repertory of movable and combinable parts that had been developed by decades of experiment. Some of the formulae also turned up in tragedy, and nearly all of them found their way into pastoral drama, as the various species of this mixed genre began to appear from the mid-1550s on.

The idea that there was no important connection between Shakespeare and Italian drama (as distinct from Italian narrative literature or Italian Renaissance culture in general) was reiterated as recently as 1978 at the Columbia and Harvard International Congress on Northern Italian Renaissance Theater, in a reference to the "incontro mancato" between two movements that should have met.[5] This is a notion that time has long hallowed but must now pass by. Its survival is made possible only

Four woodcuts used in Curzio Gonzaga's literary comedy *Gli inganni* (Venice, 1592). In addition to the illustrations of stage groups, there are two groups of detached figures, some distinguished by features specifically associated with the commedia dell'arte. One of these figures, a Pantalone, is shown above.

Below: In *Gli inganni*, Act 1, scene 4, Ginevra-Cesare, the transvestite *innamorata* belives herself to have a homosexual love for Lucrezia (who turns out to be Scipione).

Gli inganni, Act 2, scene 3. Filippa with the real Lucrezia, Scipione's sister.

Gli inganni, Act 5, scene 6. Recognitions, reconciliations, and weddings in the happy untying of the knotted plot.

by ignoring the late cinquecento repertory of theatrical structures, generic figures and frames, or "theatergrams,"[6] that are identifiable as movable parts also handled expertly and innovatively by Shakespeare. They were available in abundance, exported from Italy not only by the accounts of travelers and of Italian musicians employed at the English court, but in the innumerable editions of plays by the literary *commediografi* and in the performances of touring *comici dell'arte*, who continually refurbished their stock of scenarios for improvisation from the latest printed comedies, pastorals, and tragedies, in addition to acting many of them as written. If the areas of resemblance between Shakespearean practice and the commedia dell'arte reviewed in Ninian Mellamphy's essay seem to be contiguous with the common theatrical repertory I am identifying, it is because they are. The commedia dell'arte and the literary comedy were intimately related in the late cinquecento, so much so that the only true historical understanding of either is one derived from looking at them together.

The theatergrams in the general repertory range from units of action or character to thematic patterns or to metaphoric use of intrigue structure. The figure of the *innamorata* as transvestite page to her beloved or as a secular saint performing miracles of constancy; dialogues in which class differences become bases for material-spiritual contrasts, between the lusty coarseness or cynicism of servingmen or nurses and the naïveté or idealistic enthusiasm of wellborn *innamorati*, for example (in some pastoral plays the encounter would be recostumed as a contrast between rustic *pecorai* and elegant *pastori*); rigged trials of claims to valor or virility; Arcadian metamorphoses into animals, trees, or statues, incarceration in *camere terrene* of characters reputed to be mad or bad, balcony scenes between lovers; themes such as jealousy, unjust suspicion, fidelity or false appearances, used to integrate multiple actions and the interpretation of complex plot with unexpected, or even paradoxical, final peripety as an image of the labyrinth of human error made clear by the benign irony of providence: these are some of the verbal, gestural, and structural theatergrams in which characters, situations, and ideas of various provenance were customarily brought on stage in Italy.

Twelfth Night is unique among Shakespeare's plays in having a contemporarily acknowledged primary debt to Italian comedy, but a large number of his other works, comic and noncomic, when compared to their immediate sources, reveal principles at work that correspond to those underlying late cinquecento Italian theater: *contaminatio* of multiple sources, dramatized, linked, and framed through theatergrams, the whole enterprise aiming at inclusiveness and at hybrids of different sorts. Shakespeare's freedom in hybridizing produced a series of experiments in genre in which the shuffling or extension of the standard parts created sharp distinctions from play to play, even among those closest to one another in kind of plot. It is misleading to contrast the combined actions of mistaken-identity-of-twins and reconciliation-of-lost-relatives in *The Comedy of Errors* and *Twelfth Night* on the basis of their presumed immediate sources, respectively Plautine comedy and Italian comedy, for ultimately the two Shakespeare comedies and the Italian sources of *Twelfth Night* all are Plautine, in the way that scores of literary *commedie* were Plautine in blueprint.

   Twelfth Night is not more Italianate than *The Comedy of Errors*—if anything, it is less so, or, at any rate, it is less like the most common kind of *commedia erudita.* Time and place are more elastic in *Twelfth Night* than in the standard Italian example of the genre, lyricism more pervasive, the social ambience more elegant. The differences between *Twelfth Night* and *The Comedy of Errors* most interesting for dramatic theory are not the results of differences in their sources, but are, rather, the results of experimentation in genre, of choices and combinations of theatergrams subsequently subjected to different Shakespearean development, tonal, thematic, and psychological. What needs to be emphasized is not that Shakespeare improves upon his materials—no surprises there—but that he does so as if participating in the quest for mixed genres, aware of Continental theatrical trends while taking advantage of his English license to infringe neoclassical rules and to essay bolder variations and mixtures.

Testing Generic Possibilities

   His testing of generic possibilities is fairly obvious in *Romeo and Juliet* and in *Othello.* Both are structures of comic units, movement and patterns, which are thwarted into tragedy. Both are contaminations of Italian comic theatergrams made to swerve aside from their generic destinations by different means and with different tragic results. Da Porto's tale of Romeo and Giulietta and its many retellings invited dramatization in either of the regular genres. Borghini adapted portions of it as *commedia grave* in *La donna costante* (1578), and in the same year Luigi Groto used it as the principal source of his tragedy *L'Adriana.* Shakespeare's tragic version is compact of theatergrams from *commedia grave:* the Nurse is an earthy *balia* of comedy rather than the sententious *nutrice* of tragedy; the mischievous boy, the boisterous menservants, and the bantering young gentlemen and their encounters planned so as to underline the domestic and local urban character of the action—these are among the features that establish as comedy a play that thereafter redefines itself as tragedy. For *Othello* another novella is theatrically repopulated with unique Shakespearean transformations of the stock types of comedy: jealous husband, deceitful underling, disenchanted waiting-woman, courtesan, foolish suitor, and so on, drawn into a stock pattern of false appearances that itself proves illusory by becoming tragic. In *Romeo and Juliet* a plot steered by ill-fortune twists in a direction opposite from the one forecast by the generic signals. In *Othello* the plot follows characters who overpower the comic function for which the types they grow from are usually programmed.

Variations among Shakespeare's plays with happy endings are less drastic and more subtly revealing of awareness of contemporary fashionable Italian attempts at a third genre. In *Measure for Measure* a plot that Giraldi had introduced as a novella and later dramatized as a *tragedia di fin lieto*, *Epitia*, is recast as English *commedia grave*. Adding from comedy the underworld characters, the theatergrams of the cast-off betrothed, the unwed parents, and the secular saint that he varied in creating Isabella, as well as the outcome in which her virginity is saved and no one is executed or even punished, save by marriage, Shakespeare makes his play more regularly comic than Whetstone's earlier adaptation of the story, while simultaneously making it more serious and noble. Then, after defining its genre as *commedia grave*, Shakespeare proceeds to take the play beyond generic definition, to make it sui generis.

A Midsummer Night's Dream is an English version of the Ovidian *favola pastorale*, minus its Arcadian decor. Similar to the pastoral mixture of Luigi Pasqualigo's *Gli intricati*, it contains magic potions, physical metamorphoses, dreams, otherworldly spirits, joined with a comedy *intreccio* of misdirected passions and parental opposition, linked to the celebration of a noble wedding, and ending with the acquisition of self-knowledge, multiple happy loves, and hints of hermetic neoplatonism.

The Winter's Tale is a juxtaposition of tragedy and comedy in the elevated Guarinian "verisimilar" manner, but mixing matters more daringly than Italian rules allowed. Untrammeled by limitations of time or place, Shakespeare begins with tragedy and modulates into comedy by means of pastoral, switching the locales of his source in Greene's *Pandosto* so that Bohemia becomes Arcadian while the action at Leontes' court acquires a pastoral aura by virtue of the mythic associations clinging to the name of Sicily. The other changes also make for generic inclusiveness. The tragicomic resurrection from death that Shakespeare adds to Greene's narrative takes the form of Paulina's restoration of Hermione as a statue, a rationalized version of the transformations by sorceresses in another kind of Italian pastoral. Shakespeare obtains the wonder of the theatergram of transformation proper to one subgenre by adapting it to the more severe surroundings of the high tragicomic pastoral genre of *Il pastor fido*. He also makes his venture into this kind of pastoral tragicomedy more technically tragic in its first half than Guarini's single-set *tragicommedia* could be by setting the action in a royal court, the "regular" scene for tragedy.

The earlier stages of Shakespeare's career represented by *The Comedy of Errors* and *Twelfth Night* show him already alive to the challenge of mixing genres and in command of the Italian repertory. Although Manningham in 1602 identified *Twelfth Night* as a version of "Inganni," it has been demonstrated that the generic units Shakespeare used in it are not all to be found in the celebrated *Ingannati* of the Intronati nor in any comedy called *Inganni* (Niccolò Secchi's or Curzio

Gonzaga's) nor in the plays of different titles (Secchi's *L'interesse*, Della Porta's *Cinzia* and others) that employ some of the most salient theatergrams. In combining the lovesick transvestite heroine (by this time so worn a coin in Italian currency that some justifying new twist had to be given it by any *commediografo* claiming to be in fashion) and her look-alike brother, with an unmarried version of the figure of the courted rich young widow in Olivia, the got-up duel between reluctant participants, the material/spiritual comic contrast between downstairs feasting and up-stairs fasting for or from love, the imputation of madness and the im-prisonment in the basement, Shakespeare drew on theatergrams used and reused in *commedie erudite* but not used all together in any single one but his. Even the aristocratic Illyrian milieu is a reference to a commonplace of Italian comedy—the coastal city of Ragusa, the Dalmatian Venice, that was the scene of action in some *commedie* and more often the source of the figure of the *raguseo*, usually a seafarer, recurrent in Italian comedy and represented in Shakespeare's by the "Ragozine" of *Measure for Measure.*

The framing theatergram that holds the others is the metaphoric labyrinthine intrigue by which physical and moral recognitions put an end to misfortunes that in retrospect appear fortunate. What happens in *Twelfth Night* is, as Manningham noted, like what happens in *The Comedy of Errors.* The difference is achieved not only by the choice of different theatergrams of character, such as the transvestite *innamorata*, but by the modifications in genre effected by integration, reducing the farce and laminating the frolic with the tragicomic romance action (though without dissipating the force of concentration within limits) and by infusing the plot of mistakes and social clashes with music and with the introspective and transformational emphasis on love's kind and workings that in Italy had become most common in pastoral drama.

If *Twelfth Night* and other Shakespearean plays demonstrate con-siderable variation on Italian generic practice, *The Comedy of Errors* is closer than any of them to the most standard *commedia grave* of the second half of the cinquecento, even to the degree of unity of time and place Shakespeare chose to observe, tighter only in *The Tempest.* In *The Comedy of Errors* the materials he quarried from two Plautine comedies and from a number of other nondramatic sources are mixed and de-veloped by the Italianate technique of multiple *contaminatio*, to bring comedy near to tragedy without transgressing the neoclassical ground rules, to achieve the fullest measure of complexity in pattern and to fit the whole as a metaphor for the appearance/reality relation of fortune/providence. The doubling of characters and actions; the elaborated themes of love, marriage, and jealousy; the probing of the device of phy-sical resemblance to extract deeper perceptions about identity; the pro-vidential pattern created by the nearly tragic plot of Egeon, which is handled in a manner less integrated than Shakespeare's usual way with exposition, but reveals a concern for accomplishing profound contrasts in plot and atmosphere without sacrifice of immediacy or compression: these are principles and theatergrams developed in the Italian repertory. In *The Comedy of Errors* Shakespeare was not adapting an Italian play but performing a fashionable neoclassical *contaminatio* of the kind of materials (primarily Roman comedy and medieval narrative) preferred for the genre in modern dress and succeeding to a degree that showed mastery of a continental approach to comedy and to generic mixtures that might enlarge its capacity.

Notes

1. References in this paragraph are to Madeleine Doran, *Endeavors of Art: A Study of Form in Elizabethan Drama* (Madison: University of Wisconsin Press, 1954); G. K. Hunter, "Italian Tragicomedy on the English Stage," *Renaissance Drama*, New Series, 6 (1975), 123-48; Arthur C. Kirsch, *Jacobean Dramatic Perspectives* (Charlottesville: University of Virginia Press, 1972); J. W. Lever, Introduction to the Arden Edition of *Measure for Measure* (London: Methuen, 1965); Richard Cody, *The Landscape of the Mind: Pastoralism and Platonic Theory in Tasso's Aminta and Shakespeare's Early Comedies* (Oxford: Oxford University Press, 1969); Jackson I. Cope, *The Theater and the Dream: From Metaphor to Form in Renaissance Drama* (Baltimore: The Johns Hopkins University Press, 1973); Leo Salingar, *Shakespeare and the Traditions of Comedy* (Cambridge: Cambridge University Press, 1974).

2. Oddi and Della Porta were represented in Aldo Borlenghi's collection, *Commedie del cinquecento* in 1959, Della Porta and Girolamo Bargagli in Nino Borsellino's *Commedie del cinquecento* in 1962 and 1967, and the 1970s have produced new work including Florindo Cerreta's on Bargagli, Walter Temelini's on Pino, Giulio Ferroni's on Borghini, and Pasquale Stoppelli's on Castelletti.

3. The *commedia erudita* was also qualified by other adjectives, including *osservata*, to indicate that it observed "rules" derived from classical Roman comedy, and *grave*, because it was a structured and serious work of comic art containing food for thought and models of style in imitation of Terence.

4. The variety of pastoral drama is discussed in L. G. Clubb, "The Making of the Pastoral Play: Some Experiments Between 1573 and 1590," *Petrarch to Pirandello*, ed. J. A. Molinaro (Toronto: Toronto University Press, 1973), pp. 45-72, and in "La mimesi della realtà invisibile nel dramma pastorale italiano e inglese del tardo rinascimento," *Misure Critiche*, IV, 6-9 (1974), 65-92.

5. See the discussion during the final session of the congress, in the Acts to be published under the editorship of Maristella Lorch.

6. The term *teatrogrammi* (theatergrams) was proposed to me by Mario Baratto at a 1977 meeting of the Circolo Filologico Linguistico of the University of Padova. It is useful as a name for the basic patterns of character, situation, encounter, language, disposition, and thematic significance of action that *commediografi* used to make a dramatic script out of stories and other source materials. Theatergrams are compositional structures that are to a theatrical text roughly what *narremes* are to a narrative.

Bibliographical Note

Some basic books and articles attempting to account for the Elizabethan-Jacobean response to Italian drama are Madeline Doran, *Endeavors of Art* (Madison: Univ. of Wisconsin Press, 1954); G. K. Hunter, "Italian Tragicomedy on the English Stage," *Renaissance Drama*, N. S., 6 (1975), 123-48; Arthur C. Kirsch, *Jacobean*

Dramatic Perspectives (Charlottesville: Univ. of Virginia Press, 1972); Richard Cody, *The Landscape of the Mind* (Oxford: Oxford Univ. Press, 1969); Jackson I. Cope, *The Theater and the Dream* (Baltimore: The Johns Hopkins Univ. Press, 1973); and Leo Salingar, *Shakespeare and the Traditions of Comedy* (Cambridge: Cambridge Univ. Press, 1974). To these should be added three articles that I have written: "Italian Comedy and *The Comedy of Errors*," *Comparative Literature*, XIX (1967), 240-52; "Italian Renaissance Comedy," *Genre*, IX (1976-77), 469-88; and "Woman as Wonder: A Generic Figure in Italian and Shakespearean Comedy," *Studies in the Continental Background of Renaissance English Literature*, ed. D. B. J. Randall and G. W. Williams (Durham: Duke University Press, 1977), pp. 109-32.

For the pastoral drama, see Cody, *Landscape of the Mind* (mentioned above), and two articles of mine: "The Making of the Pastoral Play: Some Experiments Between 1573 and 1590," *Petrarch to Pirandello*, ed. J. A. Molinaro ((Toronto: Toronto University Press, 1973), pp. 45-72, and "La mimesi della realtà invisibile nel dramma pastorale italiano e inglese del tardo rinascimento," *Misure Critiche*, IV, 6-9 (1974), 65-92.

12

Pantaloons and Zanies: Shakespeare's "Apprenticeship" to Italian Professional Comedy Troupes

NINIAN MELLAMPHY

The incidence of references to improvising comedians, magnificoes, panta-loons, pedants, and zanies in later Elizabethan literature,[1] coupled with historical records of the activities of Italian actors in England and of English players in Europe,[2] makes it virtually certain that Shakespeare's contemporaries had a more than casual knowledge of the commedia dell'arte. That this is true of Shakespeare himself was suggestively demon-strated by Ferdinando Neri's *Scenari delle Maschere in Arcadia* in 1913, with its analogues for *The Tempest*. Scholars in the following decades showed that Shakespeare in his apprenticeship to the craft of comedy was able to avail himself of the well-established conventions of the Italian professional troupes. Whether Jaques had swum in a gundello or no (*As You Like It* 4.1.36), he seems to have an appreciation of the clowning and the "good set terms" (2.7.17) of motley fools abroad, for in his famous "All the world's a stage" speech, he describes the vicissitudes of human misery in an extended theatrical metaphor that reveals some knowledge of the conventional character types developed in the com-edy of Italy's famous and influential professional acting companies from about the mid-1550s onwards.

Jaques's description of man in the presenility stage of life, that of "lean and slippered pantaloon/With spectacles on nose and pouch on side" (2.7.157 ff), is a vivid picture of Pantalone, the "first old man" of typical commedia dell'arte plot, and the probable prototype for a number of Shakespeare's comic old men: especially theatrically-generically-modally-aware Polonius in *Hamlet* and the cantankerous and fussy Brabantio of *Othello.* Usually, Pantalone[3] is a Venetian merchant (when not a Venetian *magnifico* of the Brabantio sort), an authoritarian father and wealthy miser, a conservative and hypocrite, a slanderer and crank, an oldster as capable of dignity and affection as of outbursts of rage and invective: a suggestive model, surely, for nonmerchant Shylock in *The Merchant of Venice.*[4] Indeed, if we are properly to view the role of Shylock in the context of Renaissance theater, we must not utterly ignore a well-known comic tradition that emphasized the hilarious aspects of the old man's rages and of his servant's disrespect, as well as of the eloping daughter's defiance of paternal will—a tradition rich in stage business of a kind that gives to Shylock's knife-whetting (4.1.121) unqualified dimensions of the farcical.

What stage Jaques has in mind when he speaks of the variety of man's roles in life in terms of exits and entrances and the playing of many parts is clearly open to question. But since the typical commedia dell'arte scenario provided little more than exits and entrances, and since the typical *commedia* company of ten found the duplication of roles an artistic and economic necessity, one might detect in the seven-ages-of-man speech further signs of Jaques's familiarity with the popular professional comedy of the South. His lover, whose woeful ballad immortalizes the disdainfully arched eyebrows of an indifferent mistress, may well, like a love-sick Romeo, have sighed as a conventional stage *innamorato.* The same is true of his soldier, whose oaths, pride, and quarrelsomeness have not necessarily developed close to any cannon mouth but, like Don Armado's, may be those of a braggart soldier such as Francesco Andreini's Capitano Spavento in productions of the admired Gelosi company.

To argue that Jaques's bearded Justice, "full of wise saws" and so on is a bombastic pedant like macaronic Doctor Gratiano might be to protest too much; yet the Shakespeare who created Jaques had already fleshed forth Holofernes in *Love's Labor's Lost.* And Holofernes, like the doctor from Bologna in Italian improvised comedy, has feasted on scraps from the tables of the learned; his wise saws are charged with a verbosity that depends, inordinately and characteristically, on a toting of the fardels of circumlocution and pleonasm over well-trodden pathways of triteness. And, to put it mildly, is it not striking that, in the carnival world of linguistic fireworks shot off by Holofernes and Armado, Costard, should not only utter *honorificabilitudinitatibus* trippingly on the tongue, but that thereby he should enter into a tradition of spurious Latinisms that includes—as Vito Pandolfi shows in a sample list of Gratiano's multisyllabicalities—

the monumental affirmative, *certificabilitudiniprimamente?*[5]

Commentators on the sources of Shakespeare's plays have tended to consider Shakespeare more as a litterateur than as a practical playwright. Hence, it is not surprising that in our classrooms we still focus our attention on art forms governed by "the law of writ" and pay little attention to what Polonius may have in mind when he speaks of "the liberty" (*Hamlet* 2.2.409).[6] This is especially true of those of our predecessors who have explored the tributaries flowing from the Parnassus of European literature into the mainstream of Shakespeare's talent as he composed *The Two Gentlemen of Verona*. Some have tried to estimate the play's indebtedness to comedies such as Girolamo Parabosco's *Il Viluppo*, to Montemayor's romance *Diana*, and to the lost *Felix and Felismena* of the 1580s, which may have been a somewhat muddled source of details from *Diana*.

The source-seekers, failing to account for elements in the play that cannot be attributed to literary founts, leave us to discover in the pages of Flaminio Scala's *Il teatro delle favole rappresentative* (1611)[7] entire scenarios, occasional scenes, and general dramatic characteristics that show a remarkable similarity to the work of Shakespeare in his early comedies. Some of Scala's plays date back to the 1580s and 1590s, so Shakespeare could well have heard of them. Kemp could well have seen some.[8] Whatever the date of Scala's *Flavio Tradito* (*Giornata* 5), it enables us to discover in the principal characters, Flavio and Oratio, interesting parallels to Valentine and Proteus and, what is more, a parallel treatment of the theme of ideal friends. Neither Flavio nor Valentine is tainted by the least perfidy to the laws of friendship; and each, by refusing to repay his false friend in the currency of resentment, provides the precise dramatic basis for the inevitable happy ending of romantic comedy.

New Light on the Italian Influence on Shakespeare's Comedies

To study what earlier twentieth-century scholars such as Winifred Smith, Kathleen M. Lea, Daniel C. Boughner, and Oscar J. Campbell have taught us about Shakespeare's probable debts to the professional comedians of Italy,[9] and to examine their conclusions in the light of materials made available by Pandolfi and of assessments of the commedia dell'arte tradition by Allardyce Nicoll and Roberto Tessari[10] is to find that Shakespeare probably learned from the art and craft of masters of improvised comedy when most he needed to and that their conventions of characterization, character groupings, staging, comic business (*lazzi*), as well as the convention of having less exalted characters banter in prose, were all timely grist for his mill. It is to discover limits to his originality in his departures from and improvement upon the traditions of English comedy, but it is especially to discover that what is finally most interesting is his genius in transcending the limitations of what he chose to exploit.

In *The Two Gentlemen of Verona*, the influence of Italian comedy seems strong, but there is never any doubt in this play or in any other that Shakespeare ever borrows simply to imitate. He uses the ideas of other men, of other schools, of other theaters, subordinating them to his own poetic and dramatic purposes. Speed and Launce are an excellent example of this type of adaptation. They reflect—they almost duplicate—their corresponding types on the Italian comic stage, but they, especially Launce, are of functional importance in the plan of the drama in a way that no improvising actor or scenarist could be. Launce's dog had brother curs on the Italian stage, but there is no evidence in any of the scenarios that allotted a clown his dog or a braggart Capitano his hawk (often a barnyard cock) that these pets served any but a diversionary purpose.

Crab, on the other hand, is used by Shakespeare as an ironic parallel to the haughty mistress of Proteus and to Silvia's later loathing of him, and, of course, as a type of the ungrateful friend. Shakespeare delicately counterbalances the courtly language and sentiments of the lovers with the shallow, ridiculous, and pedestrian speeches of the clown to his dog. And the silence of the dog, a silence of incomprehension, is set off against the silence of Julia when, wordless at her sense of loss, she bade farewell to Milan-bound Proteus. Indeed, the parallels and antitheses between the actions of the servants and their betters are many:[11] Launce's caution about disclosing information regarding the girl he may marry contrasts with Valentine's indiscreet disclosures about the hopes he shares with his beloved. Even his going with Speed to down a "Christian" glass or two counterbalances the un-Christian deeds of his master, whose meeting with Valentine at court is the beginning of well-meditated discord.

The clowns, who play such Italianate roles, are a promise of Shakespeare's later genius in making individual scenes and even images of immense importance in the structure of each play. They are important to literary history, for they show us how Shakespeare as a young dramatist could wisely use characters and techniques of proven popularity and use them in a very individual way for his own artistic purposes.

Zanies in Shakespeare's Comedies

In *Love's Labor's Lost*, the scenes featuring Spanish braggart, Latinophile pedagogue, and *Zanni*-like figures such as Costard and Moth function in much the same way as do the Falstaff scenes in the *Henry IV* plays—not merely as amusing interludes but as an extension of, and comment upon, the main action. In other words, far from being the follies of a playwright serving an apprenticeship to his own future excellence, these very scenes show us the capable craftsman giving a striking sense of dramatic unity to a play that comprises the disparate actions, attitudes, and dialogue of kings and clowns, scholars and dunces.

There is a possibility that the Pageant of the Worthies (like "The most lamentable comedy . . . of Pyramus and Thisby" later on in *A Midsummer Night's Dream*) should be performed in commedia dell'arte fashion. This entertainment, when we first hear of it, is to be played in the "posteriors" of that very day (5.1.89), with Armado, presumably, as chief scenarist. When it is staged, the speeches of Holofernes and Armado are so similar to their habitual style of discourse and so crammed with their particular kinds of allusion that they simply *must* be improvised, and the performances of Nathaniel and Costard suggest that whatever they had in the line of the improvised comedians' *zibaldoni* (commonplace books) were of little help to them. Indeed when the swain, who made a slight fault (of memory?) in his reference to Pompey the Great, says he hopes he was perfect (5.2.544-57), we realize that his zeal—and the zest for acting exhibited by all the others—is hopelessly outbalanced by his inability.

This is true of the contrast between the zeal of the King and his courtiers and their sudden lapse from the conditions of their oath, as the ladies clearly realize. The faults of King and gentlemen have been parodied for the audience by Shakespeare's handling of Spaniard, pedant, and servants. When the play-within-the-play (a frequent device in improvised comedy) mocks its protagonists, the aristocrats' folly is lampooned before their unseeing eyes. Thus does Shakespeare give the Italian traditional stage techniques a typically Italian comic purpose, but his consistency in such mirroring of the main action, even in the Worthies' bungled pageant, is much more thorough than we can expect the collective genius of professional acting troupes ever to have effected.

Pantaloons in Shakespeare's Comedies

In the Bianca story in *The Taming of the Shew*, Shakespeare is closer to a scenario entitled *Flavio Tradito* than to Gascoigne's *Supposes* in giving the young lady three suitors. He not only molds Gremio along the lines of the traditional "Pantaloon" (1.1.47 s.d.) but also creates servants, Tranio and Grumio, who in dramatic function and personal qualities have much in common with the menservants of improvised comedy. Winifred Smith has directed us to what look like more than coincidental parallels between *The Taming of the Shrew* and Scala's *Il Dottore disperato* (*Giornata* 13) with respect to the Vincentio-Biondello-Tranio relationship.[12] A perusal of Flaminio Scala's scenarios leads one to discover similarities between the role of the Mantuan "mercatante or . . . pedant" (4.2.63) and that of the Pantaloon Cassandro in *La Finta Pazza* and *Li Duo Amanti Furiosi*, and to the suspicion that Tranio may share common origins with the clown Zanni.

However, here it is Grumio who has the liberty of the harlequinesque imp. Grumio's teasing the hungry Kate in Act IV, scene 3, might be considered a piece of devilment ordered by his master. However, in his conjuring up visions of juicy neat's-foot and tempting helpings of beef and mustard (4.3.1-3) only to deny them on the grounds that the first is "too choleric a meat" (l.22) and that the second might be too hot, we see that same delight in teasing and in causing discomfort to others that we witnessed when he invited curious Curtis to lend an ear and, to his own great delight, summarily smacked it (4.1.59). This scene with Curtis is primarily a piece of comic stage business—what the Italians termed a *lazzo*—just as is the taunting of the tailor a few scenes later and, of course, Kate's walloping of Grumio in Act 4, scene 3, following his "mustard" fun.

But Shakespeare, while treating us to snatches of action that seem to contribute little to the plot—and that seem to have the mere design of causing us to laugh—sometimes invests such scenes with a significance that we can only appreciate later. In the exchange of bawdy jests and general lively chatter between Curtis and Gremio, we learn that Kate, despite her unenviable trials on the purgatorial honeymoon journey, was overcome with concern for the abused servant whom Petruchio mistreated in her stead (4.1.73-76). Here we are informed of the first noticeable change in Katharina, and we realize that the taskmaster has almost tamed his hawk—or, it may be, that the wife, who seemed so shrewish, is beginning to reveal a compassion and betray a warm sympathy that she has too long kept hidden. The *lazzo* of harlequinesque raillery and the tradition of laughter-provoking beatings are used by Shakespeare for the purpose of an unexpected revelation that effectively prepares us for the comic resolution.

The Comedy of Errors, possibly the earliest and certainly the shortest Shakespearian comedy, has the *Menaechmi* of Plautus as its ultimate, if not immediate, model. Since, like the *Menaechmi*, it depends more on chance than on character for its primary entertainment value, there would seem to be little purpose in considering the characterization of the dramatis personae in the light of any tradition of personality portrayal. In this comedy Shakespeare is so obviously dedicated to effectively handling a plot in which the hero is Chance that we can hardly be disconcerted when he uses the abbess as a dea ex machina to resolve the final difficulties and bring about a happy ending.

Because of its close relation to classical comedy, one rightly approaches the study of *The Comedy of Errors*, as one does Gascoigne's *Supposes*, by using the same critical tools one applies to the "learned comedies" of sixteenth-century Italy (that is, plays conventionally composed by an author and learned by the actors). Shakespeare here exercised his dramatic and poetic talents in much the same way as did that anonymous Sienese member of the Intronati academy who based his *Gl'Ingannati* on the *Menaechmi*. But upon comparing *The Comedy of Errors* with the original Latin play, we discover that many of the obvious discrepancies and additions are not only un-Plautine, but are distinguished by elements that are more characteristic of Italian improvised comedy than of anything else.

The *Menaechmi* is, in the strictest sense, sheer farce. The plot development is independent of human motivation; the chief concern is with what happens to people in a given situation rather than with what they happen to do. The action springs from an external situation, the improbable but not impossible coincidence that identical twins, separated in infancy, should both be in Epidamnus on a certain afternoon and that, in their busy ramblings through the streets, they should not meet until a series of mistaken identities have resulted in discomfort and confusion for themselves and all who encounter them. Thought is not carried over into action, so the protagonists are merely flesh-and-blood puppets reacting to Fortune's playful trifling with the strings of circumstance, while Time and Chance engage in a duel that is the only central conflict in the play. What matters is plot manipulation, quickness of pace, and such a contriving of misapprehensions that the audience must concentrate on and delight in rampant confusion, which accelerates with every entrance and exit of the baffled dramatis personae, who do not discover the truth until the top note of the crescendo of bewilderment is sung.

Many details of *The Comedy of Errors* are obvious reflections of Plautine situations. Antipholus of Syracuse, like Menaechmus of Syracuse, is considered mad by his "acquaintances," though he does not put an antic disposition on. Dromio's interest in dining (1.2.66) resembles the main concern of paunchy Peniculus. The traveling master in both plays hides his surprise at being familiarly greeted by strangers in order to enjoy to the utmost the unaccountable munificence of his newfound friends. The business of the ornamental chain and the rope's end, as well as the precarious money transfers, is transacted in the Plautine manner. Adriana is, like Mulier, a voluble faultfinder, though she wears her shrewishness with a difference. The unpleasantness of these ladies drives their husbands to find comfort in meretricious arms, though Antipholus of Syracuse, unlike the Epidamnian gift-giver, is guilty only of a momentary lapse. The use of two pairs of doubles would seem to be a successful attempt to out-Plautus Plautus, but the inspiration for it is implicit in the *Amphitryon*. The similarities may be glaringly obvious, but the equally obvious differences persuade us, when we examine them, that the conventions of Plautine farce may not be the sole models for what Shakespeare, man-of-the-theater, not humanist pedant, here attempts.

Shakespeare's Originality

It would be absurd to try to explain departures from Plautus without due allowance for Shakespeare's originality. The play's the thing, not the sources. In terms of the tone of *The Comedy of Errors*, for example, the characterization of the Citizen's wife is an interesting and "promising" deviation. Adriana is, indeed, a shrew, but she in no other sense corresponds to Mulier. The Roman matron is ferocious and unloving, a butt for the humor of her father, who is ready to defend her man's adultery, and of her husband, who, in deciding to depart with his newfound twin, derisively proclaims himself willing to let her go to the highest bidder—while implying that there will be no bids. Adriana is one of Shakespeare's instruments for taking *The Comedy of Errors* out of the realm of unmitigated farce. Through her conversations with her sister, Luciana, she gives the play a set of moral concerns that are entirely absent in the pagan *Menaechmi*. Gentle Luciana, when first we see her, reproves Adriana for impatience. Adriana is no shrew here; she is a wife who regrets her husband's thoughtlessness (Act 2, scene 1). Both women discuss the respective roles of man and wife in marriage, with a seriousness that is nowhere found in the Plautine world. The originator of their implicit theme, that wives should submit to their husbands as to the Lord, was not well known for his comedy and, here, his is the measure by which Adriana's "shrewishness" may best be measured.

The seriousness of the debate is underlined by Adriana's upbraiding of her husband in the street (Act 2, scene 2). She rails, but not in the Plautine wife's manner of nagging for nagging's sake. Adriana, realizing, as Hamlet will, that "man and wife is one flesh," claims that, because of Antipholus' commerce with the courtesan, she herself is "possessed with an adulterate blot" (2.2.141). The basic earnestness of such speeches suggests that Shakespeare may have chosen Ephesus as the location of the action because of his fellow countrymen's association of that city with Christian dicta regarding marital love. Then, when the abbess appears in what we have previously called a dea ex machina situation, the Christian element of this philosophy of marriage is stressed again, for the Ephesian abbess, like a latter-day Paul, converts the shrewish, loving wife to a patient one and thus assures us that both of her sons will face the future with (whatever the Marvins may make of it) ideal wives. How diametrically opposite this is to the finale of *Menaechmi*! Source-hunting may be of little value in this respect.

Still, this perhaps too Pauline response to what is serious in the play cannot be said to alter essentially the central action. The main appeal of *The Comedy of Errors* is in the confusion that engulfs the Antipholus brothers and the Dromios, and this is nothing if not farce. And evidence abounds to support the view that in the artifice of certain non-Plautine elements Shakespeare may not have depended solely on his own invention. He would seem to have availed himself of numerous stage tricks and plot entanglements that had long appealed to Italian audiences of both humanistic comedy and the commedia dell'arte.

Modern scholars have shown how such writers as "learned comedy" as Bibbiena, Cecchi, Trissino, and Firenzuola played their parts as great thieves of Plautus.[13] Collectors of commedia dell'arte plot descriptions have provided a panoramic view of how the professional companies of the sixteenth and seventeenth centuries availed themselves of the stuff of learned comedy, exploiting any and every situation suitable to the art of stage improvisation. Scenarios based on the *Menaechmi* abound (Pandolfi gives us a few dozen), and in them we find echoes of almost every variation and augmentation of Plautus that might be attributed to the erudite playwrights—and a few more besides. Kathleen M. Lea long ago drew our attention to resemblances between *The Comedy of Errors* and such scenarios as *Li Dui Simili di Plauto*, *Il Tradito*, *Zanni Incredibile con Quattro Simili*, and *Li due Trappolini*. She usefully argued that the most obvious debt to Italian improvised comedy lies in the handling of the two Dromios, whose antics and fortunes are much more those of the Harlequin or Zanni than of the slaves of classical comedy.[14] Lea marshalls limited but convincing evidence that Shakespeare's Dromios, in being battered by their betters, in the misdelivery of messages and misplacing of valuables, and particularly in the ructions about the money of Antipholus of Syracuse (in *Li due Trappolini*) prove Shakespeare a sensible thief in his own way.

Lea shows us, too, that the writings of Isabella Andreini (1562-1604), the accomplished actress, poet, and scholar who was prima donna of the Gelosi company, prove that Adriana was not without her counterparts in the history of professional comedy, for Isabella frequently found occasion to philosophize on the role of woman in courtship and marriage and to express the heartbreak of the disappointed loved one. Lea seems to have ignored, however, *Le due Schiave*, another scenario in the Locatelli collection of 1617, which features a mother whose sole function seems to be to clear up confusions surrounding the coming together of her separated twin daughters and to create harmony in the manner of the Abbess of *The Comedy of Errors*.[15] The date of *Le due Schiave* is, perhaps, impossible to determine; hence the parallel is not essentially interesting. What is interesting is to know of the parallel, even while one may rightly insist that Shakespeare had no great need of any model, Italian or otherwise, to attempt his Aemilian coup.

In a discussion such as this, there is danger in insisting too much on the force of one tributary influence on the mainstream of Shakespeare's art. This danger is all the more remarkable because the Italian professional troupes were tireless purloiners of what Professor Clubb has taught us to call "theatergrams" from the erudite comedy of their age. In any single case of Italian influence on the art of an Elizabethan comic dramatist, it may be impossible to determine precisely the extent of indebtedness to the professional, internationally errant players. This discussion attempts to tip the balance in one direction—but with the purpose of reminding those who teach the comedies of Shakespeare in high school and college classrooms of what many of us tend to ignore or forget: the long-established success and recognition of the art of improvised comedy inevitably influenced the character of comedy and the substance of comic acting in Shakespeare's England and in Shakespeare's work. To fail to bring this to the attention of students is to deprive them of knowledge of a dynamic and influential theatrical tradition whose excellencies Shakespeare—like many modern directors of his plays—exploited so effectively.

Notes

1. For examples of references in Shakespeare to improvised comedy see *Henry IV, Part 1*, 2.4 and *Antony and Cleopatra*, 5.2.216; to the Magnifico, *The Merchant of Venice*, 3.2.280, *Othello*, 1.2.11; to the Pantaloon, *Taming of the Shrew*, 3.1.36, *As You Like It*, 2.7.157; to the Pedant, *Love's Labor's Lost*, 5.2.539, *Taming of the Shrew*, 4.2.63; to the Zany (*Zanni*), *Love's Labor's Lost*, 5.2.463, *Twelfth Night*, 1.5.89. Shakespeare does not mention Harlequin, but many of his contemporaries do: see Kathleen Lea, *Italian Popular Comedy* (1934; rpt. New York: Russell and Russell, 1962), II, 339-455.

2. See Winifred Smith, *The Commedia dell'Arte* (1912; rpt. New York: Benjamin Blom, 1964), pp. 170-99.

3. For descriptions of Pantalone's characteristic garb, values, habits, and preoccupations, see Allardyce Nicoll, *Masks, Mimes and Miracles* (New York: Cooper Square Publishers, 1963), p. 254, and Giacomo Oreglia, *The Commedia dell'Arte* (London: Methuen, 1968), pp. 78-81.

4. For a thorough discussion of this, see Walter L. Barker, "Three English Pantalones: A Study in Relations Between the Commedia dell'Arte and Elizabethan Drama." Diss., Univ. of Connecticut, 1966.

5. *La Commedia dell'Arte: Storia e Testo* (Firenze: Sansoni, 1957), II,32.

6. This is true of recent works such as Leo Salingar's *Shakespeare and the Traditions of Comedy* (Cambridge Univ. Press, 1974). Robert Weimann's *Shakespeare and the Popular Tradition in the Theatre* (Baltimore: Johns Hopkins Univ. Press, 1978) makes only passing reference to improvised comedy.

7. Translated by Henry Salerno as *Scenarios of the Commedia dell'Arte* (New York: New York Univ. Press, 1967).

8. See Louis B. Wright, "Will Kemp and the *Commedia dell'Arte*," *MLN*, 41 (1926), 516-20.

9. I refer to the already cited books by Smith and Lea, as well as to Winifred Smith, "Italian Actors in England," *MLN*, 44 (1929), 375-77; Campbell, "*Love's Labour's Lost* Re-Studied" and "*The Two Gentlemen of Verona* and Italian Comedy" in *Studies in Shakespeare, Milton and Donne*. Univ. of Michigan Publications, I (New York: Macmillan, 1925) and "The Italianate Background of *The Merry Wives of Windsor*," in *Essays and Studies in English and Comparative Literature*. Univ. of Michigan Publications, VIII (Ann Arbor, 1932); Boughner, "Don Armado and the *Commedia dell'Arte*," *SP*, 37 (1940), 201-24.

10. Nicoll, *The World of Harlequin* (Cambridge, 1963) and Tessari, *La Commedia dell'Arte nel Seicento: 'Industria' e 'arte giocosa' della civiltà barocca*. Biblioteca di "Lettere Italiane" VIII (Florence: Leo S. Olschki, 1969).

11. See Harold S. Brooks, "Two Clowns in a Comedy (to say nothing of the Dog): Speed, Launce (and Crab) in 'The Two Gentlemen of Verona,'" *Essays and Studies*, XVI (1963), 91-100.

12. *The Commedia dell'Arte*, p. 198, n. 60.

13. See, for example, Marvin T. Herrick, *Italian Comedy in the Renaissance* (Urbana: Univ. of Illinois Press, 1960), chap. III, and Geoffrey Bullough, *Narrative and Dramatic Sources of Shakespeare* (London: Routledge and Kegan Paul, 1957), I, iv.

14. Lea, II, 438-43 and 591-609.

15. Vito Pandolfi, *La Commedia dell'Arte: Storia e Testo* (Florence: Sansoni, 1957-61), V, 230.

Bibliographical Note

Readily available books in English on Italian improvised comedy are an anonymous translation of Maurice Sand's two-volume *Masques et Buffons* (Paris: Lévy, 1858) entitled *The History of the Harlequinade* (New York: Benjamin Blom, 1915), Winifred Smith's *The Commedia dell'Arte* (1913; rpt. New York: Benjamin Blom, 1964), Kathleen M. Lea's two-volume *Italian Popular Comedy* (1934; rpt. New York: Russell & Russell, 1962), Allardyce Nicoll's *The World of Harlequin: A Critical Com-*

mentary on the Commedia dell'Arte (Cambridge Univ. Press, 1963), and Giacomo
Oreglia's The Commedia dell'Arte, trans. L. F. Edwards (London: Methuen, 1968); the
latter, lacking notes and bibliography, is of little use to the serious student. In Italian,
Benedetto Croce's essay "Intorno alla Commedia dell'Arte," in Poesia Popolare e
Poesia d'Arte (Bari: Laterza, 1931), is important, as is Roberto Tessari's La Commedia dell'Arte Nel Seicento: 'Industria' e 'Arte Giocosa' della Civiltà barocca
(Florence: Olschki, 1969). Ferdinando Neri's Scenari delle Maschere in Arcadia (Città
di Castello, 1913) offers an essay on the commedia dell'arte and The Tempest and five
appropriate pastoral scenarios. Vito Pandolfi's six-volume La Commedia dell'Arte:
Storia e Testo (Florence: Sansoni, 1957-61) gives a skimpy history and an extensive
but incomplete printing of texts of extant scenarios, memoir-extracts, and fragments—
an imperfect work, but essential; it supersedes A. Bartoli's Scenari inediti della Commedia dell'Arte (Florence: Sansoni, 1880), which is narrower in range. Henry F.
Salerno's Scenarios of the Commedia dell'Arte (New York: New York Univ. Press,
1967) is a very readable translation of Flaminio Scala's Il Teatro delle Favole
Rapprensentative (Venice, 1611).

PART 5

THE POPULAR TRADITION: ORALITY, VILLAINY, AND DOUBLING

13

Comedy, Orality, and Duplicity: *A Midsummer Night's Dream* and *Twelfth Night*

TERENCE HAWKES

This essay attempts to link two established views of comedy and to relate them to a third. In the process, it aims to generate a consolidated notion that may be usefully applicable to Shakespearean comedy in general and to *A Midsummer Night's Dream* and *Twelfth Night* in particular.

The first view is Northrop Frye's account of the design of Shakespearean comedy as expressed in his essay "The Argument of Comedy" (*English Institute Essays*, 1948, New York: Columbia Univ. Press, 1949) and the later *A Natural Perspective* (New York: Columbia Univ. Press, 1965). Frye's view is essentially "structuralist":

> A comedy is not a play which ends happily: it is a play in which a certain structure is present and works through to its own logical end, whether we or the cast or the author feel happy about it or not.
>
> (*A Natural Perspective*, p. 46)

If we combine the arguments of the earlier essay with those of the later book, the case emerges that the themes of Shakespeare's comedies may be said to derive not from the mysteries or the moralities or the interludes, but from a fourth dramatic tradition of folk ritual, represented by the St. George play, the mummers' plays, the feasts of the Ass and of the Boy Bishop, and so on. These dramas of the "green world" embody and record the triumph of life over the waste land, of spring over winter, in a two-step rhythmic movement that can be discerned in the body of Shakespearean comedy.

It has three stages: first, that of an anticomic "old" society that imposes restrictive laws from the "outside": a world of uninvolved "spectators." Second, there is a stage of confusion and loss of identity, socially and sexually (boy-actors playing girls "disguise" themselves as boys and so on). The third stage occurs when the confusion is resolved, socially and sexually, through the institution of marriage. The result is a "new" society whose laws are permissive because concrete: felt, lived, and internalized by people who function, not as spectators of, but as participants in the society.

Festival, Carnival, and Shakespearean Comedy

The second view focuses upon that "fourth dramatic tradition" and resides in the notions of Festival and Carnival developed respectively by C. L. Barber (*Shakespeare's Festive Comedy*, Princeton Univ. Press, 1959) and Mikhail Bakhtin (*Rabelais and His World*, trans. Helen Iswolsky, Cambridge, Mass.: MIT Press, 1968).[1]

Barber sees the roots of Shakespearean comedy in the community observance of those feast-days and holidays that formed periodic alternatives to, and inversions of, the pattern of everyday medieval and Elizabethan life. He proposes a kind of subculture (allowed by the dominant culture) that, at regular intervals (Candlemas, Shrove Tuesday, Hocktide, May Day, Whitsuntide, Midsummer Eve, Harvest Home, Halloween, Twelfth Night, and so on) offered custom-prescribed ways of release from the constraints of "normality."

Bakhtin similarly argues for a tradition of folk carnival existing as a structured opposition to "the feudal culture" (p. 4). This world of Carnival (erupting at regular intervals, it occupied on average a total of three months of the year in medieval Europe) offered a wholly involving "second world" and a "second life" within it of a nonofficial, extrapolitical nature to the mass of ordinary people. "Carnival is not a spectacle seen by the people: they live in it . . . it is the people's second life" (pp. 7-8). The basic mode of this life involved a "special carnivalesque marketplace style of expression," a "special idiom" featuring a special logic of "turnabout," with a universal displacement from top to bottom, front to rear:

From the wearing of clothes turned inside out and trousers slipped over the head, to the election of mock Kings and Popes, the same topographical logic is put to work: shifting from top to bottom, casting the high and the old, the finished and completed, into the material bodily lower stratum for death and rebirth [p. 82].

The ideas of Frye, Barber, and Bakhtin meet in the amalgamated notion of a confusing "green" "topsy-turvy" Festive or Carnival world whose operation upon the normal world of everyday that it opposes involves a kind of redemptive duplicity: it serves, by a process of benign, mirroring reversal to change that world to a better place. Clearly, a contrary view is also possible that would take the Carnival world as a simple mirror-image *reinforcement* of the everyday world: it acts as a safety valve and so dissipates opposition. In this view, the everyday world might well seek to encourage Carnival, since the three Carnival months serve to sustain the hegemony of the everyday nine.

Orality as the Defining Mode of Comedy

The third view of comedy focuses upon a particular and central aspect of Elizabethan society: its commitment to oral rather than written language as its defining mode. The major art form that derives from and celebrates orality is, of course, that of drama. Within drama, comedy must stand as the genre in which the factor of orality is raised to the highest power. Its mode is fundamentally interactive and interlocutory. A joke, a comic remark or situation, a funny gesture, all these demand a *response*: not necessarily laughter, but an interjection or reaction or interpolation of some kind from the audience. In this sense, comedy can be said to be an art of the audience: the audience's participation finally constitutes the comedy. This is the same principle that Bakhtin recognized as fundamental to Carnival: it isn't a given spectacle which we passively *watch*, but a "second life" which we *construct*, by actively taking part in it.

This view suggests, therefore, that in addition to, or as part of, their involvement with the "green" topsy-turvy world of Carnival, Shakespeare's comic plays show a corresponding and defining commitment to oral interlocution as the fundamental mode of a total way of life whose aptest symbol is the circular, "including" and "globe"-like structure of the theater itself. In this context, comic plays offer not merely entertainment or distraction, but by the same token, their opposites: positive involvement in and engagement with the fabric of social life. To use Frye's terms, the structure of comedy mirrors that of actual experience in the Elizabethan theater: it serves to unite the "extremes" of man and nature by means of art, man's "second" nature. In such a setting, "drama is doing through the identity of myth and metaphor, what its ritual predecessors tried to do by the identity of sympathetic magic: unite the human and the natural worlds" (*A Natural Perspective*, p. 46). Such a unity cannot be achieved in the world of ordinary experience in which man is an alienated spectator. It can only take place in the theater, where, paradoxically, the world of the spectator vanishes, and we become participants in the play, which, as art, is identical with nature at its highest level.

Shakespeare's comic plays can thus be seen not merely to assert the topsy-turvy values of Festival and Carnival in the face of a hegemonic "everyday," but to do so in quite specific terms, asserting the interactive values of orality and community in the face of literate, book-committed Puritan opposition to the theater. And they also assert the central importance of drama's oral mode as a model for, and emblem of, a "good," participating, creating society, in the face of a "bad," passive, inert society of consumer-spectators.

A Midsummer Night's Dream

In terms of Frye's analysis, the three stages of *A Midsummer Night's Dream* are quite distinct. First, the "external" forces of Athenian law supported by parental authority prohibit love in an anticomic "old" world (Act 1). Next, a carnivalesque state of affairs develops in the adjacent but separate "green world" (the wood near Athens): topsy-turviness reigns, men are translated into beasts, magic potions reverse normal perceptions, and so on (Acts 2 and 3). Finally, all the confusions are resolved. Love achieves dominance over law, and a "new" society emerges that acquires, or regains, an organic cohesion whereby its laws are shaped to fit the nature of its participants (Act 4).

The play, however, additionally and concomitantly celebrates the oral values embodied in and represented by drama in a nonliterate community. It is full of "audiences" involved in "performances." Oberon watches (and becomes a participant in) the interrelationships of the lovers. He acts as audience to Titania's duping. Theseus, Hippolyta, and their court watch the lengthy performance of *Pyramus and Thisbe*, whose rehearsals have been overseen and interfered with by Puck. And, of course, the playhouse audience's sense of its own standing in respect of the larger play is constantly reinforced in the process.

In fact, *A Midsummer Night's Dream* focuses a good deal of attention on the nuts and bolts of its own art. The rehearsals of *Pyramus and Thisbe* rank amongst its most memorable moments, and with the central plot virtually concluded by the end of Act 4, the last act devotes itself almost entirely to the performance of the mechanicals' play and the response which that elicits from its stage and playhouse audiences.

This notable emphasis on "playing" and on witnessing and giving audience seems to acquire a particular social bearing largely as a result of the subtle interconnection between the fictions of drama and the reality of social life so endearingly probed by the mechanicals. Their naive and heavy-handed manipulation of established conventions serves, in effect, to make manifest the complex nature of the relationship that drama maintains between performer and audience in any community. This, surely, is the serious point animating Bottom's famous injunction:

> Nay, you must name his name, and half his face must be seen
> through the lion's neck, and he himself must speak through,
> saying thus, or to the same defect—"Ladies",—or "Fair ladies—
> I would wish you"—or "I would request you"—or "I would
> entreat you—not to fear, not to tremble: my life for yours.
> If you think I come hither as a lion, it were pity of my life. No,
> I am no such thing. I am a man, as other men are." And there
> indeed let him name his name, and tell them plainly, he is Snug
> the joiner.
>
> (*A Midsummer Night's Dream*, 3.1.35 ff.)

The essence of that relationship is seen to lie not in its capacity to afford entertainment or distraction from social reality, but in the reverse: its capacity to confirm, reinforce, and so perhaps invigorate and strengthen the social fabric. For to be "a man as other men are" clearly involves, in this setting, commitment to a *social* role over and above one's temporary, liberating Carnival or dramatic role in a play. It is this social role that finally imprints itself orally upon its bearer in the form of a name: one is plainly and openly Snug the Joiner (or, an emphasis the play makes at our first introduction to the mechanicals, Bottom the Weaver, Quince the Carpenter, Snout the Tinker, Starveling the Tailor, and so on)—or one is nothing.

Oral commitment to and involvement in the community is, of course, signaled directly by the use of trades as names in this fashion. Names and nature, speech and way of life, personal identity and social identity acquire intimate links in the larger process that it exemplifies. John of Gaunt's own embodiment of the same ancient unifying principle—he is Gaunt by name and gaunt by nature—is given memorable status as emblematic of a rooted and venerable British way of life in *Richard II*. Amongst the family names listed in the current Coventry and District telephone directory—which includes Stratford-upon-Avon—there remain twelve joiners (or joyners), fifty weavers, seventy-three carpenters, and one tinker, and three pages of tailors (or taylors) to remind us of it.[2]

That one's inherited social role, imprinted in the utterance of one's very name, provides the solid basis for any temporary carnivalesque abandonment of that role, must be a first principle of a society whose way of life is fundamentally oral in mode. Everyone must know, by means of talking and listening, exactly who everyone else "really" is. That temporary abandonment of it does not diminish but rather strengthens and reinforces that role, appears as a governing idea not only of *Pyramus and Thisbe*, but of *A Midsummer Night's Dream* itself and, it can be argued, of comedy at large. Just as carnival effectively strengthens and reinforces "everyday," so the acted role serves to revitalize, renew, and perhaps guarantee the social role from which each temporary actor derives his real quotidian identity. A theater in such a community may thus legitimately call itself *The Globe* and adopt as its motto the wholly apt precept, *totus mundus agit histrionem* (all the world's a stage).

> In short, the "hempen homespuns," the barely literate
> Hard-handed men, that work in Athens here,
> Which never labored in their minds till now
> > (*A Midsummer Night's Dream*, 5.1.72-3)

have a clear message for all comic art. And when Hippolyta complains that "This is the silliest stuff that ever I heard" (5.1.210), she is properly rebuked, in the name of Bottom and his colleagues, by Theseus. For the performance of *Pyramus and Thisbe*, ludicrous on one level, nonetheless draws forth a warm, human, humorous, oral response from its stage audience, which offers a model of comedy's best relationship to the community that generates it. As we watch spectators translated into participants there upon the stage and as we experience the same process beginning its operation here in the auditorium, we can recognize with Theseus that such events need "no excuse" (5.1.355). The process of joining and weaving together carnival role and social role, actor and audience (does this constitute the ultimate "marriage" that the play celebrates?) can be safely left in the hands of those whose names offer an oral guarantee of their abilities in that sphere.[3]

Twelfth Night, or, What You Will

In the case of *Twelfth Night*, it is clear that the eruption of "green world," carnival confusion in the play is on a massive and complex scale. Its well-known commitment to topsy-turviness permits role-confusion, sex-confusion, and confusion over motives to proliferate. Once more the three-stage structure noted by Frye emerges quite clearly. An initial, anti-comic "external" prohibition is placed upon love and merrymaking by the uninvolved Olivia and Malvolio. A complex confusion of roles and identities follows: Viola becomes Cesario; the Puritan becomes a cross-gartered lover; the clown becomes a priest, and so on. Finally, in the third stage, a new society clearly appears in which the strictures of Puritanism are banished, together with the stilted "literary" loving of the play's beginning. A more natural, unlearned, and implicating mode of good fellowship and affection (its apogee marriage) replaces them.

The most obvious effect of this structure is to focus attention upon

Malvolio and to make him a central figure at every stage. As a result, his predominant anticarnival, antiplaying stance serves to foreground the playing/carnival dimension of the play.

This has various effects. Primarily, it pushes the *theatricality* of the play to the fore. Like *A Midsummer Night's Dream, Twelfth Night* has a notable dimension of self-reference. It constantly draws attention to its own "playing" mode, invoking in the process multiple levels of irony, which undermine the standard presuppositions on which the polarities of fiction and truth, appearance and reality rest. Fabian's "If this were to be played upon a stage now, I could condemn it as an improbable fiction" (3.4.131-2) supplies an appropriate epigraph for the process.

And "playing," of course, constitutes the means by which the confusions of the second stage are mounted. Viola plays Cesario; Feste plays Sir Topas; Sir Andrew Aguecheek plays a valorous knight. In fact, "playing" finally functions as the chief means whereby the Puritan Malvolio is mocked, for he is required to become a "player" himself, to wear carnivalesque regalia (yellow stockings and cross-garters).

The same general concern provides the basis for what Maurice Charney has termed the play's many "vigorous affirmations of oral discouse"[4] and, eventually, it reinforces and makes telling the implied context of the action: the carnivalesque Feast of the Epiphany, or Twelfth Night. The play's subtitle, *What You Will*, itself hints at the abandonment or topsy-turvy reversal of accepted categories and distinctions, and comedy of the "turnabout" sort depends wholly, of course, on the interjected responses of an audience whose knowledge of the "normal" or "right" order of things provides the essential basis for the actors' reversal of them. The somersaults, oaths, absurd "dressing-up" and parodies of Carnival require an active response of everyday "right way up" awareness in order to generate the humor. The job of deliberately invoking this response and of reinforcing and cementing the play's interactive relationship with its audience falls naturally to its Lord of Misrule, Toby Belch, whose name orally reinforces the Bakhtinian principle that Carnival asserts the lower aspects of the body (the belly) above the higher ones (the head).

Overall, it might be said that the "double" or interactive nature of oral interchange serves in this play as a model that illuminates and is illuminated by the double or interactive nature of drama, especially comic drama, and the "double vision" this implies. Effectively, orality involves doubleness: an engagement between at least two persons who alternately speak and listen and, in so doing, have two roles. In comic drama, that which is *single* is anticomic: as we have said, a joke requires another's response to "complete" it (Rosaline explains the same point in *Love's Labor's Lost*, 5.2.861 ff). The player, like the speaker-hearer, like the participant in Carnival, is two people at the same time: a "real" person and a "dressed-up" or "topsy-turvy" version. The values of comic drama seem somehow to inhere in this interactive, carnivalesque, oral-aural duplicity.

Duplicity certainly stands as a central feature of *Twelfth Night*. Nothing is what it seems to be, "Nothing that is so, is so" (4.1.9). In general terms, the play seems to put the case that the perspective on the world afforded in it proves the more appropriate and the more coherent by reason of the "double" nature of its vision. The theater itself links the world the actor inhabits on the stage with the one we inhabit in the auditorium: his world "doubles" or mirrors ours. That benign duplicity, finally symbolized in *Twelfth Night* perhaps by the "doubling" of Viola/Cesario or of the identical twins at the end of the play, who combine, as actors do, "One face, one voice, one habit and two persons" (5.1.215), offers a mode wholly appropriate to our human, social nature. It is, in the Duke's words, "A natural perspective" which both "is and is not" (5.1.216). For to an audience, most of whose members probably engaged in acting in carnival or festive occasions at various points of the year, the duplicity of the player's activity and the doubling, interactive mode of life that it implies must have connoted, to a degree far in excess of our modern experience, the truly natural.

On the other hand, Malvolio's commitment to the single vision of Puritanism is seen to deny the fruitful duplicity that Carnival and playing enshrine. Appropriately, his punishment requires him to be "carnivalized" and to take part in that dressing-up. Only in the structured Carnival confusion between holiday and everyday—or, in the versions of that which the art of an oral society raises to great heights, such as the duplicity of meanings celebrated by the pun, the *double entendre* or the confusion between male and female, stage and auditorium—is the good society constituted. In comedy, the double worlds of Carnival and everyday find themselves at first opposed, then fruitfully intertwined, and finally essentially twinned.

Since interactive "conversation" between these worlds generates, it seems, all that we know of the natural and the real, it is important to grasp that its model is the human interaction that orality involves: that characteristic human activity of talking and listening which forms the raw material out of which plays are made. The union between stage and auditorium that occurs at the end of a play, when spectators inherit their own "doubling" roles as participants, can stand as a continuing memorial to that oral process. Malvolio's single-minded Puritan denial of cakes and ale is also a denial of the "second," oral world of drama; of those improbable fictions that, as *Twelfth Night* and *A Midsummer Night's Dream* tell us and as experience confirms, in fact, constitute a considerable part of reality.

Notes

1. More recently, Robert Weimann's *Shakespeare and the Popular Tradition in the Theatre* (Baltimore: Johns Hopkins Univ. Press, 1978) has stressed the wide-reach-

ing implications of the native comic tradition and pointed to the contribution of other studies such as S. L. Bethell's *Shakespeare and the Popular Dramatic Tradition* (London: Staples, 1944) in establishing its firmly rooted nature.

2. It also lists thirty-six Shakespeares, only two of whom live in Stratford.

3. James Burbage, father of the actor Richard Burbage and the first builder of playhouses (he built *The Theatre* in London in 1576), was a joiner by trade. See S. Schoenbaum, *William Shakespeare, A Compact Documentary Life* (Oxford, 1977), p. 131.

4. Maurice Charney, "Comic Premises of Twelfth Night," *The New York Literary Forum*, I (1978), 162.

Bibliographical Note

This essay draws chiefly on the following works:

Northrop Frye. "The Argument of Comedy," *English Institute Essays, 1948*. New York: Columbia Univ. Press, 1949.

————. *A Natural Perspective*. New York: Columbia Univ. Press, 1965.

C. L. Barber. *Shakespeare's Festive Comedy*. Princeton: Princeton Univ. Press, 1959.

Mikhail Bakhtin. *Rabelais and His World*. trans. Helen Iswolsky. Cambridge, Mass.: M.I.T. Press, 1968.

Terence Hawkes. *Shakespeare's Talking Animals*. London: Edward Arnold, 1973.

Robert Weimann. *Shakespeare and the Popular Tradition in the Theatre*. Baltimore: Johns Hopkins Univ. Press, 1978.

Maurice Charney. "Comic Premises of Twelfth Night." *The New York Literary Forum*, 1 (1978), 151-65.

————. *Comedy High and Low*. New York: Oxford Univ. Press, 1978.

14

Comic Villainy in Shakespeare and Middleton

MAURICE CHARNEY

It is becoming increasingly obvious that no firm line can be drawn between the comedies and the tragedies of Shakespeare and his fellow
dramatists. They are separated more by metaphysical and philosophical
commitments—and especially some view of the role of Nature and Providence—than by hard and fast generic distinctions. Comedies are not
generically disturbed by tragic materials; they can syncretize these into a
movement that is predominantly optimistic or at least moving towards
the happy ending. Tragedies, as Susan Snyder has recently made us so
eloquently aware,[1] can also very profitably generate and process comic
materials without disturbing a generally pessimistic movement toward
death and judgment.

Comic villainy is a vivid example of the interpretation of tragedy and
comedy that we are proposing. The villains in Shakespeare and Middleton
—to pair two Elizabethan playwrights most temperamentally akin—
emerge from that practical round of daily life that is the world of comedy.

The villains are never tragic but are the catalysts of tragedy in the noble but deeply flawed heroes they attack. Comic villainy defines the evil in the play from the point of view of the very vicelike villain. The evil only becomes ethical, moral, and spiritual—and therefore tragic—when we see it through the eyes of the tragic protagonists.

Both Shakespeare and Middleton had an understanding of evil that sets them apart from other Elizabethan dramatists. Next to the sensational, baroque excesses of Marston, Webster, and Tourneur, Shakespeare and Middleton seem relatively uninventive in their imaginations of villainy. This partly defines their preoccupation with moral evil—the evil of the heart—rather than with the more flamboyant evils of a world gone mad. Both Middleton and Shakespeare are interested in the psychological immediacy of their villains, who are firmly set in a believable world of daily life and ordinary human beings. In this sense, the villains are always very persuasive and even very likable figures from the world of comedy. They may precipitate the misfortune and even the tragedy of others, but they are never tragic in themselves. Their lineage to the Vice figure of the morality plays is always frankly acknowledged.

Bernard Spivack has explored this tradition of the Vice/Villain in rewarding detail in *Shakespeare and the Allegory of Evil*, which is most notable for its insistence that the Vice figure does not create real moral ambiguities or at least does not seek to exploit them. He is naturally involved in plays that posit extremes of high seriousness and broad hilarity, yet he always manages to move with agility in this double world because of "the radical difference between the nature of the Vice and the nature of his victim."[2] The victim comes from a moral world of rewards and punishments, whereas the Vice is an amoral intriguer and entertainer, seemingly impervious to the blandishments of good and evil. Spivack sums up the Vice's professional qualities:

> Free from human limitation, he is equally free from human passion and responsibility, and his residual emotion is a limitless, amoral merriment, heightened by his jubilation over the success of his intrigue. Professional and impersonal, he is immune to the gravity of his aggression—a gravity that exists everywhere in the play except in him. Nor, by the same token, is his pleasure actually malignant, for such a feeling would render him personal and passionate; and although the anthropomorphic tendency at work upon him frequently invests his speech with the language of such emotions, it is a language without real content, without genuine relevance to the color and tone of his life in the play [pp. 195-96].

"A language without real content" brilliantly defines the Vice's

---

amorality. It is a worldly, manipulative language set apart from the moral reality in which it functions. It is also a language that is consistently ironic because consistently deceptive; it appears to refer to moral truths that don't actually exist for the speaker, but which are very much alive for his hearers. The comic villainy of the Vice can only function in an atmosphere of moral truth. As Iago gloats so characteristically about his generous and high-minded victim:

> The Moor is of a free and open nature
> That thinks men honest that but seem to be so;
> And will as tenderly be led by th' nose
> As asses are.
>
> (*Othello* 1.3.390-93)

In other words, in a world of Iagos, Iago could not function. Cassius, too, has only contempt for the moral Brutus' gullibility: "If I were Brutus now, and he were Cassius,/ He should not humor me" (*Julius Caesar* 1.2. 334-35)—a strangely withering remark from a character normally expected to be sympathetic.

How does this idea of comic villainy apply to Middleton? It is generally recognized that the world of Middleton's plays is more pervasively amoral than Shakespeare's and that Middleton is constantly deploying the metaphor of life as a game. This is a very apt expression of the intrigue formula: if life is a game, then there are only winners and losers with no one in between. Clever persons win and foolish persons lose, often because of moral scruples that blind them to the true nature of reality. In *A Chaste Maid in Cheapside*, Sir Walter Whorehound seems to lord it over the complacent cuckold, Allwit, but Allwit has an uncanny sense of reality that turns the tables on his seemingly predatory rival. We have completely mistaken poor Allwit's mettle. Once a foolish concern with honor is dropped, his insight into his own comfortable position as cuckold is startling:

> I walk out in a morning; come to breakfast,
> Find excellent cheer; a good fire in winter;
> Look in my coal-house about midsummer eve,
> That's full, five or six chaldron [a dry measure of 32 bushels]
>   new laid up;
> Look in my backyard, I shall find a steeple
> Made up with Kentish faggots, which o'erlooks
> The water-house and the windmills: I say nothing,
> But smile and pin the door.
>
> (1.2.22-29)[3]

All this is wonderfully complacent, but not at all ironic. Allwit is genuinely proud of his triumph over the foolishly laborious Sir Walter, who is distinctly overburdened by middle-class pretensions. In his own world, Allwit knows himself a winner:

> I see these things, but like a happy man
> I pay for none at all; yet fools think's mine;
> I have the name, and in his gold I shine. . . .
>
> (1.2.38-40)

He clearly expects us to participate in his elation.

When Sir Walter's fortunes have turned at the end of the play, both Allwit and his wife have only the most merciless contempt for their former benefactor:

> I must tell you, sir,
> You have been somewhat bolder in my house
> Than I could well like of; I suffer'd you
> Till it stuck here at my heart; I tell you truly
> I thought you had been familiar with my wife once.
>
> (5.1.141-45)

And the good wife supports her husband with the most unctuous self-righteousness:

> With me? I'll see him hang'd first: I defy him,
> And all such gentlemen in the like extremity.
>
> (5.1.146-47)

Like Sir Epicure Mammon in Jonson's *Alchemist*, Sir Walter is justly punished for his "voluptuous mind"—his "itch of mind" (4.5.82, 101).[4] The Allwits' contempt is purely histrionic. We are not meant to believe that they, too, have undergone a moral reformation of their own. They have always held the most intensely middle-class values, they have always been insufferable snobs, and they have always worshiped the appearances both of morality and bourgeois comfort—all of which defines perfect amorality.

Allwit wants the audience to admire him and to share in his triumph. He appeals for their understanding and support in the classic manner of the Vice, who always represents himself as the practical good guy, without illusions and without any affected claims to a morality higher than that of the audience. Allwit's soliloquy in Act 1, scene 2, from which I have been quoting, is spoken in an expansive mood that appeals to the audience to feel his joy in his ample coal-pile, wood-pile, breakfast on the table, fire in the hearth, "sugar by whole loaves," "wines by runlets" (1.2.37). This is the poetry of daily life, and who could be so niggardly as to question its dubious origins?

Like Allwit, Shakespeare's Richard, Duke of Gloucester, also wants desperately to make us like him. He confesses at once to his own deformity and ugliness—nay, even emphasizes his own physical repulsiveness, as if to rub our noses in his hump, but all to prepare us clearsightedly for his determination "to prove a villain" (*Richard III* 1.1.30). He shares his plans with us, lets us in on his ingenious duplicity, and all without the slightest moral mitigation: "I am subtle, false, and treacherous" (1.1.37). We are meant to admire him for his candor and his wit.

Edmund, too, in *King Lear*, immediately sets himself apart from his scrupulous and perhaps effeminate brother, Edgar. He is much abetted in his role by the villain's conventional self-address to the audience—the victim is given no comparable speech of rebuttal—in which he is allowed to characterize himself as bluff, hearty, manly, plainspoken, practical, strong in speech and action. In short, he presents himself almost entirely within the value-structure of the audience. There is no way of getting around the tremendous amiability of the villains in Shakespeare and Middleton. This is the true heritage of the Vice of the morality plays, but it also serves to confound any clear and simple notion of tragedy.

In *Othello*, Iago is certainly more "likable" than Othello, who is perhaps too fussy, too abstract, too high-minded, too romantic, too unsure of his worldly position for our tastes. Iago draws on the convention of the bluff, honest, plain-dealing soldier to baffle us with his mastery of daily life. He parodies his own jealousy plot by casually projecting images of Emilia's adultery with Othello and perhaps with Cassio, too:

> I know not if't be true,
> But I, for mere suspicion in that kind,
> Will do, as if for surety.
>
> (1.3.379-81)

Iago's mind is idle and improvisatory. He is not at all diabolical in the sense of having a fixed purpose that he executes with relentless energy. Except in the perspective of the whole play, he is hardly even evil, but rather he is someone who plays games and who is intent on winning each round as it comes up. He is an innovator, a sleight-of-hand man who depends on the inspiration of the moment: " 'Tis here, but yet confused:/ Knavery's plain face is never seen till used" (2.1.311-12). Iago is imperturbably comic because he is always more than adequate for the occasion; he is an expert at delivering the last word and the *quid pro quo*, and he is never to be put down. His wit, in all senses of this most complex word, is inexhaustible. Othello is no match for Iago because the noble Moor's range and versatility are hampered by the narrow moral commitments of tragedy. In a more restricted framework, Hotspur is no match for Prince Hal for much the same reason.

Shakespeare and Middleton interpenetrate on this matter of comic villainy. Both playwrights draw heavily on the traditions of the Vice, whose intrigues are usually self-propelled and without any motivation to confute moral values. If morality is discomforted, even temporarily, it is purely incidental to the Vice's compulsion to play games that he will win. The overall effect of the Vice role may seem diabolical, if not actually terrifying, because so irresistible; but in practice it is perceived as a series of small but continuous triumphs. In this perspective, the tragic protagonist is always a victim and a loser, although Middleton tends to people his plays almost entirely with crafty and self-seeking persons who are set against each other in various degrees of villainy.

Iago's true heir is almost certainly Livia in *Women Beware Women*. Livia is much less spectacular than Iago, much less histrionic, and perhaps also much less overtly evil, but that is beside the point, since both operate not so much out of any desire for personal gain or aggrandizement, but more purely from the impulse to display their art, their cunning, their mystery (in the Elizabethan sense of a secret, professional skill). The elaborately staged seduction of Bianca, for example, doesn't bring Livia any direct rewards from the Duke, as it does Guardiano. His motives are basely materialistic, as he confesses in an aside: "Well, advancement,/ I venture hard to find thee" (2.2.404-5).[5] Livia's final soliloquy in this scene is spoken in an entirely different spirit. The seduction of Bianca confirms Livia's confidence in her own urbane sophistication. It is a triumph of her lively cynicism and, with it, her vision of a courtly, decayed world:

> Are you so bitter? 'Tis but want of use—
> Her tender modesty is sea-sick a little,
> Being not accustomed to the breaking billow
> Of woman's wavering faith, blown with temptations.
> 'Tis but a qualm of honour, 'twill away,
> A little bitter for the time, but lasts not.
> Sin tastes at the first draught like wormwood water,
> But drunk again, 'tis nectar ever after.
>
> (2.2.470-77)

Both Livia and Iago are masters of a simple, persuasive, colloquial diction and syntax. Everything they say is perfectly natural and unpretentious.

When Livia agrees to satisfy the ripe, incestuous longings of her brother, Hippolito, by seducing her niece Isabella, it is an even stronger demonstration of her imaginative art than the seduction of Bianca. Livia has her own special longing to dazzle her brother with what she can accomplish:

> 'tis but a hazarding
> Of grace and virtue, and I can bring forth
> As pleasant fruits as sensuality wishes
> In all her teeming longings. This I can do.
>
> (2.1.29-32)

We know that this is no idle boast, and we wait eagerly for Livia (in the words of Fats Waller) "to strut her stuff." There is a playful exuberance in Livia that is not matched anywhere else in the plot:

> Sir, I could give as shrewd a lift to chastity
> As any she that wears a tongue in Florence:
> Sh' had need be a good horsewoman, and sit fast,
> Whom my strong argument could not fling at last.

(2.1.36-39)

Livia is splendidly unconcerned with issues of mere moral responsibility, and Isabella, too, gets exactly what she wants from her aunt's heavily varnished tale of bastardy. If one of the points of the play is "women beware women," then another must surely be: "it's a witty age" (2.2. 396). Perhaps both Shakespeare's *Othello* and Middleton's *Women Beware Women* are our most illustrious examples of the tragedy of wit.

We know that Middleton was born in 1580, about sixteen years after Shakespeare. He didn't begin writing seriously for the theater until the first decade of the seventeenth century, and his early comedies are mostly written for children's companies. Middleton's comparability with Shakespeare is obviously not based on historical sources. We don't know what either playwright thought of the other, although Shakespeare must surely have been aware of Middleton's complicated and sardonic comedies of London life at the very moment that Shakespeare was turning to a very different kind of romantic comedy. Middleton was in a position to be influenced by Shakespeare's example, although specific echoes and borrowings are few.

The comparison between Shakespeare and Middleton depends as much on defining what is Shakespearean as what is Middletonian. The question of Middleton's strong affinities with Shakespeare is more and more often being posed by serious students of the new Elizabethan drama.[6] But the counterquestion of what is characteristically Middletonian about Shakespeare has, I venture to think, never been asked. The mere formulation sounds strange and seems to violate established priorities. Yet any meaningful comparison must depend upon both sides of the equation. The relations between Shakespeare and his fellow dramatists have too long depended on verbal similarities and especially verbal echoes—after-vibrations of Hamlet with the skull, the mad Ophelia, and the raging Lear on the heath. The larger parallels in dramatic construction, scenic form, creation of character, equilibration of rhetoric and purpose—all that fundamental area of dramaturgic assumptions—have generally been ignored. Verbal links lend themselves better to demonstration than the broader analogies of style and form.

Both Middleton and Shakespeare are skillful in projecting psychological immediacy and especially a kind of psychological realism that depends strongly on moral assumptions. Beatrice-Joanna's slow recognition that she is "the deed's creature" in *The Changeling* is surely a Shakespearean touch, just as much as Othello's anticipatory awareness that Desdemona is totally innocent—"O, the world hath not a sweeter creature! She might lie by an emperor's side and command him tasks" (4.1.185-87)—is surely a Middletonian touch. It is a wild burst of nostalgic, emotional fantasy right at the very moment that Othello is resolving to strangle his beloved. He knows something of the pity of it, "O Iago, the pity of it, Iago" (4.1. 198), just as Beatrice-Joanna evokes memories of her former life as if it had all passed away in time immemorial: "Oh come not near me, sir, I shall defile you:/ I am that of your blood was taken from you/ For your better health" (5.3.149-51).[7] She has now been tragically joined with those "things corruptible" (155) that represent her fate.

Similarly, the corruption of Bianca in *Women Beware Women* reminds us inescapably of the corruption of Cressida in *Troilus and Cressida*. Both are changed, changed utterly, but their transformation seems inescapably to realize the original premises of their character. Both are "sluttish spoils of opportunity/ And daughters of the game" (*Troilus and Cressida* 4.5.62-63), and their erotic immediacy is seen from up close. Shakespeare and Middleton don't need any vulgar, sexual touches to define an intensely sexual reality. The Duke's seduction of Bianca only acts out a wish-fulfillment scenario grander than anything Leantio could provide. "Come poison all at once" (2.2.426), says the ravished Bianca, who certainly is not a lady who protests too much, and Cressida is abundantly ready to accept the new reality of the Greek camp: "Troilus, farewell. One eye yet looks on thee/ But with my heart the other eye doth see" (5.2.104-5). Middleton and Shakespeare have a genius for defining a self-indulgent moral weakness in powerfully psychological terms. The tragedy is wrought from the mysterious ways in which characters unwittingly act out their destiny. Although in good faith as the world defines it, Othello, Beatrice-Joanna, Bianca, and Cressida cannot withstand the irresistible attraction of the very natural and very convincing force of evil that eventually destroys them.

The larger question is what each dramatist represented for the other.[8] At their best, both dramatists can capture an extraordinary sense of psychological and moral immediacy. The representation of evil is deliberately toned down and understated, so that their villains seem to emerge from the amoral, comic traditions of the Vice in the morality plays. By muting the flamboyance of evil, both Shakespeare and Middleton create believable and persuasive villains of daily life. They are villains who want to be admired for their practicality, their intelligence, their bluff lack of pretension, and their full commitment to a witty and inventive reality. They are stylists, performers, and magicians of ordinary experience. With black comedy making so many inroads into the territory that used to be reserved for tragedy, we now realize how powerfully Shakespeare's and Middleton's villains define and energize the world in which the tragic protagonists move.

Notes

1. Susan Snyder, *The Comic Matrix of Shakespeare's Tragedies* (Princeton: Princeton Univ. Press, 1979).
2. Bernard Spivack, *Shakespeare and the Allegory of Evil* (New York: Columbia Univ. Press, 1958), p. 195. All subsequent references will be given in the text.
3. Thomas Middleton, *A Chaste Maid in Cheapside*, ed. R. B. Parker (London: Methuen, 1969), The Revels Plays.
4. Ben Jonson, *The Alchemist*, ed. Alvin B. Kernan (New Haven: Yale Univ. Press, 1974).
5. Thomas Middleton, *Women Beware Women*, ed. J. R. Mulryne (London: Methuen, 1975), The Revels Plays.
6. See, for example, T. B. Tomlinson, *A Study of Elizabethan and Jacobean Tragedy* (Cambridge: Cambridge Univ. Press, 1964), and Maurice Charney, "Webster vs. Middleton, or the Shakespearean Yardstick in Jacobean Tragedy," in *English Renaissance Drama: Essays in Honor of Madeleine Doran & Mark Eccles*, ed. Standish Henning, Robert Kimbrough, and Richard Knowles (Carbondale: Southern Illinois Univ. Press, 1976), pp. 118-27.
7. Thomas Middleton and William Rowley, *The Changeling*, ed. N. W. Bawcutt (London: Methuen, 1958), The Revels Plays.
8. See Ch. 5 of Howard Felperin, *Shakespearean Representation: Mimesis and Modernity in Elizabethan Tragedy* (Princeton: Princeton Univ. Press, 1977).

Bibliographical Note

For the structural affinities of Shakespeare and Middleton, there is a good deal of material in Richard Levin, *The Multiple Plot in English Renaissance Drama* (Chicago: Univ. of Chicago Press, 1971). There is also interesting speculation on the relation of *Macbeth* to Middleton's *Hengist, King of Kent, or The Mayor of Queenborough* in R. C. Bald's edition of the play (New York: Scribner's, 1938). For the general issue, see T. B. Tomlinson, *A Study of Elizabethan and Jacobean Tragedy* (Cambridge: Cambridge Univ. Press, 1964), and Howard Felperin, *Shakespearean Representation* (Princeton: Princeton Univ. Press, 1977). See also Maurice Charney, "Webster vs. Middleton, or the Shakespearean Yardstick in Jacobean Tragedy," in *English Renaissance Drama: Essays in Honor of Madeleine Doran & Mark Eccles*, ed. Standish Henning, Robert Kimbrough, and Richard Knowles (Carbondale: Southern Illinois Univ. Press, 1976), pp. 118-27, and "Shakespeare—and the Others," *Shakespeare Quarterly*, 30 (1979), 325-42.

On the general subject of the interrelations of comedy and tragedy, with a good account of the historical background, see Susan Snyder, *The Comic Matrix of Shakespeare's Tragedies* (Princeton: Princeton Univ. Press, 1979). *The Comedy of Evil on Shakespeare's Stage* by Charlotte Spivack (Rutherford, N.J.: Fairleigh Dickinson Univ. Press, 1978) is particularly useful for its discussion of the medieval notion of evil as privative and, therefore, worthy of laughter. The medieval Vice and his lineage figure importantly in Bernard Spivack, *Shakespeare and the Allegory of Evil* (New York: Columbia Univ. Press, 1958).

15

The Doubling of Parts in Shakespearean Comedy: Some Questions of Theory and Practice

AVRAHAM OZ

One of the major points of difference between tragedy and comedy has to do with the ways each is pursuing dramatic fulfillment. If a linear, irreversible course of action is nearly always a hallmark of tragedy, comedy is usually marked by a sense of circularity that makes its progress highly conducive to repetitions, mirror effects, and variations on a theme—so much so that we often regard the use of a subplot in tragedy (in *King Lear*, for example) as a borrowed comic technique, since it tends to slow down the vigorous pace of the main tragic plot. Whereas the tragic hero, hitting the one-way road leading him toward some ultimate goal, "runs through the world [like Büchner's Woyzeck] as an open razor," his comic counterpart is commonly provided by the author with a round-trip ticket.

These contrasting attitudes ostensibly affect the differing representations of character in tragedy and comedy. Both genres would imply, as it were, that one's true identity, like death and the sun in La Rochefoucauld's famous phrase, cannot be stared at with a steady eye (or "saucy looks"[*Love's Labor's Lost* 1.1.85]to cite Berowne's version). Whereas the tragic hero eagerly accepts the challenge even at the price of plucking out his eyes, the comic hero is constantly involved in disguising whatever may still be betrayed of his true identity, so that no genuine part of it would be seen. And so the whole question of identity in comedy, as Maurice Charney justly reminds us, "is often reduced to a matter of costume."[1] Once our Rosalinds or Violas have assumed the apparel of some Ganymede or Cesario, their detachment from their former identity may amount to an entirely new attitude towards experience or, in some cases, to a total change of character.

Like his tragic vision, Shakespeare's comic genius contributes in a major way to his long quest for the genuine identity of man in a world growing alienated and, indeed, disguised. But as Shakespearean comedy normally pertains less to patterns of individual psychology than to the formal orchestration of themes and situations (which, of course, is why the comedies, unlike the tragedies, are rarely named after a particular character), the boundaries of identity are less determined here than in the tragedies. Thus, in throwing surprising perspectives on the dramatic action and uncovering its deeper structures, the comic *peripeteia* may go further than redeeming the integrity of the disguised. The final harmony of comedy often tends to bring together separate characters as "the semblance of . . . [each other's] soul" (*The Merchant of Venice* 3.4.20).

The Merchant of Venice is, indeed, a case in point. Like most of Shakespeare's comedies from *The Comedy of Errors* to the late romances, it clings to traditional comic devices such as disguise or mistaken identities. And yet the problem of identity plays, it seems, a greater role in the thematic and structural framework of the play. The keynote for this theme is struck in the very first speech of the play, where Antonio's ambiguous difficulty of "knowing himself" qualifies the riddle of his sadness as well as the three successive attempts, by Salerio and Solanio, Gratiano, and Bassanio, to solve it that inform the implicit structure of the entire opening scene. The same question is then pursued on various levels of meaning and form, from the assignment to which Portia's suitors become committed (namely, to find her real self in the caskets), through the clash between Shylock's self-assertion as the sum of his "eyes . . ., hands, organs, dimensions, senses, affections, passions" (*The Merchant of Venice* 3.1.57-58), and Antonio's scarcely less problematic self-immersion in the image of the "tainted wether" (4.1.114), or Jessica's dilemma concerning her identity as her "father's child" (2.3.17), down to Launcelot's harsh "identity game" with his father. It is Portia's prophetic insight into the ways in which "an egal yoke of love" (3.4.13) may forge spiritual and moral unions, transcending the boundaries of the individual self, which is finally responsible for the attainment of a sense of harmony (if heavily flawed and relative) at the end of the play.

Such a breach of the solid barriers that are supposed to protect the individuality of characters may give rise to yet another mode of repetition, which is extrinsic to the written text and thus optional, though by no means less significant. The doubling of parts is a common practice in the theater, if not necessarily dictated by the playwright himself. In a useful little study, Professor Arthur Colby Sprague provides several instances of popular, and some less popular, doublings of parts from the recorded history of Shakespearean productions.[2] Among the more popular ones one may find the doubling of Polonius (or, alternatively, Rosencrantz) and the Gravedigger; the Ghost and Laertes; Poins or King Henry and Justice Shallow; Launcelot Gobbo and the Duke of Venice; Hermione and Perdita (and sometimes Viola and Sebastian); Thomas Mowbray and the Bishop of Carlisle. Since it would be fair to believe that the practice was originally initiated by needs of economy, one is not surprised to find it habitual among early companies to try and conceal the doubling (often by coining fancy names in the programme, such as Mr. Silver and Mr. Gold playing Forest and Deighton in *Richard III*, or the assignment, in Sheffield, of Rosencrantz, Francisco, and Priest to Messrs. East, West, and South respectively).[3] Only at a later stage would companies and directors openly confess to the use of an actor in more than one role, virtually admitting that there was nothing wrong, from the artistic point of view, in such a practice.

Some Reasons for Doubling

The economic motives for the use of doubling are obvious enough: the size of a regular company, whether in Shakespeare's times[4] or in our own, would scarcely permit such an abundance in human resources as most of Shakespeare's plays require, were each single part to be entrusted to a different actor. And yet beyond this practical need there is a sense in which the doubling of parts may conform with a purely artistic principle, thus turning necessity into virtue. When Sir Thomas More (in the play bearing his name) learns from the Chief Player that there are three women's parts in *The Marriage of Wit and Wisdom* (the interlude to be presented at his house), "And one boy play them all," one may wonder whether there is any reason except the "husbandry" of production accounts for that boy being thus "loaden" (to quote Sir Thomas' reaction). But when the coupling of Theseus and Oberon, Hippolyta and Titania and Philostrate and Puck in Peter Brook's production of *A Midsummer Night's Dream* is claimed to have been practiced "for no clear reason except economy,"[5] the account seems less than satisfactory. For if in tragedy doublings such as the Ghost with the First Player in *Hamlet* may be easily justified on purely thematic grounds,[6] in comedy such doublings have come to be regarded as one of the stock devices designed to enhance the comic effect. Among the cases of doubling mentioned by Sprague, that of Christopher Sly and Petruchio sounds particularly promising, no less than does the now fashionable *A Midsummer Night's Dream* triple coupling. In both cases, a careful use of doubling follows the inner logic of the play. Sly's dream of Petruchio as his self-image may result in many ingenious points of interpretation in a clever production of *The Taming of the Shrew*, just as the encounter of the lovers (and, on another plane, the mechanicals) with the same commanding triumvirate both in Theseus' Court and Oberon's Wood may prove creative and significant for a similar production of *A Midsummer Night's Dream*.

Examples of Doubling

In *The Merchant of Venice*, the traditional doubling of Launcelot Gobbo (or Old Gobbo) and the Duke seems pretty fortuitous and stems chiefly from practical needs. But the play's crucial involvement in the riddle of identity may also call for more significant doublings, with a stronger bearing on its themes and structure. Such, for instance, was the doubling we used in our production of *The Merchant of Venice* at the Cameri Theatre of Tel Aviv in 1972.[7] In attempting to bridge the much discussed discrepancy between Bassanio's portrayal as a careless youth and his unconvincingly virtuous choice of the right casket, we suddenly realized that just as the three caskets contributed to a single moral problem, so did the three suitors stand for three optional attitudes to this single problem. What, then, if they were to suggest (however elusively) one continuous process of a single mind rather than three independent characters looking at the problem from totally different stances? In the last act of the play, Portia plays a rather cruel trick on Bassanio in dividing herself into both the learned doctor and the provoked wife. What if this were suggested, at least at one level, to be an act of revenge on Bassanio for having played a similar trick on her?

What followed was the decision to have Bassanio play both Morocco and Arragon. The idea seemed almost prescribed by the play itself (though, as far as we could check, never mentioned in stage history). Only one minor dislocation of scene was made for the sake of convenience rather than necessity. Act 2, scene 1 was combined with Act 2, scene 7, a change, incidentally, that has been frequently made in the past for different reasons. Launcelot's scene, which followed Act 1, scene 3 directly, served well as a comic relief between the bargain scene and Bassanio's preparations to set sail for Belmont. Moreover, his appearance on stage while Shylock's reference to "the fearful guard/ of an unthrifty knave" (*The Merchant of Venice*, 1.3.172-3) still echoed in the air, seemed perfectly well-timed. Beside this minor change, everything fitted into the structure of the play as if Shakespeare himself had the same idea in mind. Bassanio had plenty of time to assume the fancy appearance of the Moor between his exit at the end of Act 2, scene 2 and his entrance at Act 2, scene 7. There was some pressure for Morocco to dress up as Arragon during the rather short exchange between Salerio and Solanio at Act 2, scene 8, but time enough for Arragon to become Bassanio again while

In the Cameri Theatre (Israel) production of *The Merchant of Venice*, 1972, Itzhak Hizkiya plays Bassanio (above), doubles as Morocco (middle), and as Prince Arragon (below). *Photographs by Mula and Haramaty.*

Shylock was lengthily harassed on stage in Act 3, scene 1.

The triple change of costume was hardly elaborate, however, since it never aimed for a total concealment of the game of identity. Writing on the practice of doubling in the Elizabethan theater, William J. Lawrence speculates:

> The technical difficulties which regularly confronted the early professional players were so abundant that one is forced to the conclusion either that they possessed wondrous personative powers, a rich gift of mimicry, and an uncommon knack of disguise, or—what seems more likely—that the public of their time had the child's imagination and illimitable capacity for make-believe.[8]

Whether this be a fair judgment of an Elizabethan audience or not, it could scarcely hold true for a modern one. Therefore, no attempt was made to deceive the audience by elaborate costume; on the contrary, the trick was played forward. And if on one thematic level it made a point of having the same actor pronounce, "A golden mind stoops not to shows of dross" (*The Merchant of Venice*, 2.7.20); "I will assume desert" (*The Merchant of Venice*, 2.9.50); and "So may the outward shows be least themselves" (*The Merchant of Venice*, 3.2.73), on the level of sheer comedy, it played with the idea that it might have been Bassanio himself who was playing safe, exhausting all the possible answers by trial and error.

These added levels of comic action lent fresh meaning to the theme of appearance and reality investing the entire riddle contest. Their effect could be noticed from the very first words of Morocco, which were suddenly charged with a surprising double meaning: "Mislike me not for my complexion" (*The Merchant of Venice*, 2.1.1) says Morocco-Bassanio to the half-suspecting Portia and goes on in the same vein:

> Bring me the fairest creature northward born,
> Where Phoebus' fire scarce thaws the icicles,
> And let us make incision for your love
> To prove whose blood is reddest, his or mine.
> (The Merchant of Venice, 2.1.4-7)

Then, with a touch of some racy joke:

> (I tell thee, lady, *this aspect* of mine)
> Hath feared the valiant. By my love I swear,
> The best-regarded virgins of *our* clime
> Have *loved it* too.
> (The Merchant of Venice, 2.1.8-11)

And, finally, he comes back to the double-entendre implied by his opening lines:

> I would not change this hue
> *Except to steal your thoughts*, my gentle queen.
> *(The Merchant of Venice*, 2.1.11-12)

This, of course, he will do soon enough. The same irony holds for Portia's
answer, and toward the end of her speech it may even serve to mend, to
some extent at least, the bad impression normally left by her "sweet"
discourse.

> Yourself, renowned Prince, then stood as *fair*
> As any comer I have looked on yet
> For my affection.
> *(The Merchant of Venice*, 2.1.20-21)

Her shrewish comments in private to Nerissa upon receiving news of
Morocco's arrival in Belmont still live in our memory and put in question the sincerity of the sentiment expressed by this later comment. If,
however, she may suspect some double-dealing on his part (though
this point was never driven home in the production), the discrepancy
between her two statements could be taken more lightly. And so the
elusive guessing game goes on, strengthening the comic tension between
Portia and her suitors, adding another ironic dimension to the casket
plot, and tightening its unity. It reaches an effective climax when Portia,
having betrayed her feelings at the beginning of Act 3, scene 2, throws her
own "fancy" song into the game, a song that, even when its suspicious
rhyming with "lead" is ignored, contains an obvious allusion to the right
choice of caskets.

At least one other significant doubling seems to be suggested by
The Merchant of Venice: an interesting comic effect would be produced
if Shylock himself were to play Old Gobbo. This doubling is made possible by the play, and the dual image of "fatherhood" it may suggest
would make more of Launcelot's relevance to the play, as well as reflect
upon Shylock's own fatherhood of Jessica (a moral problem raised by
Jessica herself one scene later).

Though in *The Merchant of Venice* the play on identities is particularly emphasized, the same technique applies to most of the other
comedies. In *As You Like It*, on its inherent division into two complementary worlds, the doubling of parts may enhance the effect of Forest
and Court reflecting each other. I have discussed elsewhere[9] the successful mirroring effect created by an intricate doubling strategy in Peter
James's production of *As You Like It* (The Cameri Theatre of Tel Aviv,
1973 and 1978): Duke Senior doubled with Frederick (a doubling already
recorded in the past), courtly Le Beau with Amiens; a clever blocking

made the intellectual contest between Touchstone and William bring back to mind the wrestling match of Act 1, where William was Charles and Touchstone served as a referee; and every single character in the forest found his counterpart in Frederick's court. Only Jaques remained undoubled, an odd figure reminding Arden of the bitter undertones of "natural freedom." These are just a few reflections about the special significance one comic technique can lend to the circular world of Shakespearean comedy. In a time when the "Shakespearean revolution" still provides us with a host of fresh interpretations, doubling is a comic practice that richly deserves to be explored.

Notes

1. Maurice Charney, *Comedy High and Low* (New York: Oxford Univ. Press, 1978), p. 53.
2. Arthur Colby Sprague, *The Doubling of Parts in Shakespeare's Plays* (London, The Society of Theatre Research, 1966).
3. Ibid., pp. 11-12.
4. See William J. Lawrence, "The Practice of Doubling and Its Influence on Early Dramaturgy," in his *Pre-Restoration Stage Studies* (Cambridge, Mass.: Harvard Univ. Press, 1927), pp. 43-78.
5. J. L. Styan citing Benedict Nightingale in *The Shakespeare Revolution* (Cambridge: Cambridge Univ. Press, 1977), p. 229.
6. And a similar case can be made for tragicomedy: for example, William Gaskill's clever doubling of Lady Ager (who is falsely accused of being a whore in the "serious" main plot) and Meg the bawd (in the comic subplot), in his recent production of Middleton and Rowley's *A Fair Quarrel* at the National Theatre, London (1979).
7. Directed by J. Ysraeli and translated by Avraham Oz.
8. Lawrence, p. 54.
9. Avraham Oz, "Shakespeare in Israel," *Shakespeare Quarterly*, 30 (1979), 279-81.

Bibliographical Note

The chief sources for understanding doubling are William J. Lawrence, "The Practice of Doubling and Its Influence on Early Dramaturgy," *Pre-Restoration Stage Studies* (Cambridge, Mass.: Harvard Univ. Press, 1927), pp. 43-78, and Arthur Colby Sprague, *The Doubling of Parts in Shakespeare's Plays* (London: The Society for Theatre Research, 1966). See also Avraham Oz, "Shakespeare in Israel," *Shakespeare Quarterly*, 30 (1979), 279-81, for the production of *As You Like It* discussed in this article.

PART 6

COMIC CHARACTERS: FALSTAFF AND MALVOLIO

16

Falstaff and
the Life of Shadows

LEO SALINGAR

> *THESEUS. The best in this kind are but shadows; and the*
> *worst are no worse, if imagination amend them.*
> *HIPPOLYTA. It must be your imagination then, and not theirs.*
>
> A Midsummer Night's Dream, 5.1.211-14

What is it that makes us laugh about Falstaff? This is perhaps a naive, unanswerable question. In his magisterial lecture on "The Rejection of Falstaff," Bradley set even a part of it, the query why we laugh *at* the fat knight, judiciously aside. Nevertheless, it is still tempting to assail the indefinable and, throwing caution to the winds, to try to sprinkle salt on the tail of that particularly large but paradoxically lively bird, even at the risk of losing, along with the caution, the salt. It is particularly tempting if we want to examine the general nature of comedy and—a related but distinct set of questions—the place Falstaff occupies in the two parts of *Henry IV*.

Some of the unavoidable niggles that beset this sort of inquiry are that we do not all, as readers, laugh at the same things or even twice at the same place; that we are much more prone to laugh in company than alone; and that, even in the theater, our laughter depends to some extent on accidents of the occasion. Further, the impulse to laugh, when studying Shakespeare, is to some extent lumbered with the ponderous gear of annotations. And, more generally, a perfect, utopian theory of laughter would take care of the difference between the occasions when we laugh outright and the occasions when we merely feel an inclination to laugh. But the present essay—caution having been disregarded—cannot pause over such niceties (just as it will only be concerned with the canonical or *echt* Falstaff, as the two historical plays body him forth).

Perhaps the best starting-place is Bergson's theory of laughter, insufficient though it is. According to Bergson, then, we laugh when we perceive "something mechanical encrusted on something living," the physical encroaching upon the sphere of mental freedom, a human being behaving like a physical object; at bottom, our laughter is prompted by *raideur* rather than *laideur*, by "the unsprightly" rather than "the unsightly."[1] In comedy, it is directed against the personage who has sunk his individuality in the routines of a social or professional or temperamental type, who has forfeited his waking spontaneity to some automatism of behavior resembling absentmindedness. And, since mechanical thought or behavior, though necessary within limits, is ultimately hostile to social evolution, or the *élan vital*, the underlying function of comedy is to marshal our collective and corrective laughter against such obstacles to freedom. This theory applies well to a great deal in Molière, and to Labiche, Bergson's second choice for purposes of illustration; equally, it could apply almost intact to the superbly intricate contraptions for laughter devised by Bergson's contemporary, Georges Feydeau.

However, Bergson's purview is limited by assumptions traditional with criticism, especially in France, such as the assumption that comedy and laughter are very nearly the same thing. Even within those limits, he pays no attention to those characters who make us laugh *with* them and not at them. And, as Albert Thibaudet noted in his study of Bergson, the philosopher's analysis of stage comedy, even in Molière, omits the indispensable factor of mobility: "a comedy is a movement, I don't mean necessarily an action."[2] For Thibaudet, this is a correlative to the subliminal movement we experience inwardly when responding to any work of art. However, by the same token, it is also an expression of Bergsonian *élan*. And perhaps one can carry this observation a step further and save the appearances for Bergson's theory of the comic by supposing that those stage characters who make us laugh intentionally, and not inadvertently, have become, at least for the time being, delegates for the author by anticipating some threatened incursion of the mechanical upon the vital and triumphantly reversing the flow. If so, they represent the upsurge of spontaneity over automatism, a process more fundamental to comedy than any enforcement of social correction. This line of reasoning may account also for those stimuli to laughter that other theorists have emphasized, though they are only marginal from Bergson's point of view, such as the laughter due to surprise or incongruity or to release from the breaking of a taboo. Although in cases like those our laughter may not have been prompted by "something mechanical encrusted on something living," it could still be argued that the cause of it was the mental jolt of expecting to see a logical or a moral rule at work but finding instead that the mechanism of the rule had been overcome. This still has less to do with social solidarity than with the subconscious pleasure of release. But in the theater there is surely also a further level of interplay on some such lines between the mechanical and the vital. Once the train of laughter has been set going, we seem to store up a reserve for extra additional laughter precisely in our altered uncertainty as to when next and which way the cat is going to jump.

Falstaff is surely the grand example of such multiplicity, or deep duplicity, in the causes of laughter. "The brain of this foolish compounded clay, man," he can fairly claim, "is not able to invent anything that intends to laughter more than I invent or is invented on me. I am not only witty in myself, but the cause that wit is in other men" (*Henry IV, Part 2*, 1.2.7-10). When Bradley and like-minded critics gloss over the causes why others laugh *at* Falstaff, it must be because they seem so obvious—"gross as a mountain"—and not because they are unfathomable. First, of course, his fatness, a classic instance of what Aristotle would call the ludicrous arising from a defect that is not destructive or what Bergson would call the physical encroaching upon the mental (since it is represented as a consequence of his chosen way of life). Then his drinking, his cowardice (or, if you prefer, his "instinct" not to be heroic), his apparently compulsive lying. Poins and the Prince foresee very well what mechanisms they will spring in him when they plan their "jest" at Gad's Hill. And Shakespeare has made him a perpetual comic butt, because, as Harry Levin has pointed out, he has staged him as a walking paradox, a Renaissance knight without a horse; "uncolted" (*Henry IV, Part 1*, 2.2.39) by the Prince, and commissioned with nothing better for the war than "a charge of foot" (2.4.550).[3]

On the other hand, when Poins anticipates "the incomprehensible" (the illimitable) "lies that this same fat rogue will tell" (*Henry IV, Part 1*, 1.2.183-4), he hints at just the opposite side of Falstaff, his inventiveness, his inexhaustible resilience, his predictable unpredictability. These have to do with the reasons why we laugh *with* him. He is always quick at changing an awkward subject. And his lies are foxy evasions, not empty fantasies like the boasts of Baron Munchausen or the daydreams of Walter Mitty. They match the positive resourcefulness of his wit, his ability to play with words and, beyond that, to disconnect and recombine the accepted rules of moral judgment. In thought as in act, he is the archopponent of regularity: "Give you a reason on compulsion? If reasons were as plentiful as blackberries, I would give no man a reason upon compulsion, I" (*Henry IV, Part 1*, 2.3.239-42). We laugh, one may suggest, at sallies like this both because he is cornered and knows he is cornered and because he can nevertheless trump up something almost indistinguishable from a valid reply, unexpected and, in the fullest sense, diverting. We laugh because he is caught out, because just the same he has been too quick for us, and further (I believe) because we are not sure which of these thoughts is uppermost. This kind of uncertainty is fundamental in comic tradition.

Falstaff's Language

Falstaff's puns form one of his ways of circumventing mechanisms of thought, by taking advantage of what are possibly no more than accidental associations of ideas in language. He can treat "reasons" like "blackberries," for instance because the word was pronounced *raisins;* thereby evading an awkward truth. Or he can pun spontaneously, from high spirits, as when, later in the same tavern scene, he enjoins his companions to "clap to the doors. Watch tonight, pray tomorrow" (*Henry IV, Part 1*, 2.4.279-80)—out of sheer relief on learning that the stolen money he thought he had been filched of could be used for his benefit after all. His biblical "Watch and pray" not merely pretends to sanctify their proposed drinking-bout (or *watch*), but also recalls his fellow-thieves to their predatory highway code, thus covertly reinstating his own manliness at the same time.[4]

He is similarly inventive in the vocabulary of aggression, protestation, belittlement, and abuse. If the others will not credit his valor on Gad's Hill, he is "a shotten herring" (*Henry IV, Part 1*, 2.4.131) or "a bunch of radish." Hal, disbelieving him, becomes "you starveling, . . . you dried neat's-tongue, you bull's pizzle, you stockfish" (2.4.246-7). All this Carnival, or Billingsgate, raillery is, of course, part of the game that he shares with the Prince. In their first scene together, when Hal has disobligingly knocked down his attempts to find expressions for his alleged "melancholy," Falstaff retorts, "Thou hast the most unsavory similes, and art indeed the most comparative, rascalliest, sweet young prince (*Henry IV, Part 1*, 1.2.80-82). Set point to the "fat-witted" knight; but it seems clear enough why the Prince should enjoy his company.

The game they play calls for stylistic agility (for the copiousness in words the Elizabethans admired and for skill in calculated breaches of literary decorum) besides licensing a free-for-all of mock-aggression. It was fashionable in the 1590s and was related to the new literary conception of wit that was then emerging. Nashe, for example, relishes what he calls the "sport" of railing; after a two-page effusion over a literary enemy, he characteristically adds,

---

Redeo ad vos, mei auditores [back to you, listeners]: have I not
an indifferent pretty vein in spur-galling an ass? If you knew
how extemporal it were at this instant, and with what haste it
is writ, you would say so. But I would not have you think that
all this that is set down here is in good earnest, for then you go
by St. Giles the wrong way to Westminster; but only to show
how for a need I could rail if I were thoroughly fired.[5]

Shakespeare's courtly wits, as in *Love's Labor's Lost*, indulge themselves
in a similar vein. But it is specially appropriate to a Bohemian or
adventurer of the pen like Nashe; indeed, it becomes Nashe's principal
stock in trade, as he bawls his academically certified wares in the marketplace. And it is peculiarly appropriate to Falstaff's position as a gentle-
bred adventurer who compensates through language for deficiencies in
the more solid advantages due to his rank. In language, Falstaff is a lord.
He commands a ruffianly composure of speech, a leisured pace permitting
lightning thrusts, and a compendious range of tone including masterful
coarseness. It is the coarseness that Hotspur wants to hear from Lady
Percy when she swears (*Henry IV, Part 1*, 3.1.245-54). It distinguishes
Falstaff completely from a mere "swaggerer" of the day and ranter of
playhouse tags like Pistol; style is his real, and his only real, ground of
equality with the Prince. Yet his speech is repeatedly ambiguous in tone,
corresponding to the indeterminateness of his social position. As William
Empson has put it, "Falstaff is the first major joke by the English against
their class system; he is a picture of how badly you can behave, and still
get away with it, if you are a gentleman—a mere common rogue would
not have been nearly so funny."[6]

Whether his tone for the moment is aggressive or not, Falstaff
habitually asserts himself by defeating expectation. His very first appearance must have come as a surprise to the Elizabethans; they could
have anticipated a wild gallant or a rumbustious clown to accompany
Hal onto the stage, but not a corpulent, benevolent, apparently delibera-
tive grayhead. On his opening words, noncommittal in tone ("Now, Hal,
what time of day is it, lad?" [*Henry IV, Part 1*, 1.2.1]), the Prince
pounces with the imputation that his proper qualities are gluttony and
sloth, which are much what stage tradition, if not historical legend, would
attach to such a personage:

> Thou art so fat-witted with drinking of old sack, and unbutton-
> ing thee after supper, and sleeping upon benches after noon,
> that thou hast forgotten to demand that truly which thou
> wouldest truly know. What a devil hast thou to do with the
> time of the day? [1.2.2-6]

But Falstaff at once shows that he has, on the contrary, a concern of sorts
with the passage of time, by asking a series of questions about the future,

---

in the course of which, far from admitting to sloth or gluttony, he fleetingly adopts the voices of manly "resolution," "melancholy" solicitation,
and even sorrowful "amendment of life" (1.2.103). He may resemble
Gluttony or Sloth—or alternatively, Riot—but in himself, his manner
implies, he is not to be identified with any of them (any more than
Jaques's melancholy is the scholar's or the musician's or the courtier's,
"but it is a melancholy of mine own, compounded of many simples, ex-
tracted from many objects" [*As You Like It*, 4.1.15-17]).

And Falstaff's personality seems always in movement, going against
the stream of opinion. He repeatedly advances the idea of his own worth,
not simply by bragging when occasion favors, but by jocular assertion and,
especially in his early scenes, by insinuating that the standards he could
be criticized by, the yardsticks that society commonly applies to worthi-
ness, are habitually misconceived or misplaced. He does not expect his
assertions to be taken "in good earnest" any more (or any less) than
Nashe; and, at least before the battle scenes, he does not single out any
one of society's values for direct criticism (which might seem to fix him
in the vulnerable position of a malcontent or satirist). Instead, he works
through parody and calculated irrelevance, or the dissociation of received
ideas. His counterattack on public values is mobile and indirect, as, in
the opening dialogue, when he responds to the Prince's sarcasm by dig-
nifying (or affecting to dignity?) his occupation as a thief:

> Indeed you come near me now, Hal; for we that take purses go
> by the moon and the seven stars, and not by Phoebus, he, that
> wand'ring knight so fair [which disposes of Hal's question about
> "the time of the day."]
> And I prithee, sweet wag, when thou art king . . . let not us
> that are squires of the night's body be called thieves of the day's
> beauty. Let us be Diana's foresters, gentlemen of the shade,
> minions of the moon; and let men say we be men of good
> government, being governed, as the sea is, by our noble and
> chaste mistress the moon, under whose countenance we steal.
>
> (*Henry IV, Part 1*, 1.2.14-17; 24-30)

Hearing this, an Elizabethan audience must have been so sidetracked, or
delighted, by the pell-mell parodies of euphuism, balladry, popular
romance, and even of the worship of Cynthia, mistress of the sea, herself,
that they could not muster any of their proper indignation at the naked
proposal Falstaff is putting forward or at his hint that it is only fancy
names, arbitrary titles, that distinguish the honest citizen from the thief
(as Gadshill supportively observes a few scenes later, " 'homo' is a common name to all men" [2.1.97-8]).

Whatever else Falstaff may be set to do in *Henry IV*, he has begun
with the ancient comic operation of turning the world upside-down. And
soon he returns to this even more insidiously. After the Prince has re-

buffed him with reminders about the gallows and has teased him with the promise of a hangman's job, instead of the momentarily hoped-for office of a judge, Falstaff shifts his key to the Biblical:

> But, Hal, I prithee trouble me no more with vanity. I would to God thou and I knew where a commodity of good names were to be bought.

and, as if mounting the pulpit:

> An old lord of the council rated me the other day in the street about you, sir, but I marked him not; and yet he talked very wisely, but I regarded him not; and yet he talked wisely, and in the street too.
>
> *(Henry IV, Part 1,* 1.2.82-7)

Part of Falstaff's ploy here is to pretend, in all generosity, that he has been receiving blame because of Hal and not the other way about. And in the midst of his sermonizing he can suddenly swerve into a good, down-right tavernly oath: "I'll be damned for never a king's son in Christendom" (1.2.7-8). But as soon as Hal, taking his cue from this, quips him with a reminder about taking purses, Falstaff reverts to his Biblical strain: "Why, Hal, 'tis my vocation, Hal. 'Tis no sin for a man to labor in his vocation" (1.2.105-6). Critics, noting Falstaff's very frequent allusions to the Bible (particularly the book of Proverbs and the parable of the Prodigal Son), are fond of explaining that he is ridiculing the language of Puritanism; but it was equally the language of the Book of Homilies and the established Church.[7] As far as parody goes, his subversiveness is comprehensive.

Falstaff's Roles

Yet he is not simply a stage jester any more than he is simply a rogue. None of the roles that critics or other characters on the stage attribute to him define him adequately as a character or as a figure in the play. He is not, for instance, a Morality-play Vice, however he may be compared to such. Apart from anything else, it makes nonsense of his relations with Hal to think of him as a personification of the Prince's human proneness to sin or to speak as if he ever tempts the Prince successfully in the course of the play or gains any ascendancy over his will. He is not a traditional braggart soldier, if only because he is far too intelligent. He is not exactly a Lord of Misrule; if he can be said to preside over revels in Eastcheap, it is more in our imagination than in the view of his company as a whole. Nor is he exactly a trickster, or ironic buffoon, in the line of classical comedy, in spite of his aptitude for turning the world upside-down. He neither pursues any ingenious intrigue in the manner of New Comedy (though he swindles Mrs. Quickly and Shallow) nor consistently entertains any world-changing fantasy like a hero from Aristophanes. He is too deeply enmeshed in common reality to imagine that he can change the world, and he takes his adventures as they come. He is constantly improvising, assuming a role. In the extemporized play scene that marks the highest point of his concord with Hal, he revels in parodying an actor; but through all his assumed voices we can hear a voice of his own, coming out most clearly perhaps in soliloquies—of which he has more than any other speaker in the play. It seems no accident that he became, in his own name, a legendary figure, as quickly and as lastingly as Hamlet. We seem to be in the presence of a richly complex personality, with a reserve of self-awareness underneath all his clowning.

In Maurice Morgann's apologia for Falstaff, there is a striking footnote where Morgann outlines the principles that, in his view, require a critic of Shakespeare to explain the characters of Shakespeare's people "from those parts of the composition which are *inferred* only, and not distinctly shewn," and "to account for their conduct from the *whole* of character, from general principles, from latent motives, and from policies not avowed."[8] The "historic" or biographical method of interpretation that Morgann erected upon this insight has been thoroughly, perhaps too thoroughly, exploded. And in Falstaff's case, such apparently solid biographical facts as we are given—that as a boy he had been "page to Thomas Mowbray, Duke of Norfolk" and had known John of Gaunt—are not disclosed until the second half of the second play (*Henry IV, Part 2*, 3.2.26-73, 328). Nevertheless, one can hardly deny that Morgann brought out something vital about the *impression* (to use his own term) that Shakespeare gives us about Falstaff and gives us from the outset. Only, Shakespeare's methods were not biographical in anything like the way that (for example) Ibsen's methods could be so described. One of the means that Shakespeare uses is to suggest through the dialogue that a particular role will fit Falstaff or that he will display a particular disposition of mind, and then almost at once to make the character belie it. As Falstaff speaks, we perceive that the characteristics we have been led to expect of him are incorrect or incomplete or shadowy approximations at best. It quickly turns out that Hal's first description of him as Sloth and Gluttony is no more than a caricature. When he has behaved like a braggart soldier, he can switch to the ironic buffoon. When he is patently and professedly acting ("as like one of these harlotry players as ever I see!" says the Hostess [*Henry IV, Part 1*, 2.4.400-1]), it turns out that he is pleading his own cause. He is reputed to be misleading the Prince, but Falstaff himself says just the opposite, and in any case we never see him do it.

Watching or reading the play, of course, we do not sift such conflicting bits of evidence and work out a decisive verdict that would satisfy a jury in a court of law. There is nothing like the question whether Hal is really the irresponsible his father and the others suppose him to be, a question Shakespeare takes care to set at rest very soon. But with Falstaff, allegations and half-truths are allowed to remain at the back of our minds, without being clearly dispelled. We neither confirm nor reject them completely but are allowed and even prompted to imagine that they may be true, but only to limited facets of his character, or true to something in his unseen conduct off-stage. These half-defined approximations are like shadows in a picture that throw the figure into relief. To defeat our expectations, then, is part of Falstaff's comic tactics, and to keep us uncertain about the essential Falstaff is part of Shakespeare's strategy as a comic playwright. But further, Shakespeare has given Falstaff hints of an inner consciousness, at variance with his outward roles, that go some way towards justifying Morgann's search for "latent motives" and "policies not avowed."

Critics have been reluctant to consider that Falstaff has anything like a conscience or any doubts about himself. Hazlitt praises his "absolute self-possession" and "self-complacency,"[9] and Bradley insists that we laugh *with* Falstaff precisely because he is so "happy and entirely at his ease" in "his humorous superiority to everything serious, and the freedom of soul enjoyed in it."[10] And in W. H. Auden's view, "time does not exist" for Falstaff (but then Auden holds that the essential man belongs to *opera buffa*, and is out of place in *Henry IV*).[11] However, Falstaff (a "proud Jack" [*Henry IV, Part 1*, 2.4.11] to the tavern-drawers, according to Hal) is not remarkable for *bonhomie;* and he never expresses himself as cheerful or satisfied for long. On the contrary, his favorite terms of reference for his favorite subject, himself, imply, if they are taken in earnest, a sense of injury and regret for neglected valor, lost innocence, and either material or spiritual insecurity. His first speeches are questions about the future, which we are given no reason to think are totally flippant. If he can loudly contradict his years in the heat of the robbery scene ("What, ye knaves, young men must live" [2.2.92-3]), his next scene shows him affectedly brooding over them: "There lives not three good men unhanged in England; and one of them is fat, and grows old" (2.4.131-3). This cadence swerves, of course, into ludicrous self-mockery—"I would I were a weaver; I could sing psalms or anything" (2.4.133-5)—and this whole speech (125-35) is a typical mock-diatribe or mock-complaint, in which Falstaff's claims of "manhood" and self-righteousness are incongruous with one another and doubly incongruous in the light of his behavior.

Still, these are his two most frequent themes, with particular emphasis on the theme of religion. "Before I knew thee, Hal," he has affirmed, "I knew nothing; and now am I, if a man should speak truly, little better than one of the wicked" (*Henry IV, Part 1*, 1.2.93-6). And later, with no one more appreciative than Bardolph to hear him:

> Well, I'll repent, and that suddenly, while I am in some liking
> . . . And I have not forgotten what the inside of a church is
> made of, I am a peppercorn, a brewer's horse. The inside of a
> church! Company, villainous company, hath been the spoil of
> me.[12]

> (3.3.4-11)

Naturally, each of these outbursts of elderly grumbling, sorrowful grie-
vance, or rueful contrition on the part of "Monsieur Remorse," as Poins
calls him, strikes us as yet another of Falstaff's jokes. And whenever he
alludes to repentance, he quickly veers away from it. Nevertheless, persistent jokes on the same topic tell us something about what weighs on a
man's mind; it seems as if Falstaff were one of those fat men in whom a
thin man is struggling to get out. Without probing into "latent motives,"
Shakespeare has portrayed in him, not "absolute self-possession," but the
condition of mind of a man of intellectual power, wounded in his self-
esteem and conscience, who cannot bring himself to do anything about it,
but finds an escape from his self-image in joking. Far from expressing
"self-complacency" or complete "freedom of soul," his "humorous
superiority to everything serious," if it exists, seems to be gained at the
cost of self-mockery—which mocks the world as well, in order to redress
the balance. But without the potential, camouflaged seriousness in his
jokes (together with the background of seriousness in the political action
in the play), many of them would lose their force and point.

To return to his first scene for an example:

> But, Hal, I prithee trouble me no more with vanity. I would
> to God thou and I knew where a commodity of good names
> were to be bought. . . .

> (*Henry IV, Part 1*, 1.2.82-4)

The word *vanity*, which initiates Falstaff's diversion to Biblical parody, is
not simply a pretended rebuke to Hal's "unsavory similes" (1.2.80) but
also an oblique acknowledgment of the seriousness running through their
previous talk, particularly by way of Hal's references to hanging. And
the irony about "good names" (loaded with the word *commodity*, which
usually has a smack of skulduggery about it in Shakespeare)[13] would lose
half its dramatic point if it were no more than a capricious quip or satiric
sidethrust against the established order. There is the second irony that
Falstaff is pretending to be in earnest, while hinting to the Prince, without
openly admitting, that on another level he is seriously engaged as well.
That the two ironies should work against one another both contributes
to the continuity of Falstaff's part in the play and adds to the store of
laughter from uncertainty in the minds of the audience.

By way of contrast, consider the tone Shakespeare was to give to an
ironist of a different stamp, Iago:

> Good name in man and woman, dear my lord,
> Is the immediate jewel of their souls.
> Who steals my purse steals trash; 'tis something,
> > nothing. . . .
>
> > > > (*Othello*, 3.3.157-9)

These are the sententious accents of hypocrisy. Iago is quite indifferent to the maxim he is manipulating, and must be felt to be indifferent so that we can concentrate on the effect of his words upon Othello, whereas Falstaff knows very well that he is not really pulling the wool over the eyes of the Prince, but he is personally, if covertly, involved in what he says.

Once or twice in *Part 1* this concern shows more directly. When Falstaff has to hide from the sheriff, Hal tells the others, "Now, my masters, for a true face and good conscience" (2.4.506-7) while Falstaff exists with an aside—"Both of which I have had; but their date is out, and therefore I'll hide me" (2.4.508-9). And as he approaches the battle-field, he is given his second soliloquy. Since he comes on here in the con-temporary guise of a fraudlent recruiting officer and since this is the first time he has gained any profit in the course of the play, we should expect to find him in a mood of malicious glee if he were simply a conventional stage rogue or Morality Vice. But instead, he is unexpectedly "ashamed":

> If I be not ashamed of my soldiers, I am a soused gurnet. I
> have misused the king's press damnably . . . No eye hath seen
> such scarecrows. I'll not march through Coventry with them,
> that's flat. . . .
>
> > > (*Henry IV, Part 1*, 4.2.11-13; 38-40)

He shrugs off this mood almost at once:

> There's not a shirt and a half in all my company . . . But that's
> all one; they'll find linen enough on every hedge.
>
> > > > (42-3.47-8)

We are very nearly back to the atmosphere of Eastcheap and Gad's Hill. All the same, the tone of genuine surprise, a novel tone in Falstaff's voice, shows that there has been a progression in his part. The war becomes a testing experience for Falstaff as, on a very different scale, it becomes a testing experience for Hal. It imparts a continuous movement to Fal-staff's share in the play, from his early, half-comic protest to Hal—"I must give over this life, and I will give it over!" (1.2.46-7)—to the slyly condi-tional resolution or prediction in his last soliloquy, which is also his closing speech:

> If I do grow great, I'll grow less; for I'll purge [*repent*], and
> leave sack, and live cleanly, as a nobleman should do.
>
> > > > (5.4.161-4)

From beginning to end in Part 1, Falstaff is engaged with the passage of time, with concern about the future.

Falstaff and the Theme of Time

The theme of time is crucial to Shakespeare's presentation of what Edward Hall had described as "The Unquiet Time of King Henry IV." The guiding thought in the overplot of *Part 1* is the thought of "redeeming time," with implications at once religious,[14] financial, chivalric, and political. In financial terms, it branches out by way of talk about ransom and theft, auditing, debt, and repayment, to return, as it were, to the main line of the action by way of Hal's determination to "pay the debt I never promised. Redeeming time when men think least I will" (1.2.206; 214). In the opening scene, though he does not use the word, Henry IV dwells on the thought of the Redeemer (1.1.18-27). Shakespeare has antedated his project to lead a crusade, treating it as Henry's intended means of absolving England from civil war and, by inference, absolving himself from his guilt as an usurper.[15] Hotspur, eager to "redeem" "drowned honor," (1.3.205), tells his father and uncle that "yet time serves wherein you may redeem/ Your banished honors" (1.3.178-9)—by changing allegiance for a second time in rebellion.[16] On his side, Hal promises to "redeem" his reputation "on Percy's head" and his father confirms that he has "redeemed . . . lost opinion" in the battle (3.2.132; 5.4.46). For the leading political actors, "time serves," not to achieve honor, like knights-errant, but to redeem the honor they have already lost, or appear to have lost.

Falstaff and the Political World

With his ignoble ambition to find out "where a commodity of good names were to be bought," (*Henry IV, Part 1*, 1.2.83-4) Falstaff is a parody of this political world. In Hal's company he is like a grotesque father-substitute, and he echoes the king in his grumbles over time misspent. His lawlessness and braggartism throw light on Hotspur. Above all, Falstaff is a man in a false position, just as the king, Hotspur, and Hal are all, in their different ways, men in false positions. But Falstaff, of course, has the saving grace of humor. He has an inclusive, if usually ironic, self-awareness that men like Henry IV and Hotspur cannot afford, though some of it seems to have rubbed off onto Hal. This is the obverse of his comic "remorse": not a "superiority to everything serious" or simply an addiction to the pleasures of the flesh, but a warm belief in the immediacy and, in the end, authenticity, of his personal existence. "Banish plump Jack, and banish all the world!" (2.4.484-5) he exlaims to Hal, as their improvised play-acting breaks down in a moment of truth;

and then, as he prepares to hide from the sheriff, "Dost thou hear, Hal? Never call a true piece of gold a counterfeit" (2.4.496-7). This cryptic admonition takes on fuller significance later, in the battle scenes. Falstaff's development there, in close proximity to the political actors, is far from one-sided. His cynical betrayal of his troop of "rag-of-muffins" (5.3.36) matches Worcester's double dealing. His low-minded "discretion" is pitched against Hotspur's high-minded but futile "valor" (117-8). The conclusion to his famous "catechism," that "Honor is a mere scutcheon" (*Henry IV, Part 1*, 5.1.140) cannot efface the resplendent heroism that Shakespeare gives the Prince, though it still leaves the purely chivalric motives in war and politics open to question.

But at the same time, as at the beginning of the play, the dramatist sets Falstaff in relation to the king, by his arrangement of the kaleidoscopic battle episodes. Taking a hint from Holinshed's statement that at Shrewsbury there were several knights "apparelled in the king's suit and clothing" (but reducing the chronicler's emphasis on the king's "high manhood"),[17] Shakespeare shows two episodes in which Douglas is engaged with the "likeness" or the "shadows" or the "counterfeit" of the king. In the first (*Henry IV, Part 1*, 5.3.1-29) Douglas kills Sir Walter Blunt, as he says he has already killed Lord Stafford, believing him to be the king himself, until Hotspur undeceives him ("The king hath many marching in his coats"). In the second (5.4.23-36), meeting the king in person, he can hardly believe that Henry is not "another counterfeit." Hal drives Douglas off. Then, while Hal encounters Hotspur in resonantly epic style, in the action to which the whole course of the play has pointed, Douglas reenters briefly and, in dumb show, apparently kills Falstaff.

But as soon as Falstaff has been left alone on the stage, he jumps up again, undercutting the lofty tones of the champions' verse in his savory prose:

> 'Sblood, 'twas time to counterfeit, or that hot termagant Scot had paid me scot and lot too. Counterfeit? I lie; I am no counterfeit. To die is to be a counterfeit, for he is but the counterfeit of a man who hath not the life of a man; but to counterfeit dying when a man thereby liveth, is to be no counterfeit, but the true and perfect image of life indeed. . . .
> (*Henry IV, Part 1*, 5.4.111-17)

In this folk-play-style sham resurrection, and in his farcical sham killing of Hotspur immediately afterwards, Falstaff counteracts the high talk of politics and war. Courage in battle has been shown as a reality in the play, and the need for royal authority has been vindicated. But the political scenes have revealed expediency, double dealing, and even a kind of inward privation, not because Henry IV has been shown as a downright Machiavellian like Richard III, but because his rule has been established on false foundations and because the forward drives of conflicting political interests have generated their own ruthless momentum. Falstaff's counterfeiting here revives basic human impulses which the affairs of state would have thwarted or excluded.

The Function of Shadows in the *Henry IV* Plays

At Shrewsbury, Henry has safeguarded his life by the employment of "shadows." In another sense also, Shakespeare has extensively used "shadows" in both parts of the play to give life and imagined reality to the world in which Henry and Falstaff belong. History could be said to require that the action should shift across the country between north and south and that the main actors should refer to characters and events that are not shown on the stage. But in *Henry IV* Shakespeare has taken particular pains, more I think than in any other of his plays, to go beyond the strict requirements of dramatizing history and conjure up the thought of England as a country and, even more strikingly, to conjure up images of individuals offstage, known to the speakers in the play though unrecorded by the chroniclers.

What is at stake in the Percies' rebellion is the territory of England— "this soil," as Henry calls it in his opening lines (*Henry IV, Part 1*, 1.1.5). Shakespeare imagines this, in its continuity and specific variety, as no other poet before him had done. In the first scene of *Part 1*, for instance, we hear of "stronds" and "fields" and "acres," of Herefordshire and Windsor, and all "the variation of each soil/ Betwixt that Holmedon and this seat of ours" (64-5). Later, in the scene between Hotspur, Mortimer, and Glendower, a map is an essential property. And when Hotspur falls, Hal reflects that

> When that this body did contain a spirit
> A kingdom for it was too small a bound;
> But now two paces of the vilest earth
> Is room enough. The earth that bears thee dead
> Bears not alive so stout a gentlemen.
>
> (5.4.87-91)

Meanwhile, we have heard, for instance, of "Severn's sedgy bank" and of Berkeley Castle (the name Hotspur cannot remember [1.3.97; 240-6]) of Moorditch and the Wild of Kent and Falstaff's route through Coventry. And in *Part 2*, to say nothing of Falstaff's boasted acquaintance with "all Europe" (2.2.133), we hear of Northumberland's "worm-eaten hole of ragged stone" at Warkworth (Induction 135), of Oxford and Stamford fair, and particularly of localities in or near London—Eastcheap, the St. Alban's road, Clement's Inn, Mile-End Green, Turnbull Street, Windsor, the Jerusalem chamber, the Fleet. Both parts are busy with the images of messengers, especially horsemen, hurrying with instructions or news or rushing to or from a battlefield. And each virtually begins with a striking image of this sort, of Sir Walter Blunt "new lighted" (*Henry IV, Part 1*, 1.1.63) after his long ride from Holmedon or of the unnamed gentleman met by Northumberland's servant, Travers, "spurring hard" and "almost forspent with speed" on his "bloodied horse," who had paused only to ask the road to Chester and then "seemed in running to devour the way" (*Henry IV, Part 2*, 1.1.36; 37; 38; 47) in his headlong flight from Shrewsbury. Amid all this evocation of England's place-names and roads and "uneven ground" (*Henry IV, Part 1*, 2.2.25) the earthy and earthbound figure of Falstaff seems solidly congenial; he "lards the lean earth as he walks along" (2.2.111-12).

Even closer to the sense of animated reality in both parts of the play are the allusive sketches of nonhistorical characters whom we hear of though never see. In *Part 1*, they range from the "old lord of the council" who (allegedly) had "rated" Falstaff about Hal "the other day in the street" (1.2.85-6) by way of Hotspur's acid sketch of the "popingay" who had "so pest'red" (1.3.49) him after the fighting at Holmedon (the "certain lord" whose "chin new reaped/ Showed like a stubble land at harvest home" [1.32-4]—men and country are thought of together), on to the "mad fellow" by the wayside who had taunted Falstaff about his troop of "tattered prodigals," and to the prodigals' victim, "the rednose innkeeper at Daventry" (4.2.36; 34-5; 47). These marginal, off-stage figures, shadowlike but with separate lives of their own, intensify our sense of varied life in the stage characters themselves. They supply precisely what Morgann would call "those parts of the composition which are *inferred* only, and not distinctly shewn."

They are even more numerous in *Part 2*, especially in direct or indirect contact with Falstaff. Falstaff's first dialogue opens with a sarcasm reported from his doctor and with the knight's abuse of that "yea-forsooth knave" (1.2.36), his obdurate mercer, Master Dummelton. (It is striking how, in *Part 2*, off-stage characters, as well as minor actors on the stage, are now given expressive, caricatural names).[18] Through Mrs. Quickly's chatter, we hear of her "gossip," "goodwife Keech, the butcher's wife" (2.1.92-3) and of "Master Tisick, the deputy," who had admonished her while "Master Dumbe, our minister" (2.4.86; 89) was standing by. And in Shallow's scenes, at least (on my count) sixteen off-stage characters are identified, mostly by the aging justice himself—from the three invisible Silences he asks after, and the four "swinge-bucklers" and old Double (the bowman beloved of John of Guant), recalled from his "Inns o' Court" days (3.2.23) back to the "arrant knave" (5.1.42) William Visor of Woncot, whom nevertheless his servant Davy trusts he will "countenance" (5.1.39) in a lawsuit. With the help of names like Keech (butcher's fat), Simon Stockfish, Jane Nightwork, and Silence's champion fat man, "goodman Puff of Barson" (5.3.93-4) as well as with drinking episodes and snatches of song, these Boar's Head and Cotswold scenes project a continuing, subdued impression as of a sort of scrimmage between representatives of Carnival and of Lent. From another point of view, it is a confused medley between everyday rascality and everyday law, complicating and enriching the historical theme of high justice, now central to the main plot. And with grimly sympathetic touches, sharp as engravings by Callot, these profusely inventive comic scenes bring home the rhythm of insignificant lives and insignificant deaths that shadow the high historical drama of war and statecraft. Moreover, they contribute something vital to the state of mind or quality of experience projected by *Part 2* as a whole, especially by way of Justice Shallow, that marvellous late-comer to *Henry IV*, with his trivial comforts and his senile reminiscenes.

The predominant experience conveyed by *Part 2*, it seems to me, is the experience of uncertainty. It is the uncertainty, suspense, indecision that Northumberland expresses when he says:

> 'Tis with my mind
> As with the tide swelled up unto his height,
> That makes a still-stand, running neither way.

> (2.3.62-4)

Shakespeare makes the historical action unexciting, by contrast with *Part 1*, showing the rebellion suppressed, well before the end, by cold-blooded stratagem, not by fighting. He reduces even the death of Northumberland in battle to an incidental anticlimax, stripping it of the animation of circumstantial report (*Henry IV, Part 2*, 4.4.97-101). He treats the the passage of history he is dealing with as an interim period, a period of waiting rather than doing, thus throwing new emphasis on the way the actors perceive themselves as "time's subject" (1.3.110), peering into the future, reconsidering the past. One of his innovations in both parts of *Henry IV*, concurrent with the use of so many off-stage personalities, is the way Shakespeare now makes his characters recall past events at length, and this is particularly noticeable and effective in *Part 2*. The historical speakers think back to the battle of Shrewsbury and its antecedents—even, while Henry is dying, to the time before Richard II, as the anxious princes recall omens and popular beliefs preceding the death of Edward III:

> The river hath thrice flowed, no ebb between,
> And the old folk, time's doting chronicles,
> Say it did so a little time before
> That our great-grandsire, Edward, sicked and died.

> (4.4.125-8)

This speech echoes both Northumberland's image about the tide and the theme introduced in the prologue by Rumour, the theme of "surmises" and "conjectures," of "Conjecture, expectation, and surmise" (Induction 16; 1.3.23).

Throughout the play, remembrance of the past is set in tension against "likelihoods and forms of hope" (*Henry IV, Part 2*, 1.3.35) about the future or else "forms imaginary" (4.4.59) of apprehension, which run from the uncertainities agitating the rebel camp in the early scenes to the anxieties, even in victory, surrounding the deathbed of Henry IV. It is this form of mental tension, this general human experience, that Shakespeare is dramatizing here (though it must have struck a specially contemporary chord at the moment when the play first appeared). About midway (in Act 3, scene 1), there is a turning point in the speeches rehearsing past events, when Henry has been questioning his whole troubled career and Warwick tries to explain that "There is a history in all men's lives" (3.1.80) linking past and future in intelligible sequence. Whereupon the king exlaims, "Are these things then necessities?/ Then let us meet them like necessities" (3.1.92-3). But even here, what emerges is the expression of a frame of mind, not any decision affecting the plot. It is the characters' attitude towards current realities that Shakespeare is concerned with. As in *Part 1*, they are conscious of the pressures of "time." But in *Part 2*, it is more especially "the condition of these *times*" that preoccupies them—"The times are wild" . . . "these coster-mongers' times" . . . "the revolution of the times"—together with the signs they seem to hold about the "times that you shall look upon" (4.1.99; 1.1.93; 1.2.70-1; 3.1.46; 4.4.60).

"Old folk" dominate the stage in *Part 2*, whereas youth is either dead and gone with Hotspur or subject to fears about the future with Hal (whose glory gained at Shrewsbury is kept, for good dramatic reasons, out of sight).[19] As L. C. Knights has pointed out, *Part 2* dwells on "age, disappointment and decay."[20] But this elegiac mood is countered in the comic scenes by the enjoyment of immediate, if trivial, pleasures, such as Mrs. Quickly's appreciation of goodwife Keech's "good dish of prawns" (2.1.95) or Shallow's enjoyment of "any pretty little tiny kickshaws" to be produced by "William cook" (5.1.28) and his anticipation of eating "a last year's pippin of [his] own graffing, with a dish of caraways, and so forth" (5.3.2-3). On the other side, Hal is obliged to regret that his princely appetite can still "remember the poor creature, small beer. But indeed," he adds, "these humble considerations make me out of love with my greatness" (2.2.10-12). Such "humble considerations" are made to seem relatively timeless; particularly where, towards the climax for Falstaff, Shakespeare cuts from the scene of preparations for dinner at Shallow's house (Act 5, scene 1) to the scene at London announcing Henry IV's death and showing Henry V's reconciliation with the Chief

Justice, and then back to Shallow's house for the fruit (Act 5, scene 3)—
as if, for the moment, the national crisis belonged not only to a different
world but to a different order of time. Yet the distinction between the
low world and the high is finely shaded. There is no more than a shaky
grasp of reality in Mrs. Quickly's muddled, rambling, suggestible mind,
and in Shallow's gullible self-importance and his vanity about the past.
Doll Tearsheet and Silence are complementary, if opposite, types. Altogether, since he is kept at a distance from the Prince, Falstaff's chosen
company in *Part 2* is more easygoing, less sharp-witted, than his company
in *Part 1*.

There are corresponding changes in Falstaff himself. In spite of the
credit he has gained, with the help of Rumour, from Shrewsbury, he still
depends ultimately on patronage from Hal. But he is thrown more upon
his own resources, so that his capture of a prisoner of war seems like an
accident; and the main line of his action, until the last moments of the
play, is a spiraling progress from debt to debt. We see more of his social
versatility than before, but we also hear more of his private reflection, as
he sizes up himself and his world. He can inspire affection, at least the
maudlin affection of Doll and Mrs. Quickly. He is given less to outbursts
of "remorse" than before and more to exploiting the world as he finds
it: "A good wit will make use of anything. I will turn diseases to commodity" (something he can sell, this time, not something he wants to buy
[*Henry IV, Part 2*, 1.2.250-1]). He will fleece Justice Shallow if he can,
on the strength of their old acquaintance, in sardonic complicity with
"the law of nature" (3.2.336). He is as evasive and resourceful as before,
but less impulsive, more detached and calculating. We hear more of the
mellow, observant, leisured cadences in his prose. He is more of a philosopher and more of a rogue.

A recurrent subject of wryly amused reflection with Falstaff, in
connection with the Page and then Prince John and finally Shallow, is
the inequality between the Fat and the Lean. What occupies his mind is
not so much thoughts of his own age and sickness, which he will evade if
he can, as the contrast between his sense of implantation in life and the
unsteadiness of his fortunes. His antipathy to Prince John inspires his
most elaborate set speech (*Henry IV, Part 2*, 4.3.86-125), his soliloquy of
mock-humanistic encomium in praise of drink and of wine-inspired wit,
"apprehensive, quick, forgetive, full of nimble, fiery and delectable
shapes" (4.3.99-101). This is his most defiant plea for laughter and his
own style of life. But his meeting with Shallow has begun to elicit another style from Falstaff, more objectively humorous but also more
contemplative, as he measures the squire's history against his own. "Lord,
Lord, how subject we old men are to this vice of lying!" (3.2.307-8) is a
spontaneous (if ironic) reflection, not a set speech. And his first, richly
grotesque, soliloquy about Shallow and how "This same starved justice
hath done nothing but prate to me of the wildness of his youth" (3.2.

308-10) is also Falstaff's first excursion of any length into his own past (3.2.305-37); but—"now has he land and heeves" (3.2.332). His second soliloquy on the same topic (5.1.64-88) is more detached, with exactly balanced clauses of amused observation:

> If I were sawed into quantities, I should make four dozen of such bearded hermits' staves as Master Shallow. It is a wonderful thing to see the semblable coherence of his men's spirits and his. They, by observing him, do bear themselves like foolish justices. He, by conversing with them, is turned into a justice-like serving-man. . . . It is certain that either wise bearing or ignorant carriage is caught, as men take diseases, one of another. Therefore let men take heed of their company. . . .
>
> *(Henry IV, Part 2*, 5.1.64-71; 77-80)

This has the ring of shrewd, almost homely, unforced practical wisdom, so much that the dramatic irony in the last sentence is almost submerged. This speech marks the high point of Falstaff's role as an unruffled humorous critic of mechanical behavior in other men. He goes on to anticipate how he will make "Prince Harry" laugh over Shallow, though with a rueful glance at the gap between jester and patron—"a fellow that never had the ache in his shoulders!" (*Henry IV, Part 2*, 5.1.80-2; 85-6). In his next scene (Act 5, scene 3), the news that Pistol (of all select companions) brings from court releases a mechanism in Falstaff himself, in the wild dream that "the laws of England are at my commandment" (5.3.140-1).

It seems almost impossible for critics to agree about the rejection of Falstaff. Perhaps this shows a flaw in the writing of the play as a whole. Admittedly, there is a jarring note in Henry's rejection speech, though on the other hand the whole action ends on an unheroic note of subdued expectation, on the *diminuendo* of a half-line of verse. But perhaps also those who, like Bradley, deplore the dismissal of a comic spirit of freedom and those who, like Dover Wilson, justify the regal severity of Henry V, both minimize the comic side of Falstaff's downfall and his own share in bringing it about. A Falstaff temperate enough to approach the new king for favors privately or submissive enough to wait until sent for would be less funny than the Falstaff we see. A more amiable separation from Hal would be less in keeping with the character of Falstaff and less true to the logic of comedy, which does not require benevolence, still less indulgence, so much as what Shaw called disillusionment or, rather, a developed engagement between our sense of reality and fixed habits of human behavior or else between realism and voluntary fantasy. But a realistic appraisal of the sustained business of government cannot be the province of comedy, as distinct from satire, at all.

The two Parts of *Henry IV* form an unprecedented study of statecraft and of the relations of statecraft to other sides of life. More than any other English plays, I think, they suggest the continuousness of the life of a whole people, through space and time and the mixture of typical human qualities. As such they must include more than comedy. On the other hand, the inclusive vision they contain of the ways men and women of different sorts confront social reality gives perspective and more salience than entirely comic surroundings could provide to the uniquely comic figure of Falstaff.

Notes

1. Henri Bergson, *Laughter* (1900), Eng. trans. in Wylie Sypher, ed., *Comedy* (Garden City, N.Y.: Doubleday, 1956), pp. 79, 97.

2. Albert Thibaudet, *Le Bergsonisme* (Paris, 1923), II, 93; cf. pp. 59-60.

3. See Harry Levin, "Falstaff Uncolted" (1946), in *Shakespeare and the Revolution of the Times* (New York: Oxford Univ. Press, 1976).

4. See A. R. Humphreys, ed., *1 Henry IV*, New Arden ed. (London: Methuen, 1960), p. 71n.

5. Thomas Nashe, *Pierce Penniless* (1592), in *Selected Works*, ed. Stanley Wells (Stratford-upon-Avon Library, London: Arnold, 1964), p. 55. Cf. parallels with Nashe in *1 Henry IV*, ed. John Dover Wilson, New Cambridge ed. (Cambridge: Cambridge Univ. Press, 1946), pp. 191-6.

6. William Empson, "Falstaff and Mr. Dover Wilson" (1953), in *Shakespeare, Henry IV, Parts I and II; a Casebook*, ed. G. K. Hunter (London: Macmillan, 1970 [referred to below as *Casebook*]), p. 145.

7. See Richmond Noble, *Shakespeare's Biblical Knowledge* (London: Society for Promoting Christian Knowledge, 1935), pp. 169-81.

8. Maurice Morgann, "As Essay on the Dramatic Character of Sir John Falstaff" (1777). in *Eighteenth Century Essays on Shakespeare*, ed. D. Nichol Smith, 2d ed. (Oxford: Oxford Univ. Press, 1963), p. 230n.

9. William Hazlitt, *Characters of Shakespear's Plays*, in *Liber Amoris and Dramatic Criticism*, ed. Charles Morgan (London: Peter Nevill, 1948), p. 309.

10. A. C. Bradley, "The Rejection of Falstaff" (1902), in *Oxford Lectures on Poetry*, 2d ed. (London: Macmillan, 1909), pp. 261, 269.

11. W. H. Auden, "The Prince's Dog" (1959), in *Casebook*, p. 188.

12. Cf. *Henry IV, Part 1*, 1.2.83-4; 2.2.10-20; 3.4.334-6; 3.3.172-6; and so on.

13. Cf. *King John*, 2.1.561-98; *Measure for Measure*, 4.3.5. (Perhaps Falstaff is thinking of *Proverbs*, xxii.1 at this point; cf. Noble, p. 169.)

14. See Paul A. Jorgensen, " 'Redeeming Time' in Shakespeare's *Henry IV*" (1960), in *Casebook*, pp. 231-42.

15. See Holinshed, in *Narrative and Dramatic Sources of Shakespeare*, ed. Geoffrey Bullough, IV (London: Routledge, 1962), p. 276.

16. *Henry IV, Part 1*, 1.3.84-7; 178-80; 183-4; 203-5.

17. Holinshed, in Bullough, IV, 191.

18. See A. R. Humphreys, ed., *2 Henry IV*, New Arden ed. (London: Methuen, 1966), p. 20n; Levin, "Shakespeare's Nomenclature" (1963), in *Shakespeare and the Revolution of the Times*, pp. 70, 75.

19. See Humphreys, ed., *2 Henry IV*, Intro., p. xxvi.

20. L. C. Knights, "Time's Subjects: The Sonnets and *2 Henry IV*," in *Some Shakespearean Themes* (London: Chatto and Windus, 1959) (*Casebook*, p. 174).

Bibliographical Note

This essay has been based in part on Bergson's *Laughter*, in Wylie Sypher's collection, *Comedy*, with some help from W. D. Howarth's Introduction to *Comic Drama, the European Heritage*, ed. Howarth (Methuen: London, 1978) and in part on Morgann's essay on Falstaff and modern studies represented in the *Casebook*, ed. G. K. Hunter. A. R. Humphreys' Introductions to his New Arden editions of *Henry IV, Parts 1* and *2* have been particularly useful.

17

Strategies of Inconclusiveness in *Henry IV, Part 1*

ELIZABETH FREUND

The Mimetic Predicament

> . . . *the purpose of playing . . . both at the first and now, was and is, to hold as 'twere the mirror up to nature . . .*
> Hamlet *3.2.20-22*

"The truest poetry of the most feigning," Touchstone informs his witless country wench (*As You Like It* 3.3.18-19). His pun, as indeed his mock-romantic context, compresses a latent theory of Shakespearean comedy in the implosive linkage of "desire" and "duplicity."[1] "Through duplicity to desire" may prove an interesting attempt to recast C. L. Barber's authoritative comic formula along the lines of those rhetorical models whose antithetical and paradoxical configurations Renaissance writers so virogously and lovingly explored. It may be even more germane to take our cue from Touchstone's conflation of "true" and "false," an interplay of opposites which invites particular attention to the complexly self-conscious and self-referential rhetoricity of Shakespeare's mimetic modes.

Critical consensus fosters the commonplace that Shakespearean comedy is identified by a teleological form whose end is the reaffirmation of an ideal of concord and reconcilement usually celebrated in marriage. The Shakespearean comic idea postulates an action informed by a dialectical design that moves through knots of misconceptions, mistaken identities or misconstrued values, inhibitory complications and perturbations, all of which are ultimately remedied by timely reversals and (self) recognitions. Such formulations abide by a rigorously Aristotelian notion of plot as a working through to an ending that will satisfactorily resolve and conclude entanglement, combining all elements in some idyllic and harmonious integration.

Not that the less-than-complete nature of this achieved harmony has passed unnoticed. Debate continues to thrive around the shadow cast by a rejected Shylock or a Malvolio. The equivocal success of Katherine's "taming," the implausibility of Bertram's reformation, the aborted "revels" in Navarre, or the perfunctory resolution in Vienna are all matters that reopen the issue of conclusiveness and its intrinsic relationship to comic form. For these and other like instances of dissonance, ambiguity, or discontinuity, which obstinately resist the notion of integration, resolution, and conclusiveness, we have coined the handy and flexible class of "problem plays," available in a large variety of darker or lighter tones. This type of debate or reclassification, however, merely implies that these plays are experimental sallies and deviations from a firmly rooted and normative idea of comic form and, therefore, essentially reconfirms its currency in the critical tradition.

The teleological view of comic form is also related to the tacit and no less hardy notion that all of Shakespeare's plays, whether cheerfully comic, problematic, or tragic, "hold the mirror up to nature." The mirror, we are asked to believe, displays Life or Nature or some great universal Truth, either in the form of reality-as-is or reality-as-wished. The speculative and suspiciously tautological nature of such mirroring has only recently become a topic of investigation.[2] Trompe l'oeil perspectives and their verbal analogues subvert our preconceptions of "plot" and "character" as lifelike imitations.[3]

It is not my intention to contribute one more theory of comedy to the existing roster, but rather to offer a few tentative and empirical reflections upon the constraints and limitations of organicist and mimetic theories of comic form. My point of departure is deliberately oblique and confined: *Henry IV, Part 1* is Shakespeare's most exuberantly comic creation, though not strictly speaking (that is, generically, teleologically, or thematically) a comedy. It is my belief that Shakespeare's comic history, sui generis, can serve as a remarkably instructive instance of the limits of our thematically (and, by extension, didactically) oriented discussion of form.

This is the case of a plot whose main thrust is discovered in strategies

of delay, dallying, and evasion. The representation exhibits historical
characters locked in the deliberately obscure motives of calculating and
reckoning an unaccountable debt. The protagonists' attempts to recon-
stitute what really happened are mocked and obfuscated by the confusing
interplay of desire and duplicity to which memory is prey. Above all,
they are, like Feste, veritable "corrupters" of words, and the representation
of motive is enmeshed in the duplicitous rhetoric of a language inescapably prone, as Puttenham was acutely aware, "to deceive the eare
and also the minde, drawing it from plainnesse and simplicitie to a certain
doublenesse, whereby our talke is the more guileful and abusing."[4]   The
evasiveness of the play's rhetoric is matched and reinforced by the action's
shuttling nonprogression toward the inconclusive nonending of the Battle
of Shrewsbury. The entire mode is informed by an ironic interplay of
multiple perspectives. Such an extreme and self-proclaimed case of inconclusiveness may serve as a worthwhile gloss upon Shakespeare's mimetic
craft and the dramaturgy of feigning. It is as if, for an entire performance,
we watch Touchstone's text writ large.

When Is a Recognition Scene Not a Recognition Scene?

> PRINCE.   These lies are like their father that begets them—
> gross as a mountain, open, palpable. Why, thou clay-brained
> guts, thou knotty-pated fool, thou whoreson obscene tallow-
> catch—
> FALSTAFF.   What, art thou mad? Art thou mad? Is not the
> truth the truth?
>
> Henry IV Part 1, 2.4.226-31

The tavern in *Henry IV, Part 1* is an exemplary experimental stage
for the rehearsing and mastering of the art of feigning. On this stage are
projected scenes of densely manipulative enactments of both duplicity
and desire, as Hal and Falstaff practice answers and practice upon each
other. Proleptically they play, but only to delay, the mandatory recognition scene in the mock rejection of Falstaff. The dynamics of their
play, their impersonations, pretences, and deceptions provide a prototype
of the ironic strategies of the play at large and the practice of these
strategies upon us, the audience, to sweep us into the experience of inconclusiveness.
    In the "men in buckram" sequence, the motive of Falstaff's escalat-
ing, braggadocio recounting of his heroic engagement with two-four-
seven-eleven men, though greatly entertaining, remains obscure. Part of
the fun derives from the straightforward irony of our superior awareness
of the circumstances of the robbery (exhibited two scenes earlier) and our
complicity with the masked Hal and Poins as they stalk their prey. Such
gaps of awareness are the source of an effect of privileged one-upmanship

traditionally recognized as dramatic irony. That, after all, was the point of the ruse: "The virtue of this jest will be the incomprehensible lies this same fat rogue will tell us when we meet at supper: how thirty, at least, he fought with, what wards, what blows, what extremities he endured; and in the reproof of this lives the jest" (1.2.183-87). And that is precisely how the action proceeds to unfold as Hal's litotes threatens to explode Falstaff's outrageous hyperbole: "Mark how a plain tale shall put you down. Then did we two set on you four and, with a word, outfaced you from your prize" (2.4.256-59).

At this juncture of the game, before Falstaff's astonishing about-face, we have a perfect example of the essentially dramatic origins of irony: a contest between two kinds of duplicity, in which the *eiron*—sly, resourceful, dissembling subject—regularly triumphs over his object, the boastful *alazon.* But when Falstaff proceeds to counter with his own ironically ludic-ruse, "I knew ye as well as he that made ye" *(Henry IV, Part 1,* 2.4 270-71), he undermines the original deployment of awareness and the situation becomes a case of handy-dandy—which is the *eiron* and which the *alazon*?—as the *alazon* contrives to absorb into his imposture the ironic stance of omniscient and superior awareness.

It is the transformation rather than the typology that is my concern. When the imposter, supposedly unmasked by a plain unvarnished tale, is dialectically absorbed into the ironic dissembler, the strategy has become an ingeniously tricky and unsettling variant of the classical theatrical contest. Who is the mocker and who is the mocked? The moment of expanding complacency that accompanies our expectation of impending exposure suddenly narrows into an uncertainty of perception: for the quick agility with which Falstaff turns the tables has the paradoxical effect of planting a flickering doubt in our minds that what we know to be a lie may indeed be a truth. Perhaps he did know them all the time and was taking them on in a shrewd and masterful performance of their own game of one-upmanship. After all, the circumstantial evidence is contradictory and inconclusive. The hacking of swords and tickling of noses with speargrass suggest elaborate tactics of camouflage for the purpose of deceiving.

Yet Falstaff exuberantly and recklessly subverts his own labors to create the illusion of verisimilitude with wildly imprudent exaggerations that beg to be disbelieved. Besides, Hal's contemptuous account of how Falstaff roared for mercy and still ran and roared is not exactly corroborated by the stage directions in the robbery scene. Little wonder, then, that critics have been led into passionate debates about whether Falstaff is or isn't a coward. The truth about this matter is, of course, entirely beside the dramatic point. And so to a certain extent is the computation of inconclusive evidence for and against. More immediately germane to our experience of this moment in the dramatizing process is the contrivance of instant reversibility (and hence uncertainty), effected through verbal mask. "What goes forth as A returns as non-A" is Kenneth Burke's overall formula for the dialectic of irony.[5]

Such transformations of the relationship between disjunctives have the consequent effect of creating, dismantling, and recreating doubts about every motive. Falstaff is surely the case of the theater's greatest comic *alazon*, who is simultaneously its shrewdest and most subversive *eiron*. As such, he is a superb manifestation of what Richard Lanham calls the rhetorical type of life, "forever rehearsing a spontaneous real life" with no reassuring, referent reality to fall back upon, no center to keep faith with except its own pleasure and expediency.[6]

The Rhetoric of the Counterfeit Self

> *As if a man were author of himself*
> *And knew no other kin.*
>
> Coriolanus 5.3.36-37

The problemized motivation behind the actions in the tavern directs us toward the further perception that it is a rhetoric of feigning which functions to construct character. Its histrionic counterpart is the mask. There is an inherent and irresolvable paradox in a mask. By definition it conceals, yet by the same token the mode of concealing exhibits, displays, even magnifies some other face. This presence of two centers of reference creates an anxiety of authenticity analogous to Puttenham's ethical concern with the slippery ambivalence of figures. "As figures be the instruments of ornament," he says, "so be they also in a sorte abuses or rather trespasses in speech. . . . For what els is your *Metaphor* but an inversion of sence by transport; your *Allegorie* but a duplicitie of meaning or dissimulation under covert and darke intendments. . . . *Aenigma* . . . *Paremia* . . . *Ironia* . . . *Sarcasmus* . . . *Hyperbole*, and many other waies seeking to inveigle and appassionate the mind."[7]

The elliptical double foci that bedevil Puttenham's conception of figurative language (and perhaps all language, recent investigations lead us to believe, is figurative and infinitely elusive) similarly "appassionate" the mind's perception of fictional characters that reflect on their own antic dispositions.

The rhetoric of the counterfeit self is openly inaugurated by Falstaff in Act 1, scene 2 (although it is demonstrably there from the play's first scene and throughout, but that must remain outside the scope of this paper) when he playfully turns to his "most comparative, rascalliest, sweet young prince . . . I would to God thou and I knew where a commodity of good names were to be bought" (1.2.81-84). The self-conscious irony of the jest is that M. Remorse need not venture far afield. He engenders names, roles, selves in truly Gargantuan fashion. It is his "vocation" (1.2. 105). "Vocation" is cunningly ironic because of its ambiguous referent: "amendment" or "purse-taking."

And "amendment of life" further splinters into the two notions of religious reformation on the one hand and its playful parody—the reformation of the self, the repeated engendering of new modes of being, which is indeed Falstaff's vocation in the play. This proliferation reinforces the utterly self-subverting usage of the personal pronoun with its poly-referentiality in the preceding tirade: "Before I knew thee, Hal, I knew nothing and now am I, if a man should speak truly, little better than one of the wicked. I must give over this life, and I will . . . and I do not, I am a villain" (1.2.93-97). In the paradoxical context of playing selves and mercurial impersonations (and the playing in the tavern particularizes this again and again), the "I" is restlessly self-created, then self-destroyed to make room for the next creation.

In the style of Shakespeare's witty fools (the style of "minding true things by what their mock'ries be" [*Henry V*, Act 4, prologue, l. 53]), Falstaff guides us into the hermeneutics of the play's mode. He shams remorse, yet irony advertizes that he is saying the opposite of what he means. But deception paradoxically becomes an inverted form of honesty, since Falstaff's candid amorality constitutes an incisive critique of all sham and other politic forms of remorse and self-righteousness. But then again Falstaff offers no alternative to poor "government," the imposture ailing the commonwealth; indeed, he is himself a powerful threat to all forms of government.

But the rhetorical strategy and the play's action contrive to engulf us in the unmitigated self-contradictoriness of the rhetorical paradox of Epimenedes the Cretan, who said, "All Cretans are liars." Rosalie Colie has succinctly expounded the senses in which this paradox "folds into itself," equivocating tautologically by dealing with itself as both subject and object.[8]

What I am suggesting is that the strategy of characterization in *Henry IV, Part 1* is best understood in rhetorical terms as a labyrinthine self-engendering, self-circling masquerade of impersonation and self-presentation, rather than in the traditional terms of mimesis. Hal, too, presents himself, is represented, in the self-contradictory mode of the impersonator. Like Falstaff, he is "enselfed" (the word is Lanham's) in a multiplicity of self-created and irreconcilable masks. "I know you all" is virtually the ironic posture par excellence, the "I" (the pun is intended) of superior awareness. And in another sense, the "I" that "so offend[s] to make offence a skill" is a punning mask behind which both an ethical-political "I" and an aesthetical-histrionic "I" jostle. "You can define a pun," says Geoffrey Hartman, "as two meanings competing for the same phonemic space or as one sound bringing forth semantic twins, but, however you look at it, it's a crowded situation."[9] It is precisely such a crowding of self-contradictory roles that sets off the ironic shuttle, as the "I's" are successively self-created and self-consumed in the changing contexts of their playful transactions and transgressions.

How can one tell the masker from the mask in such a congested figuring forth of personae? Trapped in the inherent paradox of mask, Hal can simply never be what he appears to be. "I am not what I am" is, as Stanley Fish has argued, unsettling in the extreme and diabolically self-consuming.[10] It is the riddle of permanent uncertainty all over again. Consider Hal's declaration to his father: "I shall hereafter my thrice-gracious lord / Be more myself" (*Henry IV, Part 1*, 3.2.93-94). "Myself" can never escape from the ironizing shadow of its doubles. In whatever way we choose to credit this transformations of offense into defense, we must necessarily concede the contradictory readings that the statement insists upon because we have no point of reference to turn or return to except the fictional (the feigned "true" or "false") or the histrionic (the double-focused elliptical mask which both hides and reveals).

Inconclusiveness and the Ironic Dilemma

> *Our wooing doth not end like an old play*
> *Jack hath not Jill. These ladies' courtesy*
> *Might well have made our sport a comedy.*
> Love's Labor's Lost, 5.2.872-74

The destabilizing rhetorical mode of *Henry IV, Part 1* draws particular attention to itself because it is also thematized. Shamming is the play's core action, its central political theme, its pivotal image, its most fertile jest. The images of an argument, a contest, again and again invade the mind. "An irony has no point," William Empson wrote in a seminal discussion of this play, "unless it is true in some degree, in both senses, for it is imagined as part of an argument . . . it is not the joke that is fundamental but the conflict."[11] In *Henry IV, Part 1* the ironic conflict is compellingly manifested on every level of dramatic expressiveness: in the articulation of parallel and contrasted scenes, the interlacing of plots, the self-referentiality of the characterization, the decontextualization and loosening of words from their semantic moorings ("What is honor?") in witty manipulations of disjunctiveness.

It is the play's dominant strategy to thrust us into an inconclusive *medias res* (midst of things) of verbal and physical combat and there to abandon us. G. K. Hunter takes us directly to the point when he says that "the play does not tell us what to prefer; it implicates us in the action of preferring, and this is the heart of the dramatic experience."[12] Having thus engaged us, the play proceeds to frustrate and undercut every choice or preference in favor of which it has seduced us. The contest remains irreducibly "dialogical"[13] in its refusal to grant superior validity to either of the competing sides. It is this equitable calibration that finally generates the recognition of their inability to integrate or synthesize without loss.

The Shrewsbury scenes and the play's fifth act are perhaps Shakespeare's most intense and uninhibited realization of ironic enactment. Kaleidoscopic shifts of scenes and encounters articulate the changes of mood, tone, and perspective, impelling us to recognize the coexistence of incongruities and their incompatibility. Ultimately, the failure to resolve doubts and battles; to terminate the contest for authority, identity, legitimacy, and authenticity; to attain a perfect image of desire stripped of the imperfections of duplicity; the failure, in short, to come to a point, extends beyond both tavern and Shrewsbury field to lodge in the mind of the spectator.

When there is a rider to every affirmation that the play enacts, coherence and conclusion can be discovered only in the mind's ability to reflect and sustain the self-criticizing, self-appraising, self-regulating mechanism of inconclusiveness. The exasperating evenhandedness of this mechanism is reminiscent of Falstaff's mock-predicament with regard to the slippery hostess: like the otter "she's neither fish nor flesh; a man knows not where to have her," even though from her point of view this is a wicked misrepresentation: "Thou art an unjust man in saying so. Thou or any man knows where to have me, thou knave, thou!" (3.3.134-38). Would it be too much to read this little argument as a parable of one's reflections upon the dialogical predicament of interpretation in its attempts to comprehend a verbal event or an action which tugs with equal persuasiveness in contrary and contradictory directions?

Like the hostess, it is possible to insist upon a redeeming single-mindedness of univocal vision. It is a pragmatic fact, canonized in the annals of critical interpretations of this play, that unity may be discovered in a monological medieval morality structure of choice, the agent of which is Hal. An updated and psychologized version of the same structure is a *"Bildungs-spiel"* reading of the education of a prince. Conciliatory readings imply the perception of the totality of events in the play *sub specie comoediae* (under the appearance of comedy). On the other hand, it is a notable fact that *Henry IV, Part 1* has no natural or ritualized closure such as a marriage or a coronation. Hotspur's death, the conventional tragic closure, quickly moves from solemnity to the hilarity of a comic mock-resurrection and is swept into the wheeling thrusts and counter-thrusts of ironic articulation. It is the interplay of rival and unintegrated points of view that makes it possible to argue for a perception of the totality of events *sub specie ironiae* (under the appearance of irony).[14]

The whirligig of time is always at odds with our illusion of the timeless "ever after" of happy endings. In most of Shakespeare's comedies this residue of temporal disjunctiveness lurks to a lesser or greater degree, although understated, and it tends to be absorbed into the cathartic unmaskings and recognitions. In *Henry IV, Part 1*, however, the single, unequivocal recognition permitted is that disjunctive equivocation is total and unrelenting. The play represents a world of *homo rhetoricus*, "a world of contingent purpose, of perpetual cognitive dissonance, plural orchestration."[15]

SHAKESPEAREAN COMEDY

At the risk of schematizing my argument to within an inch of its life, I will suggest that the particular ironic form that I have attempted to describe, a form subversive of our received notions of mimesis and organicism, is disjunctively yoked to the Aristotelian grid of Shakespearean comic form. The dialectic or ironic form runs counter to the linearity of temporal realization of plot and fails to break through release into clarification or duplicity into desire but suspends spectacle, spectator, and critical speculation indefinitely in the cycle of inconclusiveness. In some plays, conclusion, when it comes, can feel closer to dread than to the image of desire. *Troilus and Cressida* and the second part of *Henry IV* are certainly cases in point.

The dramaturgy of Shakespearean comic history invites a reevaluation of our structural and thematic approaches to dramatic forms. Poised between the strictures of a neoclassical aesthetic rooted in principles of unity, symmetry, and harmony, *Henry IV, Part 1* is powerfully informed (indeed deformed) by the menace of immanent disintegration. Its openendedness is made the vehicle for an inescapably ambivalent vision of experience that inhabits a no-man's-land between containment and anarchy, perfection and imperfection, a vision whose nondidactic tenet is that actions (or interpretations) which profess to comprehend multidimensional and contradictory experience must be viewed through a relentlessly bifocal, refracting glass. Perhaps darkly, but also playfully.

Notes

1. It will be clear from my essay that I use the words *desire* and *duplicity* here in their simplest denotative sense. The psychological patttterns and possibilities of such a formula, explored in works such as René Girard's *Deceit, Desire and the Novel* (Baltimore: Johns Hopkins Press, 1965) or Leo Bersani's *A Future for Astyanax* (Boston: Little, Brown, 1969), are no doubt relevant but are beyond the scope of this paper, which confines itself to a discussion of form.

2. See, for example, Ernest B. Gilman, *The Curious Perspective: Literary and Pictorial Wit in the Seventeenth Century* (New Haven: Yale Univ. Press, 1978).

3. The theatrical equivalent of the Renaissance perspective glass is found in all those self-reflexive moments of a Shakespearean play that both privilege and depreciate the status of art and the nature of its hold upon the imagination. Such moments may be located in a single rhetorical figure. The pun is the analogue of the perspective's doubling in

> One face, one voice, one habit and two persons—
> A natural perspective that is and is not.
>
> (*Twelfth Night*, 5.1.215-16)

In the mise-en-âbime, mirroring is always the crux. In some plays, art's ambiguous self-reflexivity is the core image informing the entire play.

4. George Puttenham, *The Arte of English Poesie*, ed. Gladys Doidge Willcock and Alice Walker (London:Cambridge Univ. Press, 1936), p. 128.

5. Kenneth Burke, *A Grammar of Motives* (Berkeley: Univ. of California Press, 1969), p. 517. First published, 1945.

6. Richard A. Lanhan, *The Motives of Eloquence: Literary Rhetoric in the Renaissance* (New Haven: Yale Univ. Press, 1976), p. 6. My approach is deeply indebted to this work.

7. Puttenham, p. 154.

8. Rosalie L. Colie, *Paradoxia Epidemica: The Renaissance Tradition of Paradox* (Archon Books, 1976), pp. 6-11.

9. Geoffrey H. Hartman, *Beyond Formalism: Literary Essays 1958-1970* (New Haven: Yale Univ. Press, 1970), p. 347. The quotation is from "The Voice of the Shuttle."

10. My notion of the counterfeit self is related to Stanley Fish's aesthetics of the self-consuming artifact and to his analysis of the structure of response as a "decertainizing" experience. See *Self-Consuming Artifacts: The Experience of Seventeenth Century Literature* (Berkeley: Univ. of California Press, 1972).

11. William Empson, *Some Versions of Pastoral* (London: Chatto and Windus, 1935), p. 56.

12. G. K. Hunter, ed., *Shakespeare: Henry IV Part 1 and 2: A Casebook* (London: Macmillan, 1970), p. 20.

13. The coinage is Bakhtin's and is used to describe the polyphonic structure of Dostoyevsky's novels, in contradistinction to "ideological." Mikhail Bakhtin, *La Poétique de Dostoievski*, trans. Isabelle Kolitcheff (Paris: Editions du Seuil, 1970).

14. For a recent version of the morality reading, see Alan C. Dessen, "The Intemperate Knight and the Politic Prince: Late Morality Structure in *1 Henry IV*," *Shakespeare Studies*, VII (1974), 147-72. For a contrary, ironic reading, see Norman Council, *When Honour's at the Stake* (London: George Allen & Unwin, 1973). The best ironic reading, to my mind, is still A. P. Rossiter, *Angel with Horns*, ed. Graham Storey (London: Longmans, Green, 1961), pp. 40-64. Ruth Nevo's forthcoming *Comic Transformations in Shakespeare* at Methuen relates the Henriad and the figure of Falstaff to Shakespeare's experiments with comic form.

15. Lanham, p. 7.

Bibliographical Note

The variorum of interpretations of *Henry IV, Part 1* or of the two-part play or of Shakespeare's historical tetralogy would exceed the length of my essay. I confine myself, therefore, to listing only a half dozen studies that have contributed significantly in shaping my approach to the questions of rhetoric, irony, and the dialectic of drama:

Burke, Kenneth. *A Grammar of Motives.* Berkeley: University of California Press (1945), 1969.
Empson, William. *Some Versions of Pastoral.* London: Chatto and Windus, 1935.
Fish, Stanley E. *Self-Consuming Artifacts: The Experience of Seventeenth Century Literature.* Berkeley: University of California Press, 1972.
Lanham, Richard A. *The Motives of Eloquence: Literary Rhetoric in the Renaissance.* New Haven: Yale University Press, 1976.
McCanles, Michael. *Dialectical Criticism and Renaissance Literature.* Berkeley: University of California Press, 1975.
Muecke, D. C. *Irony.* The Critical Idiom, 13. Gen. ed. John D. Jump. London: Methuen, 1970.

My discussion of inconclusiveness leans in particular on Richard Lanham's *The Motives of Eloquence*. The core of his thesis is that "the western self has from the beginning been composed of a shifting and perpetually uneasy combination of *homo rhetoricus* and *homo seriosus*, of a social self and a central self. It is their business to contend for supremacy. To *settle* the struggle would be to end the Greek experiment in a complex self" (p. 6). The "serious" view of life posits an interiorized, platonic, central self (soul); the "rhetorical" view of life posits a social, playful, and dramatic self. Lanham argues for a poetics of Renaissance literature based on the rhetorical self. It seems to me self-evident that drama can project only rhetorical "selves" and that the agonistic "experiment" or experience is actualized in a collaborative act between reader and text or spectacle and spectator.

18

Malvolio:
Comic Puritan Automaton

PAUL N. SIEGEL

The Puritan, says R. H. Tawney, "disciplines, rationalizes, systematizes, his life." In so disciplining himself, he "is like a steel spring compressed by an inner force, which shatters every obstacle by its rebound."[1] It was this discipline of spirit that contributed to the victory of the Puritans in the English Civil War. But this very self-discipline, which is a source of strength, can also seem comical. The person who behaves in a predictable way, always impelled by the same spring, is comical in his automatism, which gives him the aspect of a marionette. The comic character, says Bergson, is dominated by a "mechanical element which resembles a piece of clockwork wound up once for all and capable of working automatically."[2] Whereas "the hero of a tragedy represents an individuality unique of its kind," the great comic characters tend to be supreme representatives of stock types. "We say 'a Tartuffe,' but we should never say 'a Phèdre' " (p. 166).

Such a comic character is Shakespeare's Malvolio. Malvolio, whose name connotes ill will, is the Puritan spoilsport in the midst of gaiety. His role as a killjoy has been generally recognized, but because of the misunderstanding of an oft-cited passage he has been regarded not as a representative of the Puritans but as some one who merely bears some resemblance to them. The consequence is that much of his comic self-repetition has been missed, as has the full significance of the prank played on him, a prank that involves what Bergson calls a variation of repetition, "an inversion of *rôles*, and a situation which recoils on the head of its author" (p. 122).

The passage in question is the one in which Maria says of him, "Marry, sir, sometimes he is a kind of Puritan" (2.3.140). A moment later she states: "The devil a Puritan that he is, or anything constantly but a time-pleaser" (146-47). William P. Holden, after observing that "recent opinion does not make him a Puritan," concurs: "She does not quite say that he is a Puritan . . . She does say that 'sometimes he is a kind of Puritan.' In other words, in some ways, he on occasion acts like a Puritan. A few lines later she says that he is not a Puritan; she is not contradicting herself because she never said that he was one."[3]

But Holden's own research indicates that this interpretation is wrong. He cites Thomas Dekker on the sin of "politick bankruptisme" in *The Seven Deadly Sinnes of London:* "Sometimes hee's a Puritane, . . . wrapping his crafty Serpents body in the cloake of religion, he does those acts that should become none but a Divell" (p. 56*n*). "Sometimes hee's a Puritane" here means that Puritanism is only one of the guises of this deadly sin; the devil performs his evil under the cloak of a religion in which he does not really believe. This was a standard charge made against Puritans: they do not really believe in their religion or any other religion but use it as a means to hide the evil they perform to advance their material interests. Thus a contemporary attack on usury states that the "dissembling gospeller" "under the colour of religion overturneth all religion, and bearing good men in hande that he loveth playnesse, useth covertlie all deceypte that may bee, and for pryvate gayne undoeth the common welfare of man. And touching thys sinne of usury, none doe more openly offende in thys behalfe than do these counterfaite professours of thys pure religion."[4] So, too, Robert Greene says of a usurer who dies advising his sons to study Machiavelli to learn how to amass money, "He was religious too, neuer without a booke at his belt, and a bolt in his mouth, ready to shoote through his sinfull neighbor."[5] When Maria says, therefore, that Malvolio is not constantly a Puritan or anything else but a "time-pleaser" (that is, one who adapts his conduct to the opportunities afforded by the time), she is merely making the charge that was made against Puritans generally: they are concerned with their religion only insofar as it serves their profit.

"The devil a Puritan that he is" is not only a denial of the sincerity of Malvolio's religious professions, but also an allusion to the frequently voiced idea of the devil taking the form of a Puritan. "There is," says Holden, "the general tradition that the devil is a Puritan, that is, that any sort of bad deed from a dissenter indicates that the spirit of Satan, or of true dissent, is within him; . . . 'the devil turned precisian' simply means vice compounded" (p. 114).

"A kind of Puritan" does not mean that Malvolio acts like a Puritan without being one. Holden quotes a passage in Marston's *What You Will* in which the attendant at a brothel, on being asked "What is your mistress?" replies, "A kind of puritan" (p. 116n). The attendant goes on to say in a speech immediately following, which Holden does not quote, that he is "a kind of page," even though he is of the lowest order of pages, and that his petition should be heard among "the particular grievances of each sort of pages."[6] "A kind of page" means a member of one of the various divisions of pages, and "a kind of puritan" would seem likewise to mean that the prostitute is an adherent of one of the Puritan sects, which are casually confounded with each other.[7] So today a staunch proponents of the status quo who knows little of the various radical doctrines will say, "He's some kind of Red," implying that distinctions are scarcely worth making. The same is true of the application of the phrase to Malvolio.

Epithets Applied to Puritans

An abusive term, "niggardly rascally sheep-biter" (2.5.4-5), Sir Toby uses for Malvolio gains significance if we perceive him to be a Puritan. The Signet edition glosses this phrase "sneaky dog" and the Riverside edition glosses it "malicious sneak." The New Arden edition, however, noncommittally states that J. W. Lever, in glossing "sheep-biting" in the New Arden edition of *Measure for Measure*, "suggests that 'sheep-biter' was applied to a hypocritical Puritan."[8] Lever's reference is to Nashe's "An Almond for A Parrot," in which Nashe speaks of "a Precisian," a "zealous sheepebyter." The idea, as Lever's further reference to Vaughan's *The Golden-groue* makes clear, is of a wolf in sheep's clothing who has stolen in among the fold of Christians. "Niggardly rascally sheep-biter" means "miserly, cheating Puritan," miserliness and cheating in business being associated with Puritans (Holden, pp. 42, 114-15; Tawney, p. 209). Although Malvolio is not shown as either a miser or a cheat, Sir Toby, in speaking of him as a Puritan, makes use of the stock epithets for Puritans.

These epithets express the antagonism of Sir Toby, a member of the older aristocracy, with its roistering habits and militaristic way of life, toward the social classes among whom Puritanism was strong. "To contemporaries," says Tawney, "the chosen seat of the Puritan spirit" was "the trading classes of the towns, and of those rural districts which had been partially industrialized" and "some of the gentry," "where the feudal spirit had been weakened by contact with town life" (p. 168). As steward, Malvolio manages a large estate and household that might number as many as 500 persons. Such men were often of the gentry.[9] The position, however, was a socially ambiguous one: Viola and Olivia refer to him as a "gentleman" (5.1.276, 279), but Sir Toby taunts him with "Art any more than a steward?" (2.3.115-16), and the purported letter from Olivia urges him not to be content with being "a steward still, the fellow of servants" (2.5.152).[10]

The steward had to maintain control over the brawling armed retainers and aristocratic kinsfolk and hangers-on who constituted part of a great household. In the rules governing his houshold the second Viscount Montague enjoined his steward to "reform . . . by his grave admonitions and vigilant eye over them, the riotous, the contentious and quarrelous persons of any degree" (Byrne, p. 204). If Malvolio lacked tact, his position did call for the preservation of discipline. The Puritan steward Malvolio, then, embodies what Christopher Hill calls "the connection between religious discipline, self-discipline and labour discipline."[11] His rebuke to Sir Toby, "You waste the treasure of your time" (2.5.75-76), is an expression of the Puritan bourgeois ethic like the modern businessman's "Time is money." He is opposed to the very spirit of the twelve days of Christmas culminating in Twelfth Night, with its extended merrymaking.

It is, as Maria says, Malvolio's "grounds of faith" that he is "crammed . . . with excellencies" (2.3.149-51). Pride was often attributed to Puritans, whose faith taught them that they were members of the elect (Holden, p. 151). Like the Puritan Angelo, who thought that he did not have the frailties of other men, "studied" "state," and took "pride" in his "gravity" (*Measure for Measure* 2.4.7-10), Malvolio evidently prides himself on being "virtuous" (2.3.116), that is, morally superior to others; "cons state" (2.3.148); and fancies himself for his "austere regard of control" (2.5.64), his grave demeanor. His pride makes him oblivious to his own defects. "Is there no respect of place, persons, nor time in you?" (2.3.92-93), he pompously exclaims, bursting in upon the trio of Sir Toby, Sir Andrew, and Feste singing in the middle of the night. But he himself violates order in presuming to aspire to the hand of Olivia. "A comic character," says Bergson, "is generally comic in proportion to his ignorance of himself" (p. 7), for then he continues to behave as he always has behaved. "Rigidity, automatism, absentmindedness [that is, obliviousness to reality] and unsociability are all inextricably entwined; and all serve as ingredients to the making up of the comic in character" (p. 156). This is almost a description of Malvolio.

Maria knows her man. She is sure that in "the obscure epistles of love" she will leave in his way he will "find himself most feelingly personated" (2.3.154-58). The letter merely confirms Malvolio's opinion of Olivia's love for him and makes him behave in a manner he has already dreamed about. Before he reads the letter urging him to "embrace" "thy Fates" (2.5.142-43), he has already told himself, " 'Tis but fortune; all is fortune" (21). Before reading its command, "Be opposite with a kinsman, surly with servants" (145-46), he has imagined himself married to Olivia and lecturing Sir Toby: "Cousin Toby, my fortunes having cast me on your niece, give me this prerogative speech. You must amend your drunkeness" (67-71).

Puritan Nonconformism

But it is not merely in his imagination that Malvolio acts imperiously. The letter makes him act as in his daydream, but this is only an exaggeration of the way he has already behaved in sternly admonishing Sir Toby and speaking sourly to Feste. The command of the letter, "cast thy humble slough and appear fresh," is therefore amusingly ironic—Malvolio has never been humble—but in his self-ignorance he is unaware of it. "Let thy tongue tang arguments of state," the letter continues. "Arguments of state" means "topics of statecraft." One of the charges made against Puritans was that they were seeking to meddle not only in church government, which should be the prerogative of the church hierarchy, but in matters of state, which should be the prerogative of the aristocracy (Holden, p. 63). The command is merely an extension of Malvolio's dream of becoming "Count Malvolio" and indulging in "the humor of state" (2.5.33, 50). When he says in response to this command, "I will read politic authors" (157), "politic authors" does not merely mean "writers on statecraft," as it has been generally glossed, but has the usual Elizabethan pejorative sense, suggesting the Machiavelli read by Greene's hypocritical, self-serving Puritan usurer.

The next command of the letter is "put thyself into the trick of singularity." "Trick of singularity" is commonly glossed "affectation of eccentricity" without explanation as to why the letter advises Malvolio to assume such an affectation and what should be the nature of the eccentricity. James F. Forrest notes, however, that the word *singularity* "had acquired an almost technical connotation as pejoratively applied to Puritans, who with their 'new-fangleness' and 'innovations' were already . . . rocking the precariously settled order of the established church."[12] Of the many illustrative examples that he gives, we may refer particularly to one. Edmund Grindal, Archbishop of York, spoke of the Puritan Thomas Cartwright's "love of contention and liking of novelties," stating that, "besides the singularity above rehearsed, the said Cartwright is not conformable in his apparel" (pp. 260-61).

Not only were the Puritans nonconformists in matters of church doctrine, but also in their attire. This casts light upon the command "Remember who commended thy yellow stockings and wished to see thee ever cross-gartered," which has occasioned a good deal of controversy. The editors of the New Arden edition comment: "Both articles of dress seem chosen for their conspicuousness rather than for their significance. If both were 'probably old-fashioned' (Wilson), Malvolio would not have worn them; more probably they were associated with jolly young bachelors. Hence the incongruity in the often-quoted remarks from Overbury's *Characters*, 1616 ('If he [a country gentleman] goe to

Court, it is in yellow stockings') and Ford's *The Lover's Melancholy*, 1629, 3.1 ('As rare an old youth as ever walked cross-gartered')" (p. 71). But cross-garters were not only old-fashioned; they were worn "chiefly by old men, Puritans, pedants, footmen, and rustic bridegrooms."[13] Henry King says in one of his poems that a play would have been successful at court if in it there had "appear'd some sharp cross-gartered man/ Whom their loud laugh might nick-name Puritan."[14] The Puritans in their sedate sobriety objected to the showy new fashions of dress.[15] Possibly, yellow stockings, also old-fashioned, were, therefore, one of the items in which they were not "conformable" in their apparel and were, with cross-garters, part of their attire when they wished to appear in their best clothes.

Certainly, Olivia's supposed command does not tell Malvolio to wear what he has not worn before. The very phrasing of the command ("Remember who commended thy yellow stockings") indicates that he had worn them previously. That he has yellow stockings and cross-garters in his wardrobe is borne out by his statement: "She did commend my yellow stockings of late, she did praise my leg being cross-gartered" (2.5.161-63). There has been some confusion about the contradiction between this statement and Maria's "He will come to her in yellow stockings, and 'tis a color she abhors, and cross-gartered, a fashion she detests" (194-96). But the point seems clear: Malvolio is so carried away, put "in such a dream" (189) by the letter, that he actually imagines remembering Olivia complimenting him on his yellow stockings and cross-garters, as the letter says she did.

Like other comic characters, Malvolio has a one-track mind. He molds reality to suit his own preconceptions and "proceeds with the certainty and precision of a somnambulist who is acting his dream" (Bergson, p. 179). This is the significance of the "fustian riddle," "M. O. A. I. doth sway my life" (105-07), which has caused scholars' ink to flow in their attempting to work out an answer to it. The riddle, however, is not meant to have an answer: it has been contrived by Maria with the knowledge that Malvolio will force an interpretation of the line to suit his wish. "Observe his construction of it" (2.3.174), she says in delighted anticipation.

The Letter

The letter, says Malvolio, "set down the manner how" he is to behave: to maintain "a sad face, a reverend carriage, a slow tongue" (3.4. 75-78), that is, to continue more than ever with his customary supercilious manner and pompously polysyllabic mode of speech. Bergson's words are apropos of Malvolio's "sad face": "Automatism, *inelasticity*, habit that has been contracted and maintained, are clearly the causes why a face makes us laugh" (p. 76). Malvolio has the funereal Buster Keaton countenance without the endearing traits of the Buster Keaton character.

The sober-faced Malvolio, played by Laurence Olivier, dressed in the black garb and plain band of the Puritan and wearing cross-garters, regards his mockers, Maria and Sir Toby, played by Angela Baddeley and Alan Webb, in Act 3, scene 4, of the Royal Shakespeare Company's production of *Twelfth Night* at Stratford-on-Avon. *Photograph by Angus McBean. Courtesy of the Harvard Theatre Collection.*

But in complying with the command in the postscript "in my presence still smile" (172-73)—carefully separated from the rest of the letter, it is the only command at variance with Malvolio's usual conduct—he disarranges his face with mechanical regularity. In addressing Olivia, after each kissing of his fingers by way of compliment and after each conclusion of a sentence, he distends his lips and exposes his teeth in a forced smile, the only kind of which he is capable. These smiles only make him seem the more an automaton.

Precisian that he is, he obeys "every point of the letter" (3.2.75), no matter how absurd it is to a rational person. His forced construction of "the obscure epistles of love" recalls the Elizabethan allegations about the Puritans' fantastic interpretations of the Bible and their wresting it to suit their purpose.[16] He is, says Maria, "turned heathen, a very renegado; for there is no Christian that means to be saved by believing rightly can ever believe such impossible passages of grossness" (3.2.67-70). Her words, suggestive of contemporary criticism of the Puritans, are paraphrased by Simmons: "Malvolio, as a result of his 'precise' following of the letter, is no longer a Christian but a 'Heathen,' an apostate: Christians achieve salvation by correct belief, belief to be derived from the Bible; but Malvolio has interpreted and believed obviously impossible and gross passages in a perversity of spirit which would prevent his reading the Bible and 'believing correctly' " (p. 182).

Malvolio's Madness

Maria is able to foretell how he will behave when he sees Olivia. "I know my lady will strike him. If she do, he'll smile, and take't for a great favor" (3.2.79-81). She is wrong about Olivia, who is moved not to rage but to concern about Malvolio's apparent madness, but she is right about Malvolio. He continues "like a machine in the same straight line" (Bergson, p.66), acting out his dream, disregarding Olivia's actual behavior, and putting the same forced construction on her words that he did on the words in the letter.

The tricks played upon Malvolio while he is treated as a madman, it used to be said in the nineteenth century, arouse sympathy and make him pathetic. Even today this view is sometimes expressed. "Malvolio's credulity . . . is chastised so severely," says Herschel Baker, "that he becomes, as Lamb observed, an almost tragic figure."[17] But Shakespeare so handles the matter that Malvolio remains a comic figure throughout.

In the first place, we are reassured from the beginning that the joke will not go so far that Malvolio will be driven to madness. "Why," says Fabian, "we shall make him mad indeed" (3.4.137), but Sir Toby replies: "We may carry it thus, for our pleasure and his penance, till our very pastime, tired out of breath, prompt us to have mercy on him." After they have had a good laugh and Malvolio has been properly punished for his arrogance, presumptuousness, and self-righteousness, they will be merciful and he will be released. In fact, rather than driving him to madness, they rouse him, albeit rudely, from his absurd daydream of marrying Olivia, which is akin to madness. In dreams, says Bergson, "we find the same associations of ideas as we do in lunacy, the same peculiar logic as in a fixed idea. . . . *Comic absurdity is of the same nature as that of dreams*" (p. 180).

Then, too, Malvolio's punishment is amusingly appropriate. In musing over the letter and working it out to his satisfaction, he had become, in the words of Maria, "a contemplative idiot" (2.4.17), just as the Puritans were often regarded as religious maniacs in the fantasizing prompted by their zealous reading of the Bible (Simmons, pp. 184-85; Holden, p. 110). It is appropriate, therefore, that he be treated as a madman.

The darkness in which he is confined is also appropriate, for it is in conformance with his spiritual blindness and lack of self-knowledge. "I say," says Feste in his role as Sir Thopas the parson, "there is no darkness but ignorance, in which thou art more puzzled than the Egyptians" (4.2.43-45). Moreover, darkness is associated with hell, which would be regarded as the appropriate abode of religious dissidents with the list of sins assigned to the Puritans. "Though we have light mistresses," says the brothel attendant in Marston's *What You Will* who had stated that his mistress was "a kind of puritan," "we are made the children and servants of darkness" (2.383). "Children and servants of darkness" here refers, of course, to the members of the brothel in which the "act of darkness" (*King Lear* 3.4.86) is performed, but it also refers to the inmates of hell, just as Othello, pretending to believe that Emilia is the madam of a brothel, says that she keeps "the gate of hell" (4.2.91). When, therefore, Malvolio speaks of his place of confinement as being as dark as hell (36), the audience would have accepted this as appropriate enough for one who belongs to the forces of darkness.

Puritans, as we have seen, were spoken of as incarnations of the devil, the chief occupant of hell. Feste addresses as Satan the devil he pretends to believe is speaking through Malvolio, and when he goes off with Malvolio's letter to Olivia, he sings a song comparing himself to a Vice going off in the service of the Devil, a song that, says Bernard Spivack, "recaptures the typical features of the comic passages between the Vice and the Devil, whenever in the moralities the former comes to the aid of the frustrated demon . . . and badgers him unmercifully."[18]

Comic justice is also served by an inversion of roles in which Malvolio takes the place of Feste and Sir Toby. He, who had said, "I protest I take these wise men that crow so at these set kind of fools no better than the fools' zanies" (1.5.88-89), indeed becomes a "zany," a subordinate clown, to Feste. He is made a fool of by the Fool, who, he had said, has no more brains than an idiot. "I am as well in wits, fool," he entreats Feste in the mad-cell scene, "as thou art." "But as well?" retorts Feste. "Then you are mad indeed, if you be no better in your wits than a fool" (4.2.90-92).

So too he, who had exclaimed "I will baffle Sir Toby" (2.5.157-58), is at the end said to have been "baffled" (5.1.369) by Sir Toby and the others.

Also, it should be noted, the role of madman, which Malvolio is forced to enact, is enacted by almost everyone else. Everyone in the play except the sharp-witted Maria and Fabian, who acts as lawyer at the conclusion for Sir Toby, Feste, and Maria, at one time or another calls himself mad or is so called by others. This madness lends itself to comedy. "It is comic," says Bergson, "to wander out of one's self. It is comic to fall into a ready-made category" (p. 157). Orsino and Olivia, normally, as we are told, a noble duke and a great lady in full command of themselves, wander out of themselves and fall into the category of humor-ridden lovers, behaving with amusing predictability, he a captive of constantly changing moods and she a captive of headlong precipitousness.

Illyria is a realm of madcap mirth and of dreamlike illusion like unto madness. Passage through this realm of illusion is necessary before one finds one's true love. One must let one's self go, giving in to the magic of the place. "How runs the stream?" exclaims Sebastian when an unknown great lady entreats him to love. "Or I am mad, or else this is a dream./ Let fancy still my sense in Lethe steep;/ If it be thus to dream, still let me sleep!" (4.1.61-64).

But Malvolio is far too tightly disciplined to give himself up to either love or mirth. "My masters, are you mad?" (2.3.87) he exclaims as he bursts in upon the foolery and song of Sir Toby, Sir Andrew, and Feste. Refusing to join in the holiday revelry, he is willy-nilly dragged into it. If he does not enjoy it, it is his own fault for not having entered into the spirit of the game. It is a game, a play, in which he has been assigned a role. "If this were played upon a stage now," says Fabian of Malvolio's persistence in delusion, "I could condemn it as an improbable fiction" (3.4.131-32). A moment later when Sir Andrew comes on with his fatuous letter challenging "Cesario," Fabian exclaims, "More matter for a May morning"—that is, another subject such as Malvolio's ridiculous behavior for a May Day game or playlet. And when Feste exults over Malvolio at the conclusion, he tells him, "I was one, sir, in this interlude, one Sir Topas, sir" (5.1.372-73): the Fool had his part in the little play, as did Malvolio.

Holiday Festivities and the Puritans

May Day festivities, with their summer lords and ladies presiding over outdoor sports and games, and Christmas season festivities, with their lords of misrule presiding over the indoor hearty eating, drinking, and reveling, were equally objected to by the Puritans, who "attacked the very numerous and irregular festivals that had hitherto marked the seasons" as unsuited to "the regular and continuous rhythms" of an emerging urban society (Hill, p. 146). Anti-Puritan satirists, responding to the Martin Marprelate pamphlets, attacking the church hierarchy, made use, C. L. Barber points out, of the holiday motifs to which the Puritans objected. The anti-Martinist pamphlets "show a curious mingling of buffoonery and invective, of relish for the opponent with scorn, which goes with the satirist's playing the fool to make a fool of his antagonist. The likeness of this tone to a Lord of Misrule's vaunting and abuse is suggested by several passages alluding to the games." One pamphlet observed that "Martin 'took it very grievously, to be made a May game upon the stage' . . . The phrase 'to make a May game' of somebody implies that one need only bring an antagonist into the field of force of May games to make him ridiculous. A pamphlet promises its readers a 'new work' entitled *The May game of Martinism* and gives a preview . . . [that offers] an example of the practice of mocking individuals by identifying them with traditional holiday roles. Various prominent Puritans, along with Martin, are put in the game."[19] Although Barber does not refer to Malvolio as playing a role similar to that of Martin, his description of the holiday motifs in the anti-Martinist pamphlets casts light on the mockery of Malvolio, who was made "matter for a May morning" by Sir Toby, the Lord of Misrule, and Feste, the spirit of holiday festivity.

In the final scene Olivia acts as the dispenser of justice. Her words, "He hath been most notoriously abused" (5.1.380), have been taken as a vindication of Malvolio. But this is to disregard what happens in the scene. After Olivia tells Malvolio, "Thou shalt be both the plaintiff and the judge/ Of thine own cause," Fabian comes forward with the plea: "Good madam, hear me speak,/ And let no quarrel, nor no brawl to come,/ Taint the condition of this present hour." He goes on to inform her of the trick that the trio played on Malvolio because of his "stubborn and uncourteous parts," saying, "How with a sportful malice it was followed/ May rather pluck on laughter than revenge,/ If that the injuries be justly weighed/ That have on both sides passed."

Fabian has seized the time shrewdly. Olivia, happy in her marriage, is in no mood for meting out severe justice. She says nothing about punishing Fabian and Sir Toby, and Malvolio evidently sees that he will not be able to dictate any terms of justice. She expresses sympathy for Malvolio, as she had expressed sympathy for the comically limping Sir Toby, who, crippled by drink, had been soundly beaten by Sebastian, an appropriate rough justice for the drunken brawler who had disturbed her household. In each case, her expression of sympathy does not alter the comic justice. Her expression of sympathy for Malvolio, moreover, has an undercurrent of light mockery: "Alas, poor fool, how have they baffled thee!" "Poor fool" is here, condescending and recalls how he has been made a fool of by the Fool, just as "baffled," we have seen, recalls how Malvolio has vaunted about how he would "baffle" Sir Toby. "He hath been most notoriously abused" echoes Malvolio's words in the darkroom scene, "Fool, there was never man so notoriously abused" (4.2.89-

90), and also his words earlier in this scene ("Madam, you have done me wrong,/ Notorious wrong" [5.1.327-28]; "made the most notorious geck and gull" [5.1.343]), the mocking repetition suggesting that she is not taking him too seriously.

As for Malvolio, his last words, "I'll be revenged on the whole pack of you!" (5.1.378-9) have often been regarded as spoken with a snarl in a frenzy of rage. But this would be untrue to his character, whose dominant trait is pride, not choler, and unfitting to the tone of the conclusion. Just as Joseph Surface in *The School for Scandal*, although thoroughly exposed, maintains in his departure his hypocritical pose of benevolence, "moral to the last drop," so does Malvolio maintain his haughty demeanor. Uttered in response to Feste's "And thus the whirligig of time brings in his revenges" (5.1.376), his words to Feste and Fabian are a vain attempt to regain his dignity: "*I'll* be revenged on the whole pack of *you*!" So had he left, speaking in a high-and-mighty fashion, when, treated with mock solicitude as being insane, he had been firmly convinced of his impending marriage: "Go hang yourselves all! You are idle shallow things; I am not of your element. You shall know more hereafter" (3.4.127-29). He now likewise stalks off with his nose in the air, speaking with a superciliousness laughable in the situation.

Malvolio is to be urged to a peace. He will continue as steward of Olivia's household, but his dream of assuming command of her estate has been exploded. His absurd aspiration, if it could ever have been realized, would have been a disaster, as would have the continued reign of Sir Toby Belch as the lord of misrule. Instead, the conclusion brings the order and harmony resulting from the marriage of Olivia and Sebastian. "Fear not, Cesario," said Olivia when Viola denied in wonderment having married her. "Take thy fortunes up;/ Be that thou know'st thou art, and then thou art/ As great as that thou fear'st" (5.1.147-49). The words are an echo of those in the letter to Malvolio: "Be not afraid of greatness. . . . Thy Fates open their hands; let thy blood and spirit embrace them . . . Thou art made, if thou desir'st to be so" (2.5.140-51). In an ironic reversal, it is Sebastian, of whom "Cesario" is an image, not Malvolio, who has greatness thrust upon him. But, unlike Malvolio, he is a true gentleman, "free, learned, and valiant" (1.5.258), with the generous spirit and the balanced personality of a gentleman, and he, therefore, deserves his fortune. All that Malvolio gets, however, is what he deserves: the laughter roused by his automatism, the essence of the comic character described by Bergson.

Notes

1. R. H. Tawney, *Religion and the Rise of Capitalism* (New York: Penguin Books, 1947), pp. 167-68.
2. *Comedy by George Meredith and Laughter by Henri Bergson*, ed. Wylie Sypher (Garden City, N.Y.: Doubleday, 1956), p. 156.

3. William P. Holden, *Anti-Puritan Satire, 1572-1642* (New Haven: Yale Univ. Press, 1954), pp. 123*n*., 126. Critics and editors after Holden have continued to reiterate this interpretation of Maria's words.

4. Thomas Wilson, *A Discourse Upon Usury* (1572) (New York: Harcourt Brace, 1925), p. 178.

5. Robert Greene, *The Life and Complete Works*, ed. Alexander B. Grosart (London, 1881-83), XII, 104.

6. John Marston, *Works*, ed. A. H. Bullen (London: John C. Nimmo, 1887), II, 383.

7. Satirists used the alleged sexual practices of the Puritan sect, the Family of Love, to tar the other Puritans, making Puritan wives to be either easily seduced or prostitutes. In one satire, twenty-nine sects are said to exist in London. "Sexual irregularities are common among them. But the worst of all is, as usual, the Family of Love" (Holden, p. 58).

8. *Twelfth Night*, ed. J. M. Lothian and T. W. Craik, New Arden ed. (London: Methuen, 1975), p. 62.

9. M. St Clare Byrne, "The Social Background," *A Companion to Shakespeare Studies*, ed. Harley Granville-Barker and G. B. Harrison (Garden City, N. Y.: Doubleday, 1960), p. 203.

10. So, too, Kent objects to the steward Oswald because he puts on the airs of a gentleman and wears a sword at his side. Cf. *King Lear* 2.2.74-75.

11. Christopher Hill, *Society and Puritanism in Pre-Revolutionary England* (London: Secker and Warburg, 1964), p. 226.

12. James F. Forrest, "Malvolio and Puritan 'Singularity,' " *English Language Notes*, 11 (1973), 260.

13. M. C. Linthicum, *Costume in the Drama of Shakespeare and His Contemporaries* (1936), p. 264. Quoted by Leslie Hotson, *The First Night of Twelfth Night* (New York: Macmillan, 1954), p. 113.

14. Henry King, "To His Friends of Christ-Church," *English Poems* (New Haven: Yale Univ. Press, 1914), p. 28. King's poems were published in 1664 as his juvenalia.

15. The Puritan Ananias in Ben Jonson's *The Alchemist* declaims against the "slops" (wide, puffy breeches) and the large ruff, calling them "profane/ Leud, superstitious, and idolatrous breeches" and "that ruffe of pride" (*Works*, ed. C. H. Herford and Percy Simpson, Oxford Univ. Press, 1937, V, 384). In the next line of the poem quoted in footnote 14, King returns the compliment, saying that the cross-gartered Puritan wears "factious breeches and small ruffe."

16. J. L. Simmons, "A Source for Shakespeare's Malvolio: The Elizabethan Controversy with the Puritans," *Huntington Library Quarterly*, 36 (1973), 182-86.

17. Introduction to *Twelfth Night* in *The Complete Signet Classic Shakespeare*, p. 878.

18. Bernard Spivack, *Shakespeare and the Allegory of Evil* (New York: Columbia Univ. Press, 1958), pp. 202-3.

19. C. L. Barber, *Shakespeare's Festive Comedy* (New York: World Publishing Co., 1966), pp. 52-53.

Bibliographical Note

The chief sixteenth- and seventeenth-century sources are as follows: Robert Greene, "Greene's Groat's Worth of Wit," *The Life and Complete Works*, ed. Alexander B. Grosart (London: 1881-83), vol. 12, 94-150; Ben Jonson, "The Alchemist," *Works*, ed. C. H. Herford and Percy Simpson (Oxford Univ. Press, 1937), vol. 5, 282-408; Henry King, "To His Friends of Christ-Church," *English Poems* (New Haven: Yale Univ. Press, 1914), pp. 28-29; John Marston, "What You Will," *Works*, ed. A. H. Bullen (London: John C. Nimmo, 1887), vol. 2, 317-419; Thomas Wilson, *A Discourse Upon Ursury* (1572) (New York: Harcourt Brace, 1925).

The other chief sources are as follows: C. L. Barber, *Shakespeare's Festive Comedy* (New York: World Publishing Co., 1966); Henri Bergson, *Laughter* (1900) in

Comedy by George Meredith amd Laughter by Henri Bergson, ed. Wylie Sypher (Garden City, N. Y.: Doubleday, 1956); M. St Clare Byrne, "the Social Background," *A Companion to Shakespeare Studies*, ed. Harley Granville-Barker and G. B. Harrison (Garden City, N.Y.: Doubleday, 1960), 186-219; James F. Forrest, "Malvolio and Puritan 'Singularity,' " *English Language Notes*, 11 (1973), 259-64; Christopher Hill, *Society and Puritanism in Pre-Revolutionary England* (London: Secker and Warburg, 1964); William P. Holden, *Anti-Puritan Satire, 1572-1642* (New Haven: Yale Univ. Press, 1954); Leslie Hotson, *The First Night of Twelfth Night* (New York: Macmillan, 1954); J. L. Simmons, "A Source for Shakespeare's Malvolio: The Elizabethan Controversy with the Puritans," *Huntington Library Quarterly*, 36 (1973), 181-201; Bernard Spivack, *Shakespeare and the Allegory of Evil* (New York: Columbia Univ. Press, 1958); R. H. Tawney, *Religion and the Rise of Capitalism* (New York: Penguin Books, 1947).

PART 7

THEORY OF COMEDY:
PSYCHOANALYSIS
AND
SEMIOTICS

19

Errors in Comedy: A Psychoanalytic Theory of Farce

BARBARA FREEDMAN

The widespread assumption that farce is light, inherently meaningless comedy derives from a no less reputable source than the *Oxford English Dictionary*. Here we learn that farce is "a dramatic work (usually short) which has for its sole object to excite laughter." This definition has been largely responsible for the two major attitudes toward Shakespearean farce. The first is represented by that group of critics who know that Shakespeare never wrote anything solely to make us laugh and so argue that Shakespeare never wrote farce at all. Anne Barton, in the Riverside Shakespeare introduction to *The Comedy of Errors*, observes that "despite its emphasis on plot and situational absurdity, despite the merry violence in many of the scenes, it is not really possible to contain *The Comedy of Errors* within the bounds of farce as defined by the *Oxford English Dictionary*."[1] She therefore concludes that what Coleridge termed "this legitimate farce in exactest consonance with the philosophical principles and character of farce" is in fact no farce at all. E. M. W. Tillyard offers a similar assessment of this comedy's generic status, complaining that "when an example of a lesser literary kind reaches a certain pitch of excellence, it is apt to transcend the kind to which it belongs.''[2] The more popular critical approach, however, is to agree that Shakespeare wrote farce, but to consider *Errors* (as well as Shakespeare's other predominantly farcical plays) to be nonsensical *insofar* as they are farce. The plays are pronounced ''two-dimensional only, unsubstantial, not intended to be taken seriously.''[3] The editor of the Pelican edition of *Errors*, for example, laments that ''there is left over nothing really to think about—except, if one wishes, the tremendously puzzling question of what so grips and amuses an audience during a play which has so little thought in it.''[4]

The reasoning behind these arguments appears to be that if a farce should do more than arouse laughter, it is no longer a farce, and if it does no more than arouse laughter, it is not a serious or viable art form. Obviously, the *OED*'s stipulation that farce's sole object is laughter only makes sense when reworded so as to stipulate that farce's essential aim is laughter. In this way, the definition does not exclude those intellectual, emotional, and aesthetic aims that differentiate a Chaplin masterpiece from the tasteless films of the Three Stooges, or a work of art from a mere simulacrum. The latter complaint is substantive, however; the charge that farce is inhospitable to meaning has riddled, if not undermined, the very concept of farce criticism.

This essay calls for a re-evaluation of Shakespearean farce in light of a psychoanalytic theory of the dynamics of meaning in farce. It suggests that the critical neglect and disparagement of the farces is largely due to the plays' own insistence on their meaninglessness, an insistence which by no means should be accepted at face value. Rather, I shall argue that a strategic denial and displacement of meaning is intrinsic to the genre and essential to the humorous acceptance of normally unacceptable aggression which it allows. I shall confine my proof to *The Comedy of Errors*; those Shakespearean plays which share the same generic background, *The Taming of the Shrew* and *The Merry Wives of Windsor*, would be equally suitable subjects for analysis. A major assumption of this study is that without an appreciation of the role of farce in these plays and a more sophisticated understanding of the dynamics of meaning in farce, the ''nonromantic'' comedies will never be properly understood.

The association of farce with that which is insignificant and insubstantial is deeply rooted in the word's history. Our use of ''farce'' may be traced back to the Old French (*farsir*) and the Latin (*farcire*), meaning ''to stuff,'' and appears to be a metaphorical use of its longstanding, and still popular, equation with ''stuffing.'' As early as the thirteenth century, the latinized form of ''farce'' was used to refer to Latin phrases, and even rhymed passages in French, interpolated in any set liturgical formula. Its use was ultimately extended to include the improvised clowning which was similarly inserted in religious dramas. It was at this point, apparently, that the word became permanently associated with the nature and quality of the matter interpolated, rather than its interpolated status. For most of us, "farce" now signifies the recasting of what we normally consider serious in a foolish and insubstantial light.

While the *OED*'s definition of farce as a drama "which has for its sole object to excite laughter" may be considered historically accurate, it fails to take into account contemporary usage of the term. Briefly, the definition is misleading in ignoring the changes that occur when an interpolated form becomes a full-length play and viable genre, as farce has today. It ignores the distinctions between "farce" and that which is "farcical" (the former striving for much more than laughter), and it ignores the basic, accepted differences between farce and other forms of purely comic drama, such as folk comedy, intrigue comedy, and burlesque. Obviously, farce does more than arouse laughter, and it does so in ways which are recognizably different from other forms of comedy. Finally, the description of a genre solely in terms of affective response is problematic in itself, but particularly so when the affect is laughter. Since there is no critical consensus about the causes of laughter, we are left with a definition of farce as a mysterious response to an undefinable object.

A survey of definitions of farce in dictionaries, encyclopedias, and literary and theatrical glossaries, however, provides us with three basic structural elements to which this mysterious response may be attributed: an absurd situation, normally unacceptable libidinal action, and flat, surrealistic characters.[5] A valid definition of farce might only list these three characteristics; a valuable one would discover what is essential in these elements and why. It would, ideally, determine their relationship as a dynamic, functional modality, which would enable us to understand how farce is constructed and how it can be deconstructed analytically. Considered as interdependent, functional units, the one dynamic element would seem to be farce's normally unacceptable libidinal action. The key to farce, as Eric Bentley reminds us in *The Life of the Drama*, is that we laugh at violence; the unacceptable becomes acceptable, even enjoyable. What Bentley sidesteps in his brilliant treatment of the genre is how the characteristic elements of farce interact in a functional manner to enable us to enjoy the unacceptable.

Fowler's *Dictionary of Modern Critical Terms* anticipates a functional analysis in its suggestion that farce's "encapsulated universe encourages a comedy of cruelty since the audience is insulated from feeling by the absence of motive, and by the response being simultaneously more and less aggressive than real-life response."[6] Fowler thus views farce's absence of cause and effect, its absence of logic and realism, in a functional manner. The first and last terms of our classic definition—an absurd situation (here translated as absence of cause) and stereotyped, flat characters (translated as absence of effect)—may be viewed positively, as making possible a certain type of humorous response determined by the definition's second term: unacceptable aggression.

One might choose, however, to reverse Fowler's ordering and suggest that it is not the encapsulated universe that encourages a comedy of cruelty, but cruelty that encourages—indeed demands—the anesthetizing removal of cause and effect, thus creating comedy. In other words, it is not the absence, but the denial of the cause and effect of farce's violence that enables its expression and renders it safe. Were we not able to disown intent for aggression through error or dissolve remorse for its consequences through denial, the characteristic humor that ensures farce's popularity could never be achieved. On the other hand, were some initial, meaningful aggression not present to be disowned or denied, farce would lack both pleasure and humor. Like dreams, farce couples a functional denial of significance with often disturbing and highly significant content. The union of the absurd and the significant is essential to farce; a mother-in-law is mistakenly barraged with cream pies, a son mistakenly marries his father's mistress, a troop of policemen just happen to chance upon a street lined with banana peels. A taboo is always both broken and not broken.

Clearly, farce cannot function in a moral vacuum; it is not anesthetic, and its violence cannot operate in the absence of meaning. It is the denial of meaning that makes farce work. Yet if it is the denial and displacement, as opposed to the mere absence, of meaning and affect that characterizes farcical aggression, then these displaced elements can be reconstructed to reveal meaningful dramatic action. Illogic, contradiction, omission, and mistakes become signifiers of a functional dislocation of meaning through which the absurd becomes meaningful. Hence, a definition: farce is a dramatic genre deriving laughter chiefly from the denial of the cause (through absurdity) and the effect (through surrealism) of aggressive action upon an object. And hence, as well, a model of analysis.

The argument that farce's aggression is meaningful has long been implicit in the descriptions of anxiety, paranoia, horror, and menace that accompany critics' discussions of this supposedly carefree genre. Bentley, for example, claims to view farce as an exhilarating world of children without parents, action without consequences, id without superego: "Farce affords an escape from living, a release from the pressures of today, a regression to the irresponsibility of childhood."[7] Yet his language points to a sense of malevolent and punitive action, to a sense of the terrors of childhood as well: "Human life in this art form is horribly attenuated. Life is a kind of universal milling around, a rushing from bedroom to bedroom driven by demons more dreadful than sensuality. The kind of farce which is said to be 'all plot' is often much more than ingenious, it is maniacal."

The maniacal demons which inhabit the farcical world can, however, be identified. Bentley offers a clue: "Melodrama and farce are both arts of escape and what they are running away from is not only social problems but all other forms of moral responsibility. They are running away from the conscience and all its creations. . . ." I would agree only if we add that if farce involves running away from the conscience, it re-enacts that chase with the conscience as a strong contender. Bentley's descriptions of being driven from bedroom to bedroom by demons, of a loss of free will and control to something which "bristles with menace," something which threatens, in turn, to lose control, suggest that farce enacts something like a primitive superego punishment for the characters' libidinal release in the form of a maniacal plot which both arranges libidinal gratification and punishes for it. This would explain why the more the characters lose control in farce, the more tightly the plot is wound up; why the more the characters seek gratification, the more severely the plot punishes them for it. The lawless plot aggression in farce is, paradoxically enough, punitive superego aggression. Only conscience, primitive conscience, enjoys violence without guilt or cost. The characteristic sense of anxiety and menace in a highly elaborated, paranoid plot; the celebrated chase, the hallmark of farce; the series of blows mistakenly delivered—all are signs of a comedy of the superego. The secret of the strange enjoyment of farce may be that although we enjoy fulfilling forbidden wishes, we enjoy punishing them just as much, if not more, particularly when we can do so in a plot which is apparently devoid of logic, meaning, and harm.

Our understanding of farce has shifted, then, from an art form which simply enjoys libidinal release and gratification to a form which expresses, instead, a dialectic of gratification and punishment as gratification. (Hence the relation of bedroom farce to slapstick: the former provides the usual content of farce, the transgression; the latter the informing principle of the action, the form of farce, the punishment.) Although there is no literature on this dialectic in farce, Norman Shapiro discusses the theme of punishment in the works of that consummate farceur, Georges Feydeau. Shapiro is careful to distinguish between two different forms of punishment in Feydeau's plays: absurd punishment "which delights in recreating . . . the absurdity and inexplicability of everyday life"[8] and meaningful punishment, which satirizes human pretensions. His examples, however, negate that distinction, because they offer a striking similarity to dream episodes in which the gratification of an illicit wish is coupled with an apparently absurd yet obviously displaced punishment. Hence Shapiro designates punishment in a thinly disguised Oedipal plot as absurd and unwarranted. The only real distinction between the two groups is the degree to which the characters' transgressions, and hence the logic of the punishment, is disguised. Farce is not the typical product of a world view which enjoys contemplating "the absurdity and inexplicability of everyday life," then, but the product of a world in which life is considered all too explicable and moral values are regarded all too seriously—so seriously, in fact, that aggressive action taken both against certain laws and in the name of those laws provides much needed relief in the form of laughter.

What is of chief importance in understanding farce, then, is the recognition that the plot's aggression is punitive, and meaningfully so—a recognition in turn dependent upon the reconstruction of the characters' disguised, denied transgressions. We may gather these perceptions into a working model of farce as follows: farce is a type of comedy deriving laughter chiefly from the release and gratification of aggressive impulses, accomplished by a denial of the cause (through absurd situations) and the effect (through a surrealistic medium) of aggressive action upon an object, and functioning through the plot in a disguised punitive fashion which is directly related to the characters' disguised libidinal release.

The perfect psychoanalytic description of farce is in fact the punishment dream:

> In these dreams, as in so many others, the ego anticipates guilt, that is, superego condemnation, if the part of the latent content which derives from the repressed should find too direct an emergence in the manifest dream. Consequently, the ego's defenses oppose the emergence of this part of the latent content, which is again no different from what goes on in most other dreams. However, the result in the so-called punishment dreams is that the manifest dream, instead of expressing a more or less disguised fantasy of the fulfillment of a repressed wish expresses a more or less disguised fantasy of punishment for the wish in question, certainly a most extraordinary "compromise" among ego, id, and superego.[9]

There is no better description of the underlying dynamics of meaning in farce. The identification of farcical drama as a type of punishment dream or fantasy explains both the extensive disguise of its characters' libidinal transgressions (whether in content, cause, or effect) and their minimization in favor of audience and author identification with punitive plot action against those transgressions, disguised solely in terms of cause and effect.

Although *The Comedy of Errors* has been proved a thematically harmonious play, its imaginative direction still appears disjunctive to critics. There has been no successful attempt to uncover a method to the mad confusion of the twins' identities in the main plot or a reason for its envelopment by a frame plot concerning their father's woes. The cause of this critical standstill is a plot rife with contradictions, omissions, discontinuities, and disclaimers. The play appears to meander from the initial romance plot of Egeon's mysterious crime and debt, through his sons' farcical confrontation of mistaken punishment and payment for debt, back to his own miraculous forgiveness and redemption. The patterns of crime-punishment-forgiveness and debt-payment-redemption assert plot logic; the use of mystery, mistakes, miracle, and a disjunctive double plot deny it. The simultaneity of logic and absurdity, transgression and innocence, meaning and mistake, suggests that the play employs the disjunctive double plot and the device of errors to disperse and deny the meaning of one original, meaningful plot that can be retrieved.

The key question is whether the apparently absurd farcical aggression in the main plot is indeed meaningless or, in fact, punitive; whether it is causally related to some disguised transgression in the play and, if so, what transgression. Actually, the plot offers us two transgressions, Egeon's violation of Ephesian law in the frame plot and his sons' run-ins with domestic law in the main plot. Not only does the dual status of both culprit and crime wonderfully confuse the issue, but the fact that both transgressions are invalidated—either by ignorance of the law or mistaken identification of the culprit—further complicates matters, because it renders the punishment either perversely arbitrary or comically absurd. There is, at least, an interesting similarity in the two transgressions. The twins are mistakenly punished for each other's mistakenly unpaid debts, all of which are either due to a woman and are marital in nature or function as symbolic payment for the marital claim, whether in the form of a chain (symbolizing relationship) or a ring. Egeon's doom is also the result of an inability to pay a debt, however much the transgression resulting in that debt is obscured by lack of significant information. Although both transgressions involve unpaid debts, then, Egeon's debt is actual, obscure, and monetary, whereas his sons' debts are mistaken, meaningful, and marital. Thus, on the one hand, the play is obsessed with confronting, punishing, and forgiving debts, that action following a logical pattern and accompanied by significant emotional reaction. On the other hand, the play either invalidates those debts or obscures their significance, thereby denying any meaning to the characters' punishment. It appears that the play is denying what it desires to confront and disguising what it must enact.

Presented with a knockabout farce obsessed with the anguish and punishment of unpaid debts, yet notably devoid of any significant and valid debt, we are led to consider the hypothesis that the play is censoring or dislocating the debt's significance and validity; further, that it is this censoring activity which enables the play of otherwise unacceptable aggressive content associated with the debt. More simply, the hypothesis is that the play's harsh confrontation and punishment of unpaid debts is only made acceptable, indeed humorous, by disguising and dislocating its content and validity. Our strategy would then be to seek possible points of dislocation or displacement in the pattern of debts that might lead to the recovery of meaning.

For example, the play has been repeating and developing one theme, one situation, that of Egeon's debt. Yet it has been so developed as to add marital to monetary debts, mistaken debts to actual debts, sons' debts to a father's debt. Critics often overlook the fact that the twins' mistaken debits and credits are bracketed by the situation of Egeon's actual debt and redemption. This play, like so many of Shakespeare's early comedies, is set up in terms of a framework of problem (here bondage to the law in the form of indebtedness to and separation from others) and solution (here release from bondage, from debt, into union with others). The middle part of the play (the farce proper) must, therefore, present the working out of the problem, the means to a solution. Somehow, the twins' confrontation of mistaken debts, as well as their mistaken fulfillment of debts, is a means of paying a real debt, of working out Egeon's redemption. The denial of the significance of the twins' confrontation of debts is thus invalidated. Furthermore, were the twins not confronting Egeon's actual debt, this advance from his bondage to his freedom would be unwarranted. We are thus left with the thesis that the validity of the twins' debts is to be found in Egeon's situation; perhaps the meaningful content of Egeon's debt and the transgression associated with it may be found in the twins' situation.

Whereas the twins' confrontation of debts would seem to apply to Egeon's situation, the content of their debts does not. For the recurrent lectures, jokes, and reminders of unpaid debts in the main plot refer to a significant breach of marital obligations, while Egeon's debt is an apparently arbitrary, monetary one. Psychoanalysis has taught us, however, that fantasies of obscure yet fatal monetary debts are often disguised expressions of guilt over unmet personal obligations, especially when the monetary debts appear meaningless. Yet without substantiation of a valid marital debt in the play, this theory of its displacement would be inapplicable.

Adriana's copious complaints of marital neglect, coupled with the kitchenmaid Nell's equally relentless marital demands, strongly argue the existence of a valid marital debt or, at the very least, a considerable disjunction between male and female perceptions of what constitutes marital obligations in Ephesus. Even if we grant, however, that Adriana's jealousy undermines the validity of her complaint, there is one claim of hers concerning her husband's neglect of marital obligations that remains undisputed, and further, which corresponds to Egeon's situation. Adriana rightly believes her husband to be guilty of not returning home that day (2.1.1), and Antipholus of Ephesus admits that wrong in conceiving of the work on the gold chain as an excuse for his absence (3.1.1). The highlight of Egeon's story is equally a failure to return home, which, while it is melodramatically presented to us as the result of "cruel fate," is not the first such incident in his biography. It is, however, the one instance in which Egeon's separation from his spouse is attributed to external forces, earlier separations being attributed once to business (1.1.39-43), and once, most significantly, to personal preference (1.1.58-60).

That the action of cruel fate which separated Egeon from his wife was seconded by his own guilty wish for independence is further suggested by the fact that Egeon allows eighteen years to escape without searching for Emilia and is only motivated in his present journey to Ephesus by the loss of his Syracusan son. The crime of marital neglect, in the form of a failure to return home for a significant lapse of time, provides a genesis for the plot, explaining such problematic issues as Egeon's curiously passive acceptance of a decidedly obscure punishment, the significance of the twins' prolonged punishment for neglected marital obligations at the hands of Adriana and Nell, and the means by which that punishment wins Egeon's redemption.

Finally, the fact that Egeon's initial situation couples indebtedness with separation from others, whereas his release from debt results in his re-union with his wife, also suggests that his debt is indeed marital rather than monetary. Thus there is a sense in which the marital debt is both significant and valid and provides a meaningful link between the frame plot and the main plot. Since the monetary debts contracted do not ful-fill this condition, it seems justified to consider that they are a disguised expression of the marital debt and that the meaningful content of Egeon's debt is disclosed in the marital debts that his sons confront.

To summarize: true to its farcical design, the play is censoring the meaning and validity of its debts and the aggression associated with them, displacing logic by splitting the truth of one plot into two. The play is only working out one debt, the twins in the main plot serving as symbolic representatives of their father. The validity of their mistaken debts resides in Egeon's actual crime; the nature of Egeon's vague, impersonal, mone-tary debt resides in the specific marital debts that his sons confront. The errors are meaningful and project a disguised means of enacting self-punishment for neglected marital obligations.

The hypothesis that the twins represent Egeon is borne out by an analysis of the function of their status as "doubles." In *The Comedy of Errors*, as in many of Shakespeare's early works, the trope equating the self with the beloved and, hence, separation from the beloved with self-division is in plentiful evidence. In Act 2, Adriana describes her hus-band's separation from her in terms of his self-estrangement:

> How comes it now, my husband, O how comes it,
> That thou art then estrangèd from thyself?
> Thyself I call it, being strange to me,
> That, undividable, incorporate,
> Am better than thy dear self's better part.
> Ah, do not tear away thyself from me. (2.2.120-25)

To be separated from one's spouse is associated with a splitting of one's identity into two distinct, opposing selves: a shared marital persona, the undividable and incorporate "thou"; and a single, dear persona, the "thyself." This speech relates to neither of the Antipholi; it does relate, however, to their father, Egeon, who has been separated from his spouse for over twenty years. If, by implication, Egeon is estranged not only from his wife but from his marital identity, divided into single and marital personae, we might consider his twin sons as symbolic of his self-division. It is only after Egeon's first separation from his wife and when his wife comes to see him in Epidamnum—or, as Adriana would put it, only when

Egeon's past (marital) and then present (single) identities confront each other—that the concept and fact of doubleness are engendered: Emilia gives birth to twins. The symbolic function of the twins is explained here by the fact that one can only conceive of selfhood as a duality when one has severed one's identity from the past, rather than conceiving of identity as constant and unified in time, and when one is confronted with that past.

The twins' symbolic function becomes especially evident when one notes the exact correspondence of their opposing characteristics to Egeon's marital and postmarital, past and present, unified and divided identities. Antipholus of Ephesus is quite literally the part of Egeon that has remained lost with his wife since the storm finally separated the couple; Antipholus of Syracuse is that part of Egeon that has remained with him. Antipholus of Ephesus is married to a demanding wife, as his father was long ago, while Antipholus of Syracuse is a bachelor, as Egeon is now. Although there is some confusion about the order of the twins' births, the married brother is twice referred to and commonly accepted as the older of the two, which relates him to Egeon's past, whereas the single brother is the younger, which relates him to Egeon's present. Antipholus of Ephesus has no knowledge of his brother, hence no awareness of, no condition of split identity; as Egeon's identity in the past, he has no premonition of future self-division. Antipholus of Syracuse, as Egeon's present identity, is aware of his divided condition and seeks to remedy it.

Antipholus of Syracuse is further associated with Egeon's present, divided state when he is advised by a friend to deny his birthplace and call his home Epidamnum, thereby recalling Egeon's separation from birthplace, wife, and past when he left for Epidamnum. The Syracusan twin thus lodges at the Centaur, sign of a divided state, whereas the Ephesian brother who must be recovered lodges at the Phoenix, sign of rebirth. The Ephesian twin, lost with Egeon's wife, is the stable, secure marital identity of Egeon's youth; the Syracusan twin is the fragile identity of Egeon's present, the single traveler seeking to recover what has been lost in time, to find his other half, to integrate himself, to be reborn: "So I, to find a mother and a brother, / In quest of them, unhappy, lose myself" (1.2.39-40). The part of the self that has been lost and is sought by Egeon is his past marital identity, represented realistically by his separation from his wife in the frame plot, and symbolically by Antipholus of Syracuse's search for his long-lost married brother in the main plot.

The play, then, is not simply about the payment of debts or the physical division and reunion of a family, but about the psychic division and integration of a personality, the reintegration of a long-denied part of oneself through psychological payment as well. That the path to the integration of Egeon's personality should involve the "mistaken" identification of single and married twins with each other may seem immediately less problematic. That the "miraculous" recovery of Egeon's past marital identity depends upon the "mistaken" confrontation of marital debts may also seem more logical. The farcical misunderstandings of identity, the absurd series of debts directed at the "wrong" man, are not as nonsensical as they at first appear. The two actions are one; the errors no errors at all.

Notes

1. Anne Barton, "Introduction" to *The Comedy of Errors*, The Riverside Shakespeare (Boston: Houghton Mifflin, 1974), p. 79.
2. E. M. W. Tillyard, *Shakespeare's Early Comedies* (London: Chatto & Windus, 1965), p. 69.
3. Berners A. W. Jackson so characterizes the two farces, along with *The Two Gentlemen of Verona*, in his Introduction to the latter play in The Pelican Shakespeare (Baltimore: Penguin, 1969), p. 55.
4. Paul A. Jorgenson, "Introduction" to *The Comedy of Errors*, The Pelican Shakespeare, p. 116.
5. See Bernard Sobel, ed., *The New Theatre Handbook* (New York: Crown Publishers, 1959), p. 282; Phyllis Hartnoll, ed., *The Oxford Companion to the Theatre*, 3rd ed. (London: Oxford Univ. Press, 1967), p. 308; Walter Parker Bowman and Robert Hamilton Ball, eds., *Theatre Language: A Dictionary of Terms* (New York: Theatre Art Books, 1961), p. 131; Glynne William Gladstone Wickham, "Farce," *The Encyclopaedia Britannica* (Chicago: William Benton, 1972), pp. 67-68; John Russell Taylor, comp., *The Penguin Dictionary of the Theatre* (Harmondsworth, England: Penguin Books, 1966), pp. 97-98; and M. H. Abrams, *A Glossary of Literary Terms*, 3rd ed. (New York: Holt, Rinehart, & Winston, 1971), p. 27.
6. Roger Fowler, ed., *A Dictionary of Modern Critical Terms* (Boston: Routledge & Kegan Paul, 1973), p. 70.
7. This quotation and all following references to Bentley are from the chapters "Farce" and "Comedy" in *The Life of the Drama* (New York: Atheneum, 1967).
8. Norman R. Shapiro, "Suffering and Punishment in the Theatre of Georges Feydeau," *The Tulane Drama Review*, 5 (1959), 126.
9. Charles Brenner, *An Introductory Textbook of Psychoanalysis* (1955; rpt. Garden City, N.Y.: Doubleday-Anchor, 1957), p. 184.

Bibliographical Note

This essay is indebted to Eric Bentley's pioneering work in drama studies, *The Life of the Drama* (New York: Atheneum, 1967), and to Norman Holland's classic study of the potential contributions of psychoanalytic theory to literary criticism, *The Dynamics of Literary Response* (New York: Oxford Univ. Press, 1968).

20

Semiotics and Shakespeare's Comedies

MARION TROUSDALE

I begin with a received view that of Northrop Frye. In *A Natural Perspective* and at greater length in *Anatomy of Criticism*, Frye argues that
literature is a secular displacement of myth, that the mythical background
of all literature is the cycle of nature, and that comedy reflects the second
half of this cycle, the movement from winter to spring.[1] Such a definition from origin purports to be historical, but as in Freud, origins define
essences, and the underlying nostalgia for a lost primitivism renders
Frye's definition antihistorical. Comedy's authenticity lies rather in a
Vicovian *verum factum*—tales created by man to impose order on his
world. Thus Shakespeare's conventions in comedy work because of their
primitive origins: they are attached in some way to a submerged part
of our being, and he works toward uncovering a primeval, archetypal
form.[2] It is a form whose dialectic importance seems for Frye to have the
force of magic. "The action of a Shakespearean comedy, then, is not
simply cyclical but dialectical as well: the renewing power of the final
action lifts us into a higher world, and separates that world from the
world of the comic action itself."[3]

If genre is, in Rosalie Colie's words, a fix on life; if, as Frye says, comedy's formula "is deeply involved with a structure in which redemption from death or even revival from death, is a central element,"[4] then such a form is expressionistic as well as archetypal. It expresses the individual's and the community's needs. Shakespeare's comedies usually begin "with an anticomic society, a social organization blocking and opposed to the comic drive, which the action of the comedy evades or overcomes. . . . at the same time the irrational society represents social reality, the obstacles to our desires that we recognize in the world around us, whereas the society of the conclusion is the realizing of what we want but seldom expect to see."[5] But Frye also uses the Aristotelian assumption that the workings of drama and of art generally are mimetic and that departure from what is credible—a definition in some respects of comedy— depends for its success on a total suspension of disbelief. Shakespeare's audience, he remarks, is not allowed to think. It is not allowed to think because the comic conventions with which Frye is concerned seem unnatural to him. But forms which take their shape from nature and which are mimetic cannot be unnatural. Hence, their truth must lie below the surface. This truth can be Freudian as well as Vicovian. "In the action of a Shakespearean comedy," Frye writes, "the kind of force associated with 'wish fulfillment' is not helpless or purely a matter of dreams. It is, in the first place, a power as deeply rooted in nature and reality as its opponent; in the second place, it is a power that we see, as the comedy proceeds, taking over and informing the predictable world."[6]

It is instructive to set beside the Frye for whom comedy is a societal rite the other Frye who looks at literature as a series of texts and at its structures as autonomous and self-generating, made up not of anachronistic rituals but of viable societal signs. This second Frye sees character as a function of plot and value as a dramatic postulate. And he remarks at one point that at least some of Shakespeare's comedies use conventions not to present a hidden reality but in order to explore the convention itself. Such comedies use comic conventions the way we use the word *dog* when we say, "*Dog* is a noun." The Shakespeare that emerges from such views is neither childlike nor naive. A comedy is no longer a play which ends happily. It is rather "a play in which a certain structure is present and works through to its own logical end."[7] This 'structuralist' Frye has suggested that dramatic texts grow out of other texts, that comic structure is autonomous and self-generating, that conventions, as nouns and verbs, partake of the nature of distinguishable signs. Such descriptions of genre are concerned not with what genre represents, the hypothetical object behind the structure and that the structure 'means,' but with the structure itself. My argument will be that generic structure is a semiological structure and that the system of relationships to which we respond is different in degree but not in kind from the system of relationships that Saussure observed in ordinary language.[8]

In Saussure's view, meaning is linked to a perception of *difference*, and elements of a system are defined by their relation to other elements of that system. We distinguish the word *tell* from the word *fell* by distinguishing the difference between a *t* and an *f*. In the same way comedy, the name that we give to a particular structure of events on the stage, is discernible as structure only in relation to tragedy. Shakespeare might have had Hero die in *Much Ado About Nothing.* We classify the fact that he didn't according to a preestablished scale that has comedy at one end and tragedy at the other. That Hero doesn't die, we might say, makes it possible for us to classify the play in which Hero appears. But we know at the very beginning of the play that she won't die. Such patterns are language patterns rather than mimetic actions and we respond to those patterns in the same way in which we respond to language. That is to say, we "read" both the actor and the action as we watch them on stage. And we read them not in terms of meaning in Frye's sense but in terms of function. That is the essential "meaning" a convention has. We know that Hero cannot die, just as we know that Claudio will marry her and that Don John will somehow be thwarted. We place each character and each action according to a recognized grammar. And as with subjects and verbs in traditional grammar, we know according to this grammar, how each character is going to act. Thus action that seems mimetic is actually functioning very much as parts of speech function in a sentence. If one knows the code well enough, the relationship of part to part in all important senses is predictable. *When*, introducing a clause, tells us that a noun or a pronoun with its modifiers will follow. In the same way we know that Duke Frederick in *As You Like It* will banish Rosalind and that she will in the end have her Orlando. As Frye has pointed out, there must be an obstructing action at the beginning that there might be a resolution at the end. But it is not that we suspend disbelief in watching Rosalind woo Orlando. Belief is never in question so long as the syntax is correct. What we are apt to question are violations of an established code.

Predictability then seems to me an essential characteristic both of grammatical structure and of genre. Structure in this sense is structure of plot and predictability is a predictability of function. At the level of function we always know the plot and it is that knowledge that makes it possible for us to watch the play. It is within the context of this knowledge of a known convention that we make distinctions and that we "read." Thus we distinguish *The Comedy of Errors* from *Twelfth Night* not only by noting the different ways in which the protasis (exposition) is handled in both plays, but also by observing how in the one, mistaken identity in its simplest sense provides the ground for the entire plot, whereas in the other there are many kinds of mistaken identity. Nonetheless, we recognize Malvolio as belonging to the same group of characters as Antipholus of Ephesus, and I would argue that the beginning of *Twelfth Night* is like the beginning of *The Comedy of Errors* in much the same way in which *John hit the ball* is like *Mary bit the cat.* We are not surprised in either play that mistakes in identity result in confusions in love.

The distinctions we make are distinctions of kind, between comedy and tragedy and between comedy and comedy. And meaning is created as it is in an ordinary language sentence by means of differences, not by reference to a world elsewhere. Similarly, within an individual play our sense of Beatrice in *Much Ado* is in part created by our sense of Hero, and our awareness of Rosalind in *As You Like It* results from her differences from Celia. Plot itself is structured in this fashion. Frye sees the anti-comic world at the beginning of the play as antisocial forces overcome in the end to create a new society. If we understand that that reading is generated by the differences defining the form's structure, then we can partially agree with Frye. But insofar as such difference is characteristic of language generally, we should recognize that, rather than some myth about nature, the structure of comedy reflects the linguistic aspect of signifying systems. The structures which we invest with meaning themselves determine the shapes of those meanings, just as the activity of reading itself gives birth to new texts.

What then can be said about theme in comedy? Frye remarks that certain formulas recur—the storm at sea, identical twins, the heroine disguised as a boy, the retreat into the forest, the heroine with a mysterious father, and the disappearing ruler.[9] I shall return to these semantic kernels because they provide further proof of just how linguistic Shakespeare's comedies actually are. But before looking at such thematic shapings, I want to explore the use of folk ritual from which these formulas are said to come. Although Frye claims that Shakespearean comedy is dependent on folk festivals, and mentions in particular St. George and the Dragon, it is actually C. L. Barber who has convinced us of the importance of popular ritual in comedy. And it is easy to see in the folk festivals that Barber's *Shakespeare's Festive Comedy* describes, forms of language. It is as forms of language that they find their way into Shakespeare's plays.

Barber points out, for instance, that in *A Midsummer Night's Dream* Shakespeare is "developing a May-game action at length to express the will in nature that is consummated in marriage."[10] We have here a specific instance in which Shakespeare uses a folk festival that continues today. In the sixteenth century men and women celebrated by "gadding over night to the woods . . . where they spend the whole night in pleasant pastime."[11] In Shakespeare's play the lovers do not go into the woods because of May Day. Rather, Hermia and Lysander are on their way to Lysander's widow aunt, who lives seven leagues from Athens. They are followed by Helena and Demetrius, each in pursuit of her or his beloved. Here the confusion associated with a night of sexual license is created first by the lovers getting lost in the woods and subsequently by the manipulations of Puck. The play's confusion is identified both with magic and love, but its association with license is oblique. Let us for the moment use the categories developed by Saussure and amplified by Roland Barthes[12] and think of May Day as *signifier*, and license, madness, and love as *signified*—two sides, as Saussure says, of the same piece of paper cut out in a particular shape. In Shakespeare's version of the festival, the confusion arising from lawful sexual license, is expressed by what Barthes has described as second level language. May Day as a sign has been emptied of its primary meaning and the identification of May Day with a particular kind of sexual confusion operates as signifier of the kind of confusion Hermia and Helena experience, a confusion arising from mistaken love.

The playwright handles the fairies in similar fashion. Latham noted in 1930 that Shakespeare's fairies seem more benign than Elizabethan fairies in general were thought to be.[13] The source most often cited for Puck as Robin Goodfellow is Reginald Scott's treatise on witchcraft. In this treatise Scott not only remarks that Robin Goodfellow heretofore was as terrible and also as credible to the people "as hags and witches be now," but he argues that good Christians have no business believing in fairies at all.[14] Again, to sketch out very crudely what Shakespeare seems to have done, he takes the folk beliefs of the fairy lore, that is, superstitious credulity, and equates them both with magic—they are not as bad as you think, or perhaps, they are not what you think—and the frailty of art. The sign is again emptied of its original meaning, and both signifier and meaning are used as sign. But a trace of the original sign remains. Shakespeare is not simply using the semiotic systems available to him as the means of his art. He is rather creating a new language which grows out of a critical exploration of the old.

We can see in these two instances how this "new language" is expressed. Comedy as genre can still be defined as societal in origin and in use, but its devices would seem to be semiological ones by means of which new codes are made. Puck with his broom makes us aware of the Robin Goodfellow who does the household chores, but in becoming aware of Robin Goodfellow, we notice that that kind of magic has even less substance than the art of Shakespeare's play. In a similar way Viola teaches Olivia and us that romantic love is a code. The same observation can be made about the language in *As You Like It* and *Love's Labor's Lost*. As Barber remarks, "in a self-conscious culture, the heritage of cult is kept alive by art which makes it relevant as a mode of perception and expression."[15] My only disagreement is one of emphasis. The cult, obviously, was already a mode of expression, so we can say that Shakespeare's examination of modes of expression is characteristic of his comedy. Barber saw the comedies as organizing experience and clarifying the relationship between man and nature. The first activity is a semiotic one, and it is our relation to signs that is clarified rather than our relation to nature.

But the troubling question of theme is yet to be faced, and any attempt to deal with genre cannot ultimately escape it. Comedy and tragedy are themselves signs. They are, as Saussure's *langue*, shapes cut out of pieces of language, and the *signified* cannot be separated from the *signifier.* What we find attached to the *signified* side of this shape, insofar as comedy is concerned, is a collection of topoi. I have argued earlier that predictability is one of the characteristics of genre and one of the functions of various aspects of the plot. The scope of that predictability can be extended to include theme. I am using this word as Albert Lord uses it in his discussion of the characteristics of oral literature: themes are the "group of ideas regularly used in telling a tale in the formulaic style of traditional song."[16] Themes in that sense also partake of the nature of formulas. They are semantic kernels attached to generic situations.

If we look again at Frye's list—storm at sea, identical twins, disappearing ruler, heroine disguised, retreat into the forest, the heroine with a mysterious father—we see a collection of various items. *Storm at sea* might be a description of setting or of exposition; *identical twins* refers to character; and *disappearing ruler* seems to be a piece of plot. Such formulas become theme to my mind when they are verbally exploited as subject matter and through recurrence made part of the semantic texture of the play. Thus Antipholus of Syracuse, in *The Comedy of Errors*, says of himself: "I to the world am like a drop of water/ That in the ocean seeks another drop" (1.2.35-36), and in *The Tempest* Ferdinand hears that "Full fathom five" (1.2.399) his father lies and that he has suffered a sea-change into something rich and strange. In a similar way the music heard on stage in *Twelfth Night* becomes a controlling part of the play's language and, as John Hollander has shown, is used within a context of musical ideas made more explicit in *The Merchant of Venice*. We might see such semantic threads as received ideas woven through the plays as threads of meaning. Yet their use suggests something different from our usual sense of meaning as intentional content.

Thematic formulas appear to be attached to situations which themselves recur in the genre. They are then in some ways stock responses. Madness, for instance, is attached to mistaken identity. The extent to which this is so can be seen in Sebastian's remarks after he has been received by Olivia: "And though 'tis wonder that enwraps me thus/Yet 'tis not madness" (4.3.3-4). It is an explanation and a verbal association he rejects, something he could not do were the association not there to be rejected. Similarly, Leontes like Iago remarks on paddling palms and pinching fingers and consoles himself, as Othello had done earlier, with the observation that this is a bawdy planet and that the pinch of adultery comes only from the knowledge of it (*The Winter's Tale*, 2.1.36; *Othello*, 3.3.342).

The almost mechanical way in which Shakespeare amplifies such semantic kernels can be seen in his use of sources in *The Comedy of Errors*. As Bullough observes, the remarkable thing is the complexity he wove within the simple Plautine plot. He did this in the first instance by the addition of the twin servants which he found in another Plautine play, expanding the play as one might expand a sentence with additional clauses, modifiers, and prepositional phrases. Insofar as meaning governs his choices, it governs them only, I would say, in the ways in which semantic concerns are involved in any use of signs. Twin servants make it possible to increase significantly the number of errors. The twin servants are then generated by the title and can be accounted for as rationally as examples of a thesis sentence. In a similar way we can see how the change of Ephesus for Epidamnum generates not only insistence on a town "full of cozenage," but also an interpretation of Antipholus of Ephesus as possessed, with the need for an exorcist rather than a *medicus* or doctor to cure him.

No one would deny that Shakespeare's comedies are made up of language. That stage action itself should often be semantically generated may seem more problematic. What is suggested is an assembling of parts that is rule-governed and linguistically based. Louise Clubb in discussing Italian comedy of the sixteenth century has usefully identified the repertory of dramatic patterns available to sixteenth-century playwrights as theatergrams—a collection of movable and combinable parts which in her description range from units of action or character to thematic patterns or metaphoric uses of intrigue structure. Thus in *Twelfth Night* she notes Shakespeare's use of the love-sick transvestite heroine, the aristocratic Illyrean milieu, the courted rich young widow, the got-up duel between reluctant participants, the imprisonment in a dark room—all of which had been used and reused in *commedie erudite* but never in that particular combination, and all of which can be seen in other Shakespearean plays.

Such structures as signs are capable of transformations, as is the English sentence, and can generate other verbal shapes. The assumed infidelity of a Hero can by generic transformation become the assumed infidelity of a Desdemona, even as a prince who has lost his father and woos Ophelia can by semantic and syntactic transformations become a Helena who has lost her father and woos a prince. Leontes and Othello we know appear in different kinds of plays. The same observation has to be made in talking about themes. Love, death, friendship, madness, dream, illusion, wit, nature are among the topoi attached to Shakespeare's romantic comedies. But these topoi appear to be generated by patterns smaller in kind than we might at first imagine, and it is these smaller units which are made part of larger structures and, as part of these structures, transformed. Both dream and madness are an important part of *Hamlet*, a play in which disguise has a purpose different from *Twelfth Night*. And nature, so important in *As You Like It*, cannot be separated from the tragedy of *Lear*. We have looked earlier at Shakespeare's association of madness with disguise and remarked briefly on his variation of that set association in the remarks of Sebastian after he had been received by Olivia. The uses of this topos in *The Comedy of Errors* and in *Twelfth Night* show us something about how Shakespeare employed theatergrams, and it is with examples from each play that I should like to conclude.

After he has met Adriana, Antipholus of Syracuse remarks:

> What, was I married to her in my dream?
> Or sleep I now and think I hear all this?
> What error drives our eyes and ears amiss?
>
> (2.2.183-185)

Having been attacked by Sir Andrew and received by Olivia, Sebastian remarks:

> What relish is in this? How runs the stream?
> Or I am mad, or else this is a dream.
> Let fancy still my sense in Lethe steep;
> If it be thus to dream, still let me sleep!
>
> (4.1.61-64)

Were we to explicate Antipholus' response, we would have to say that sleep and dream as used here blur the sharp outline of reality, at least from Antipholus' point of view, and we might, if we liked, attach his observations to his earlier ones in which he sees himself as a drop of water and feels himself to be lost. Sebastian, on the other hand, uses dream in such a way that it acts as a compliment to Olivia and this compliment is heightened in the last two lines of the speech to suggest the true pleasure he takes in Olivia's company. The bewilderment as such has deepened into an expression of love.

Similarly, Antipholus later in the same scene says:

> Am I in earth, in heaven, or in hell?
> Sleeping or waking, mad or well advis'd
> Known unto these, and to myself disguised
>
> (2.2.213-15)

As we have seen above, Sebastian remarks that though wonder enwraps him, yet it isn't madness. Some thoughts about Antonio follow, and he then says:

> For though my soul disputes well with my sense,
> That this may be some error, but no madness,
> Yet doth this accident and flood of fortune
> So far exceed all instance, all discourse,
> That I am ready to distrust mine eyes,
> And wrangle with my reason that persuades me
> To any other trust but that I am mad,
> Or else the lady's mad; yet if 'twere so,
> She could not sway her house, command her followers,
> Take and give back affairs, and their dispatch,

With such a smooth, discreet, and stable bearing
As I perceive she does. There's something in't
That is deceivable.

(4.3.9-21)

We see Shakespeare handling a theme in much the same way in which we earlier saw him handling folk conventions. Sebastian's exploration of the commonplace is in essence an examination of the commonplace to see how and in what ways it might be applied. As a result, his character is more deeply etched than that of Antipholus, and *Twelfth Night*, filled with such craft, more profound in its considerations and more original than *The Comedy of Errors*. Such explorations are certainly a part, and an essential part, of Shakespeare's comedies. They provide, if not release, at least a kind of clarification, though that clarification may involve nothing more than a clear sense of how madness and dream, given a shipwreck and twins, might be used to create two very different plays. What makes both plays comedies is not this clarification as such, but the ordering of the theatergrams out of which they are made.

The assessment of such critics as Frye of what is central to human experience, or perhaps to human existence and by extension to our art, is that we are as human beings in essence nonverbal, and that is a view with which I simply disagree. We are deemed nonverbal in the sense that, among other possible explanations of our actions, what is intuitive is thought most significant. Shakespeare's comedy is a derivative but nevertheless intuitive form. We are thought nonverbal beyond that because we were once primitive, and what we once were, in spite of the overlay of history and civilization, we continue in a Lawrentian fashion to be. But genre, it behooves us to remember, like Saussure's *langue*, is a purely abstract entity, and that entity has been verbally and conceptually abstracted from a variety of linguistic forms. Gerard Genette in talking about Aristotle's *Poetics* remarks that tragedy to Aristotle marks the intersection between the modal and the thematic.[17] I would say rather that the thematic in genre is modal and that it is because of this fact that topoi recur, with those differences out of which we generate meaning. And these differences occur more often than not in the exploration of established themes.

When we say that comedies end happily we are making much the same kind of observation about a play as we make about a declarative sentence when we say that the subject precedes the verb. In a semiotic system we are describing the functional relationships between the constitutive parts. This is not to say that the happy ending has no meaning. *Joan bit the cat* describes an action. But the fact that *bit* follows *Joan* is an arbitrary convention of order by means of which, having learned the code, we are able to read. If we agree that such order is arbitrary, then we can see that meanings as such cannot be used to account for that order. There is nothing intrinsically declarative about subject-verb. Insofar as order as such defines both the declarative sentence and genre, one can obviously argue that a happy ending is one of the distinguishing marks of comedy.

But the ending itself, like the topoi we looked at earlier, comes into being not because of an act that the form seeks to imitate, as Frye suggests, but rather because of accepted linguistic patterns to which such endings and such topoi are attached. This is proved in part by the fact that the topoi, attached to patterns smaller than those that constitute genre, recur in large structures in which the patterns of order change. I have called such uses of what we like to think of as meaning "modal" because such uses are relational rather than substantive. They involve certain kinds of order rather than certain kinds of theme. When Northrop Frye sees in comic resolution a renewed sense of social integration, a kind of moral norm, he is giving us a reading of comic closure that grows out of a knowledge of tragic closure. He certainly recognizes the code, but he confuses the meanings that are generated with the structure generating these meanings. Obviously, comic structure can generate many meanings. But crucial to any definition of that structure is the mechanism by means of which we recognize and anticipate the function of its parts. It is this aspect of genre that Frye describes when he says that a comedy is not a play that ends happily, but "a play in which a certain structure is present and works through to its own logical end."

Notes

1. *Anatomy of Criticism* (Princeton: Princeton Univ. Press, 1957), pp. 163-86 and passim. See also "The Argument of Comedy," *Myth in the Later Plays of Shakespeare,* ed. J. A. Robertson, Jr. (New York: Columbia Univ. Press, 1949), p. 65.
2. *A Natural Perspective* (New York: Harcourt, Brace, 1965), p. 58.
3. Ibid., p. 133.
4. Ibid., p. 139. He is discussing *All's Well That Ends Well.*
5. Ibid., p. 73-75.
6. Ibid., p. 123.
7. Ibid., p. 46.
8. This is to assume that the rules of phonology entail rules of semantics. For the difficulties in this view, see Neil Smith and Deirdre Wilson, *Modern Linguistics* (Harmondsworth, England: Penguin Books, 1979).
9. *Natural Perspective,* p. 7.
10. *Shakespeare's Festive Comedy* (Princeton: Princeton Univ. Press, 1959, 1972), p. 132.
11. *Festive Comedy,* p. 119. Barber is quoting Phillip Stubbes.
12. *Elements of Seminology,* trans. by Annette Lavers and Colin Smith (Boston: Beacon Press, 1970), p. 35-57; *Mythologies,* trans. by Annette Lavers (New York: Hill and Wang, 1957), pp. 109-127.
13. Minor White Latham, *The Elizabethan Fairies* (New York: Columbia Univ. Press, 1930).
14. *Narrative and Dramatic Sources of Shakespeare,* ed. Geoffrey Bullough (New York: Columbia Univ. Press, 1966), I, 395-96.
15. *Festive Comedy,* p. 15.
16. *The Singer of Tales* (Cambridge: Harvard Univ. Press, 1960), p. 68.
17. "Genres, 'types', modes," *Poétique,* 32 (1977), 389-421.

Bibliographical Note

The most useful recent works include Terence Hawkes, *Structuralism and Semiotics* (Berkeley: Univ. of California Press, 1977); Umberto Eco, *A Theory of Semiotics* (Bloomington: Indiana Univ. Press, 1976); Pierre Guiraud, *Semiology*, trans. George Gross (London: Routledge, Kegan Paul, 1975); Roman Jakobson, *Coup d'oeil sur le développement de la sémiotique* (Bloomington: Indiana Univ. Research Center for Language and Semiotic Studies, 1975); Julia Kristéva, *Sémiotiké* (Paris: Editions du Seuil, 1974); and, of course, the work of Roland Barthes, particularly *Elements of Semiology*, trans. Annette Lavers and Colin Smith (Boston: Beacon Press, 1970) and *Mythologies*, trans. Annette Lavers (New York: Hill and Wang, 1957). The work of Ferdinand de Saussure is available in English as *Course in General Linguistics*, ed. Charles Bally, Albert Sechehaye, Albert Riedlinger, trans. Wade Baskin (New York: The Philosophical Library, 1959), and a useful book on Saussure has been written by Jonathan Culler, *Saussure* (Glasgow: Fontana Modern Masters, 1976).

The most recent work in linguistics is discussed in depth by Neil Smith and Deirdre Wilson in *Modern Linguistics* (Harmondsworth, England: Penguin Books, 1979). One should look as well at the very important work of Jacques Derrida, particularly *Of Grammatology*, trans. Gayatri Chakravorty Spivak (Baltimore: The Johns Hopkins Univ. Press, 1976); *Speech and Phenomena*, trans. David B. Allison (Evanston: Northwestern Univ. Press, 1973); and *Writing and Difference*, trans. Alan Bass (Chicago: Univ. of Chicago Press, 1978). The works of Northrop Frye that I have used for this paper include "The Argument of Comedy," *Myth in the Later Plays of Shakespeare*, ed. D. A. Robertson, Jr. (New York: Columbia Univ. Press, 1949), pp. 58-73; *Anatomy of Criticism* (Princeton: Princeton Univ. Press, 1957); and *A Natural Perspective* (New York: Harcourt, Brace, 1965). Useful analyses of Frye can be found in *Northrop Frye in Modern Criticism*, ed. Murray Krieger (New York: Columbia Univ. Press, 1966).

PART 8

TEXTS
AND
DOCUMENTS

21

Ancient Theories of Comedy: The Treatises of Evanthius and Donatus

S. GEORGIA NUGENT

The Significance of the Text

The text that follows forms the preface to a collection of commentaries on the comedies of Terence, which is attributed to Donatus.[1] This treatise excites considerable interest for two reasons. The first (discussed by Susan Snyder and Ruth Nevo in this volume) is the great influence the work exercised on later comic theory and practice, particularly in the sixteenth century. In *Comic Theory in the Sixteenth Century*, Marvin Herrick sums up this aspect when he says, "It was Donatus who taught the sixteenth century what the pattern and function of both comedy and tragedy ought to be."[2]

The second reason why particular interest attaches to Donatus is that the theory of comedy in antiquity is a subject about which we are rather remarkably uninformed.[3] In *Comedy High and Low*, Maurice Charney calls attention to our contemporary lack of a shared critical discourse for discussing the comic.[4] Interestingly enough, ancient literary theory shows this same gap. G. M. A. Grube, in his study of the subject, comments on the strange lack of a well-articulated consideration of comedy, even by authors such as Plato, who were clearly excellent practitioners of the comic art:

> It is curious that Plato, so adept at humour, irony, sarcasm, and even farce, should have reflected so little on the nature of the comic. It is even more curious, though this may be accidental, that we have very little more on this subject from Aristotle or any other Greek writer.[5]

The one genre, of course, which was thoroughly treated in antiquity was tragedy, in Aristotle's *Poetics*. For comedy, we possess no such treatise. The *Poetics*, however, as well as the *Rhetoric*, contain allusions to a treatment of comedy, which was apparently comparable to the study of tragedy in the *Poetics*. The existence of such references has led to the theory, now widely accepted, that there originally existed either a second book of the *Poetics* or another, separate Aristotelian work that did treat of comedy and is now lost.

We do possess, however, a curious document known as the *Coslinian Tractate*.[6] The text was first printed in 1839, from a tenth-century manuscript in the De Coislin collection at Paris. The *Tractate* is a very brief (approximately three-page) treatment of comedy that alternates between bare outlines (subdividing topics into headings, which appear on the page much like a genealogical table) and short, discursive definitions. Opinions on the date of this document, its value, and its place in a peripatetic tradition vary widely. On the one hand, Lane Cooper has used it to reconstruct what might have been the Aristotelian treatment of comedy in the lost book of the *Poetics*. At the other extreme, A. P. McMahon doubts that there ever was a second book of the *Poetics* and does not rate very high the value of the rather mystifying *Tractate*. Grube, on the whole, follows McMahon in downplaying the significance of the *Tractate* in the peripatetic tradition.

Whatever the work's claim, however, to filling the gap in Aristotelian theory, one thing is clear. The *Coslinian Tractate*, through its definition and division of comedy, as well as its discussion of the aims and means of the comic art, does represent an attempt to treat the genre on an abstract, theoretical level. Slight though the work may be, it clearly proceeds from important questions such as, What is comedy? What is the purpose of comedy? How does it accomplish that purpose? This is one reason why considerable attention has been paid to the *Tractate*, and particularly to the most interesting section of it, which attempts to detail the causes of laughter. For our purposes, then, the importance of the *Tractate* is the standard it provides, sketchy though it be, of what a theoretical treatment of the genre might entail. The discussion of comedy in the Donatan corpus may be measured against this standard. Before analyzing the contents and structure of the Donatan treatise, however, one must have some

---

familiarity with the history of the work.

The History of the Text

This little treatise on comedy has a curious and disputed history.[7] Although it appears here and in editions of the Terentian commentaries as one unit, it is in fact believed by modern scholars to be the compilation of two texts, written by two authors: Evanthius and Donatus. Of Donatus we know little, of Evanthius almost nothing. Both were grammarians of the mid-fourth century, and both are mentioned in the universal history of St. Jerome, who was in fact a pupil of Donatus. In his chronicle for the year 353 A.D., Jerome records the entry, "Victorinus and the grammarian Donatus, my teacher, were held in high regard at Rome." In the year 358 we read, "Evanthius, the most learned of the grammarians of Constantinople, died." Several other ancient references to Donatus and his commentary on Terence exist in the works of Jerome, Priscian, and others. Jerome's notice of Evanthius' death, however, provides half of all the information we possess on this author.

The second of the two ancient references to Evanthius supplies the evidence on which our text is attributed to his hand, for it includes two citations from the work. The grammarian Rufinus, writing on the metrics of Terence, notes that "Evanthius, in the commentary on Terence entitled *On Drama*, that is *On Comedy*, speaks of 'coherent plot, realistic characterization, useful sayings, clever witticisms, and harmonious meter' and later says, 'Even though it is true that the old poets had composed rather freely in the iambic meter, to the extent that they permitted substitution in the second and fourth feet, nevertheless Terence surpassed them in the resolution of this meter, so that it was broken down as much as possible into the form of prose speech.' " Because both of the passages cited by Rufinus appear in the text as we have it, it is believed that the section of the treatise which contains them should be attributed to Evanthius.

Not only the history of this opening treatise, but also the history of the entire commentary of Donatus on the comedies has presented a difficult problem to classical scholars. In his long article tracing the history of the question, Sabbadini calls attention to the discrepancy between the universal admiration of Donatus' commentary in the fifteenth century and the judgment of his own day—his article was published in 1894—which held the text to be full of *lacunae*, corrupt, and in places incapable of yielding a true reading. The sixteenth-century scholar, Giano Parrasio, first called attention to the incoherent state of the textual commentary by pointing out repetitions and direct contradictions in the notes on the *Andria* and the *Eunuchus*. Subsequent editors have continued on this path, indicating how differences in diction and critical attitude among the *scholia* (as well as the doubling, contradiction, and conflation found in the notes) make it impossible to believe the commentaries the work of a single author.

Nonetheless, it is universally agreed that the foundation, at least, of the commentary is Donatan. This leaves two questions: (1) How can the genuine *scholia* of Donatus be decanted from this corrupt text? (2) How did such corruption originally occur? Solutions to the first question, as might be imagined, are as various and imaginative as the editors who have pored over the text. The grounds on which distinctions have been made include peculiarities of diction, judgments on the critical value of individual *scholia* (those the editor considers most insightful invariably being attributed to Donatus), and pure caprice (or, as Wessner calls it, *merum arbitrium*).

The generally accepted answer to the second question holds that the text as we have it has gone through a process of unification, disunion, and reunification. As Sabbadini envisions it, the scenario would run as follows: Donatus' commentary was originally written as a continuous text; then notes (both polemic and illustrative) were added to the margins of that text. Later, these notes were copied as marginalia into an edition of the comedies themselves. Finally, the text we have was compiled by someone who, using both a continuous text of the notes and an edition of the comedies with notes copied into it, recombined the two into one compendium, probably adding comments of his own in the process. One can understand how ingenious proposals, based on various critical principles, have been employed to disentangle the genuine Donatan *scholia* from those believed to have been added by one, two, or three more hands.

The introductory treatise on comedy, of course, would not have suffered a similar history (that is, it would scarcely have been fragmented into notes on individual lines). Nevertheless, the critical principles by which an editor tests the genuineness of the *scholia* are generally also applied to the preface, and on these grounds some sections of the opening tract as well have been considered spurious. Perhaps because of the difficult and intriguing problems which the text itself has presented, although considerable philological attention has been lavished on the establishment of a true text, modern scholars have paid little attention to the actual contents of the treatise on comedy.

Evanthius: De Fabula, hoc est, de Comoedia

The first section of the treatise on comedy, that supposedly by Evanthius, follows an antiquarian program. In fairly logical, if somewhat repetitive order, it treats the history of the genre. The text first proposes a ritualistic, evolutionary theory of drama, according to which drama grew out of religious ceremonies. This is followed by the presentation of possible etymologies—first for tragedy, then for comedy. The ordering of tragedy before comedy is seen to be no accident in the next section, which presents perhaps the most provocative suggestion of the work, namely, that the history of the dramatic arts mirrors the evolution of society. Just as man's life was at first cruel and harsh but gradually progressed toward mildness, so tragedy was the first dramatic form, but comedy developed with civilization. The first authors of tragedy and of comedy are then named, although, in fact, Homer may be considered the father of both forms—of tragedy in the *Iliad*, comedy in the *Odyssey*.

At this point tragedy is explicitly left behind, so that the author can focus exclusively on comedy, on "those plays which Terence imitated." Again, the text follows a logical, evolutionary order. The way in which individual actors were gradually separated from the unified chorus is discussed first, and then the history of the genre is taken up, with a discussion of the advantages and drawbacks of each successive stage, from Old Comedy through satire to New Comedy. Having now reached his true subject—the New Comedy for which Terence is famous, the author again begins at the beginning with a few remarks on prologues. The text now concentrates entirely on praise of Terence, considering in turn his prologues, metrics, characterizations, emotional tone, clarity, and handling of plot. Returning to his historical program, the author lists the types of drama, both tragic and comic, which the Latins developed after New Comedy. There follow two sections of the type which seem endemic to our author, with his almost scholastic passion for organization. One notes (after listing the types of Roman tragedy and comedy) that the first author of both was Livius Andronicus; the second proposes three, not-very-imaginative divisions of comedy, which might be rendered, "active, not active, and in-between."

Interspersed with these notes, however, are two sections that rank—along with that comparing artistic development to social development—among the most illuminating of the work. The first discusses what it is that distinguishes tragedy from comedy:

> Although there are many differences between tragedy and comedy, these are the chief distinguishing features: in comedy, the fortunes of men are ordinary, the onslaughts of difficulties minor, the outcomes of actions happy. But in tragedy everything is the opposite: the characters are outstanding, the fears great, the outcomes disastrous. Then again, in comedy the beginning is stormy, the end calm, but in tragedy the opposite holds true. In tragedy a life is portrayed which one must flee, in comedy a life which one ought to seek. Finally, all comedy deals with fictional plots, whereas tragedy is often sought in historical reality.

The other illuminating section, which concludes the work, discusses the function performed by each part of a comedy: prologue, *protasis*, *epitasis*, and *catastrophe:*

Ancient Theories of Comedy: Evanthius and Donatus

The prologue serves as a kind of preface to the play; it is the only part in which it is permissible to tell the audience something which is external to the plot, either for the sake of the poet or of the play itself or of the actor. The *protasis* is the first act and the beginning of the play. The *epitasis* provides the growth and development of the complications and is, one might say, the knot of the whole problem. The *catastrophe* is the turning of events to a happy outcome through the discovery of the facts being revealed to all.

On the whole, the Evanthian text is rather highly ordered. It is mainly concerned to establish the historical development of the genre up to Terence and then to praise various aspects of Terence's art. Viewed in this way, the treatise might seem to offer little in the way of an abstract or theoretical, critical discussion of the genre. Inevitably, however, the judgments rendered on Terence's plays seem to tell us what comedy ought to be, not simply what Terentian comedy is. To the extent that these sections of the treatise become prescriptive rather than descriptive, they may be seen as formulating a theory of comedy. Thus, for example, when the author praises Terence's unity of plot, we may perceive this as a quality toward which comedy in general should strive, not simply as a particular excellence of Terence.

But any such theory that might be derived from the treatise must be considered both rudimentary and highly subjective on the part of the reader. Nowhere does the author take up abstract questions as such; nowhere does he ask (as does the *Coslinian Tractate*) what the definition or the intention or the effect of comedy is—nowhere, that is, unless in the two sections mentioned above. In his discussion of the parts of the play, and especially in his differentiation of comedy and tragedy, the author does provide some theoretical guidelines for the genre, the importance of which by far eclipses the rest of the work. Overall, however, the characterization the author himself uses of those who pursue antiquarian researches—*prisca volventes* (people who turn over old matters)—applies well enough to himself.

Donatus: Excerpta de Comoedia

The second treatment of comedy, that attributed to Donatus himself, overlaps with the first treatise on a few points—notably the question of etymologies and the espousal of a ritualistic, evolutionary theory of drama. Likewise, it employs similar techniques of division, listing at times the types of drama, the types of comedy, the types of prologue, and so forth. On the whole, however, Donatus' treatment seems to follow a less coherent pattern than that of Evanthius.

The first sections of the text, rather than moving straightforwardly from one point to the next, circle about questions of origin and naming. First, several definitions of comedy are given, then an account of comedy's origins, leading to an etymology. Here the remark is interjected that comedy creates its effect through both gesture and speech. The definition of comedy as a mirror of life is introduced for the second time, now attributed to Livius Andronicus rather than to Cicero, as previously. Then the author returns to the historical origin of comedy in Athenian ritual and to its etymology. Likewise the history of tragedy and its etymology are touched upon.

Next, the Dionysian association with drama is emphasized, as it was not in the first treatise, for the author makes clear that the dramas are produced in honor of Bacchus. Returning again to history, the text makes mention of Thespis and Aeschylus, then refers us to a fourteen-line citation from the *Ars Poetica* of Horace. (The first study also contained one footnote—to Vergil's *Georgics*—but the quotation was not included as part of the text.) Next, the author moves into a section employing the straightforward techniques of division and definition. He lists the types of prologue, and so forth. In essence, throughout this section the same type of logical format is employed as in the first treatise. Here, however, the orderly flow of presentation is interrupted several times by seemingly anomalous bits of information, such as who were the first actors to employ masks, or how titles are chosen for plays. Having completed the survey of the types of drama and the parts of an individual play, the treatise ends with observations on whether title or author appears first in manuscripts, a list of the types of games for which plays were held, a long section discussing the costumes and props appropriate to certain characters, and a closing note on the musical accompaniment to comedies.

From this survey of the essay's contents, it may be apparent that, on the whole, it presents a less coherent pattern than the first. Indeed, at times it seems a collection of miscellaneous information, including observations ranging from the titles on manuscripts to the colors of costumes. Ostensibly, this random assortment of material would seem to offer a much less promising treatment of the genre than the carefully ordered researches of Evanthius. This, however, seems an odd conclusion, because as a scholiast Donatus has been held in remarkably high repute—both by the ancient references we possess and by modern editors of the *scholia*. How can Donatus' reputation as a sound and intelligent scholar be reconciled with the rather haphazard collection of thoughts attributed to him here? I would like to suggest several ways in which we might view the treatise attributed to Donatus as a more significant mine of information, revealing a more sensitive understanding of the genre than that of Evanthius.

The most obvious way in which the Donatan section deviates from a clear, Evanthian presentation is in the interjection of bits of information which do not fit into an orderly outline of the topic. In virtually every case, however, these additional notes are of two types: they are comments concerned either with the staging of comedy or with the reading of comic manuscripts. Examples of the first include remarks on the importance of gesture and speech, the presence of altars on the stage, the introduction of masks, the significance of costumes and of particular types of music. Examples of the second are the discussions of how titles are chosen, whether author or title appears first, what the markings of meter on the text indicate, where the musician's name appears, and whether there is an inscription assigning the production to a certain festival. In other words, the apparently superfluous information presented by Donatus may not be anomalous at all. It may be seen instead as an indication of the author's familiarity with and interest in the scholarly study of the manuscripts themselves, and his recognition of the importance of staging to comedy.

There seems to be another, less easily defined way in which the tone of the Donatan sections of the treatise differs from those of Evanthius. One might say that Evanthius, in most of his remarks, marshals facts like a journalist, whereas Donatus consistently seeks reasons like a theorist. Perhaps this can be seen most clearly by comparing cases in which both sections of the treatise discuss the same concept. Both authors advance an etymology for comedy from *komes*, "countryside." Evanthius presents a strictly antiquarian justification: the word comes from "country-side" because comic songs were first sung in the country. But Donatus seeks a reason in the form itself, noting that comedy depicts the lives of people who would live in the country, not in palaces like tragic characters. Likewise, both authors believe that the comic chorus originally castigated private citizens for their shortcomings. Evanthius, however, stresses the result of this custom (it was beneficial to the citizen body), while Donatus considers its purpose (the Athenians did it to safeguard Attic propriety). Finally, the two sections of the treatise contain very similar characterizations of comedy. The Evanthian citation, by its phrasing, emphasizes factual information: "comedy portrays a life which is to be sought." Donatus' definition, on the other hand, emphasizes the intention of the form: "comedy is a play from which one may learn what is useful in life and what, on the other hand, is to be avoided."

From these opening remarks on the definition of comedy to his closing observations on its musical accompaniment, Donatus tends to explore the reasons, the causes, the purposes behind comedy. Even the lengthy treatment of costuming reveals this bias. In it, he does not simply list costumes but virtually allegorizes them, explaining in most cases why a certain color carries a certain significance. The Donatan treatment, then, intersperses various types of material according to a not very logical plan. But if we are looking for a discussion which deals with theoretical questions, such as what is comedy and how does it achieve its effects, then this treatise may well come closer to the heart of the matter than the more orderly but less imaginative Evanthian text.

Notes to the Introduction

1. The best modern editions of the text of Evanthius and Donatus appear in Georg Kaibel, *Comicorum Graecorum Fragmenta* (Berlin: Weidmann, 1899), and Paul Wessner, *Aeli Donati Commentum Terenti* (Leipzig: Teubner, 1902). The text reprinted here is that of Wessner. Translations of the text have previously been included in the following works: Michael J. Hilger, "The Rhetoric of Comedy: Comic Theory in the Terentian Commentary of Donatus," Ph.D. Diss., Univ. of Nebraska, 1970; Paul Lauter, ed., *Theories of Comedy* (Garden City, N.Y.: Anchor Books, 1964); and Alex Preminger et al., *Classical and Medieval Literary Criticism* (New York: Frederick Ungar, 1974).

2. Marvin T. Herrick, *Comic Theory in the Sixteenth Century* (Urbana, Illinois: Univ. of Illinois Press, 1950), p. 57.

3. Nor has great attention been paid to this particular text as an example of ancient criticism. Russell and Winterbottom in *Ancient Literary Criticism* (Oxford: Clarendon Press, 1972) do not include the essay in their selection of literary texts. Georges Grube, in his *The Greek and Roman Critics* (Toronto: University of Toronto Press, 1965) takes very little cognizance of Donatus. Herrick, both in the study cited previously and in the first chapter of *Tragicomedy* (Urbana, Illinois: University of Illinois Press, 1962) gives the Donatan text a fuller consideration than these studies on classical criticism.

4. Maurice Charney, *Comedy High and Low* (New York: Oxford Univ. Press, 1978), p. vii.

5. Grube, p. 65.

6. The most detailed—and sympathetic—treatment of the *Coslinian Tractate* is Lane Cooper's *An Aristotelian Theory of Comedy* (New York: Harcourt, Brace, 1922). A. P. McMahon, in his article, "On the Second Book of Aristotle's *Poetics* and the Sources of Theophrastus' Definition of Tragedy," *Harvard Studies in Classical Philology*, 28 (1917), 1-46, denies the significance of the document.

7. For the history of the text see: Wessner's preface to his edition of the text, cited above, and Remigio Sabbadini, "Il Commento di Donato a Terenzio," *Studi Italiani di Filologia Classica*, 2 (1894), 1-134. The question of Evanthius in particular is treated by Eduard Scheidemantel in his dissertation, *Quaestiones Evanthianae* (Leipzig: Leopold & Baer, 1883). Herman T. Karsten, in *de Commenti Donatiani ad Terenti Fabulas Origine et Compositione* (Leiden: Brill, 1907), treats the history of the text in general, but not that of the introduction in particular.

EVANTHIUS ON COMEDY
Translated by S. Georgia Nugent

The beginning of tragedy and of comedy stems from religious ceremonies which the ancients performed to fulfill their vows of thanksgiving for the harvest.[1]

For, when the altars had been kindled and the sacrificial goat brought in, the type of song that the holy chorus delivered to Father Bacchus was called tragedy. This name may have come from the Greek phrase, *apo tou tragou kai tês ôidês*, that is, from "goat," an enemy of the vineyards, and from "song." (There is a clear allusion to this very thing in Vergil, [*Georgics* II.380 ff] .)[2] Or tragedy may be so called because the poet of this song was presented with a goat or else because a skin full of new wine was the customary reward for the singers. Or again it may be because the actors used to smear their faces with the dregs of the wine before the use of masks was discovered by Aeschylus, for in Greek, wine lees are called *truges*. For these reasons, the name for tragedy was devised.

At a time when the Athenians had not yet been gathered together into a city, when altars for religious ceremonies were built to Apollo under his names of *Nomios* or *Aguiaios* (that is, as the guardian deity of shepherds or of country districts), around the countryside, farms, villages, and crossroads of Attica, a festive song was customarily sung, which was called comedy. This name was composed, I think, from the phrase, *apo tôn kômôn kai tês ôidês*, that is, from "countryside" and "song." Or else it was from, *apo tou kômazein kai aidein* which is, "to celebrate and sing." This derivation is not unlikely, since the members of the comic chorus might be drunk on the festival day or indulging in playful love-making.

Further, when one considers the arrangement of the subject matter as well as chronology, it is clear that tragedy was produced first.[3] For just as man progressed, little by little, from uncouth and wild manners to gentleness, and cities were founded, and life became milder and more leisurely, so analogously the tragic mode was discovered long before the comic.

Those who study antiquities find that Thespis was the original inventor of tragedy, and Eupolis, with Cratinus and Aristophanes, is believed to have been the father of Old Comedy. But actually Homer, who is the most abundant source of almost all poetry, furnished models even for these types of songs. And he established virtually a kind of rule in his works, for he can be seen to have written the *Iliad* as a specimen of tragedy, the *Odyssey* in the image of comedy. And after this model of his—both excellent and extensive—clever imitators set in order and arranged all those things which still at that time were written in a disorganized way, as yet rough and rudimentary, not at all—as they later became—elegant and polished.

Now that we have spoken at the beginning about both genres for the sake of clarifying their origins, let us consider what is necessary to the subject at hand. Those things that ought to be said accurately about tragedy, therefore, we shall defer to another time. Sticking to the title of this work, let us deal now with those plays which Terence imitated.

Old Comedy generally, just like tragedy, was once a simple, undivided song, as we have already said, which the chorus—at times moving about, at times standing still, at times whirling in circles—sang with the fluteplayer, around the smoking altars.

But at first one character was detached from the singers and he, responding in alternation, that is [text corrupt],[4] served to enrich the chorus and vary the musical aspect. Then a second, then a third character was separated, and finally, when the number of characters had been increased by various authors, then the mask, the *palla* [robe], the *cothurnus* [boot], the *soccus* [slipper], and the other props and accoutrements of the actors were invented, and for each particular character an appropriate costume was discovered. Eventually, there were actors of first, second, third, fourth, or fifth roles, and the whole play was divided into a five-part action.

This type of play, in the very cradle of its origin as it were, when it had scarcely begun, was called *archaia kômôidia*, Old Comedy, and *ep' onomatos*, eponymous. It was called *archaia* on account of the fact that it is old in comparison to the things we have discovered recently, and it was called, *ep'onomatos* because it has, as it were, the historical veracity of a true narrative, and in it there is also the naming of citizens, who are freely described.

For among the ancient poets, in contrast to present practice, the plots were not entirely fictional, but the actions of citizens were rehearsed openly, often with the names of those who were involved. And this very practice in its own time was very beneficial to the morals of the citizen body, since everyone took care to avoid blameworthy action, for fear that he might provide a spectacle for the others and bring disgrace upon his household. But when the poets began wantonly to abuse this mode of composition and to wound good men indiscriminately out of caprice, a law was proposed which silenced them, so that no one would compose a scandalous song against someone else.

And from this then another type of play had its beginning: satire. It was named from satyrs, who are gods that we know are always engaged in joking and impudence. This is the origin of the name, even if some others mistakenly believe it to have another derivation. Now satire was a type of song that, although it entailed harsh and, as it were, crude jibes at the faults of citizens, yet had no attribution of proper names. But this type of comedy was also harmful to many poets, since they came under suspicion with powerful citizens of having described the activities of those citizens (and made them worse than they were) and having spoiled the genre by this kind of composition.[5] Lucilius, then, was the first to write satire in a new way, so that he made of it a poetic composition, that is, a single song composed of several books.

The poets, compelled by that difficulty which we discussed above to give up satire, discovered a new type of song, which is New Comedy. New Comedy, with its more universal story line, concerns in general all men who have moderate means. It produces less bitterness for the audience and, by the same token, considerable entertainment, through its coherent plot, realistic characterization, useful sayings, clever witticisms, and harmonious meter.

Just as there were numerous authors of Old Comedies, so New Comedy had many authors both before and after, but it is preeminently the form of Menander and Terence. Although many things might be said about it, it will be sufficient, for the sake of reminding the reader, as it were, to set out what is maintained in the writings of the ancients concerning the comic art.

In the beginning Old Comedy was a choral song, and little by little through the division of parts, it progressed to five acts. Then gradually, as the chorus was reduced and, in a sense, refined away, the form developed into New Comedy, in which not only is no chorus led onstage, but there is no longer even any place left for it.[6]   For after the spectator, in his leisure time, became more discriminating, then when the action of the play passed from the actors to the singers, the audience began to get up and leave. The poets took notice. At first, in fact, they took away the chorus but left a place for it—as Menander did for this reason, not, as some others think, for another reason. Afterwards, they did not even leave a place for the chorus. The Latin comic poets did this, and for this reason it is difficult in Roman comedies to divide the action into five acts.

In addition, the Greeks do not have prologues in the sense which the Latins have. Also, other Latin poets have *theous apo mêchanês*, that is, gods contrived for the purpose of relating the plot, in the Greek fashion; but Terence does not have them. To perform this function, Terence often uses a device which other authors do not handle with ease: *protatika prosôpa*, that is, characters drawn in from outside the plot, so that by bringing them in the plot may easily be made clear.[7]

Even though it is true that the old poets had composed rather freely in the iambic meter, to the extent that they permitted substitution in the second and fourth feet, nevertheless Terence surpassed them in the resolution of this meter, so that it was broken down as much as possible into the form of prose speech.

Then also Terence observed the rules concerning the appearance, age, duty, and roles of characters more scrupulously than anyone else. And yet he alone dared, even against the traditions of comedy, since he sought the ring of truth in his fictional plots, to introduce from time to time prostitutes who were not wicked. In these cases, however, there was both a reason why they might be good and a pleasure in the thing itself.

Since Terence had done these things extremely skillfully, it is especially admirable that he upheld tradition, in that he did write comedy, and that he tempered the mood so that it would not pass over into tragedy. This is a quality that we find, along with other things, less successfully maintained by Plautus and Afranius and [Appius], and for the most part by many comic playwrights. Also among Terence's strengths, it is remarkable that his plays are so well balanced that they neither swell to tragic heights nor sink to low farce.

Also, he brings in nothing arcane, nor is there anything which must be clarified by antiquarians. But Plautus does this more often and is more obscure in many places.

In addition, Terence is so carefully attentive to the plot and the style that he always either deletes or delicately handles anything that might get in the way. And he ties the central portion to the beginning and end so well that nothing seems added to anything else, but the whole play seems to be formed as one organic unit.

Another feature that is admirable in Terence is that in the beginning he does not mix four characters together in such a way that the distinction among them is unclear. And also he does not have an actor say any-thing to the audience as if he were outside of the comedy, which is a very common fault of Plautus.

Also this quality of his, among other things, seems praiseworthy: he chose to create richer plots by doubling what goes on. For, except for the *Hecyra*, in which there is only the love affair of Pamphilus, the other five plays have two sets of young lovers.

Now it should be recognized that after New Comedy the Latin authors produced many types of plays. For example, *togatae* (so called from their Latin settings and plots), *praetextatae* (named from the *toga praetexta*, the robe of state appropriate to tragic characters from Roman history), Atellanae (from the Campanian town where they were first acted), Rinthonicae (from the name of their author), *tabernariae* (from the lowliness of the plot and style), and mimes (from the everyday imita-tion of trivial events and unheroic characters).

Although there are many differences between tragedy and comedy, these are the chief distinguishing features: in comedy the fortunes of men are ordinary, the onslaughts of difficulties minor, the outcomes of actions happy. But in tragedy everything is the opposite: the characters are out-standing, the fears great, the outcomes disastrous. Then again, in comedy the beginning is stormy, the end calm, but in tragedy the opposite holds true. In tragedy a life is portrayed which one must flee, in comedy a life which one ought to seek. Finally, all comedy deals with fictional plots, whereas tragedy is often sought in historical reality.

The first Latin plays were written by Livius Andronicus, and the whole concept was at that time so new that he was both poet and actor of his own plays.

Comedies may be of the type called, "bustling" [*motoriae*], "calm" [*statariae*], or "mixed" [*mixtae*]. The first are frenetic, the second quieter, and the mixed consist of both types of action.

Comedy is divided into four parts: the prologue, *protasis*, *epitasis*, and *catastrophe*. The prologue serves as a kind of preface to the play; it is the only part in which it is permissible to tell the audience some-thing which is external to the plot, either for the sake of the poet or of the play itself or of the actor. The *protasis* is the first act and the be-ginning of the play. The *epitasis* provides the growth and development of the complications and is, one might say, the knot of the whole problem.[8] The *catastrophe* is the turning of events to a happy outcome through the discovery of the facts being revealed to all.

DONATUS ON COMEDY
Translated by S. Georgia Nugent

Comedy is a play that presents various manners of life of private citizens, from which one may learn what is useful in life and what, on the other hand, is to be avoided. The Greeks defined comedy in this way: "comedy is a narrative of the acts of private individuals, which does not entail danger." Cicero said that comedy was an imitation of life, a mirror of experience, an image of truth.[9]

Comedies were named from ancient customs, because among the Greeks songs of this type were first performed in country districts—as are the Italian festivals of the Lares, held at crossroads—in a motley kind of delivery, which held the audience while the acts were being changed. "Comedy," then, comes from *apo tês kômês*, that is, from the depiction of lives of men who live in the country districts because of their moderate lot in life, not in royal courts, as do tragic characters.

Comedy, moreover, because it is a work composed to be an imitation of life and a faithful representation of *mores*, depends upon gesture and speech.

Among the Greeks it is doubtful who first discovered comedy, but among the Romans it is certain: Livius Andronicus first devised comedy and tragedy and the *togatae*.

And he said, justifiably, that comedy is a mirror of daily life. For, just as we easily grasp the outlines of reality by means of the image when a mirror is held up to us, so through the reading of comedy we perceive the image of life and of daily habit without difficulty.

The invention of the comic form came about from foreign peoples and customs. For the Athenians, protecting Attic propriety, when they wanted to single out for reproach those who were living improperly, came together from all places to the country districts and crossroads and there, high-spirited and zealous, they publicly proclaimed the faults of individuals—with their names. From this custom the name was created, so that it was called comedy.

First these songs were performed in soft meadows. And there were prizes to encourage the talent of those skilled at writing. The actors were also offered gifts to induce them to use the pleasing modulation of their voices more freely for the sake of sweet praise. For a goat was given to these as a gift, because the animal was considered a nuisance to the vines. From this practice the name of tragedy arose. Some, however, prefer to say that tragedy was named from *amurca*, the dregs of oil, which is a watery humor (as if it were called "trugedy").

Since the games were performed by artists in honor of Father Bacchus, even the writers of comedy and tragedy began to cultivate and venerate the power of this god as if he were present. There is reasonable evidence for this. For at the beginning songs were produced so that they clearly celebrated and proclaimed the praises of Bacchus and his glorious deeds.

Then, little by little, the reputation of this art gained ground. Thespis was the first who brought these writings to the attention of all, and afterwards Aeschylus, following the example of the earlier man, developed the form.[10] In the *Ars Poetica*, Horace speaks about these matters:

When the genre of tragic poetry was as yet unknown, Thespis is said to have invented it—and to have formed a traveling company, for in wagons he carried about his poems, which actors declaimed and performed, their faces smeared with wine lees. After him, Aeschylus was the inventor of the mask and the tragic robe. He also constructed the stage over a scaffolding and introduced tragic diction and the use of the *coturnus* [elevated shoe used by tragic actors]. Old Comedy came next and was well received. But its free way of speaking issued in license and in violence worthy to be restrained by law. A law was brought forward, and the chorus, submitting to the judgment, silenced its abuse. Our Latin poets have left nothing untried, and those are especially praiseworthy who have dared to abandon the well-worn Greek paths and take Roman topics as their subject matter or those who have produced *praetextae* or *togatae*.

Drama is the general name; there are two major parts of it, tragedy and comedy. Tragedy, if it has a Latin plot, is called *praetexta*. Comedy has many types: *palliata*, *togata*, *tabernaria*, Atellana, mime, Rinthonica, or *planipedia*.

Now *planipedia* is so called from the lowliness of its plot and the baseness of the actors, who support themselves neither upon the *coturnus* [boot] nor the *soccus* [slipper] on the stage or platform, but stand on their bare feet. Or it may be called this because it does not deal with actions that are appropriate to characters living in towers or high places, but to those who live on level ground and in a humble place.

The first to have used masks are said to have been Cincius Faliscus for comedy and Minucius Prothymus for tragedy.[11]

The titles of all of the comedies are taken in every case from four things: from the name of a character, the name of a place, an event before the play, or an event within the play. Plays that take their titles from a character's name are *Phormio, Hecyra, Curculio, Epidicus;* from a place, *Andria, Leucadia, Brundisina;* from an event before the play, *Eunuchus, Asinaria, Captivi;* from an event within the play, *Commorientes, Crimen, Heautontimorumenos.*

There are three forms of comedy: the *palliatae* retain Greek dress, next the *togatae* (which some call *tabernariae*) require togas as the costume of the characters, and the Atellanae are fashioned with witticisms and jokes that have no appeal except that of tradition.

Comedy is divided into four parts: prologue, *protasis, epitasis,* and *catastrophe.*

The prologue is the first speech, called by the Greeks *ho pro tou dramatos logos,* or the speech coming before the real substance of the play. There are four types of prologue: *sustatikos* or introductory [*commendativus*], in which either the poet or the play is recommended; *epitimetikos* or critical [*relativus*], in which either a curse is pronounced against a rival or thanks is given to the audience; *dramatikos* or narrative [*argumentativus*], explaining the plot of the play; *mixtos* or mixed, containing all of these things.[12]

Some wish to make this distinction between prologue and *prologium*, namely, that it is a prologue when either the poet justifies himself or commends the play, but it is a *prologium* only when something about the play is stated.

Protasis is the first act of the play, in which part of the plot is unfolded, part is held back to retain the attention of the audience. The *epitasis* is the complication of the plot, which, by its cleverness, binds the play together. The *catastrophe* is the unfolding of the play, through which its outcome is made clear.

In many plays the name of the plays themselves are placed before those of the poets, in some those of the poets before those of the plays, and history indicates diversity in this practice. For when some individuals first brought out plays, the names of the plays were proclaimed before the poets were announced, lest some ill-will discourage them from writing. When, however, through the production of many plays, some authority had been acquired for the poet, at once the names of the poets were mentioned first, so that through their names attention might be given to the plays.

It is clear that the acts are ascribed to different festival occasions or games.[13] For there are four types of games which the curule aediles [officials in charge of public games] oversee as a civic duty: the Megalenses, consecrated to major gods, which the Greeks call *megalous*; the funeral games, intended to occupy the people while the procession decreed in honor of a patrician's funeral is thoroughly arranged; Plebeian games, which are given for the welfare of the populace; and Apollinares, which are consecrated to Apollo.

Two altars are customarily placed onstage: the right one to Bacchus, the left one to the god for whom the games are produced. Thus Terence in the *Andria* [4.3.11] says, "Take the sacred bough for yourself from the altar here."

They always bring Ulysses onstage in a *pilleus* [felt cap]. This may be because at one time he feigned insanity—at that time when he wished himself to be hidden, fearing that if he were recognized he would be compelled to go off to war. Or it may be because of his unique cleverness, which protected and fortified him and made him extremely useful to his companions. For his strength was always the ingeniousness of his beguiling mind. Some recount that the inhabitants of Ithaca, like the Locrians, were accustomed to wear the *pilleus*.

The characters of Achilles and Neoptolemus wear crowns, although they never held regal scepters. The reason adduced for this is that they never entered into the sacred oath to wage war against Troy with the rest of the Greek youths nor were they ever under the rule of Agamemnon.

A white costume is given to the old men in comedy, because this is thought to have been the most ancient.[14] For the youths, there is a varicolored costume. The slaves wear a short outfit, either because of age-old poverty or so that they can move about more readily. The freeloaders [*parasiti*] come with Greek cloaks [*pallia*] wound about them. A cheerful character is given bright clothing; a gloomy one, dark; the rich wear purple; the poor, red. Soldiers come onstage in a purple *chlamys* [military cloak]; young women wear exotic costumes. A pimp uses a *pallium* of various colors. The prostitute, on account of her greed, has saffron-colored clothing.

Syrmata [robes with a train] are so called from the fact that they are trailing garments, a luxury that was introduced from Ionia. The same thing worn by characters in mourning signifies their self-neglect.

In addition, woven stage curtains are spread across the stage, ever since golden tapestry was brought all the way to Rome from Attalus' palace.[15] Instead of this a later age adopted *siparia*. This is the curtain for farce, which is put in front of the audience while the acts of the play are being changed.

Actors spoke the dialogue parts in iambic lines, but the singing parts were set to music not by the poet but by someone skilled in the musical arts. And not everything was composed in the same meter in one song, but often in different meters, as is indicated by the three numbers marked on comedies that contain three songs in changing meters.[16]

The name of the person who arranged the music was put in the beginning of the play after those of the author and actor.

Songs of this type were played on flutes and, when the songs were heard, many people in the audience could tell beforehand what play the actors were about to put on, before the title of the play was announced to the spectators. The songs were played on matched pipes, that is, right and left [perhaps bass and treble] and on unmatched pipes. The right pipes, with their weightiness, announce the serious speech of comedy; the left, with their light sharpness, sound the joke. And when the action of the play calls for both right and left, both jests and serious matters are announced.

Notes to the Translation

In paragraphing, I have followed the divisions of the Latin text. Brackets have been used to indicate information that is not a part of the text—or, in a few cases, to enclose a Latin term from the text, appearing here as a gloss. My only consistent editorial bias in translating has been to change, wherever possible, the grammarian's habitual passive voice into active constructions, which are more acceptacle in modern English.

   1. This ritual theory of drama, of course, has had modern adherents, notably F. M. Cornford in *The Origin of Attic Comedy* (Cambridge: Cambridge Univ. Press, 1934).
   2.   We shall, then, sing, in native songs, our debt
        Of praise to Bacchus, bring on cakes and plates
        And lead in by the horns a sacred goat

To stand beside the altar, and proceed
To roast his fertile flesh on hazel spits.

Vergil, *Georgics* II.380 ff., in the translation of Smith Palmer Bovie, *Vergil's Georgics* (Chicago: Univ. of Chicago Press, 1956).

3. I have taken *res* here to mean the stuff of which tragedy is made, "the subject matter." The term is sufficiently vague, however, to be rather obscure. Literally translated, the line would read, "when the order has been discovered of things (*rerum*) as well as of times."

4. Various suggestions have been proposed to fill the *lacuna*, such as *hupokrīnomenē* "responding" or *amoibaiōs* "alternately." The sense is clear enough.

5. *Genus* here has been taken by some to be a reference to the class of powerful citizens just alluded to. *Deformasse genus* would then mean, "having disgraced the upper class" rather than "having spoiled the genre." My interpretation has been determined by (1) the consistent use of *genus* throughout this section to refer to a type of poetry, and (2) the transition to the next sentence: *quod primus Lucilius novo conscripsit modo*, where *quod* surely picks up *genus*, "*which* Lucilius wrote in a new way."

6. The observation that there is no *locus*, "no place" left for the chorus is ambiguous. It may refer to actual staging, but it is also an allusion to the practice (found in texts of Menander) of marking the text with a notation "for the chorus" but with no lines. Presumably this indicated an impromptu or, at least, unwritten choral interlude. It is difficult to determine how vestigial the choral part had become at this stage. It is this practice of manuscript notation—or the lack of it—which is alluded to in the end of this section: the marking, "chorus," made it easy to separate the acts from one another.

7. The author's praise here of Terence' bringing in characters from outside the plot appears to contradict his later assertion that Terence "does not have an actor say anything to the audience as if he were outside of the comedy, which is a very common fault of Plautus."

8. *Error*, which I have translated here as, "problem," is a technical term designating the real essence of the comic plot. Literally, *error* is a wandering-off; it is the mistake, misconception, or difficulty out of which the comedy is born.

9. As discussed in the introduction, some sections of this second part of the text are taken to be interpolations. In the Latin text, these sections are printed in italics. In both translation and interpretation, however, I have treated the text as we have it as an organic whole. Incidentally, this famous definition of comedy, much used by Renaissance writers (including Ben Jonson), does not appear to be quoted directly from Cicero. There is a comparable passage in *De Re Publica*, IV.11: "Numquam comoedia, nisi consuetudo vitae pateretur, probare sua theatris flagitia potuissent." ("Nor would comedy, unless the customs of daily life had so permitted, ever have been able to make its disgraceful exhibitions acceptable to the spectators.") Although *vitae* and *consuetudo* appear in this passage, as they do in Donatus' supposed Ciceronian definition, what Cicero has in mind here is surely not a definition; to understand the passage as such would be to seriously misinterpret it.

10. The text is corrupt at this point, but the sense would clearly correspond to what follows in the citation from the *Ars Poetica*.

11. It is possible that the reference here is to the first actors rather than the first masks, since *ago personam* can mean "to play a part." *Persona* means both "dramatic part or character" and "mask." The discovery of masks, however, seems the more noteworthy historical event.

12. I have included the terms from the Latin text here, thinking that some readers may be accustomed to the use of their obvious English cognates. The cognates, however, do not seem to me to convey the sense of the Latin.

13. *Inscribi* here seems to imply a designation written on the text, virtually as if it were labeled, "for presentation at the Plebeian Games."

14. A useful modern companion to this section is Catharine Saunders' study, *Costume in Roman Comedy* (New York: AMS Press, 1966). Ms. Saunders discusses each of the stock character's costumes, drawing on evidence from this and other literary texts (including the comedies themselves) and from manuscript illustrations of Terence's comedies.

15. Attalus is said to have discovered the technique of weaving cloth of gold.

16. This passage is difficult to understand but presumably refers to a practice of marking the texts to signify the meters they employ. Literally, it would read: "Nor are all things set out in the same measures in one song, but in changed ones, as those signify who place three numbers on the comedies which contain three 'songs in changed measures.' "

Bibliographical Note

The best introduction to Roman comedy is the extensive study by George E. Duckworth, *The Nature of Roman Comedy: A Study in Popular Entertainment* (Princeton: Princeton Univ. Press, 1952). Duckworth's book includes chapters on the history of the genre, its conventions, staging, language and meter, and later influence, as well as other topics. A second very good treatment is W. Beare, *The Roman Stage* (London: Methuen, 1950). Individual chapters in Beare are somewhat more specialized than Duckworth's treatments and range over a wide variety of topics, including authors such as Naevius, Pacuvius, and Accius, as well as studies on the seating and stage of a Roman theater. A narrower work, which is of special interest in the consideration of Donatus' treatise, is Catharine Saunders, *Costume in Roman Comedy* (New York: AMS Press, 1966). Duckworth's book also includes a lengthy bibliography, separated by topics, where the interested reader is referred to additional sources.

LATIN TEXT

⟨EVANTHIVS DE FABVLA⟩

I 1 Initium tragoediae et comoediae a rebus diuinis est incohatum, quibus pro fructibus uota soluentes operabantur antiqui.

2 namque incensis iam altaribus et admoto hirco id genus carminis, quod sacer chorus reddebat Libero patri, tragoedia dicebatur: uel ἀπὸ τοῦ τράγου καὶ τῆς ᾠδῆς, hoc est ab hirco hoste uinearum et a cantilena — cuius ipsius rei etiam apud Vergilium (*Geo. II 380 sq.*) plena fit mentio —, uel quod hirco donabatur eius carminis poeta, uel quod uter eius musti plenus sollemne praemium cantatoribus fuerat, uel quod ora sua faecibus perlinebant scaenici ante usum personarum ab Aeschylo repertum; faeces enim Graece dicuntur τρύγες. et his quidem causis tragoediae nomen inuentum est.

3 at uero nondum coactis in urbem Atheniensibus. cum Apollini Νομίῳ uel Ἀγυιαῖῳ, id est pastorum uicorumue praesidi deo, instructis aris in honorem diuinae rei circum Atticae uicos uillas pagos et compita festiuum carmen sollemniter cantaretur, ἀπὸ τῶν κωμῶν καὶ τῆς ᾠδῆς comoedia uocitata est, ut opinor, a pagis et cantilena composito nomine, uel ἀπὸ τοῦ κωμάζειν καὶ ᾄδειν, quod est comessatum ire cantantes. quod appotis sollemni die uel amatorie lasciuientibus [choris comicis] non absurdum est.

4 itaque, ut rerum ita etiam temporum reperto ordine, tragoedia prior prolata esse cognoscitur. nam ut ab incultu ac feris moribus paulatim peruentum est ad mansuetudinem urbesque sunt conditae et uita mitior atque otiosa processit, ita res tragicae longe ante comicas inuentae.

5 quamuis igitur retro prisca uoluentibus reperiatur Thespis tragoediae primus inuentor et comoediae ueteris pater Eupolis cum Cratino Aristophaneque esse credatur, Homerus tamen, qui fere omnis poeticae largissimus fons est, etiam his carminibus exempla praebuit et uelut quan-

dam suorum operum legem praescripsit: qui Iliadem ad instar tragoediae, Odyssiam ad imaginem comoediae fecisse monstratur. nam post illius tale tantumque documentum ab ingeniosissimis imitatoribus et digesta sunt in ordinem et diuisa cuncta, quae etiam tum temere scribebantur, ad huc impolita atque in ipsis rudimentis hautquaquam, ut postea facta sunt, decora atque leuia.

6 postquam demonstrandae originis causa de utriusque generis initio diximus, quod necesse est iam dicamus, adeo ut ea, quae proprie de tragoedia dicenda sunt, titulo propositi nunc operis instantes in alia tempora differamus et de his fabulis iam loquamur, quas Terentius imitatus est.

II 1 Comoedia fere uetus ut ipsa quoque olim tragoedia simplex carmen, quemadmodum iam diximus, fuit, quod chorus circa aras fumantes nunc spatiatus nunc consistens nunc reuoluens gyros cum tibicine concinebat.

2 sed primo una persona est subducta cantatoribus, quae respondens alternis id est ⟨* * *⟩ choro locupletauit uariauitque rem musicam: tum altera, tum tertia, et ad postremum crescente numero per auctores diuersos· personae, pallae, coturni, socci et ceteri ornatus atque insignia scaenicorum reperta et ad hoc unicuique suus habitus: et ad ultimum, qui primarum partium, qui secundarum tertiarumque, ⟨qui⟩ quarti loci atque quinti actores essent, distributum et diuisa quinquepartito actu est tota fabula.

3 quae tamen in ipsis ortus sui uelut quibusdam incunabulis et uixdum incipiens ἀρχαία κωμῳδία et ἐπ' ὀνόματος dicta est: ἀρχαία idcirco, quia nobis pro nuper cognitis uetus est, ἐπ' ὀνόματος autem, quia inest in ea uelut historica fides uerae narrationis et denominatio ciuium, de quibus libere describebatur.

4 etenim per priscos poetas non ut nunc ficta penitus argumenta, sed res gestae a ciuibus palam cum eorum saepe qui gesserant nomine decantabantur, idque ipsum suo tempore moribus multum profuit ciuitatis, cum unus quisque caueret culpam, ne spectaculo ceteris exstitisset et

domestico probro. sed cum poetae licentius abuti stilo et passim laedere ex libidine coepissent plures bonos, ne quisquam in alterum carmen infame componeret lata lege siluerunt.

5 et hinc deinde aliud genus fabulae id est satyra sumpsit exordium, quae a satyris, quos in iocis semper ac petulantiis deos scimus esse, uocitata est, etsi ⟨alii⟩ aliunde nomen praue putant habere. haec satyra igitur eiusmodi fuit, ut in ea quamuis duro et uelut agresti ioco de uitiis ciuium, tamen sine ullo proprii nominis titulo, carmen esset. quod idem genus comoediae multis offuit poetis, cum in suspicionem potentibus ciuium uenissent, illorum facta descripsisse in peius ac deformasse genus stilo carminis. quod primus Lucilius nouo conscripsit modo, ut poesin inde fecisset, id est unius carminis plurimos libros.

6 hoc igitur quod supra diximus malo coacti omittere satyram aliud genus carminis νέαν κωμῳδίαν, hoc est nouam comoediam, repperere poetae, quae argumento communi magis et generaliter ad omnes homines, qui mediocribus fortunis agunt, pertineret et minus amaritudinis spectatoribus et eadem opera multum delectationis afferret, concinna argumento, consuetudini congrua, utilis sententiis, grata salibus, apta metro.

7 ut igitur superiores illae suis quaeque celebrantur auctoribus, ita haec νέα κωμῳδία cum multorum ante ac postea, tum praecipue Menandri Terentique est. de qua cum multa dicenda sint, sat erit tamen uelut admonendi lectoris causa quod de arte comica in ueterum cartis retinetur exponere.

III 1 Comoedia uetus ab initio chorus fuit paulatimque personarum numero in quinque actus processit. ita paulatim uelut attrito atque extenuato choro ad nouam comoediam sic peruenit, ut in ea non modo non inducatur chorus, sed ne locus quidem ullus iam relinquatur choro. nam postquam otioso tempore fastidiosior spectator effectus est et tum, cum ad cantatores ab actoribus fabula transiebat, consurgere et abire coepit, res admonuit poetas, ut primo quidem choros tollerent locum eis relinquentes, ut Menander fecit hac de causa, non ut alii existimant alia. postremo ne locum quidem reliquerunt, quod Latini fecerunt comici, unde apud illos dirimere actus quinquepartitos difficile est.

2 tum etiam Graeci prologos non habent more nostrorum, quos Latini habent. deinde θεοὺς ἀπὸ μηχανῆς, id est deos argumentis narrandis machinatos, ceteri Latini ad instar Graecorum habent, Terentius non habet. ad hoc προτατικὰ πρόσωπα, id est personas extra argumentum accersitas, non facile ceteri habent, quibus Terentius saepe utitur, ut per harum inductiones facilius pateat argumentum.

3 ueteres etsi ipsi quoque in metris neglegentius egerunt, iambici uersus dumtaxat in secundo et quarto loco, tamen a Terentio uincuntur resolutione huius metri quantum potest comminuti ad imaginem prosae orationis.

4 tum personarum leges circa habitum, aetatem, officium, partes agendi nemo diligentius a Terentio custodiuit. quin etiam solus ausus est, cum in fictis argumentis fidem ueritatis assequeretur, etiam contra praescripta comica meretrices interdum non malas introducere, quibus tamen et causa, cur bonae sint, et uoluptas per ipsum non defit.

5 haec cum artificiosissima Terentius fecerit, tum illud est admirandum, quod et morem retinuit, ut comoediam scriberet, et temperauit affectum, ne in tragoediam transiliret. quod cum aliis rebus minime obtentum et a Plauto et ab Afranio et †appio et multis fere magnis comicis: inuenimus. illud quoque inter Terentianas uirtutes mirabile, quod eius fabulae eo sunt temperamento, ut neque extumescant ad tragicam celsitudinem neque abiciantur ad mimicam uilitatem.

6 adde quod nihil abstrusum ab eo ponitur aut quod' ab historicis requirendum sit, quod saepius Plautus facit et eo est obscurior multis locis.

7 adde quod argumenti ac stili ita attente memor est, ut nusquam non aut cauerit aut curauerit quae obesse potuerunt, quodque media primis atque postremis ita : nexuit, ut nihil additum alteri, sed aptum ex se totum et uno corpore uideatur esse compositum.

8 illud quoque mirabile in eo, primo quod non ita miscet quattuor personas, ut obscura sit earum distinctio, et item quod nihil ad populum facit actorem uelut extra comoediam loqui, quod uitium Plauti frequentissimum.

9 illud etiam inter cetera eius laude dignum uidetur, quod locupletiora argumenta ex duplicibus negotiis delegerit ad scribendum. nam excepta Hecyra, in qua unius Pamphili amor est, ceterae quinque binos adulescentes habent.

IV 1 Illud uero tenendum est, post νέαν κωμῳδίαν Latinos multa fabularum genera protulisse, ut togatas ab scaenicis atque argumentis Latinis, praetextatas a dignitate personarum tragicarum ex Latina historia, Atellanas a ciuitate Campaniae, ubi actitatae sunt primae, Rinthonicas ab auctoris nomine, tabernarias ab humilitate argumenti ac stili, mimos ab diuturna imitatione uilium rerum ac leuium personarum.

2 inter tragoediam autem et comoediam cum multa tum inprimis hoc distat, quod in comedia mediocres fortunae hominum, parui impetus periculorum laetique sunt exitus actionum, at in tragoedia omnia contra, ingentes personae, magni timores, exitus funesti habentur; et illic prima turbulenta, tranquilla ultima, in tragoedia contrario ordine res aguntur; tum quod in tragoedia fugienda uita, in comoedia capessenda exprimitur; postremo quod omnis comoedia de fictis est argumentis, tragoedia saepe de historia fide petitur.

3 Latinae fabulae primo a Liuio Andronico scriptae sunt, adeo cuncta re etiam tum recenti, ut idem poeta et actor suarum fabularum fuisset.

4 Comoediae autem motoriae sunt aut statariae aut mixtae. motoriae turbulentae, statariae quietiores, mixtae ex utroque actu consistentes.

5 comoedia per quattuor partes diuiditur: prologum, protasin, epitasin, catastrophen. est prologus uelut praefatio quaedam fabulae, in quo solo licet praeter argumentum aliquid ad populum uel ex poetae uel ex ipsius fabulae uel actoris commodo loqui; protasis primus actus initiumque est dramatis; epitasis incrementum processusque turbarum ac totius, ut ita dixerim, nodus erroris; : catastrophe conuersio rerum ad iucundos exitus patefacta cunctis cognitione gestorum.

DE COMOEDIA.

V 1 Comoedia est fabula diuersa instituta continens affectuum ciuilium ac priuatorum, quibus discitur, quid sit in uita utile, quid contra euitandum. hanc Graeci sic definiuerunt 'κωμῳδία ἐστὶν ⟨ἰδιωτικῶν πραγμάτων⟩ περιοχὴ ἀκίνδυνος'.

comoediam esse Cicero ait imitationem uitae, speculum consuetudinis, imaginem ueritatis.

2 comoediae autem more antiquo dictae, quia in uicis huiusmodi carmina initio agebantur apud Graecos — ut in Italia compitaliciis ludicris —, *admixto pronuntiationis modulo, quo, dum actus commutantur, populus attinebatur,* ἀπὸ τῆς κώμης, hoc est ab actu uitae hominum, qui in uicis habitant ob mediocritatem fortunarum, non in aulis regiis, ut sunt personae tragicae.

3 *comoedia autem, quia poema sub imitatione uitae atque morum similitudine compositum est, in gestu et pronuntiatione consistit.*

4 *comoediam apud Graecos dubium est quis primus inuenerit, apud Romanos certum: et comoediam et tragoediam et togatam primus Liuius Andronicus repperit.*

5 *aitque esse comoediam cotidianae uitae speculum, nec iniuria. nam ut intenti speculo ueritatis liniamenta facile per imaginem colligimus, ita lectione comoediae imitationem uitae consuetudinisque non aegerrime animaduertimus.*

6 huius autem originis ratio ab exteris ciuitatibus moribusque prouenit. Athenienses namque Atticam custodientes elegantiam cum uellent male uiuentes notare, in uicos et compita ex omnibus locis laeti alacresque ueniebant ibique cum nominibus singulorum uitia publicabant, unde nomen compositum, ut c o m o e d i a uocaretur.

7 haec autem carmina in pratis mollibus primum agebantur. nec deerant praemia, quibus ad scribendum doctorum prouocarentur ingenia; sed et actoribus munera offerebantur, quo libentius iucundo uocis flexu ad dulcedinem commendationis uterentur: caper namque pro dono his dabatur, quia animal uitibus noxium habebatur. a quo etiam tragoediae nomen exortum est. nonnulli autem ex amurca, olei faece, quae est humor aquatilis, tragoediam ⟨quasi trygodiam⟩ dici uocarique maluerunt.

8 qui lusus cum per artifices in honorem Liberi patris agerentur, etiam ipsi comoediarum tragoediarumque scriptores huius dei uelut praesens numen colere uenerarique coeperunt. cuius rei probabilis ratio exstitit. ita enim carmina incohata proferebantur, ut per ea laudes eius et facta gloriosa celebrari proferrique constaret.

9 tum paulatim fama huius artis increbruit. Thespis autem primus haec scripta in omnium notitiam protulit, postea Aeschylus secutus prioris exemplum †publicauit. de quibus ita Horatius in arte poetica loquitur

275   'ignotum tragicae genus inuenisse Camenae
       dicitur et plaustris uexisse poemata Thespis,
       quae canerent agerentque peruncti faecibus ora.
       post hunc personae pallaeque repertor honestae
       Aeschylus et modicis instrauit pulpita tignis
280   et docuit magnumque loqui nitique coturno.
       successit uetus his comoedia non sine multa
       laude: sed in uitium libertas excidit et uim
       dignam lege regi. lex est accepta chorusque
       turpiter obticuit sublato iure nocendi.
285   nil intemptatum nostri liquere poetae:
       nec minimum meruere decus uestigia Graeca
       ausi deserere et celebrare domestica facta,
       uel qui praetextas uel qui docuere togatas.'

VI 1 Fabula generale nomen est: eius duae primae partes, tragoedia et comoedia. ⟨tragoedia⟩, si Latina argumentatio sit, praetexta dicitur. comoedia autem multas species habet: aut enim palliata est aut togata aut tabernaria aut Atellana aut mimus aut Rinthonica aut planipedia.

2 planipedia autem dicta ob humilitatem argumenti eius ac uilitatem actorum, qui non coturno aut socco nituntur in scaena aut pulpito sed plano pede, uel ideo quod non ea negotia continet, quae personarum in turribus aut in cenaculis habitantium sunt, sed in plano atque in humili loco.

3 Personati primi egisse dicuntur comoediam Cincius Faliscus, tragoediam Minucius Prothymus.

4 Omnium autem comoediarum inscripta ex quattuor rebus omnino sumuntur: nomine, loco, facto, euentu. nomine, ut Phormio [Hecyra] Curculio Epidicus; loco, ut Andria Leucadia Brundisina; facto, ut Eunuchus Asinaria Captiui; euentu, ⟨ut⟩ Commorientes Crimen Heautontimorumenos.

5 Comoediarum formae sunt tres: palliatae Graecum habitum referentes, togatae iuxta formam personarum habitum togarum desiderantes, quas nonnulli tabernarias uocant, Atellanae salibus et iocis compositae, quae in se non habent nisi uetustatum elegantias.

VII 1 Comoedia autem diuiditur in quattuor partes: prologum, πρότασιν, ἐπίτασιν, καταστροφήν.

2 prologus est prima dictio, a Graecis dicta πρῶτος λόγος uel antecedens ueram fabulae compositionem elocutio, ⟨ὁ πρὸ τοῦ δράματος λόγος⟩. eius species sunt quattuor: συστατικός commendatiuus, quo poeta uel fabula commendatur;

ἐπιτιμητικός relatiuus, quo aut aduersario maledictum aut populo gratiae referuntur;

δραματικός argumentatiuus, exponens fabulae argumentum;

μικτός mixtus, omnia haec in se continens.

3 inter prologum et prologium quidam hoc interesse uoluerunt, quod prologus est, ubi aut poeta excusatur aut fabula commendatur, prologium autem est, cum tantum de argumento dicitur.

4 πρότασις est primus actus fabulae, quo pars argumenti explicatur, pars reticetur ad populi exspectationem tenendam; ἐπίτασις inuolutio argumenti, cuius elegantia conectitur; καταστροφή explicatio fabulae, per quam euentus eius approbatur.

VIII 1 In plerisque fabulis priora ponebantur ipsarum nomina quam poetarum, in nonnullis poetarum quam fabularum, cuius moris diuersitatem antiquitas probat. nam cum primum aliqui fabulas ederent, ipsarum nomina pronuntiabantur, antequam poetae pronuntiaretur, ne aliqua inuidia ab scribendo deterreri posset. cum autem per editionem multarum poetae iam esset auctoritas adquisita, rursus priora nomina poetarum proferebantur, ut per ipsorum uocabula fabulis attentio adquireretur.

2 actas diuersis ludis manifestum est inscribi. nam sunt ludorum species quattuor, quos aediles curules munere publico curant: Megalenses, magnis dis consecrati, quos Graeci μεγάλους appellant; funebres, ad attinendum populum instituti, dum pompa funeri decreta in honorem patricii uiri plene instruitur; plebei, qui pro salute plebis eduntur; Apollinares, Apollini consecrati.

3 In scaena duae arae poni solebant: dextera Liberi, sinistra eius dei, cui ludi fiebant. unde Terentius in Andria (IV 3, 11) ait 'ex ara sume hinc uerbenas tibi'.

4 Ulixen pilleatum semper inducunt, siue quod aliquando insaniam simulauit, quo tempore tectum se esse uoluit, ne agnitus cogeretur in bella prodire, seu ob singularem sapientiam, qua tectus munitusque plurimum sociis profuit; huius enim uirtus erat animi semper decipientis ingenium. nonnulli Ithacae incolas sicut Locros pilleatos fuisse commemorant.

5 Achillis et Neoptolomi personae diademata habent, quamuis numquam regalia sceptra tenuerunt. cuius argumenti probatio talis inducitur, quod numquam cum reliqua Graeciae iuuentute ad gerenda cum Troianis bella sacramenta coniurationis inierunt nec umquam sub Agamemnonis imperio fuerunt.

6 comicis senibus candidus uestitus inducitur, quod is antiquissimus fuisse memoratur, adulescentibus discolor attribuitur. serui comici amictu exiguo teguntur paupertatis antiquae gratia uel quo expeditiores agant. parasiti cum intortis palliis ueniunt. laeto uestitus candidus, aerumnoso obsoletus, purpureus diuiti, pauperi phoenicius datur. militi chlamys purpurea, puellae habitus peregrinus inducitur. leno pallio colore uario utitur, meretrici ob auaritiam luteum datur.

7 syrmata dicta sunt ab eo quod trahuntur, quae res ab Ionica luxuria instituta est. eadem in luctuosis personis incuriam sui per neglegentiam significant.

8 Aulaea quoque in scaena intexta sternuntur, quod pictus ornatus ex Attalica regia Romam usque perlatus est; pro quibus siparia aetas posterior accepit. est autem mimicum uelum, quod populo obsistit, dum fabularum actus commutantur.

9 deuerbia histriones pronuntiabant, cantica uero temperabantur modis non a poeta sed a perito artis musicae factis. neque enim omnia isdem modis in uno cantico agebantur sed saepe mutatis, ut significant qui tres numeros in comoediis ponunt, qui tres continent 'mutatis modis cantici'.

10 eius qui modos faciebat nomen in principio fabulae post scriptoris et actoris superponebatur.

11 huiusmodi carmina ad tibias fiebant, ut his auditis
multi ex populo ante dicerent, quam fabulam acturi scaenici essent, quam omnino spectatoribus ipsius antecedens
titulus pronuntiaretur. agebantur autem tibiis paribus, id
est dextris aut sinistris, et imparibus. dextrae autem tibiae
sua grauitate seriam comoediae dictionem praenuntiabant,
sinistrae [Serranae] acuminis leuitate iocum in comoedia
ostendebant. ubi autem dextra et sinistra acta fabula in-
scribebatur, mixtim ioci et grauitates denuntiabantur.

Forum Reviews

RECENT BOOKS ON SHAKESPEAREAN COMEDY

As the present volume testifies, the critical interest in Shakespearean comedy, quickened in the late fifties and early sixties by the work of C. L. Barber and Northrop Frye and sustained by a flow of strong and original books throughout the sixties and early seventies, has continued in the later seventies. Yet, to judge solely from recently published books, we have been going through a relatively calm period dominated by the balanced assessment. This is a generalization no sooner offered than qualified—for any new book on Shakespeare produces partisan arguments. Still, the best way to judge most of the recent books is less by the originality of their theses than by the vitality and variety of forces over which they preside. The most interesting books attempt the most precarious balances.

Leo Salingar. Shakespeare and the Traditions of Comedy. Cambridge University Press, 1975.

The most comprehensive of the recent assessments is Leo Salingar's *Shakespeare and the Traditions of Comedy*. Salingar's main aim is to gauge the relative influences upon Shakespearean comedy of medieval, classical, and Renaissance traditions. His scope is vast and his treatment thorough. Of Shakespeare's three lines of influence, he declares that "in broad terms, the romantic elements in his plots spring from the Middle Ages, while his sense of comic irony stems from the Roman playwrights and his feeling for comedy as festivity expresses the culture of the renaissance." Such a statement, though obviously an oversimplification, entails a number of aggressive contentions. Salingar's formulation about Renaissance festivity, for example, is an effort to remove as much as he can from the holiday reach of Barber—there are many elements of Shakespearean comedy, he is careful to insist, "which the idea of festivity will not take in at all." Salingar is similarly eager to be free of Frye, whom he accuses of reducing romantic comedies, through the idea of wish fulfillment, "to a flat level of sentimentality."

Some instability can be noticed in the book's organization. Despite

his protestations to the contrary, Salingar's two erudite chapters on classical comedy overwhelm his single chapter on medieval romances, for
though the classical chapters are the products of much compression, the
medieval one depends upon extrapolation. Yet Salingar wants to give
priority and prominence to medieval influences. He points out that the
mere survival of "sources" can be a misleading indication of influence, and
he argues that the secular romance, a genre that neither churchmen nor
printers found incentive to preserve, may have had in performance an influence we can no longer measure. The readjustment Salingar urges has
interesting implications, particularly for considering the atavistic aspects
of Shakespeare's late romances; but ultimately it is difficult to allow absent evidence more than a cautionary function. As much as we can sym-
pathize, for example, with his conviction that *The Comedy of Errors* is
not nearly so Plautine as its borrowed plot has been made to suggest, we
are unlikely to leap to the countersuggestion that Shakespeare turned to
Plautus to "strengthen" a more medieval and more romantic story of
family reunion.

A further imbalance of *Shakespeare and the Tradition of Comedy* is
the ambiguity latent in the *and* of its title. For the most part, Salingar's
subject is Shakespeare in the light of, or, at least, against the background
of, his comedic tradition; but, often enough, the discussion of traditions
loses its Shakespearean focus. The long and excellent discussion of Old
Comedy, for example, floats free of a clear connection to Shakespeare.
Similarly, Salingar's cogent analysis of the influence of Euripides upon
New Comedy is more valuable in itself than for any new light it sheds upon Shakespeare's relation to either Euripides or New Comedy. In his preface Salingar explains that this book will be followed by a sequel addressing itself more directly and continuously to Shakespeare's comedies themselves.

One of Salingar's special strengths, however, is describing the Italian
Renaissance traditions and distinguishing what is often naive, native, and
morally simple in the Italian novelle from what is self-consciously literary,
exotic, and morally agitated in Shakespeare's use of them. In general, Salingar's assertions about Shakespeare grow more frequent and gain more
weight the further he proceeds. When he declares eventually that Shakespeare's "great invention was to treat comedy lyrically" or that Shakespeare and his contemporaries were the first to take full advantage of the
metaphor of world as stage or that "the greatest creative writer whose influence can be felt widely diffused through Shakespeare's plays in Boccaccio"—the truisms have behind them the expanse of his investigations.

Salingar's later chapters also yield some fresh insights about specific
Shakespearean comedies. For example, he provides a delicate analysis of
the double plot of *The Taming of the Shrew* in its Italianate context. Elsewhere he notices that Shakespeare's princely figures, though they sym-
bolize order, are invariably associated with disruption. And most significantly perhaps, he argues persuasively that there is indeed a group of plays

well designated "problem comedies." All of the problem comedies—*All's Well That Ends Well, Much Ado About Nothing, Measure for Measure,* and *The Merchant of Venice*—complicate their novelle sources by importing a problematic sense of "law," and their apparent moral issues all evaporate in climactically theatrical trial scenes. Detached from their context, these would be interesting points; but against the background Salingar provides, they also carry considerable authority. *Shakespeare and the Traditions of Comedy* is one of the solidest Shakespeare books of the seventies. Its patient syntheses and informed distinctions are counterbalanced by enough assertive hypotheses to make it a stimulating book as well.

Lawrence Danson. The Harmonies of The Merchant of Venice. Yale University Press, 1978.

At a first reading, Lawrence Danson's *The Harmonies of The Merchant of Venice* seems balanced to the point of evasion. Danson negotiates skillfully among a range of critical viewpoints, makes graceful use of the play's theatrical history, draws deftly on contemporary legal practices, and displays a mastery of relevant Biblical backgrounds—all in broad support of his general argument that *The Merchant of Venice* is a profoundly Christian play dominated by patterns of harmonic circularity. The argument sounds routine enough; yet for all its emphasis on harmony— or rather because of that insistent emphasis—Danson's treatment is subtly contentious.

That *The Merchant of Venice* is an explicitly Christian play is itself a somewhat controversial claim these days. So strong have been the counteremphases that a critic like Robert Hunter in his *Shakespeare and the Comedy of Forgiveness* (1965) passed over *The Merchant of Venice*, with a nod toward Frye, as a play whose structure owes little to Christian ideology and much to New Comedy. Danson does not see the prevailing movement of the play overcoming a barrier or banishing a scapegoat, but fulfilling a circle of gifts back to givers. More precisely, he claims to see the play as fleshing out a Christian version of a three-part gesture advocated in Seneca's *De Beneficiis* (Danson's addition to the always growing list of texts Shakespeare must have read): "We need to be taught to give willingly, and to return willingly." This is a lesson, maintains Danson, well understood by Portia, learned in separate ways by Bassanio and Antonio, and ignored by Shylock, to his chagrin. Danson is quite willing to place *The Merchant of Venice* within a tradition of Christian homiletic literature.

Shylock, of course, is the great impediment to any successful orchestration of the play, homiletic or otherwise. In gradually approaching "The Problem of Shylock" (the title of his next-to-last chapter), Danson does some fancy sidestepping. First, he attempts to dissociate himself from the extremes of overpsychologizing and overconventionalizing the character. He has no sympathy for ironists like Leslie Fiedler who see *The Merchant of Venice* as a play about Christian hypocrisies; and he has a running, if belated, disagreement with the convention-peddling E. E. Stoll (who speaks, in Danson's quotations, however, with an endearing cantankerousness). The effect is to create the impression that Shylock, like that lesser problem, the unaccountably melancholy Antonio, can best be viewed as a "richly impure mixture" of dramatic tendencies; but this impression of interpretive latitude is one he later takes care to restrict. Eventually, Shylock must be "accommodated within the final harmony," and Danson strains to provide accommodation. His main suggestion is that Shylock embodies "the fortunate fall" of Jewry, the disbelieving remnant that makes salvation for believers possible. A secondary point is that Portia's humiliation of Shylock is not so harsh as it seems—her proviso that upon his death half of his forfeited estate will revert to Jessica and Lorenzo is one more instance of tempered mercy and another image of harmonic circularity. In the face of such explanations I reach gladly for the declaration of Alexander Leggatt in *Shakespeare's Comedy of Love* (1974) that *The Merchant of Venice* "has shown a larger world than it can finally bring into harmony."

Danson's perception of Christian harmonies dampens other characters besides Shylock. Even Portia is somewhat held down. For in emphasizing her graciousness as orchestrator, Danson plays down her wiliness as manipulator. His bias is nowhere more apparent than in his treatment of the song "Tell me where is Fancy Bred." We need not feel strongly that the "Bred," "head," and "nourished" rhymes are subtle encouragements for Bassanio's choice of the lead casket in order to find odd the vehemence with which Danson rejects that possibility : "the imputation of Antonio's homosexuality is one the play can survive intact . . . but *this* imputation . . . would make the rest of the play inexplicable."

There are other moments in which Danson's apparently sedate argument stirs excitement. Early in his chapter titled "This Strict Court of Venice," for example, Danson calls attention to the "diabolical literalism" at work in the play's theme of law. The courtroom scene troubles the deep fear in us all "of being trapped in the word itself": "the courtroom is archetypally an arena where bright logic and dark mystery mingle, where language, codified into law, assumes a virtual power of its own and becomes a potentially uncontrollable menace." This eloquent insight has resonance for both the casket scenes and the ring plots, as well as for Antonio's bond of flesh; and it lends some powerful support to Salingar's contention about the centrality of the trial scenes to problem plays. But since Danson is interested in muting the play's problems, he turns away from these perceptions in the interest of final harmonies.

Merry Wives of Windsor

Page 71

Publifhd 1 April 1798 by Edw.ᵈ Harding Pall Mall .

An engraving (1798) by William Gardiner showing Fal-
staff in Windsor Forest, *The Merry Wives of Windsor*,
Act 5, scene 5, used by Jeanne Addison Roberts as a
frontispiece for her *Shakespeare's English Comedy:
"The Merry Wives of Windsor," in Context. Courtesy of
The Folger Shakespeare Library.*

Jeanne Addison Roberts. Shakespeare's English Comedy:The Merry Wives of Windsor in Context. University of Nebraska Press, 1979

The balance Jeanne Addison Roberts attempts to strike in *Shakespeare's English Comedy: The Merry Wives of Windsor in Context* is between textual and literary criticism. Her main critical emphases are that the play is farcical but no farce, that it is more English than Italianate (Salingar sees it, despite the setting, as the most Italian of Shakespeare's plots), and that it embodies a ritual of seasonal change. One of the shortcomings of this critical portion of the book is that the language of the play is seldom allowed to speak for itself, except through the quotations of other critics. Roberts' own argument picks up the most energy in the vicinity of Frye and Barber. Perhaps the most interesting section of the book is her exploration of the ritualistic implications of the behorned Falstaff so rotundly envisioned in the engraving by William Gardiner that Roberts has chosen as frontispiece. Falstaff antlered in Windsor Forest is wide enough to be seen simultaneously as cuckold, fertility-figure, and scapegoat. Her suggestion that the play is not a spring holiday but a play about "the final fling" of mischievous fall spirits "foreshadowing worse days to come" coincides with a compelling Halloween stage conception of the play.

Roberts is less successful in some of her textual discussion. What she sees historically as "the orderly progress" toward the hypothesis, first articulated by Greg, that *Q* is a memorial reconstruction of *F*, could as easily be seen as the sporadic eruption and gradual erosion of the more far-fetched hypotheses. In her discussion of the date of the play, Roberts advances a dubious hypothesis of her own. It is her conviction "that while Shakespeare was working on *Henry IV, Part 2*, he interrupted his writing at 4.3 to supply the text of *The Merry Wives of Windsor* in time for performance in connection with the Garter celebrations of April and May 1597." There is solid evidence, compiled by William Green and others, for associating *The Merry Wives* with the garter ceremonies of 1597, but there is little warrant for Roberts' interruption theory. Her suggestion would pacify literalists who have never been able to imagine that Shakespeare or his audience could have the heart to see Falstaff so ignominiously resurrected after his rejection at the end of *Henry IV, Part 2* and his off-stage death in *Henry V*. There might be interesting comparisons between the fall of Falstaff in *Henry IV, Part 2* and his pratfalls in *The Merry Wives of Windsor*, but they need not depend on the chronology of the plays.

Barbara A. Mowat. The Dramaturgy of Shakespeare's Romances. University of Georgia Press, 1976.

If there is one recent tendency in the criticism of Shakespearean comedy likely to persist into the eighties, it is the fascination with Shakespeare's late romances. More than any other grouping of Shakespearean comedies, *Pericles*, *Cymbeline*, *The Winter's Tale*, and *The Tempest* exert a collective interest, partly because of their clear chronological proximity at the end of Shakespeare's career, but mostly because their strong affinities seem to promise mutual illumination.

Barbara A. Mowat's *The Dramaturgy of Shakespeare's Romances* is representative of recent trends. It avoids the fallacies of Shakespearean psychohistory, and it also avoids the reductive explanations of theatrical history (the suggestion that these plays are the response to the fashion set by Beaumont and Fletcher, for example, or the notion that they were written to suit the King's Men's venture with the Blackfriars Theatre). It also avoids the practice of disguising separate readings of the separate plays under some illusion of continuity; by organizing her discussion around dramaturgic topics, Mowat keeps her focus on what the romances share as theatrical performances. Many of her emphases are familiar, but she puts them to work in an effectively cumulative way. Her most persistent point is that the romances fluctuate between "representational" (illusionistic) and "presentational" (deliberately artificial) dramatic moments, a fluctuation that by its "sporadic engagement and detachment" forces us into a complex awareness. She also stresses the frequency with which narration intrudes upon action, the displacement of Shakespeare's usual mid-play climax, and the ease with which characters submerge themselves in role-playing, the dominance of surprises, and the way a sense of death permeates these plays without smothering them.

Less persuasive than this accumulation of observations is the conclusion toward which Mowat points them. Shakespeare's romances are "open form drama." It is difficult to know exactly what she means by this label. In one sense she means simply that in the romances "Shakespeare places us not, as in normal Shakespearean drama, in a position of dramatic expectancy about what will happen, but in the position of innocent, wondering auditors." But she also comes to the verge of saying that the romances have as much in common with the plays of Aristophanes or Brecht as Shakespeare's earlier comedies. The most glaring weakness of Mowat's study, however, is simply her decision to omit *Pericles* because Shakespeare's authorship of part of that play is still disputed. Shakespeare's authorship of *Pericles* is not much in doubt, but even if the play were not entirely his, it would still provide the most fertile ground for illustrating Mowat's best points.

Frances A. Yates. Shakespeare's Last Plays: A New Approach. Routledge & Kegan Paul, London 1975.

Less representative of recent trends and one book not much concerned with balance is *Shakespeare's Last Plays* by Frances Yates. Subtitled "A New Approach," Yates's study is essentially the old approach of glimpsing a play through its topical allusions. Yet Yates's view is less a glimpse than a broad and experienced vision, focused toward the two concerns that have occupied most of her distinguished career: court politics and the science of magic. Her main argument is that, early in the reign of James I, a cult of "Elizabethan revival" attached its sympathies to the martial and marital prospects of the ill-fated Prince Henry. Particular interest was drawn to James's strategy to stabilize international relations by negotiating a Spanish and a German marriage for Henry and his sister, Elizabeth. The specific correspondences she sees between contemporary circumstances and situations in Shakespeare's plays are too intricate to encapsulate here, but I can say that her chapter on *Cymbeline* offers impressive illuminations of several of the odder aspects of that play. There can be little doubt that, in the appeal to Cymbeline's noble lineage, the princely sparks of Guiderius and Arviragus, and the xenophobic portrayal of Cloten, Shakespeare was drawing on some powerfully associative political images. The question, of course, is to what extent these associations structure the play or modify its tone. Yates's searchlight approach is apt to flood the plays with stark allusiveness. Yates reads *The Tempest* in the light of her second interest. I will leave readers to their own answers to the question she asks about the influence of German Rosicrucianism:

> Dare one say that this movement reaches a peak of poetic expression in *The Tempest*, a Rosicrucian manifesto infused with the spirit of Dee, and using (like Andreae) theatrical parables for esoteric communication?

Carol McGinnis Kay and Henry E. Jacobs, eds. Shakespeare's Romances Reconsidered. University of Nebraska Press, 1978.

The most valuable recent book on Shakespeare's romances is a collection of essays edited by Carol McGinnis Kay and Henry E. Jacobs. *Shakespeare's Romances Reconsidered* is also the most balanced book on Shakespeare's late comedies, if balance can be said to result from the intersection of extremely varied techniques. The collection is highlighted by Northrop Frye's "Romance as Masque," an essay that extends, with his usual boldness, clarity, and wit, some of the propositions of *Anatomy of Criticism* and *A Natural Perspective.* His supple central contention is that Shakespeare's late romances (among which, with practiced offhandedness, he includes *Henry VIII* and *The Two Noble Kinsmen)* express one of the primary Renaissance divergences from the form of New Comedy under the pressure of the processional elements and polarized values that are impulses of Old Comedy. Connections that in a study like Salingar's must remain unhazarded or buttressed by firm evidence proceed from the web of Frye with the same provisional flamboyance that allows him to touch down fleetingly, but never quite irrelevantly, on Fabergé, "ziggurat imagery," and the tedium of King James.

Frye, however, is not allowed too magisterial a place in the volume. His essay is followed, after the editor's tactful placement of a sturdy essay by the late Clifford Leech on the theme of masking and unmasking, by Howard Felperin's severe criticism of the way Frye's system, particularly his theory of modes, encourages too simple a reading of Shakespearean romance. For Frye, according to Felperin, a romantic text like *The Tempest* extensively retains its mythic shape, a version of Christian resurrection only a small way toward irony:

> Nothing is more remarkable in Frye's writings on earlier romance than the absence of any suggestion that this recuperation of pristine mythic shapes may be incomplete or problematic and may be presented as such by the romancer himself.

Felperin proceeds to his own problematic reading of *The Tempest*, finding a pattern of "demystification and remystification" analogous to Conrad's *Heart of Darkness*. I don't think that Felperin thoroughly established the basis of his disagreement with Frye, whose own essay proves subtly uncooperative with the direction in which Felperin would push him; but Felperin's essay, besides being an effective appeal for joining the study of romances to the study of romanticism, adds another voice for the dark, double-edged reading of *The Tempest* that is more than ever in vogue.

The essays of Charles R. Forker and Charles Frey are agile restatements of conventional interpretations of *The Tempest* and *The Winter's Tale*, respectively. Forker precedes his somewhat familiar Christian reading of *The Tempest* by an ingenious preliminary treatment ot *The Taming of the Shrew* and a discussion of Shakespeare's uses of plays-within-plays. Frey uses his discussion of scenic contrasts in *The Winter's Tale* to enforce what he sees as the play's inherently tragic movement toward "sacred purgation." Also included are two essays with scholarly focuses: Jean Warhol Rossi's argument that Shakespeare's use of Holinshed is more central to *Cymbeline* than is usually supposed, and David M. Bergeron's educated conjecture that Hermione's appearance as a statue is part of a revised version of *The Winter's Tale* and thus only a Shakespearean afterthought. Bergeron's hypothesis carries little conviction, but it is appealing in its puckish implications for painstaking formal analyses that find a pervasive structural element in "statue scenes."

The three other essays in *Shakespeare's Romances Reconsidered* share a technique that is becoming more and more popular and well managed—the ingenious grouping. David Young (author of *The Heart's Forest* [1972], an influential treatment of Shakespeare's "pastoral" comedies) here groups *The Tempest* with *Doctor Faustus* and *The Alchemist* in a "triangular study" that enables him to see Prospero as an extraordinary apex. Joan Hartwig cleverly groups a motley selection of characters—Cloten, Autolycus, and Caliban—and argues, also cleverly, that the three characters carry "parodic burdens" in relation to Posthumous, Leontes, and Prospero. All three are crucial to their plays, for they serve as antimasque figures who "exert dramatically an energy, sexual and physical, that the figures they parody do not generate in themselves."

The groupings of Cyrus Hoy in "Fathers and Daughters in Shakespeare's Romances" are less ingenious but more important. The father-daughter theme is very much in the critical air, and nowhere does it seem more promising than in the investigation of the late romances. Hoy's treatment of the idea is suggestive rather than complete, and it verges too much upon a kind of post-Dowden psychobiography:

> The dramatist is engaged in a quest to free the imagination from all the shrill mistress-wife-mother figures who have inhabited the late tragedies, and to create in their place an ideal of femininity on whom the imagination can bestow its tenderest sentiments, without the distraction of sexual desire.

Despite its psychological excesses, or perhaps because of them, this is an attractively bold approach. Certainly Hoy's point about the incestuous Simonides and his daughter in *Pericles* is marvelously provocative:

> Here, at the outset of the romances, we are confronted for just a moment with the disturbing possibilities which it will be a principal endeavor of the dramatist's art to supress in the plays ahead.

William O. Scott. The God of Arts: Ruling Ideas in Shakespeare's Comedies. University of Kansas Publications, 1977.

The most puzzling of the recent books is William O. Scott's *The God of Arts: Ruling Ideas in Shakespeare's Comedies*. One of its minor eccentricities is that it is the first book since 1960 on the general topic of Shakespearean comedy, as far as I know, never to mention C. L. Barber. More intriguingly eccentric, however, is the book's overall conception. Scott claims a kind of balance by directing his book toward the need for a systematic study of Shakespearean comedy at a "middle level of generality" somewhere between an immense structure like Frye's and an ad hoc approach to each play. Since "Shakespeare's comedies seem to range from the individual's puzzled encounters with the world . . . to the problems of government," he orders his chapters via seven overlapping categories that illustrate a progression from individual characters' problems of self-definition to the problems of redefining entire societies. Scott sees the chronology of the comedies as roughly matching this movement from the individual outward. Rough or not, this is a sweeping outlook to defend, and Scott, perhaps wisely, does not explicitly try to defend it.

But he does allow the impression that he is moving from the simple to the complex to create an odd thrust, as in this comment on *Cymbeline:*

> Shakespeare goes about as far as he can in this play in making re-demptions result from good actions done in ignorance or despair by exiles.

Though not without some insight about the structure of *Cymbeline*, this is a strange emphasis.

Scott's strength is his willingness to speak of the ways plots actually work upon us and of the ways a dramatist channels our feelings about characters. There is a crudeness in the way he analyzes choices open to characters that corresponds to the mechanical way we as audience construct a dramatic action and establish our expectations. In his early chapters he pays an attention to rings and vows, an emphasis that seems belabored particularly when accompanied by a comment like "rings reveal truth by recalling past obligations." Yet his point, that the tangible existence of a ring or the assurance of a love-pledge locks us firmly into a relatively narrow corridor of expectations, is well worth making.

Scott often writes about characters as if they were people with real options, and his considerations often extend to what they do *not* do: "Yet for all we know Bertram might have avoided Helena, and perhaps got the marriage annulled, if he had been willing to remain celibate long enough." As reminiscent as such extrapolations sound of the worst excesses of Victorian criticism, they touch upon a real layer of theatrical feeling that most of us have been trained to ignore. In places Scott's book is disquietingly repetitive, obscure, and banal; but it disquiets us most by making us aware, through the ease with which we see how far off-track it is, of the critical tracks on which we stand.

S. Schoenbaum. Shakespeare: The Globe & The World. Folger Shakespeare Library and Oxford University Press, 1979.

While not specifically addressed to comedy, Samuel Schoenbaum's sumptuously illustrated *Shakespeare: The Globe & The World* deserves special mention as the most festive of recent books. It is designed to accompany the Folger Library's exhibition of Shakespeareana which began its national tour late in 1979. The 350 illustrations (150 in color) in this book are exquisitely reproduced and wonderfully varied. There is a judicious sampling of evidence from Shakespeare's own documentary life, but the more luxurious view is of the life of his times as recorded in a startling array of woodcuts, watercolors, miniatures, costumes, maps, and needlepoint bible bindings. Equally remarkable are Shakespeare's manifestations in after-times, whether in the splendid reproductions of paintings by Romney, Fuseli, and Rackham, or in such arresting glimpses as the Cushman sisters portraying Romeo and Juliet, a MacBird poster, or a still from *A Midsummer Night's Dream* acted by Czech marionettes. While subordinating his own text to the purposes of the exhibition, Samuel Schoenbaum moves nimbly and learnedly among the complex biographical and historical materials. In characteristic fashion, he manages to make the entertainingly arcane also entertainingly germane. This is a joyful book which will fortunately be available long after the materials of the exhibition have been returned to the Folger.

Bibliography

Abel, Lionel. *Metatheatre.* New York: Hill and Wang, 1963.

Allen, Don Cameron. *Mysteriously Meant.* Baltimore: Johns Hopkins Univ. Press, 1970.

Allen, Michael J. B. "The Chase: The Development of a Renaissance Theme." In *Comparative Literature*, 20 (1968), 301-12.

Bakhtin, Mikhail. *Rabelais and His World.* Trans. by Helene Iswolsky. Cambridge, Mass.: M. I. T. Press, 1968.

Baldwin, T. W. *Shakespeare's Five-Act Structure.* Urbana: Univ. of Illinois Press, 1947.

Barber, C. L. *Shakespeare's Festive Comedy.* Princeton: Princeton Univ. Press, 1959.

Barton, Anne. "'As You Like It' and 'Twelfth Night': Shakespeare's Sense of an Ending." In *Shakespearian Comedy*, ed. by Malcolm Bradbury and David Palmer. New York: Crane, Russak, 1972, 160-80, Stratford-upon-Avon Studies, 14.

Bear, Andrew. "Restoration Comedy and the Provok'd Critic." In *Restoration Literature: Critical Approaches*, ed. by Harold Love. London: Methuen, 1972.

Beare, W. *The Roman Stage.* London: Methuen, 1950.

Bentley, Eric. *The Life of the Drama.* New York: Atheneum, 1967.

Bergson, Henri. *Laughter* (1900). In *Comedy*, ed. by Wylie Sypher. Garden City, N. Y.: Doubleday, 1956.

Bermel, Albert C. "Farce." In *The Reader's Encyclopedia of World Drama*, ed. by John Gassner and Edward Quinn. New York: Crowell, 1969, 262-65.

Bethell, S. L. *Shakespeare and the Popular Dramatic Tradition.* London: Staples, 1944.

Boughner, Daniel C. "Don Armado and the *Commedia dell'Arte.*" In *Studies in Philology*, 37 (1940), 201-24.

Brooks, Harold S. "Two Clowns in a Comedy (to say nothing of the Dog): Speed, Launce (and Crab) in 'The Two Gentlemen of Verona.'" In *Essays and Studies*, 16 (1963), 91-100.

Burckhardt, Sigurd. *Shakespearean Meanings.* Princeton: Princeton Univ. Press, 1968.

Burke, Kenneth. *A Grammar of Motives* (1945). Berkeley: Univ. of California Press, 1969.

Campbell, Oscar James. "The Italianate Background of *The Merry Wives of Windsor.*" In *Essays and Studies in English and Comparative Literature*, Univ. of Michigan Publications, 8 (1932).

———. *"Love's Labour's Lost* Re-Studied" and *"The Two Gentlemen of Verona* and Italian Comedy." In *Studies in Shakespeare, Milton and Donne*, Univ. of Michigan Publications, 1. New York: Macmillan, 1925.

Charney, Maurice. *Comedy High and Low.* New York: Oxford Univ. Press, 1978.

———. ed., *Comedy: New Perspectives. New York Literary Forum*, 1, 1978.

———. "Comic Premises of *Twelfth Night.*" In *New York Literary Forum*, 1 (1978), 151-65.

———. "Shakespeare—and the Others." In *Shakespeare Quarterly*, 30 (1979), 325-42.

———. *"Twelfth Night* and the 'Natural Perspective' of Comedy." In *De Shakespeare à T. S. Eliot: Mélanges offerts à Henri Fluchère.* Paris: Didier, 1976, 43-51.

———. "Webster vs. Middleton, or the Shakespearean Yardstick in Jacobean Tragedy." In *English Renaissance Drama: Essays in Honor of Madeleine Doran & Mark Eccles*, ed. by Standish Henning, Robert Kimbrough, and Richard Knowles. Carbondale: Southern Illinois Univ Press, 1976, 118-27.

Clubb, Louise George. "Italian Comedy and *The Comedy of Errors.*" In *Comparative Literature*, 19 (1967), 240-52.

———. "Italian Renaissance Comedy." In *Genre*, 9 (1976-77), 469-88.

———. "The Making of the Pastoral Play: Some Experiments between 1573 and 1590." In *Petrarch to Pirandello*, ed. by J. A. Molinaro. Toronto: Univ. of Toronto Press, 1973, 45-72.

———. "Woman as Wonder: A Generic Figure in Italian and Shakespearean Comedy." In *Studies in the Continental Background of Renaissance English Literature*, ed. by D. B. J. Randall and G. W. Williams. Durham: Duke Univ. Press, 109-32.

Cody, Richard. *The Landscape of the Mind.* Oxford: Oxford Univ. Press, 1969.

Cohn, Ruby. *Modern Shakespeare Offshoots.* Princeton: Princeton Univ. Press, 1976.

Colie, Rosalie L. *Paradoxia Epidemica: The Renaissance Tradition of Paradox.* Princeton: Princeton Univ. Press, 1966.

——— *Shakespeare's Living Art.* Princeton: Princeton Univ. Press, 1974.

Cooper, Lane. *An Aristotelian Theory of Comedy.* New York: Harcourt, Brace, 1922.

Cope, Jackson I. *The Theater and the Dream.* Baltimore: Johns Hopkins Univ. Press, 1973.

Cornford, F. M. *The Origin of Attic Comedy*. Cambridge: Cambridge Univ. Press, 1934.

Council, Norman. *When Honour's at the Stake*. London: Allen and Unwin, 1973.

Cunningham, J. V. *Collected Essays*. Denver: Swallow Press, 1977.

Danson, Lawrence. *The Harmonies of "The Merchant of Venice."* New Haven: Yale Univ. Press, 1978.

Dessen, Allan C. "The Intemperate Knight and the Politic Prince: Late Morality Structure in *1 Henry IV.*" In *Shakespeare Studies*, 7 (1974), 147-72.

Doran, Madeleine. *Endeavors of Art*. Madison: Univ. of Wisconsin Press, 1954.

Duckworth, George E. *The Nature of Roman Comedy*. Princeton: Princeton Univ. Press, 1952.

Empson, William. *Some Versions of Pastoral*. London: Chatto and Windus, 1935.

Evans, Bertrand. *Shakespeare's Comedies*. London: Oxford Univ. Press, 1960.

Felperin, Howard. *Shakespearean Representation*. Princeton: Princeton Univ. Press, 1977.

Fish, Stanley E. *Self-Consuming Artifacts*. Berkeley: Univ. of California Press, 1972.

Forrest, James F. "Malvolio and Puritan 'Singularity.' " In *English Language Notes*, 11 (1973), 259-64.

Frye, Northrop. *Anatomy of Criticism*. Princeton: Princeton Univ. Press, 1957.

——. "The Argument of Comedy." In *Myth in the Later Plays of Shakespeare*, ed. by D. A. Robertson, Jr. New York: Columbia Univ. Press, 1949, 58-73, English Institute Essays, 1948.

——. *A Natural Perspective*. New York: Columbia Univ. Press, 1965.

——. *The Secular Scripture: A Study of the Structure of Romance*. Cambridge, Mass.: Harvard Univ. Press, 1976.

Galinsky, G. Karl. *Ovid's Metamorphoses*. Oxford: Blackwell, 1975.

Gardner, Helen. "*As You Like It.*" In *More Talking of Shakespeare*, ed. by John Garrett. London: Longmans, Green, 1959.

Geertz, Clifford. *The Interpretation of Cultures*. New York: Basic Books, 1973.

Gesner, Carol. *Shakespeare and the Greek Romance*. Lexington: Univ. Press of Kentucky, 1970.

Gilman, Ernest B. *The Curious Perspective: Literary and Pictorial Wit in the Seventeenth Century*. New Haven: Yale Univ. Press, 1978.

Hartman, Geoffrey H. *Beyond Formalism: Literary Essays 1958-1970*. New Haven: Yale Univ. Press, 1970.

Hartwig, Joan. *Shakespeare's Tragi-Comic Vision*. Baton Rouge: Louisiana State Univ. Press, 1973.

Hawkes, Terence. *Shakespeare's Talking Animals*. London: Arnold, 1973.

Herrick, Marvin T. *Comic Theory in the Sixteenth Century.* Urbana: Univ. of Illinois Press, 1950.

——. *Tragicomedy.* Urbana: Univ. of Illinois Press, 1955.

Holden, William P. *Anti-Puritan Satire, 1572-1642.* New Haven: Yale Univ. Press, 1954.

Holland, Norman. *The Dynamics of Literary Response.* New York: Oxford Univ. Press, 1968.

Hollander, John. "*Twelfth Night* and the Morality of Indulgence." In *Sewanee Review*, 68 (1959), 220-38.

Hotson, Leslie. *The First Night of Twelfth Night.* New York: Macmillan, 1954.

Hunter, G. K. "Italian Tragicomedy on the English Stage." In *Renaissance Drama*, N. S., 6 (1975), 123-48.

Hunter, R. G. *Shakespeare and the Comedy of Forgiveness.* New York: Columbia Univ. Press, 1965.

Jeffrey, Violet M. *John Lyly and the Italian Renaissance.* New York: Russell and Russell, 1969.

Jones, Thora Burnley, and Bernard de Bear Nicol. *Neo-Classical Dramatic Criticism: 1560-1770.* Cambridge: Cambridge Univ. Press, 1976.

Kay, Carol McGinnis, and Henry E. Jacobs, eds. *Shakespeare's Romances Reconsidered.* Lincoln: Univ. of Nebraska Press, 1978.

Keach, William. *Elizabethan Erotic Narratives.* New Brunswick: Rutgers Univ. Press, 1977.

King, Walter N. "Shakespeare and Parmenides: The Metaphysics of *Twelfth Night.*" In *Studies in English Literature*, 8 (1968), 283-306.

Kirsch, Arthur C. *Jacobean Dramatic Perspectives.* Charlottesville: Univ. of Virginia Press, 1972.

Krieger, Murray, ed. *Northrop Frye in Modern Criticism.* New York: Columbia Univ. Press, 1966.

Langer, Susanne K. "The Comic Rhythm." In *Feeling and Form.* London: Routledge and Kegan Paul, 1953.

Lanham, Richard A. *The Motives of Eloquence: Literary Rhetoric in the Renaissance.* New Haven: Yale Univ. Press, 1976.

Latham, Minor White. *The Elizabethan Fairies.* New York: Columbia Univ. Press, 1930.

Lauter, Paul, ed. *Theories of Comedy.* Garden City, N.Y.: Doubleday, 1964.

Lawrence, William J. "The Practice of Doubling and Its Influence on Early Dramaturgy." In *Pre-Restoration Stage Studies.* Cambridge, Mass.: Harvard Univ. Press, 1927, 43-78.

Lea, Kathleen M. *Italian Popular Comedy*, 2 vols. New York: Russell and Russell, 1962.

Leggatt, Alexander. *Shakespeare's Comedy of Love.* London: Methuen, 1974.

Levin, Harry. *Shakespeare and the Revolution of the Times.* New York: Oxford Univ. Press, 1976.

Levin, Richard. *The Multiple Plot in English Renaissance Drama.* Chicago: Univ. of Chicago Press, 1971.

——. *New Readings vs. Old Plays: Recent Trends in the Reinterpretation of English Renaissance Drama.* Chicago: Univ. of Chicago Press, 1979.

Mack, Maynard. "Introduction" to Henry Fielding. In *Joseph Andrews.* New York: Holt, Rinehart, 1948.

——. "The Jacobean Shakespeare." In *Jacobean Theatre,* ed. by John Russell Brown and Bernard Harris. London: Arnold, 1960, 11-42, Stratford-upon Avon Studies, 1.

Massey, Irving. *The Gaping Pig: Literature and Metamorphosis.* Berkeley: Univ. of California Press, 1976.

McCanles, Michael. *Dialectical Criticism and Renaissance Literature.* Berkeley: Univ. of California Press, 1975.

McMahon, A.P. "On the Second Book of Aristotle's *Poetics* and the Sources of Theophrastus' Definition of Tragedy." In *Harvard Studies in Classical Philology,* 28 (1917), 1-46.

Mowat, Barbara A. *The Dramaturgy of Shakespeare's Romances.* Athens: Univ. of Georgia Press, 1976.

Muecke, D. C. *Irony.* London: Methuen, 1970, in the Critical Idiom series.

Murdoch, Iris. *The Fire and the Sun: Why Plato Banished the Artists.* Oxford: Oxford Univ. Press, 1976.

Nicoll, Allardyce. *Masks, Mimes, and Miracles.* New York: Harcourt, Brace, 1931.

——. *The World of Harlequin.* Cambridge: Cambridge Univ. Press, 1963.

Norwood, Gilbert. *The Art of Terence.* Oxford: Oxford Univ. Press, 1923.

Oreglia, Giacomo. *The Commedia dell'Arte.* Trans. by L. F. Edwards. London, Methuen, 1968.

Otis, Brooks. *Ovid as an Epic Poet.* Cambridge: Cambridge Univ. Press, 1966.

Oz, Avraham. "Shakespeare in Israel." In *Shakespeare Quarterly,* 30 (1979), 279-81.

Palmer, D. J. "Art and Nature in *Twelfth Night.*" In *Critical Quarterly,* 9 (1967), 201-12.

Panofsky, Erwin. *The Life and Art of Albrecht Dürer,* 4th ed. Princeton: Princeton Univ. Press, 1955.

Peterson, Douglas L. *Time, Tide, and Tempest.* San Marino, Calif.: The Huntington Library Press, 1973.

Pettet, E. C. *Shakespeare and the Romance Tradition.* London: Staples, 1949.

Phialas, Peter G. *Shakespeare's Romantic Comedies.* Chapel Hill: Univ. of North Carolina Press, 1966.

Radcliff-Umstead, Douglas. *The Birth of Modern Comedy in Renaissance Italy.* Chicago: Univ. of Chicago Press, 1969.

Roberts, Jeanne Addison. *Shakespeare's English Comedy: "The Merry Wives of Windsor" in Context.* Lincoln: Univ. of Nebraska Press, 1979.

Rossiter, A. P. *Angel with Horns*. Ed. by Graham Storey. London: Long-
    mans, Green, 1961.
Rowland, Beryl. *Animals with Human Faces*. Knoxville: Univ. of Tennessee
    Press, 1973.
———. *Birds with Human Souls*. Knoxville: Univ. of Tennessee Press, 1978.
Salerno, Henry F. *Scenarios of the Commedia dell'Arte*. New York: New
    York Univ. Press, 1967.
Salingar, Leo. *Shakespeare and the Traditions of Comedy*. Cambridge:
    Cambridge Univ. Press, 1974.
Sand, Maurice. *The History of the Harlequinade* (1915, 2 vols.). New
    York: Blom, 1968.
Saunders, Catharine. *Costume in Roman Comedy*. New York: AMS Press,
    1966.
Schoenbaum, Samuel. *Shakespeare: The Globe & The World*. New York:
    Folger Shakespeare Library and Oxford Univ. Press, 1979.
Scott, William O. *The God of Arts: Ruling Ideas in Shakespeare's
    Comedies*. Lawrence: Univ. of Kansas Press, 1977.
Scragg, Leah. "Shakespeare, Lyly, and Ovid: The Influences of 'Gallathea'
    on 'A Midsummer Night's Dream.'" In *Shakespeare Survey*, 30
    (1977), 125-34.
Shapiro, Norman. "Suffering and Punishment in the Theatre of Georges
    Feydeau." In *Tulane Drama Review*, 5 (1959), 117-26.
Simmons, J. L. "A Source for Shakespeare's Malvolio: The Elizabethan
    Controversy with the Puritans." In *Huntington Library Quarterly*,
    36 (1973), 181-201.
Smith, Winifred. *The Commedia dell'Arte*. New York: Blom, 1964.
———. "Italian Actors in England." In *Modern Language Notes*, 44 (1929),
    375-77.
Spivack, Bernard. *Shakespeare and the Allegory of Evil*. New York:
    Columbia Univ. Press, 1958.
Spivack, Charlotte. *The Comedy of Evil on Shakespeare's Stage*. Ruther-
    ford, N. J.: Fairleigh Dickinson Univ. Press, 1978.
Snyder, Susan. *The Comic Matrix of Shakespeare's Tragedies*. Princeton:
    Princeton Univ. Press, 1979.
Sprague, Arthur Colby. *The Doubling of Parts in Shakespeare's Plays*.
    London: The Society for Theatre Research, 1966.
Steadman, John M. "Falstaff as Actaeon: A Dramatic Emblem." In
    Shakespeare Quarterly, 14 (1963), 231-44.
Strong, Roy. *The English Icon*. London: Routledge and Kegan Paul,
    1969.
Summers, Joseph H. "The Masks of *Twelfth Night*." In *The University
    Review*, 22 (1955), 25-32.
Taylor, Anthony Brian. "Shakespeare and Golding: Viola's Interview with
    Olivia and Echo and Narcissus." In *English Language Notes*, 15
    (1977), 103-6.

Thiébaux, Marcelle. *The Stag of Love.* Ithaca: Cornell Univ. Press, 1974.

Tillyard, E. M. W. *Shakespeare's Early Comedies.* London: Chatto and Windus, 1965.

Tomlinson, T. B. *A Study of Elizabethan and Jacobean Tragedy.* Cambridge: Cambridge Univ. Press, 1964.

Trimpi, Wesley. *The Ancient Hypothesis of Fiction.* New York: Fordham Univ. Press, 1971.

———. *The Quality of Fiction.* New York: Fordham Univ. Press, 1974.

Turner, Victor. *Dramas, Fields, and Metaphors.* Ithaca: Cornell Univ. Press, 1974.

Van Gennep, Arnold. *The Rites of Passage* (1908). Trans. by Monika B. Vizedom and Gabrielle L. Caffee. Chicago: Univ. of Chicago Press, 1960.

Waith, Eugene. "The Metamorphosis of Violence in *Titus Andronicus.*" In *Shakespeare Survey*, 10 (1957), 36-49.

Weimann, Robert. *Shakespeare and the Popular Tradition in the Theater.* Ed. by Robert Schwartz. Baltimore: Johns Hopkins Univ. Press, 1978.

Wells, Stanley. "Shakespeare and Romance." In *Later Shakespeare.* Ed. by John Russell Brown and Bernard Harris. London: Arnold, 1966, 49-79, Stratford-upon-Avon Studies, 8.

Wright, Louis B. "Will Kemp and the *Commedia dell'Arte.*" In *Modern Language Notes*, 41 (1926), 516-20.

Yates, Frances A. *Shakespeare's Last Plays: A New Approach.* London: Routledge and Kegan Paul, 1975.

Yoder, Audrey. *Animal Analogy in Shakespeare's Character Portrayal.* New York: Columbia Univ. Press, 1947.

Young, David. *The Heart's Forest.* New Haven: Yale Univ. Press, 1972.

About the Authors

DAVID M. BERGERON is a professor at University of Kansas. He is editor of *Research Opportunities in Renaissance Drama* and a member of the editorial board of *Shakespeare Quarterly*. Among his publications is the well-known book *English Civic Pageantry 1558-1642* as well as a popular introductory book on Shakespeare. He is currently preparing a book on the dark side of Shakespeare's romances.

WILLIAM C. CARROLL is a professor of English at Boston University. In addition to several articles on Shakespeare, he has written *The Great Feast of Language in "Love's Labour's Lost."* The present essay is part of a forthcoming book on metamorphosis in Shakespearean comedy. He has also written on the fiction of Vladimir Nabokov.

MAURICE CHARNEY, distinguished professor of English at Rutgers University, has published widely on Shakespeare and Elizabethan drama and is currently writing a book "Shakespeare and the Others" (the subject of a recent article in *Shakespeare Quarterly*). Author of *Shakespeare's Roman Plays* (1961), *Style in "Hamlet"* (1969), *How to Read Shakespeare* (1971), and *Comedy High and Low* (1978). As a diversion from Renaissance studies, he is presently engaged in studies of sexual fictions and Joe Orton.

LOUISE GEORGE CLUBB is professor of Italian and comparative literature at the University of California at Berkeley, author of *Giambattista Della Porta, Dramatist*, *Italian Plays (1500-1700) in the Folger Library*, and various essays on Italian and English Renaissance literature. She has recently edited and translated an example of the late cinquecento *commedia grave*, Della Porta's *Gli duoi fratelli rivali*.

ANN JENNALIE COOK has been the executive secretary of the Shakespeare Association of America since 1975. In 1976 she organized the World Shakespeare Congress in Washington, D.C. She is associate editor of *Shakespeare Studies*, and her book on Shakespeare's audience, *The Privileged Playgoers*, is forthcoming.

BARBARA FREEDMAN teaches dramatic literature at the University of Cincinnati, where she is a member of the department of English. She has articles on Shakespearean comedy forthcoming in *English Literary Renaissance* and *Shakespeare Quarterly*, is working on annotated bibliographies of the criticism on *The Comedy of Errors* and *The Taming of the Shrew* 1940-48, and is completing a book which analyzes Shakespeare's "nonromantic" comedies according to her psychoanalytic theory of farce.

ELIZABETH FREUND, lecturer at the Hebrew University in Jerusalem, is currently a post-doctoral visiting fellow at Yale. She wrote her dissertation on "Configurations of Opposition in a Selection of Shakespeare's Plays" and has published articles on *A Midsummer Night's Dream* and *The Tempest*. She will shortly publish a course on Shakespeare for Everyman's University in Israel. Her special fields of interest are drama and literary theory.

MARJORIE GARBER is the author of *Dream in Shakespeare: From Metaphor to Metamorphosis* and of many articles on Shakespeare, Marlowe, and Milton. She has recently completed a study of maturation patterns and rites of passage in Shakespeare's plays, *Coming of Age in Shakespeare*, and is currently at work on a consideration of *memento mori* figures in Shakespeare and Renaissance drama. Professor Garber formerly taught at Yale University and is now professor of English at Haverford College.

TERENCE HAWKES is a professor of English, University College Cardiff and a former visiting professor, State University of New York (Buffalo), University of Waterloo (Ontario), and Rutgers University. He is author of *Shakespeare and the Reason, Shakespeare's Talking Animals, Metaphor*, and *Structuralism and Semiotics* and is editor of *Coleridge on Shakespeare* and *20th Century Interpretations of "Macbeth"*; he is also general editor for the "New Accent" series on literature.

HARRIETT HAWKINS taught at Swarthmore and Vassar and held fellowships from the Folger and Huntington libraries, the National Endowment for the Humanities the American Council of Learned Societies, and the John Simon Guggenheim Memorial Foundation. Her latest book, *Poetic Freedom and Poetic Truth: Chaucer, Shakespeare, Marlowe, Milton* was awarded the Rose Mary Crawshay Prize by the British Academy and cited as one of the "Books of the Year" in the London *Observer.*

MALCOLM KINIRY is an assistant professor at University College, Rutgers University. He is working on a book on the collaborations of Beaumont and Fletcher and a book on recent American science fiction.

M.E. LAMB attended Wellesley and Yale, received her Ph.D. from Columbia, and is now an assistant professor of English at Southern Illinois University. In addition to her studies on Ovidian influence on Shakespeare's plays, she is working on the anonymous holograph poems of the Bright manuscript.

NINIAN MELLAMPHY, a graduate of Rockwell College, is associate chairman (undergraduate studies) of the department of English, University of Western Ontario, London, Canada. His published work includes articles on Shakespeare, Irish literature, and the theory of fiction.

RUTH NEVO, who was born in Johannesburg, immigrated to Israel and now teaches at the Hebrew University of Jerusalem. She is the author of *The Dial of Virtue: A Study of Poems on Affairs of State in the Seventeenth Century, Tragic Form in Shakespeare*, and *Comic Transformations in Shakespeare* (in press).

S. GEORGIA NUGENT, assistant professor of classics at Princeton University, has previously taught in the classics departments of Swarthmore College and Cornell University. Having just completed her dissertation on allegorical personifications in Latin epic, she is currently returning to work on the narrative technique of Ovid's *Fasti*. Her previous translations include the Cupid and Psyche tale from Apuleius and the "Spiritual Canticle" of San Juan de la Cruz.

AVRAHAM OZ is lecturer in drama at Tel Aviv University in Israel and also associate artistic director of the Cameri Theatre, the municipal theater of Tel Aviv. He is a leading translator of Shakespeare into Hebrew, of which his version of *The Merchant of Venice* was published in 1975, and an enthusiastic, acerbic commentator on the theater and other arts.

DOUGLAS L. PETERSON, a member of the English faculty at Michigan State University, has published articles on *Romeo and Juliet, Julius Caesar,* and *Measure for Measure.* He is also the author of *The English Lyric from Wyatt to Donne* and *Time, Tide, and Tempest: A Study of Shakespeare's Romances.* Professor Peterson is currently at work on studies of ideal comedy and the art of Shakespeare's comedies. The present essay on *The Tempest* is part of this book-length manuscript.

JEANNE ADDISON ROBERTS is professor of literature at The American University in Washington, D.C. She is a member of the executive committee of the Shakespeare Division of the Modern Language Association, a trustee of the Shakespeare Association of America, and a member of the editorial board of *Shakespeare Quarterly.* She is coeditor, with James G. McManaway, of *A Selective Bibliography of Shakespeare: Editions, Textual Studies, Commentaries,* and author of *Shakespeare's English Comedy: "The Merry Wives of Windsor" in Context.* She is also coeditor of the projected Variorum *Merry Wives* and textual editor of *The Tempest* for the International Shakespeare.

LEO SALINGAR is a lecturer in English at the University of Cambridge and Fellow of Trinity College. He has contributed to *The Age of Shakespeare* (1955) and other volumes of the *Pelican Guide to English Literature,* edited by Boris Ford. He is author of *Shakespeare and the Traditions of Comedy.*

CATHERINE M. SHAW teaches English at Concordia University, Montreal, P. Q., Canada. The author of numerous articles on Shakespeare and his contemporaries, Professor Shaw has also written *"Some Vanity of Mine Art:" The Masque in English Renaissance Drama* (University of Salzburg, 1980) and *Richard Brome* (Boston, 1980). She has also edited *The Old Law* by Middleton and Rowley which will be part of the Nottingham Drama Text series.

PAUL N. SIEGEL, professor emeritus, Long Island University, is author of *Shakespearean Tragedy and the Elizabethan Compromise* (1957), *Shakespeare in His Time and Ours* (1968), *Revolution and the Twentieth-Century Novel* (1979), and numerous articles in professional journals and literary magazines. He is also editor of *His Infinite Variety: Major Shakespearean Criticism Since Johnson* (1964) and *Leon Trotsky on Literature and Art* (1970).

SUSAN SNYDER is professor of English at Swarthmore College and a member of the editorial board of *Shakespeare Quarterly.* She is the editor of *The Divine Weeks and Works of Guillaume de Saluste, Sieur du Bartas* and author of *The Comic Matrix of Shakespeare's Tragedies* as well as articles on Shakespeare and other Renaissance writers.

MARION TROUSDALE, who teaches English at the University of Maryland, has written widely on questions of style and form in drama, especially in Shakespeare and the Elizabethans. Her book, *The Reason of Shakespeare's Art,* is in press.

Index

Production and Design: Editorial and Graphic Services
Calligraphy: Jeanyee Wong

Cap. Babeo.   Cucuba.   Sig.ª Lucia.   Trastullo.   S

Razullo.   Cucurucu.   Cap. Esgangarato.   Cap.º Cocodrillo   Cap.

Riciulina.   Metzetin   Cap. Babeo.   Cucuba.   R

Bello Squacio.   Couiello.   Scapino.   Cap. Esgangarato.   Ca